10/25/12
$83.99

The Nature of Dignity

The Nature of Dignity

Ron Bontekoe

LEXINGTON BOOKS

A division of
ROWMAN & LITTLEFIELD PUBLISHERS, INC.
Lanham • Boulder • New York • Toronto • Plymouth, UK

LEXINGTON BOOKS

A division of Rowman & Littlefield Publishers, Inc.
A wholly owned subsidary of The Rowman & Littlefield Publishing Group, Inc.
4501 Forbes Boulevard, Suite 200
Lanham, MD 20706

Estover Road
Plymouth PL6 7PY
United Kingdom

Copyright © 2008 by Lexington Books

British Library Cataloguing in Publication Information Available

Library of Congress Cataloging-in-Publication Data

Bontekoe, Ronald, 1954-
  The nature of dignity / Ron Bontekoe.
    p. cm.
  Includes index.
  ISBN-13: 978-0-7391-2407-9 (cloth : alk. paper)
  ISBN-10: 0-7391-2407-2 (cloth : alk. paper)
  1. Philosophical anthropology. 2. Dignity. I. Title.
  BD450.B585 2008
  128—dc22   2007044988

Printed in the United States of America

∞™ The paper used in this publication meets the minimum requirements of American
National Standard for Information Sciences—Permanence of Paper for Printed Library
Materials, ANSI/NISO Z39.48–1992.

Contents

Acknowledgments

A number of my colleagues, friends, and some of the past and present doctoral candidates in the Philosophy Department at the University of Hawaii have generously read and commented upon portions of the text that follows. In this regard, I would like to thank Arindam Chakrabarti (for drawing my attention to Schiller's "On Grace and Dignity"), Vrinda Dalmiya, Graham Parkes, Roger Ames, Eliot Deutsch, Marty Heitz, Brad Park, Matt Mackenzie, Kyle Takaki, Lara Mitias, Karl Frogner, Anderson Meyer, Rob Henderson, and most especially Jim Tiles. (Anyone familiar with Jim's *Moral Measures* will realize that he does not entirely share my sense of the weaknesses of Kant's moral theory.) Finally, I want to acknowledge that this book would almost certainly not have emerged, in the form that it now has, were it not for the failure of my second marriage. For that reason, it is dedicated to Adrienne.

Chapter One

Dignity in Eclipse

In recent decades philosophers have had a great deal to say about human dignity as something that is to be acknowledged in our treatment of others. They have considered at length what sorts of rights human beings should be thought to possess—or should be granted—in order to safeguard their dignity against assault or attrition. Much of this work has been quite valuable, and yet it is noteworthy that, in spite of all of the attention that philosophers have recently lavished on the subject of human dignity, comparatively little has been said about dignity as a moral *achievement*. This seems rather strange given that, among nonphilosophers at least, the primary meaning associated with the term "dignity" is not that of a property universally possessed by human beings that entitles them to various forms of protection. Instead, what we normally think of when we speak of someone's dignity—of Abraham Lincoln's dignity, for example, at Gettysburg while delivering his famous address—is the unusually worthy way in which the person in question bears himself under trying circumstances. Dignity in this, its primary sense, is understood to be a characteristic that different people possess to different degrees. It is also clearly a kind of virtue—a *master* virtue, as this book will attempt to show. Before we begin to examine in what sense personal dignity is a virtue and why it is a virtue especially worth cultivating, however, a significant source of confusion needs to be cleared away.

It seems at first blush that the kind of personal dignity that different people exhibit to varying degrees must be related in some important respects to the kind of dignity that we attribute to all human beings, simply by virtue of their being human. Whatever the characteristics may be that we acknowledge as being of particular importance in human beings generally when we attribute dignity to them all must surely be the same characteristics—or at least overlap with

1

those characteristics—on the basis of which, if we find them especially pronounced, we will tend to speak of some individual's exceptional dignity. That seems plausible and yet it is a problematic contention, because we do not in fact have an entirely clear sense of what the grounds are for attributing dignity to humans in general. The possession of human dignity, after all, is what we appeal to in arguing that certain *other* things—privacy, fair trials, personal property, the vote, and so on—should be possessed as rights, in that these either protect or are the appropriate accoutrements of a person's dignity. But dignity in this freestanding sense is nothing more than inclusion within the charmed circle of those who are deemed to be morally relevant—those whose welfare we have decided to take into account. It amounts to little more than an acknowledgment of one's citizenship when we appeal to it as the justification for certain narrowly held rights, such as the right to vote or the right to free speech (as this is exercised, for example, in publicly criticizing the government). With respect to more broadly held rights—the right not to be subjected to torture or slavery, for example—it amounts to little more than a declaration of how far our capacities for sympathetic identification extend. For the most part, in other words, today we tend to appeal to our shared belief in the inherent dignity of human beings without inquiring too deeply into the original grounds that were offered for attributing dignity to human beings as such. The reason for this, it turns out, is that once we do inquire into those original grounds, we find that over the past few decades they have lost much of their power to convince.

The idea of the inherent dignity of all human beings did not suddenly burst upon the ethical and political consciousness of Western civilization sometime in the eighteenth century. It has always been an important part of the Christian tradition, with its doctrine that mankind was created in God's image. But this earlier Christian conception of human dignity was radically transformed in the eighteenth and nineteenth centuries by the Enlightenment faith in the inexorability of human progress—progress that was felt to be both driven by, and tending naturally toward, the expansion of human freedom. These two identifiably separate but closely related traditions—the Christian and the North European Enlightenment—fuse most tightly in the writings of Immanuel Kant, who was one of the most penetrating of advocates for the idea of human dignity. Thus in order to lay bare the conceptual incoherence that most of us today labor under regarding the notion of human dignity, it will be useful to consider what the typical Christian, the Kantian, and the Enlightenment progressive severally meant by "human dignity," what grounds each of them had for attributing dignity to human beings, and the extent to which those grounds for belief in human dignity have been undermined by recent developments in our understanding of human nature.

By way of preliminaries, it is worth noting that the word "dignity" has a pedigree even more ancient than the Christian tradition. It derives from the Latin *dignitas*, which did not mean, however, quite what we mean today by "dignity." In ancient Rome, a man's *dignitas* was a matter of his prestige or social standing, and given that Roman society was highly class-conscious, there were many people—slaves and common laborers—who, simply by virtue of their place in society, possessed little if any *dignitas*. On the other hand, because in Rome social advancement *was* open to individuals of talent, a man's *dignitas* (or standing) was not entirely unrelated to his virtues. Personal courage, eloquence, and wisdom contributed to a man's *dignitas*, as did, and especially so, his sense of seemliness or *decorum*—by which the Romans meant a person's tendency to do the appropriate thing, taking into account specific circumstances and his own social status. An important part of seemliness, however, was liberality or the bestowing of benefits upon others as an expression of one's own munificence. To engage in significant acts of liberality, it was, of course, necessary to be wealthy. And thus we read in Cicero's *On Duties*, for example, that the construction of a splendid home—which is to say, a suitable place for lavishly entertaining guests—is the sort of thing that can provide one (as it did Gnaeus Octavius) great *dignitas*.

It was in conscious contrast to this Roman idea that one's *dignitas* or personal worthiness is a matter of one's social standing that the early Christians contended that *all* humans are in a more profound sense equally worthy, by virtue of their all being in possession of a soul and all having been created in God's image. It would be a mistake, though, to think that the Christian conception of the inherent dignity of human beings simply blotted out this earlier Roman understanding of *dignitas*. On the contrary, as our modern conception of dignity evolved, it took its primary characteristics from this Christian doctrine, and later added to these elements that came to the fore during the Enlightenment, but it preserved as well, as a distinct undertone, the Roman tendency to equate dignity with prestige. Even today we continue to hear this undertone. (And for our Enlightenment forbears, given their far greater familiarity with the Latin classics, it was much more powerfully heard. As evidence of this, we need only note the felt need of America's ruling aristocracy during the Federalist period to provide the President with a splendid home—the White House—in which to lavishly entertain guests, in order to bolster his dignity.) Nonetheless, in a democratic social climate prestige and dignity tend to be distinguished. Prestige is earned, but can, in certain cases, also come one's way by lucky accident. Dignity, by contrast, is thought to be inherent in one's nature, and insofar as this basic measure of dignity can be augmented, this is only through the cultivation of those aspects of one's nature that already account for one's innate possession of dignity. Time now to turn our attention to how this modern conception of dignity emerged.

KANT AND CHRISTIANITY

What it meant (and means) to the typical Christian to have been created "in God's image" is that, in contrast to the nonhuman animals, human beings are, by virtue of their possession of reason and free will, *responsible* for their actions. Like God, they know what morality requires of them and thus, unlike all other creatures, which are merely part of the world, human beings are suitable creatures for God to have granted *stewardship* of the world. But this idea of responsibility is intimately related to the idea of blameworthiness. Only because human beings understand the difference between right and wrong, after all, does it make sense to hold a wrongdoer accountable and punishable for his actions. Thus the Christian conception of human dignity has always been coupled with, and significantly qualified by, the notion of original sin. For if humans are created in God's image in their capacity to distinguish good from evil, they are nonetheless still closely related to the nonhuman animals, in that they are driven by lusts and are prone to temptations that they can never entirely manage to resist. Moreover, it is only because humans can distinguish right from wrong that their inability to resist temptation amounts to *sin*—a concept that is inapplicable to the nonrational animals. Only for mankind, then, do the alternative prospects of heaven and hell open up. Still, as responsible creatures, precisely as creatures for whom the stakes involved in their earthly sojourn are so much higher, humans are exalted above the other, nonrational animals, and are deserving of a respect that is not due to the latter.

Immanuel Kant makes this same point in the *Groundwork of the Metaphysics of Morals* when he remarks that rational (i.e., human) beings are always to be regarded as ends in themselves and never to be treated as mere means to the achievement of someone else's ends. For Kant too, the sharp distinction to be drawn between human beings and other, nonrational creatures is based upon our human capacity to recognize the requirements of morality. There is, however, a significant difference between what the typical Christian meant by this and what Kant intended. For the typical Christian, the demands of morality are recognized by virtue of man's ability to hear and respond when he is being addressed by God. Thus the Ten Commandments, for example, were not the products of human deliberation; rather they constituted an injunction delivered to mankind by God's spokesman, Moses. The fact that, as moral imperatives, most if not all of the Ten Commandments make good sense is not irrelevant, but the more important point is that, for the typical Christian, recognition of God's authority comes first. Thus even when the purpose of God's message is unclear to us—as, for example, it was unclear to Abraham why God should want him to offer up in sacrifice his only and much cherished son, Isaac—obedience and not debate is what is required of us. But this subordination of the human will to the Divine will raises a serious problem—that of correctly identifying those messages that genuinely come from God. Given our human capacity for self-deception, and for being deceived by others, as well as the multiplicity of religions and gods that have always been on offer, we are not in a position confidently to identify as the will of God intentions that seem strange to us.

It is for this very reason that Kant reversed the relation between religious faith and moral conviction. Given the untrustworthiness of "divine revelation," Kant denied that human beings either can or need to be informed by God about the requirements of morality. On the contrary, according to Kant, only by virtue of His undeviating and effortless compliance with what, as rational beings, we humans already and independently understand to be required by the moral law could we ever recognize God.

Earlier philosophers (most notably Aquinas, Anselm, and Descartes), appreciating the problems posed for religious faith by the unreliability of revelation, had attempted to provide strictly rational proofs of God's existence. Kant was unimpressed with these, however, and in *The Critique of Pure Reason* he examined in turn each of the three standard arguments for God's existence—the ontological, the cosmological, and the teleological—and provided devastating refutations of them. Nonetheless, in his own way, Kant himself was also a member of this long rationalist tradition that perpetually struggled to establish "within the limits of reason alone" the legitimacy of religious (that is, of Christian) faith. But, setting for himself a somewhat higher standard of rational consistency than had his predecessors in this endeavor, Kant could find no compelling argument for the necessity of God's existence.

By way of his moral theory, however, he did develop an argument that entitled us to *hope for* the existence of God—an argument that established not the necessity, but at least the plausibility, of God's existence. For as rational beings we are obliged—by our own sense of what reason requires of us—to behave morally, and yet there are grounds to believe that moral behavior will not receive its due reward in this life. For this reason, Kant argued that it would make sense if justice were done in the hereafter. Moreover, because the orderliness and beauty of the world seem at least to suggest (even if they do not, strictly speaking, demonstrate) the activity implicit within it of an ordering intelligence, we are entitled to believe that God does exist and cares about our moral standing. Ultimately, though, we have grounds only to hope for the existence of God, and not to know with mathematical certainty of his existence, because, as Kant acknowledges, the mere fact that there is a moral law which we, as rational beings, are able to recognize, does not in itself guarantee that the universe will vindicate our sense of what justice requires.

On the other hand, that there *is* a moral law, dictated by reason itself—by "pure practical reason," as he styles it—is taken by Kant to be beyond doubt. Moreover, only to the extent that individual human beings recognize and acknowledge this reason-dictated moral law—by acting in accordance with it— can they be said to be truly rational beings and thus deserving of the respect that reason commands. Human dignity does not derive, in Kant's estimation, from our having been "created in God's image" even though, as a Christian, Kant personally believed (and hoped) that mankind was created in God's image. Human dignity derives, instead, from our ability as rational beings to recognize and place upon ourselves the restraining force of moral law. Insofar as we are capable of doing this, according to Kant, we possess *autonomy*— which is to say, we are genuinely in command of ourselves. In contrast, insofar as we are driven to do what we do, not by reason, but by our own natural impulses and by objects external to ourselves—that is to say, by our fears and desires, passions and thoughtless habits—we are subject to the forces of *heteronomy*. Where heteronomy prevails, we are mere shuttlecocks, alternately driven and pulled from point to point in our lives by a combination of natural buffets and attractions that we make no effort to resist. The difference between being fully human and being merely a human animal—and thus the difference between possessing and lacking the dignity attendant upon one's humanity—is a matter of one's possessing autonomy, a matter of being a free initiator of events rather than a mere conduit for impulses provided one by nature.

Freedom, for Kant, always meant freedom from the impulses supplied to us by the material (or natural) world, but in human beings there was only one counterforce that could effectively resist these impulses. If one were not to be a slave to one's own passing inclinations, one had to receive one's guidance from a steadier, more reliable and honorable source—from the universally true moral law that is dictated by pure practical reason. What the moral law (or categorical imperative) requires of a rational being, Kant contends, is that one must always avoid acting in ways that are inconsistent with preserving the conditions that define a world the existence of which it is rationally possible to will. And how does one do this? According to Kant, when one is in doubt about the moral propriety of an action, one should frame a *maxim* or general description of the action in question and then ask whether or not one "could will that one's maxim should become a universal law." Thus if one feels an inclination, for example, to tell a lie in order to take advantage of another person's gullibility, one should first ask oneself whether one could actually wish for the existence of a world in which everyone routinely told lies. Kant claims that as soon as we frame the question in this way we recognize that lying is incompatible with the dictates of reason. For if everyone routinely told lies, no one would have grounds for believing anything that was ever said. The upshot of that state of affairs, of course, would be the effective end of all spoken or written communication. For why even bother to speak if nothing you say is going to be believed? What lying amounts to, then, is a sort of performative contradiction. In the act of lying one contradicts the purpose that is implicit in the nature of speech itself, and it is this contradiction that offends pure practical reason.

This is Kant's most convincing illustration of the principle of universalizing the maxim, and the principle almost looks plausible in this case. But it takes no great effort to think of compelling counterexamples. Should one, for example, always tell the brutal truth about the imminence of death to someone suffering from a terminal illness? There are circumstances in which (and patients for which) nothing would be achieved by this except an overall increase in misery.[1] (And it is a simple matter to formulate another maxim, readily universalizable, to the effect that one should avoid needlessly increasing a victim's pain.) Or imagine that you are confronted by a small child who wants to know whether Santa Claus is coming. Should you, as a matter of principle, feel obliged to dispel this fantasy—a fantasy that the child's parents have presumably found fit to let her enjoy?

What counterexamples such as these imply is the need to fine-tune the maxim regarding the telling of falsehoods so as to acknowledge the relevance of particular circumstances. But this is a move that Kant understandably resists. For once introduce the subject of circumstances and there can be no question any longer of knowing what must be done in a novel and complicated situation. It is not normally obvious, after all, that one should—or should not—withhold the truth about the imminence of death from a patient. With respect to an issue such as this, the clear fine-edged certainty that the categorical imperative seems to offer dissolves into a welter of conflicting considerations that must be balanced and rebalanced as further information comes to light. And once the individual's personal judgment enters into the picture, not only in determining the respective weights to be given competing considerations but also in deciding which circumstances are to be deemed relevant, what Kant sees as the crucial question—the question whether or not one has acted on the basis of a good will, and therefore laudably—becomes difficult to settle. This is because, once the process of decision-making has been complicated by the consideration of circumstances, it is easy to slide from the disinterested exercise of moral reason to an indulgence in rationalization—to finding grounds for doing whatever is convenient for oneself. This impulse is precisely what the principle of universalizing the maxim was meant to oppose. To obey the moral law, according to Kant, is to give others exactly the same consideration as oneself and never to make a convenient exception in one's own favor.

Kant opens the *Groundwork* with the declaration that a good will is the only thing that can be considered good without qualification, and that goodness of will is in no way impugned just because, as will occasionally happen, an unpleasant but wholly unintended consequence follows from it. This is intuitively a sound observation. Given our limited capacity to foresee in detail what a particular action on our part will produce in the way of consequences, it is unreasonable to hold ourselves morally culpable for any and every ill that follows upon our well-intended act. But the point is that we are not entitled, because of this limitation, to simplify arbitrarily our processes of moral reasoning. To say that we cannot possibly calculate all consequences of our actions is not to imply that we need not take into account even readily foreseeable consequences and pursue instead some formalistic conception of duty regardless of the actual results it produces.

Understandable as may be Kant's desire to identify moral merit with the possession of a good will (one that is not impugned by the actual unforeseeable consequences of its actions), there are problems involved in his attempt entirely to eschew consequentialism in his moral theory. For even if Kant does not ground the moral praiseworthiness of an action on the specific consequences that flow from it, what he means by "formal contradiction" is largely a matter of the undesirability (or of our inability to *will* the bringing about) of certain general, large-scale consequences. As John Stuart Mill observes,

> when he begins to deduce from this precept [of universalizing the maxim] any of the actual duties of morality, he fails, almost grotesquely, to show that there would be any contradiction, any logical (not to say physical) impossibility, in the adoption by all rational beings of the most outrageously immoral rules of conduct. All he shows is that the *consequences* of their universal adoption would be such as no one would choose to incur.[2]

Kant himself acknowledges this with regard to one of his other key examples—that of charity. Society would not come crashing to a halt, he admits, even if no one ever chose to extend charity to a neighbor in distress. But someone who can imagine wishing to receive charity himself in certain circumstances would exhibit an inconsistency in refusing to behave charitably toward others. True enough, but the individual who cannot imagine ever wanting charity, either for himself or anyone about whom he cares, and who genuinely would not wish it, is *not* guilty of any such inconsistency. Such an individual will no doubt be rare, but he may nonetheless exist.

Kant's other examples in the *Groundwork* are even more problematic. This is because the general, large-scale consequences that Kant appeals to in arguing that suicide and the wasting of one's talents run counter to our moral duty imply a particular view of what a human being exists *for*. It makes no sense, he argues, to kill oneself just because one's remaining days seem certain to be filled with "more evil than satisfaction" given that the feeling of self-love that is responsible for this inclination has, as its special nature, the purpose of preserving and improving life. In inclining one toward suicide, that feeling of self-love is contradicting its own *telos* or purpose, and thus one has an obligation to resist the impulse. This argument is hopelessly strained. It makes an end-in-itself, not of the individual, but of the individual's self-love and its tendency toward the preservation and improvement of life. These, on Kant's account, become masters to be served, regardless of our inclination in the matter. But if, as one might believe (given that there is no inconsistency in the belief, as Kant himself admits), there is no Divine or ultimate purpose to human existence, then why must we struggle to extend its duration even after it has lost all desirability for us? And if there were no purpose to human existence, then surely while wasting one's talents might be a shame, it could hardly be a dereliction of *duty*. One senses that the real reason that Kant opposes suicide and the dissipation of one's talents—which is to say, his belief as a Christian in God's plan for humankind—is not offered here only because, having established our recognition of the moral law as the *ground* for our belief in God's existence, Kant recognizes that to invoke God's injunction against self-slaughter (and the implicit injunction against self-dissipation) would be viciously circular.

Mill's take on the legitimacy of suicide and the wasting of one's talents is revealing here, and equally relevant to an inquiry into the nature of human dignity. For Mill, by comparison with Kant, is almost entirely agnostic on the question of the purpose of life. If there is one clear lesson to be learned from history, in Mill's estimation, it is that the all-too-human tendency to presume that we know what is best, not only for ourselves, but for others has been largely unjustified and, when insisted upon, the cause of incalculable misery. The only thing that can be said with perfect confidence about the nature of life, as Mill sees it, is that for each of us it represents an opportunity to make of that life what one wishes. But the opportunity represented by each individual human life belongs, by right, exclusively to the individual whose life it is. Thus, according to Mill, each of us should have the right to live his life as he pleases, providing only that he does not harm others or interfere with *their* liberty to live *their* lives as they may wish. The rationale for this, again, is simply that no one is in a position to declare with certainty how someone else should live his or her life so that it might turn out to be, in his or her own judgment, as satisfyingly lived as possible.

Given these assumptions, the attitude one has to adopt toward suicide is that, while it is possible that the person contemplating suicide is making a mistake, and therefore his or her friends should certainly remonstrate with the would-be suicide to make sure that the action is not being undertaken rashly, the person contemplating suicide may well be in full possession of his or her faculties and simply know better than anyone else why life will no longer be worth living. Almost all of us can appreciate that a terminal cancer patient, for example, might decide that a few extra weeks or months of life are not worth the cost in suffering endured. But Mill's point is considerably stronger than this. Even an individual in perfectly good physical health, who is experiencing "merely" spiritual or emotional distress (Sylvia Plath, say), knows his or her own nature better than anyone else could, and is therefore in principle in a better position than anyone else to judge whether suicide is warranted. For those of us left behind, even if we may not be able to bring ourselves to agree with the decision, it is our lot to acknowledge at least that the decision *may* have been right, and even *if* a mistake, that it was nonetheless the suicide's *own* mistake to make.

With regard to the wasting of one's talents, Mill makes two points. First, whether one's talents are being genuinely wasted is always a matter of interpretation. After all, each of us is born with many latent talents and our lifespans afford us the opportunity to develop only a few of these. Thus when someone else accuses one of wasting one's talents, almost invariably this is an expression of disapproval regarding which of one's talents one has chosen to cultivate. And this choice is in each case always one's own to make. Mill's second point is that even if one is, in one's own estimation, wasting one's talents, this is always a legitimate, if not an especially laudable, choice of lifestyle, given that one is answerable, in this respect, only to one's own sense of worthwhileness.

What constitutes the well-lived life is an empirical question, Mill contends, and the correct answer to this question will vary to some extent from one person to the next. For this reason, even an individual with considerable life experience should offer recommendations rather than dogmatic pronouncements to those who lack such experience. Even more important is the idea that we are all, given the uniqueness and limitations on the range of our personal experience, in a position to learn from one another about the sorts of things that are capable of adding value to a life. Thus the picture that Mill offers in *On Liberty* is one in which each individual human being can be thought of as a kind of explorer in the realm of values. Because we are not omniscient, and because the terrain of life is extraordinarily varied, we must venture into that terrain in order to discover and map its details. As with other explorers, moreover, the fruits of our explorations are fully realized only when we return to society and report what we have found.

Interestingly, Kant too feels that this is indeed how we come to understand the nature of happiness. Individual human beings vary greatly in their tastes and inclinations. Together these two facts imply, for Kant as for Mill, that inquiry into the nature of happiness and the means by which it might be achieved by the particular individual can never be exhausted. But in Kant's estimation, for this very reason the production of happiness cannot serve, as Aristotle proposed and Mill much later agreed, as the ultimate goal of ethical behavior. For it is not a goal that can be aimed at with complete confidence (as even Aristotle admits) and if, as Kant insists, morality is simply and entirely a matter of acting with a good will, there must be some way in which we can, with complete confidence, identify the goodness of the will. Kant believes that the principle of universalizing the maxim is precisely what is needed in this regard. He expects, moreover, that in some instances acting in accordance with the moral law, as the principle of universalizing the maxim defines this, will run counter to the pursuit of happiness.

But as I have shown, the principle of universalizing the maxim almost immediately runs into problems. Kant never manages, moreover, to make this an entirely coherent notion. Why, then, does he remain so adamantly devoted to it? And why does the Kantian principle of universalizing the maxim continue, in spite of its obvious failings, to attract serious consideration even today among ethicists? The answer to both questions has to do with the attractiveness of the picture of human nature that Kant offers. That human beings are animals Kant does not deny. That we are extraordinarily clever animals is also obvious. As Kant conceives of us, however, human beings are much more than even very clever animals, pursuing our individual inclinations and private satisfactions. We are, potentially at least, exemplars of reason itself— that same reason which is the very essence of divinity. It follows that in this one respect, in our capacity to understand what reason requires and to act in accordance with it, we stand before God not merely as His creatures, but as His equals. Thus the measure of dignity possessed by the individual human being whose actions arise from the impersonal exercise of reason is *Godlike* in its dimensions.

THE SIGNIFICANCE OF DARWIN

Unfortunately, however, the argument that Kant offers in support of this contention that reason constitutes the essence of human nature fails in the light of what we now know about the origins of our own species. In the *Groundwork of the Metaphysics of Morals*, Kant's argument runs as follows:

> In the natural constitution of an organized being, that is, one constituted purposively for life, we assume as a principle that there will be found in it no instrument for some end other than what is also most appropriate to that end and best adapted to it. Now in a being that has reason and a will, if the proper end of nature were its *preservation*, its *welfare*, in a word its *happiness*, then nature would have hit upon a very bad arrangement in selecting the reason of the creature to carry out this purpose. For all the actions that the creature has to perform for this purpose . . . would be marked out for it far more accurately by instinct. . . . [S]ince reason is nevertheless given to us as a practical faculty, that is, as one that is to influence the *will*, then, where nature has everywhere else gone to work purposively in distributing its capacities, the true vocation of reason must be to produce a will that is good, not perhaps *as a means* to other purposes, but *good in itself*, for which reason was absolutely necessary. This will need not, because of this, be the sole and complete good, but it must still be the highest good and the condition of every other. . . . In this case it is entirely consistent with the wisdom of nature if we perceive that the cultivation of reason, which is requisite to the first and unconditional purpose [i.e., the production of a good will], limits in many ways—at least in this life—the attainment of the second, namely happiness, which is always conditional; indeed it may reduce it below zero without nature proceeding unpurposively in the matter.[3]

In other words, because human beings are uniquely characterized by their possession of the faculty of reason, which must, by assumption, be perfectly suited to whatever purpose it was meant by nature to serve, and because what reason is good for is decision-making—which is to say, the determination of the will—the whole point of human existence must be to cultivate goodness of will—even at the expense, perhaps, of human happiness.

Kant wrote these lines long before Charles Darwin published *On the Origin of Species* in 1859, and even longer than that before the theory of evolution finally became a coherent and convincing whole in the 1940s. Given what we now know about the process of evolution by which humankind came into existence, there are two crippling errors in Kant's argument. First, it is not the case, as Kant assumes, that nature never produces any "instrument" or organ other than that which is "most appropriate" and "best adapted" for the purpose that it serves. On the contrary, organisms are not perfectly adapted to their environments (and thus their organs are not perfectly adapted to their "purposes"); rather, organisms are competitively adapted.[4] They (and consequently their organs) are well enough adapted to escape, for the most part, their predators, to survive in adequate numbers to maturity, and thus to pass on their genes and heritable characteristics to their offspring. Second, since nature has no purpose at all "in mind" in the process of evolution, nature is most certainly not aiming, in the emergence of the human species, at the production of a good will.

But then, in spite of the language that he chooses to use in this passage, Kant is not really suggesting that it is *nature*, in the sense in which we understand nature, that intends that human beings should exhibit good will in their dealings with one another. As a Christian, Kant believes that it is God's intention that is manifested in the natural world. If he hesitates, in this passage, to speak forthrightly about God's intention, this is because his goal is to establish the inescapable necessity—the categoricalness—of the moral law *without* making any reference to God, and then to use our recognition of the moral law as a basis for justifying our faith in the existence of God. As it happens, however, he cannot establish that the governing principle of human existence is the production of a good will without introducing into the argument a surrogate for God's intention, in the form of nature's intention. Human beings are *meant* to exhibit good will, and that is why they possess reason, which otherwise would be a hindrance rather than a help to them. By whom are they meant to exhibit good will? It is premature, Kant feels, to say "God" here, and so he says "nature" instead. But in so doing, he commits himself to the same assumption—that the world exhibits purposive design—that he would have if he had simply said "God" from the start.

In Kant's day it was difficult to imagine the integrated complexity of the natural world coming into existence in any other way than through intentional design. Thus even Kant's contemporary, David Hume, who made no secret of his agnosticism and who provided in his *Dialogues Concerning Natural Religion* the definitive refutation of the argument from design, confessed in the end that he had no *other* adequate explanation to offer for the world's existence. But the incapacity of Kant and Hume (and of all other eighteenth-century thinkers) to conceive of a way in which the natural world could have come into existence other than through intentional design is simply a function of their having written before Darwin. We, in contrast, have no such excuse.

But even if we accept, as the relevant scientific evidence now overwhelmingly indicates, that human beings (and all other life-forms) came into existence through a process of evolution that can be traced back approximately four billion years, one might argue that evolution is merely the means by which a Creator God realized His intentions for the world. Creation, perhaps, did not literally occur in six days, but creation it was, nonetheless. If we accept this argument, then we can preserve, it would seem, the idea that human beings were created for the purpose of achieving some particular end—perhaps the cultivation of their own good will, as Kant claimed.

We should not be sympathetic to this argument. It is in fact what it appears to be at first glance—a case of desperately clutching at straws. For on the one hand, since we now have, in the theory of evolution, a fully adequate explanation of how the integrated complexity of the natural world emerged without any need of an original creative intelligence, appealing to God is superfluous. It is rather like, once the details of a crime have been reconstructed by meticulous police work, insisting that the known perpetrator *must* have had an accomplice, even though there is nothing to suggest that he needed one and nothing to suggest that anyone else was present. Nor is this all, or even the worst. For on the other hand, an omniscient and omnipotent deity who would choose to achieve his ends through the astonishingly wasteful and brutal process of natural selection could by no stretch of the imagination be described as benevolent. If what happens in this world has any moral significance at all, God would have to be considered guilty of abominable immorality. I am referring here not to the evils that human beings have inflicted upon one another—for which God *might* be excused on the ground that He is not responsible for the human misuse of freedom—but rather to the perpetual horrors of disease, predation, and natural calamity.

The problem of evil has always posed the greatest challenge in theology. What could possibly justify, Ivan Karamazov asks, the suffering of innocent children?[5] The question is a good one, and in the face of a young child dying of cancer, for example, all a defender of God's goodness can do is insist upon the inscrutability of His motives. This way of dodging the issue has a very ancient pedigree. It goes all the way back to the book of Job, according to which, in order to make a point with Satan, God consented to have all of Job's possessions stolen, all of his children killed, and his body infested with boils. Then, as if to rub salt into the wounds, several of Job's friends, arriving to commiserate with him, observe that because the innocent are not punished, Job must be guilty of *something* to deserve such terrible misfortune. Job knows better, and finally challenges God to justify the evils to which he has been exposed. In response, God thunders intimidatingly, "Where wast thou when I laid the foundations of the earth? Declare if thou hast understanding." And Job, unable to explain how the world came into existence, abandons his questioning of God's justice and submits to the self-evidence of God's power.

A modern-day Job, however, could not be so easily put off. We can now answer the questions with which God intimidates Job. And God's power, which was something that believers always thought they could discern in the magnificence of His created works, is now an empty (because unnecessary) hypothesis. All that remains, then, is the challenge to God's sense of justice. But the problem of evil first arises as an insurmountable conceptual problem only if one accepts the theistic assumption that an omnipotent and benevolent God exists. The despairing cry "How could this have happened?" presumes the existence of a God who, in His omnipotence, could have caused things to happen otherwise, and who, in His benevolence, should have caused things to happen otherwise given that he could have. If the assumption of God's existence is incorrect, however, then to ask why the innocent should suffer in this world is to pose a meaningless question. Nothing justifies the gazelle's death in the jaws of the lion. The lion was hungry, the gazelle was unlucky. So too nothing justifies the child's death by cancer. The cancer was malignant, the child was unlucky.

To accept the sheer meaninglessness of innocent suffering, however, especially when it touches us directly, is for most people extraordinarily difficult. We want consolation, and the only thing that will effectively console us in the midst of tragedy is the idea that there has been no *real* tragedy—that present suffering is merely a price to be paid in exchange for a more than offsetting reward. But to believe this we must believe in a God with the power and inclination to make all things right, regardless of what dispassionate examination of the evidence suggests. Precisely because we want consolation in the face of tragedy, and because it is so easy to persuade ourselves that what we desperately want to be true is in fact true, we must actively resist the temptation to let our desires determine our beliefs. Whatever may have been the case before Darwin, today there is no need to appeal to the existence of God to explain the orderly complexity of our world. If we believe in the existence of God nonetheless, we find that our conception of Him as the benevolent, omniscient, and omnipotent Creator of *this* world—with all of its misery and sorrow—is incoherent, and we have to insist on the inscrutability of God's motives to preserve our faith. This is a warning sign that we are allowing our desires to govern our beliefs. Recognizing this, many intelligent people, who in an earlier age might have been believers, find today that they *cannot* believe in God.

For these people, Kant's contention that the purpose of human existence is the cultivation of good will rings hollow. The theory of evolution, after all, implies that we are here by chance. There is thus no purpose to human existence; there are merely the multifarious distinct purposes that individual human beings embrace for themselves. Some human beings may choose the cultivation of good will as one of their private goals, but Kant is clearly wrong in believing that reason requires it. In the light of evolution, we are left with nothing but hypothetical imperatives. (*If* you want to achieve *this* goal, you will have to do *that* in order to reach it. But on the other hand, if you don't, you needn't bother.) In Kant's estimation, this would mean the end of human dignity. For dignity, as he defines it, is a matter of recognizing and imposing upon oneself, as a rational being, the restraining force of the *categorical* imperative or moral law. If all we have are hypothetical imperatives, there is little if anything to distinguish us from the "lower" animals, since they too have their inclinations and pursue the satisfaction of their desires. But it is not only the Kantian conception of dignity that atheism/agnosticism undermines. Human beings cannot be deserving of a special measure of respect by virtue of their having been created "in God's image" when they have not been *created* at all (and there is no God). Thus the traditional Christian conception of human dignity is also undermined in the wake of Darwin.

INTO THE ENLIGHTENMENT

However, the modern conception of human dignity—as this emerged in Northern Europe in the eighteenth century—was not based exclusively upon Christian faith in the privileged position that God has assigned to human beings. This Christian belief certainly contributed its share, but so too did that questioning of the authority of tradition that we identify with the Enlightenment. This questioning of the tradition had already begun in earnest at least a couple of centuries earlier than the eighteenth—which is to say, in the Renaissance—but it was the thinkers of the Enlightenment who fully and intentionally embraced the questioning of authority as a fundamental principle governing the pursuit of knowledge. They did so in the recognition that individual human beings were all of them, potentially at least, explorers.

The age of exploration was initiated during the Renaissance. This took the form, most obviously, of exploration at sea—in the voyages of, among others, Dias, da Gama, Columbus, Vespucci, Magellan, and Drake. But the rediscovery of the Greek and Latin classics had released a flood of creative energy that found its outlet in a wide variety of endeavors—in science, in art, in religion, and in the marketplace.

In the burgeoning sciences (and protoscience) of astronomy, mechanics, biology, medicine, and alchemy, there was a growing reliance upon empiricism. Alchemists, lured by the false promise of gold and eternal life, became adept at experimentation, and their inquisitiveness led many of them to dedicate some of their time, and improving skills in the laboratory, to the study of mechanics, pharmacology, and chemistry proper. In astronomy and biology, enormous gains in understanding followed upon the invention of the telescope and microscope. And flowing back from the explorers of the New World were reports and specimens of all manner of bizarre plant and animal life to be assimilated by biologists.

In art, too, the Renaissance was a period not only of innovation, but of empirical investigation. Close observation of the natural world made possible both the development of the techniques of perspective and the great improvements in realistic representation in Renaissance painting and sculpture.

At no other point in history has the relation between the fine arts and the observational sciences been closer, as the prominence of Leonardo da Vinci in both fields indicates.

In religion, the empirical impulse took the form of an insistence on the part of Lutherans, Calvinists, and other Protestants that they be allowed to read and interpret scripture for themselves, and thus to take primary responsibility for mediating their own relationships to God, rather than continuing to leave that responsibility in the hands of the priesthood. In the realm of economics, the Renaissance witnessed the emergence of venture capitalism, as the newly discovered lands of the Americas, Africa, and the Indies opened extensive opportunities for economic entrepreneurship (and exploitation), and a new economic class—the financiers—grew wealthy in the process of backing these endeavors.

As the Renaissance drew to a close, René Descartes, in his *Discourse on Method*, provided the archetypal expression of the prevailing attitude of the period with his resolution to doubt everything that possibly could be doubted and to build the edifice of knowledge upon entirely new, and solidly grounded, foundations. But radical doubt and the new discoveries were upsetting to those with a conservative cast of mind, or with vested interests to protect, and thus during the Renaissance there was not only an enormous outpouring of creative energy in the sciences and in religious thought, but also ongoing efforts to violently suppress those creative activities and to restore the status quo. Resistance to the growing tendency of ordinary individuals to think for themselves came, first, from the traditional, and now increasingly threatened, authority of the Catholic Church, and second, from the centralized authority of the newly emerging nation-states such as France, England, and Spain, whose rulers sought to impose uniformity of custom and belief on the cultural mosaic of the various geographical regions and subregions that were now being forcefully unified.

Where opposition to authority was relatively feeble or disorganized, the Church could protect the status quo and the State could impose its will to uniformity by torturing and executing heretics on an individual basis, and in the process intimidating minorities into conformity. By these means, the Church kept Italy safely Catholic, and the Spanish monarchs Ferdinand, Isabella, and Philip II purged Spain of its Jews and Muslims. Where opposition was better organized and more numerous, efforts to impose religious conformity resulted in a series of devastating and atrocity-filled wars that wracked Europe throughout the late sixteenth and early seventeenth centuries—the Thirty Years' War, the Huguenot wars in France, the English Civil War, and the wars of liberation of the Protestant Netherlands against Catholic Spain.

As the wars of religious intolerance dragged on, the increasingly appalled and exhausted parties began to search for a way to escape the cycle of violence that had been unleashed. There had always been voices raised in favor of tolerance, but initially these were the voices only of the victims of oppression—the free thinkers and Protestants who could not see how their mere existence posed a threat to the authority of Church and State. As long as it seemed likely that religious conformity could be imposed by force, these voices carried no weight. Only when it had become clear that, in some places at least, religious minorities were too deeply entrenched to be extirpated was there a growing willingness to look for a modus vivendi involving compromise and the protection of religious freedoms. Philosophers and political theorists led the way in this search, and some of the most astute of them—Thomas Hobbes, for example—concluded that there simply was no solution to be found.

Hobbes took as his initial assumptions, first, the obviously self-centered inclinations and desires of ordinary human beings; second, the fact that the available resources by means of which human beings can satisfy their inclinations and desires are scarce; and third, the fact that any human being could, simply by picking his or her moment and the right tool, inflict serious injury or death upon any other human being. Hobbes believed that, taken in combination, these three facts implied that in the primordial "state of nature" (that is, the state in which human beings find themselves before they have entered into any political relations with one another) the conflicting desires of individuals would place each of them in perpetual war with all others. This unhappy situation could be escaped, Hobbes argued, only by virtue of two things: the capacity of individuals, as rational agents, to recognize the benefits to be gained—in the form of an increase in personal security as well as in cooperation—by entering into a social contract with one another; and the existence of someone who actually possessed the power to punish infractions of the social contract, and in so doing to make the contract not only desirable but real. This role was to be played by the king, but the political legitimacy of the monarch depended entirely on his ability to exercise power and preserve the public peace. If a weak monarch lost the capacity to enforce his political will, then it was sensible, prudent, and legitimate for his former subjects to seek the social stability and unity offered by a new ruler who did possess the power to punish. In this respect, even though Hobbes conceived of *Leviathan*, which he wrote during the English Civil War, as a defense of the royalist cause, his thought was too radical in its implications, too clearly committed to the proposition that "might makes right," for any political group of his day to embrace.

If Hobbes's political theory was too uncompromising to be welcomed by his contemporaries, it nonetheless provided a more convincing picture of how and why men accepted the authority of political leaders than did the traditional ideology of the "divine right of kings." Far too many kings had come by their thrones through usurpation—by repudiating the "divine right" of earlier kings—for this ideology to carry much conviction among the thoughtful. But if the "divine right of kings" was a fiction, at least it promoted stability. It was also relatively easy to graft onto it the idea that, as God's privileged servant, a king must himself observe the moral restraints imposed by "natural law." He could not tyrannize over his subjects and claim in doing so that he had the support of God. Hobbes's theory, in contrast, not only stripped the sovereign of any pretense of legitimacy extending beyond the might of his arms, it also provided a justification for any successful attempt to unseat him. And because one could not know until after a given attempt had been made whether or not it would prove successful, in this respect Hobbes's theory clearly seemed to promote political instability. Moreover, insofar as the sovereign's authority rested entirely upon his personal power, if he was confident in that power, he had no reason to accept any constraints—moral or otherwise—upon his rule. Since his will *constituted* the law for his subjects, and he himself was subject to no one, he was personally *above* the law.

LOCKE AND THE ENGLISH EXPERIENCE

Hobbes wrote *Leviathan* when the conflict in England over who should rule, King or Parliament, was at its height, and the outcome was unclear. Between then and 1690, when William of Orange defeated James II at the Battle of the Boyne and John Locke's *Two Treatises of Government* was published, the situation changed in England in such a way as to make it possible to discern how the absolutist implications of *Leviathan* might be avoided—how it might be possible, in other words, to guarantee political compromise and cooperation, and incidentally protect religious freedom, without having to rely upon the authority and good will of an all-powerful sovereign.

The English Civil War had come about because King Charles I had insisted upon what he took to be his royal prerogatives, under the prevailing political philosophy of monarchical absolutism, to rule his kingdom as he saw fit, while Parliament had insisted upon what it took to be its own traditional rights—chief among which were the right to approve temporary tax measures and, implicitly, the right at least to discuss the advisability of the foreign and domestic policies that made necessary the raising of such extraordinary revenues. This tension over the control of finances and indirectly over the control of policy was hardly a problem unique to England in the seventeenth century. War had been an expensive pastime for kings even in the Middle Ages, and in the early modern era, with the growing reliance upon substantial navies

and standing armies, both of which had to be extensively equipped with artillery and regularly paid, most monarchs found it impossible to finance their
foreign policies entirely, as the principles of feudalism required, with money
raised from their private royal estates. Not all monarchs, however, were as dependent as the Stuarts were upon the cooperativeness of their representative
assemblies.

English kings were confronted with two factors that significantly complicated the business of ruling. First, there was the English common law tradition, which encouraged jurists like Edward Coke to think of themselves as
representatives and defenders of the rule of law itself, rather than as servants
of the king. Second, and even more importantly, there was the fact that in
Britain religious fragmentation had proceeded further than it had anywhere
else in Europe, with the possible exception of Germany. It was not a matter,
as in France, of there being two camps pitted against each other, with one
clearly dominant over the other. In seventeenth-century Britain there were,
roughly speaking, three camps, no one of which was permanently able to gain
the upper hand over the other two. There were the Catholics, which included
the Stuarts themselves, their immediate circle among the nobles, and the Irish.
There were the Anglicans, which included the larger portion of the nobles, as
well as the gentry and yeomanry of the English countryside. And finally, there
were the various dissenting sects—Quakers, Methodists, Baptists, Presbyte-
rians, and so forth—whose strength lay predominantly in the urban centers
and in Scotland. Given this complication of interests, ruling Britain in the
seventeenth century required considerable tact and political acumen, qualities
that Charles I unfortunately lacked.

When the civil war that his heavy-handedness precipitated ended with
Charles's execution, England tried for a while to get along without a king.
The Roundhead general, Oliver Cromwell, governed the nation competently
as Lord Protector until his death in 1658, but declined the offer to become a
monarch. His son Richard succeeded him as Lord Protector, but quickly
alienated his father's primary constituency—the army—and found that without its support he was in no position to govern. As a result, in 1660 the Stuarts were invited to return from exile, and the eldest son of the executed
Charles I became king after all—a chastened king, however, at least initially,
with a healthy awareness of the power and rights of Parliament.

Upon his taking the throne, Charles II promised a regime of religious tolerance in England. However, he did so without first consulting the opinion of
Parliament, which passed instead a series of acts designed to repress both
Catholics and Protestant dissenters alike. The new king accepted the situation
at first. Ironically, though, it was during Charles's reign that the monarchy finally reestablished a measure of financial independence from Parliament—as

a result of the Anglo-Dutch naval wars, which, while proving to be a stand-off on the field of battle, strategically were an enormous success, multiplying English commerce many times over and filling the royal tax coffers in the process. With the freedom of action this provided them, and sensing the unwillingness of most Englishmen to face the prospect of renewed civil war, Charles tentatively, and his brother James much more openly, began to work for the restoration of Catholic rights.

In this regard, James II, who ruled for a scant three years, seriously underestimated English fear of a renewed Catholic supremacy—a fear that was exacerbated in 1685 by Louis XIV's revocation of the Edict of Nantes, which had protected Protestantism in France for almost a century, and the subsequent suppression of Huguenot congregations. Two events brought matters to a head and set the stage for another revolution. First, in June 1688 a male heir to the throne was born, creating the prospect of a Catholic succession. Second, in a heavy-handed manner reminiscent of his father, James attempted to pack Parliament with men who would oblige him by repealing the anti-Catholic Test Acts, and began to purge mayors, justices of the peace, and even Anglican bishops who would not cooperate with his efforts. This time when revolution came there was no beheading, and not much of a struggle. A number of the leading Protestants invited James's son-in-law and nephew, William of Orange, the Stadholder of the United Netherlands,[6] to replace James as king. When William arrived in Devon and began his cross-country march to London, James could only watch as his support among the people, and army, drained away. Losing heart, he fled to France, returning (to Ireland) in 1690 to make just one abortive bid to recover his throne.

The combination of the civil war and the Glorious Revolution of 1688 established Parliament's position in England as virtually a coequal authority with the crown. In actual fact, during William's reign, Parliament did not assert its authority too loudly. William had, after all, been *invited* to become king, and for his part, given his prior experience as a Stadholder of the Netherlands, William understood how to cope with a powerful representative assembly. All the same, Parliament took advantage of the fact that William and Mary were childless to lay down, before the end of William's reign, a clear declaration of Parliamentary rights and powers. No subsequent English king would ever be able to think of himself as the sort of absolute monarch that, for example, Henry VIII had been.

The reason for providing this summary of developments in England during the seventeenth century is to show how, where pure philosophical reflection (on the part of Thomas Hobbes) proved unequal to the task of explaining how the seemingly perpetual curse of political tyranny might be evaded, a fortunate combination of historical circumstances and an attentive observer (in the person of John Locke) of the delicate balance of power that these gave rise to *could* and *did* hit upon a solution to the problem.

John Locke was more than a mere interested observer of political events in the reigns of the later Stuarts. As a close friend and personal adviser of the first Earl of Shaftesbury, the most important Protestant parliamentarian of his day, Locke was not only given an insider's view of the workings of government, he was actively involved in Shaftesbury's maneuvers to prevent the succession of James II, who, unlike his brother Charles, refused even to pretend that he was not a Catholic. After Shaftesbury's efforts led to his arrest for treason in 1681, Locke, like many of Shaftesbury's supporters, came under surveillance, and in 1683, in the wake of the alleged Rye House Plot,[7] Locke fled to Holland and lived there until James II had been driven from the throne of England. In his six years in Holland, Locke had an opportunity to see firsthand how the conditions that he and his patron Shaftesbury had struggled to bring about in England—constitutional monarchy and an official policy of religious tolerance—could actually be realized in a modern nation-state.[8] In 1690, with William and Mary's accession, those policies finally triumphed in England as well and, as both a justification and exposition of constitutional monarchy, Locke published (although anonymously) his *Two Treatises of Government*.

Locke's basic presuppositions in this work are almost diametrically opposed to Hobbes's assumptions in *Leviathan*. Where Hobbes assumed that individual humans are entirely self-oriented in their activities, Locke stresses that political theory must start with the recognition that individual humans are not their own masters but are the creatures and servants of God. Thus, according to Locke, the state of nature that is supposed to exist before community is established cannot be properly characterized as a state of perpetual war of each against all, because "the State of Nature has a Law of Nature to govern it, which obliges everyone: And Reason, which is that Law, teaches all Mankind, who will but consult it, that being all equal and independent, no one ought to harm another. . . ."[9] The natural law to which Locke appeals here is God's will, which can be understood through the exercise of reason—a faculty given to us by God specifically so that we might appreciate his intent. For Locke, as for Kant, it is our possession of reason that distinguishes us from the brutes, and accounts for our freedom and equality. As Locke puts it, "We are *born Free* as we are born Rational."[10]

But not everyone, of course, does consult reason or abide by the law of nature. There are dangerous self-oriented individuals in the world even if, as Locke insists, the majority of people are rational and God-fearing. How are those who *do* recognize the natural law to relate to the dangerous self-oriented few? Locke's response is uncompromising. The individual who refuses to recognize that reason is the mode of cooperation between human beings, and who attempts to kill or enslave another, thereby denying his equality and freedom as a fellow rational creature, is liable to destruction by the injured party (acting on behalf of humankind) just as any rampaging wild beast would be. This violent resistance of another's depredations by the intended victim is not itself a lawless act, no more so than is the execution by the state of a condemned criminal an act of murder. In both cases what justifies the violence is the fact that it occurs in conformity with, and defense of, the natural law. The only difference is that in the state of nature the individual, not yet having delegated to the community his power and right to preserve justice, for the obvious reason that no such community yet exists, acts on his own authority. So long as his actions are in accordance with natural law, there is no objection to be raised.

On the basis of just this much knowledge of Locke's political theory, one can see already that he, just as readily as Hobbes, was able to justify political revolution under certain not-too-uncommon circumstances. For Locke the relevant circumstances were different than they were for Hobbes, however. Whereas Hobbes at least implied that revolution was legitimate whenever the sovereign was suspected of not actually possessing the power to enforce his will, for Locke the crucial issue was not how much power the king possessed but whether or not he exercised it in accordance with the principles of natural law. Even a powerful king, such as Charles II undeniably was by the 1680s, deserved to be challenged if his rule was despotic. For a despotic king in effect enslaved his subjects, denying their existence as fellow rational creatures, and thus put himself at odds with humanity generally. Like that of an unrestrained wild beast, his power was subject to destruction in the service of justice. Moreover, while an absolute monarch did not necessarily rule contrary to the principles of natural law, since he too possessed reason, insofar as a monarch's rule truly was *absolute*, there was the constant danger of its becoming despotic. Constitutional monarchy was thus far preferable.

In order to explain the proper relationship between those governing and those they governed, however, Locke first had to offer his own account of the considerations that led individual human beings voluntarily to enter into the social compact. Here he introduced the important concept of *property*, which referred, as he employed the term, to personal wealth, goods, and land, certainly, but also to the individual's life and personal liberties. All of these the individual possessed to a greater or lesser degree, Locke contended, *before* the political community had been established, and the individual entered into the social compact primarily for the sake of the protection that it offered for this private property.

Here again we find a major point of disagreement between Locke and Hobbes. According to Hobbes, it is not until such time as the political community has been set up that any significant property can be thought of as being privately owned. The insecurity of the individual in the Hobbesian state of nature implies that nothing, not even his own life, can be *owned* with any assurance. Locke, relying upon the presumed general acknowledgment by rational human beings of the principles of natural law, argues that there *is* already, even in the state of nature, meaningful ownership of private property, but that this ownership is not as secure as it could be, given the absence of any communal response to the dangers posed by irrational entirely self-oriented individuals.

What grounds are there, however, for thinking that *reason* recognizes the individual's right to private property? For unless the natural law, as understood by reason, implies the right to private property, Locke's argument collapses. According to Locke, private ownership of goods and land is implied by the fact that everyone owns his own body and thus also his own labor. From this it follows that those things existing in nature, the value of which one personally improves by mixing one's labor with them, one now has a legitimate claim to own as well—providing only that one's appropriation of those things leaves "enough and as good" behind for the satisfaction of the needs of others. One cannot, in other words, lay claim to the *only* piece of arable land available by tilling it, but where there is plenty of arable land to be had, the mere fact of tilling some portion of it does provide one with a rightful claim to the possession of the land that one has improved. "Thus in the beginning all the world was *America*,"[11] Locke contends, with nature's bounty waiting to be appropriated by anyone who made the effort to improve some portion of it.

The point of this argument is to show that the private ownership of property does not depend upon the common consent of mankind, given that natural law itself implies private ownership, and thus that property cannot rightfully be taken from its owner without his consent. This consent may, however, be merely implicit—as in the case where an individual, by accepting the benefits of citizenship, tacitly consents to be taxed by the duly constituted government of the nation to which he belongs, even though he may personally disagree with some of the policies to be supported by the revenues raised in this way. Because the citizens of a nation embrace the social compact voluntarily and for the sake of the protection it offers for their private property—because, in other words, they are enticed into the compact by promises, rather than driven into it by fear—the community established by the social compact *owes* them delivery on those promises. It follows that the governing power in this community cannot rule either arbitrarily or for the sake of its own benefit, but rather must govern for the benefit of the general citizenry. The executive power of government is to be understood, Locke contends, as a *trust*—in the financial sense of that word. And just as trustees who dip into their trust for personal enrichment are dismissed, and sometimes prosecuted for malfeasance, so too in the well-formed government the executive must be held to account for its actions and be removable if it abuses its authority.

This, of course, is precisely what the English themselves had done, by force of arms, with both Charles I and James II. It was to be hoped, however, that in the future the executive power could be more peacefully restrained. Parliament, after all, had *offered* William of Orange the executive authority, and made it a condition of his accepting that William understand that Parliament was not thereby abdicating any of its own legislative powers. William grasped the role that he was being asked to assume, and immediately made this clear by taking the initiative in formally recognizing the independence of the judiciary. For this new political dispensation that the English had created for themselves in the crucible of lived historical events, Locke provided a theoretical justification in his doctrine of the separation of executive and legislative powers. The familiar system of checks and balances, which has become a cornerstone of democratic political theory, is intended to guarantee that the executive authority will understand that its power is indeed a *trust* and not an invitation to tyranny.

As a work of political philosophy, Locke's *Two Treatises* (and especially the second, "On Civil Government") had enormous and immediate success. Copies of it were available in French almost as soon as it appeared in English, and the fact that the author of the work was the celebrated John Locke of *An Essay Concerning Human Understanding* was something of an open secret. In the early decades of the eighteenth century, moreover, two of the greatest French authors of the day, Voltaire and Montesquieu, lived for a time in England and immersed themselves in Locke's writings as well as in English culture generally, and through their intermediary influence, admiration of Locke's political philosophy as well as of English government became central features of French liberalism.

For all of the enormous influence that it has had, and continues to have, however, Locke's political theory contains serious flaws. It is difficult to make clear sense of his notion of property, and especially of the proviso that, in appropriating those natural resources with which one has mixed one's labor, one must leave "enough and as good" for others. How do we determine whether this proviso has been satisfied? Locke blithely asserts that there is plenty of land still available (in his day), but his remark that "in the beginning all the world was *America*," for modern readers, should make his ideas concerning property seem less plausible rather than more. After all, in America "enough and as good" was *not* left for the natives who chose to hunt rather than till, or who, like some tribes on the Eastern seaboard, chose to till in what the settlers deemed to be the wrong manner! The question to which Locke has no satisfactory answer to offer, and the significance of which he does not entirely seem to appreciate in *The Two Treatises*, is *how much* must one improve the "value" of the natural resources that provide one's living in order for one to have a right to their preservation for one's own use.

America was not empty when the European settlers arrived. Granted, those settlers managed, on average, to generate more food from a given acreage of land than the natives had. But if that fact alone is sufficient to justify their excluding the natives from what had been their hunting grounds, then as more and more land is turned over to agriculture, soon hunting as a way of life must become impossible. Does reason (or God) disapprove, then, of hunting as a way of supporting oneself? If so, why? And of course, the problem is not restricted to a conflict between hunting and agriculture. Various forms of agriculture can also conflict. In fact, if we ignore the cultural and racial dimensions of the former struggle, we can see that, as the American frontier moved westward, essentially the same (economic) conflict between settlers and natives was repeated between farmers and cattle barons. By and large, cattlemen had arrived first in the trans-Mississippi, but their method of using the land—as pasturage—was less intensive than that of the "sodbusters." Does it follow that ranching, unlike farming, does *not* give one a claim to property in land? But if ranching *does* give one a claim to ownership, why does hunting fail to do so?

Surely it cannot be the case that the more intensive usage of land *always* takes precedence in conferring ownership. For then there could be no grounds for preventing would-be "developers" from mining, or lumbering, or farming in what has been set aside as parkland. One might be tempted to reply here that once ownership has been established, as the United States established ownership over the lands that eventually became the national parks, the owner can do what he will with his property—including allowing it to lie fallow. But if, as Locke claims, property is legitimately acquired only by mixing one's labor with what had previously been unclaimed, how does a *nation* ever come to own huge tracts of fallow land—Alaska, for example? The answer, of course, *cannot* be by purchasing it from Russia, for then one must ask how Russia came to own it. There *is* an obviously correct answer here, but it is provided by Hobbes, not Locke. A nation comes to own the territory it claims by conquest—by establishing and maintaining its authority over the territory in question through force of arms. Only once the claim has been recognized by others do the niceties of negotiation and purchase become relevant. Locke acknowledges that as a matter of fact conquest does occur; he simply denies that it ever confers legitimate ownership of land or goods.

According to Locke, however, there is *one* form of property ownership that does legitimately arise from conquest. Contrary to what his opening declaration that individual humans are not their own masters but are all the creatures and servants of God might lead one to suspect, Locke does not consider slavery to be a violation in principle of natural law. Slavery is justified, he contends, when it is the consequence of crime or of a "wrongful war." The perpetrators of crime or of wrongful war, if they are overcome by the righteous, forfeit their lives to their conquerors. If their conquerors then decide to make use of them as slaves rather than kill them outright in punishment, this is within their rights. (The slaves themselves, Locke observes, have the opportunity to demand the appropriate punishment of death whenever they wish, simply by resisting to the uttermost the imposition of slavery.) But leaving aside the question of whether, when death is warranted, anything other than death (torture?) must also be legitimate, is it so clear when a war is in fact "wrongful" and when it is not? In the heat of battle, it *helps* to feel one's cause is just and one's enemy is a villain. This is why the verdict of history and cooler times is always relevant in determining whether a war actually *needed* to be fought. But if, in the flush of victory over one's "villainous" enemy, one is permitted to enslave him, what likelihood is there that the victor's cooler moments of reflection will ever suggest to him that perhaps the struggle was one over a question to which there were, after all, two sides?[12]

The fundamental problem with Locke's political philosophy is his insistence on the rational self-evidence of natural law. Locke insists, literally as a matter of faith, that reason can always recognize when property claims are justified and when a war is "wrongful." But the shortcomings of this exaltation of reason at the expense of experience have been shown already in my discussion of Kant's categorical imperative. Reason does not exhaustively comprehend on cue all that may be relevant regarding a given concrete situation requiring moral judgment. Experience is inexhaustible and there is always the possibility that something the significance of which we have so far failed to appreciate is precisely *that* consideration on which the moral judgment *should* ultimately turn. But in the meantime, of course, we must get on with living. There are difficulties to be faced, and reason—along with tradition—is clearly one of the more powerful resources upon which we can draw in dealing with them. The problem, then, is not our reliance upon reason, but rather *overconfidence* in our reliance upon it. Locke, like Kant and the Enlightenment generally, was guilty of supreme overconfidence in the powers of reason.[13]

In spite of its shortcomings, which were not nearly as apparent in the eighteenth century as they should be today, Locke's political philosophy was appealing, especially to the wealthy and well-placed, because in its oversimple picture of the challenges posed by the social interactions of human beings in community life, it promised the possibility of achieving simultaneously security from external dangers and also from internal tyrannies. In a word, Locke's account was *optimistic* where Hobbes's had been *pessimistic*, and in 1690 with James II safely removed from power, optimism was the spirit of the day. In the years to come that optimism only deepened as the success of the English experiment in mixed government demonstrated that a society could tolerate a considerable measure of internal disagreement about religion, and even about social policy, without fragmenting into warring parties because of it. This was possible, of course, provided, first, that freedom of conscience was guaranteed, and second, that there were means available—in the form of Parliament, for example—of eventually effecting widely desired political change without having to resort to force. In a broader sense, what these particular political lessons seemed to indicate was that the structure of society itself was amenable to *scientific* investigation, and that solutions could be found to the chronic problems of social organization through the exercise of reason.

THE LATER ENLIGHTENMENT

These developments of the sixteenth and seventeenth centuries—the refinement of political thought, the emergence of science, the discovery of new lands and peoples, and the growth in economic wealth that both science and exploration promoted—combined to set the stage for what has been described as the great secular religion of the eighteenth and nineteenth centuries—the Enlightenment faith in the inexorability of progress. The central doctrines of this faith were set out, with minor variations, in the many "universal histories" that were produced during this period. The most important of these were Turgot's "Universal History," Condorcet's *Picture of the Progress of the Human Mind*, Hegel's *Philosophy of History*, and August Comte's *Positive Philosophy* and *Positive Polity*. Reduced to their essence, the central doctrines ran as follows: (1) that progress was driven by the free employment of reason—in science, in the marketplace, in social organization and policy direction—as opposed to reliance upon some privileged intellectual or political authority; (2) that those who valued progress would consequently strive to increase the sphere of freedom available to individuals; and (3) that the measure of freedom actually enjoyed in a given society could thus be taken as indicative of how relatively "advanced" the society in question was. The entire thrust of history, these philosophers argued, each in his particular fashion, was toward the elimination of all forms of tyranny and toward the growth of freedom and equality. But the inexorability of progress that these thinkers read into the course of history was not underwritten by any *divine* guarantee. It was not that *God* could be counted upon to free the oppressed, on the one hand, and provide riches, on the other. An earlier age had thought this way, but by the end of the eighteenth century, progress had been demythologized. Now it was thought simply that, once reason had gained a significant foothold in a culture, its obvious advantages would tend to preserve and to extend its range of influence.

Thus all cultures—even those "primitive" cultures that had only relatively recently been discovered in the Americas, in Africa, and in the Pacific—were thought of as progressing along the same road to freedom, although they were located at the moment, of course, at very different points along that road. This self-flattering judgment on the part of West Europeans—that their own culture represented the highest expression of human civilization so far achieved, and thus a point on the highway of progress to which more primitive cultures must eventually come—allowed the seafaring Europeans to combine their idealism with the pursuit of economic self-interest. For clearly (or so at least it seemed to European colonizers) it was to the benefit of primitive peoples to be guided and educated by those who had come further and who thus knew the road still to be traveled by nonwhite cultures. And thus we come to the curious irony that lay at the heart of the Enlightenment's faith in progress: on the one hand, Western colonizers of the nineteenth century for the most part genuinely did believe that all humans were brothers[14] and that freedom was both the goal and engine of progress, and yet they were equally convinced that, by virtue of the "primitiveness" of nonwhites, and for their own benefit, their labor could and should be directed by Europeans, who would then reap the profit of that labor. It is easy to condemn the obvious ethnocentrism of self-serving Western judgments concerning the "primitiveness" of other cultures (including even the ancient and highly literate cultures of India and China). In spite of this, however, it is difficult to scoff at the Enlightenment conviction that freedom is a universal, even an ultimate, good for humankind. (And when the "primitives" revolted in one colony after another against the purveyors of these Enlightenment beliefs, it was always, of course, for the sake of freedom, rather than against it, that they rebelled.)

Where the Enlightenment ideal of freedom was misconceived—as it was right from the start—was in its failure to distinguish between the various uses of, and justifications for, freedom. After all, freedom of thought and freedom of action are very different things. And even the freedom of thought is one thing in the context of religious belief, where it constitutes an inviolable sanctuary for personal faith, and quite another in the context of scientific inquiry, where it challenges the investigator to evaluate, recognize, and cope with the best evidence available. But in the adoption of freedom as a political ideal, these nuances for the most part failed to register. *"Liberté, egalité, fraternité!"* the French revolutionaries proposed, without inquiring too deeply into the question of how one person's liberty might impinge upon and reduce another's, thus undermining both equality and fraternity. (Meanwhile the guillotine carried on with its grisly work.) So too, Thomas Jefferson, author of the lines, "We hold these truths to be self-evident; that all men are created equal; that they are endowed by their Creator with certain inalienable rights; that among these are life, liberty, and the pursuit of happiness," without doubt the most famous political pronouncement of the ideals of freedom and human dignity, was apparently only mildly disturbed by the inconsistency involved in his owning a considerable number of slaves. Repeatedly, justifications of freedom that were legitimate only with respect to the freedom of *thought*, and which were based ultimately upon the importance of promoting the free employment of reason, have been fallaciously appealed to, in the political forum, in defense of the freedom of *action*, no matter how *unreasonable* this action might be. Thus, for example, right from the start in America the freedom to pursue one's personal happiness was taken to mean the right to own property (including property in human form) and the right to grow wealthy at whomever's expense—the black slave's, the red Indian's, the propertyless recent immigrant's.

One later Enlightenment thinker who did keep clear the distinction between freedom of thought and freedom of action, although he was no opponent of the acquisition of wealth, was John Stuart Mill. As we have already seen, the central contention of Mill's *On Liberty* is that each of us should have the right to live his life as he pleases, providing only that he does not harm others or interfere with their liberty to live their lives as they may wish. Mill's justification for this claim has two sides to it. On the one hand, given the limitations of our human capacity to know, we should presume that no one other than the person *whose life it actually is* is in a better position to say how it should be lived if it is to prove as satisfying as possible. On the other hand, by tolerating one another's experiments in the art of living, we may come to learn more fully what sorts of things are capable of adding value to a life. In this sense, Mill sees continuity between the empirical attitude to be adopted in science and the empirical attitude to be adopted in ethics. Understanding the world and our place within it should be conceived, in both cases, as a collective enterprise involving the application of reason to the evidence supplied by experience.

In the collective enterprise that is science, it is a fundamental methodological principle that the opinions of other inquirers are to be respected—that is, viewed as at least potentially correct—until such time as they have been adequately tested and shown to be faulty. One implication of Mill's argument is that in ethics—and by extension, in politics as well—the same principle should hold. Not only are *opinions* to be granted a measure of presumptive respect, however, so too are the *holders* of those opinions. Because each of us is, at least in principle, capable of formulating new insights in the realm of ethics or politics, insights that may prove beneficial to the larger community, each of us is to be granted a certain measure of public respect for the sake of what we *might* contribute, regardless of whether or not a worthwhile contribution is ever actually forthcoming from us. This, of course, is a somewhat different way of conceiving of human dignity than that offered by Kant. Here the idea is that dignity attaches to human beings simply by virtue of their capacity to explore the unknown and to share their discoveries, rather than because, as "rational beings," they are (unrealistically) presumed to have the capacity to recognize and act upon objective ethical truths.

With regard to both the Kantian and Millian conceptions of dignity, moreover, we can distinguish between a weaker form of respect that is automatically due to all human beings in light of their potential and a stronger form of respect that is accorded to individuals only to the degree that they manage actually to deliver on that potential. In the Kantian framework, the stronger form of respect is due to those individuals who not only recognize the moral law but who act in accordance with it. In the Millian, inquiry-based framework, the stronger form of respect is due to those individuals who not only might make worthwhile contributions to our understanding but actually do make such contributions. It is important to recognize, however, that while in the Kantian framework the stronger form of respect takes priority over the weaker, in the Millian or inquiry-based framework the weaker form of respect takes priority over the stronger. Let us consider why.

For Kant, the goal of morality can be equally well defined in several different ways: it is the possession of a good will; it is acknowledging one's duty; it is a matter of treating other rational beings as ends rather than as means; it is possession of dignity in the strong sense of not only recognizing, but also responding to, the demands of reason. The goal of morality can be defined in all of these different ways because they are all essentially equivalent expressions. This is why, for Kant, the stronger form of human dignity takes priority over the weaker. Actually achieving the goal of morality is more important than merely being able to recognize what that goal must be. After all, the thief and the murderer, according to Kant, recognize the requirements of morality too, but as individuals governed in this respect by their inclinations rather than their reason, they allow themselves to ignore those requirements and behave in a manner unbefitting rational beings.

By contrast, Mill does not believe that the goal of morality can actually be achieved in anything like the unequivocal manner that Kant has in mind.

Whereas Kant sees moral deliberation as a matter of pure rational deduction, rather like what we encounter in mathematics, Mill takes ethics to be an empirical discipline (like geography) employing a combination of reason and experience and illuminating a realm that can never be exhaustively known. Thus, as I remarked earlier, the picture that Mill offers us in *On Liberty* is one in which each individual human being can be thought of as a kind of explorer in the realm of values—an explorer following his own unique trajectory into the unknown, and reporting back from time to time about what he has discovered there. According to Mill, moreover, it is *as* a self-directing investigator of the realm of values that a human being exhibits dignity. But in marked contrast to what we find in the Kantian framework, in this inquiry-based framework dignity is a *precondition* rather than a *byproduct* of the enterprise. (For Kant, the goal of the moral enterprise is autonomy, and the stronger form of dignity can be thought of as the byproduct of achieving autonomy.) What the individual is looking for in his forays into the unknown, according to Mill, are insights into how best to live his life. His dignity—which is to say, our acknowledgment of his right to be allowed to explore where he will—to some extent makes his explorations possible, but it is not, even indirectly, anything he sets out in search of. As an explorer who is primarily searching for insights into how best to live his *own* life, moreover, the individual is not obliged to report his discoveries either explicitly or in a timely fashion. He may be too busy simply living his life to wish to spend any time proselytizing about it. For this reason, the stronger form of respect associated with the inquiry-based framework—that is, the respect accorded to the individual who actually discovers something that others consider significant—is less important than is the weaker form of respect that first establishes the possibility of all such discoveries in the realm of values. This is because the stronger form of respect is unreliable: it may accrue to individuals whose discoveries will not in fact withstand the test of time; and it may not accrue to individuals who deserve it, simply because we are unaware of the discoveries that they have made.

For Kant, then, the form of dignity that matters primarily is an exceedingly demanding (but not entirely unattainable) ideal to which rational beings must aspire. For Mill, dignity is not something to be earned; it is something to which all human beings have a prima facie claim. And neither indolence nor foolishness on their part jeopardizes their dignity as long as they continue to respect the rights of others. In contemporary usage of the term "dignity," we hear both of these overtones, but today we hear predominantly the Millian, egalitarian strain.

The reason for this is that what I call the Millian, inquiry-based framework for dignity was by no means original with Mill. He was merely its most eloquent expositor. The idea that what constitutes the well-lived life (and so too, by extension, the well-governed state and the well-run economy) is discovered most readily when people are granted the freedom to explore and test their inclinations was one of the primary recurrent themes of the Enlightenment. There are anticipations of it in both Locke's political theory and his empiricism. The central doctrine of the Enlightenment—the insistence on freedom—was not always (as the example of Kant illustrates) justified in terms of the benefits to be gained from extending the range of human experience, but this was nonetheless probably the most commonly offered justification. And two enormously influential thinkers in the English-speaking world— Adam Smith and James Madison—had explicitly drawn this connection between freedom, experience, and sound management well before Mill did.

FREEDOM IN THE MARKETPLACE, AND IN POLITICS

Adam Smith, in advocating the benefits of economic free enterprise, was arguably the first[15] to draw attention to the tremendous flexibility enjoyed by an economy in which individuals are allowed to employ their talents, energies, and resources as they see fit. Basically, his idea is that the range of circumstances bearing in one way or another upon the production of wealth in a nation is inconceivably vast—far beyond the capacity of any one person, or small group of people, to comprehend in detail—and thus that an economy functions most efficiently when those who are actually on the scene—those who, given their direct involvement with the affairs in question, are in a position to see some means of improving efficiency—are also free to *act* upon that insight and introduce the improvement in question (or at least to run the experiment to see whether the envisaged alteration will in fact constitute an improvement). But this cannot be all there is to it, for unless those who see the opportunities are also motivated to introduce the changes that seem called for, the opportunity will go begging and there will be no improvement in economic efficiency. The easiest and most reliable way to motivate individual initiative, it is almost universally presumed, is to allow those who exhibit it to keep a substantial portion of the increase in wealth that their initiative generates. Thus, in what is probably the most widely quoted and best-known passage in *The Wealth of Nations*, Smith observes that, "It is not from the benevolence of the butcher, the brewer, or the baker that we expect our dinner, but from their regard to their self-interest. We address ourselves, not to their humanity, but to their self-love, and never talk to them of our necessities, but of their advantages." We pay them, in other words, and we pay them the more handsomely, all other things being equal, the more singular the service they provide.

Essentially the same argument that Adam Smith made regarding the requirements of economic efficiency was advanced with respect to the requirements of political justice by innumerable advocates of democracy in the eighteenth century, of whom James Madison was merely one. Here again, the basic idea is that a decision-maker—even a benign one—removed from and thus unaware of the actual detailed consequences of his decisions cannot govern with the same sensitivity to particular circumstance and lived consequence as can a system in which everyone affected has the opportunity to focus general attention upon specific problems and to propose specific solutions. As with the free-market system, the comparative strength of democracy is seen to be twofold: first, in its greater responsiveness to inefficiencies and injustices, and second, in its capacity to take advantage of insightful initiatives regardless of where they may originate.

But the reason for linking the names of Smith and Madison is that each of them was rendered somewhat uneasy by his recognition that, with respect to economics on the one hand, and with respect to politics on the other, he was advocating the adoption of a system that frankly acknowledged the pursuit of self-interest to be the drivespring of social interaction. (In Adam Smith's case, moreover, this represented something of a departure from the stance he had assumed in his earlier *Theory of Moral Sentiments*, in which he gave a much more prominent place to human sympathy.) For both Smith and Madison, there was a serious problem involved in explaining *how* self-interested human activity *could* be coordinated so as to serve the general welfare. And both hit upon the same solution—a solution that seemed more promising than that which Hobbes had offered, and more realistic than that which Locke had offered, to roughly the same problem. It was *competition*, both Smith and Madison argued, that tamed the natural rapacity of self-interest—not fear (or "awe"), as Hobbes had suggested, and not reason, as Locke had contended.

In the marketplace, it is competition for customers between providers of the same goods or services that guarantees that a fair price is set—neither too high, for then one provider will be motivated to undercut the price of another, nor too low, for then no provider can sell at a profit. By the same principle, it is competition between employers for the services of workers, and between workers for the jobs that are available, that guarantees that a fair wage is set—neither too high, for then there will be unemployed laborers prepared to work for less, nor too low, for then an employer's laborers will be inclined to work for someone who can pay more and still turn a profit. As long as competition is freely allowed, moreover, it would seem that there is no serious problem involved even when, for a time, only one provider of a particular good or service exists. If the business is profitable, and especially if the current provider is overcharging, others will be attracted into the field. In principle, then, a system of free enterprise unhampered by state interference in the form, for example, of protectionist tariffs and legal monopolies should serve the cause of economic justice. Each individual within such an economic system, while focused entirely upon the pursuit of personal gain, Smith contends, is "led by an invisible hand to promote an end [the public interest] which was no part of his intention."[16]

In the realm of politics, competition occurs between individuals but also, and more importantly, between groups of individuals—or factions. These factions, Madison argues in the tenth and fifty-first numbers of *The Federalist Papers*, have their origin in self-interest and tend to pursue that self-interest unrelentingly—to the detriment of sober reflection on public policy and even to the point of violating the rights of minorities. While factionalism is an inherent and inescapable evil in a democratic republic, Madison argues that there are means available by which its excesses can be curtailed. The first is to multiply the organs of power—without, however, making them unworkable in the process. This is the ultimate rationale for the American (and widely copied) practice of strictly separating the legislative, judicial, and executive branches of government, and for further subdividing into two chambers the legislative branch (as being the strongest of the three). But this expedient, while important, might yet be ineffective in a democracy with relatively few, and thus at least one or two comparatively large, factions. In the age of the religious wars, it was precisely because the relevant factions were usually only the Catholics and the Protestants (often locally represented by a single sect), that factional conflict was so unremitting and bloody. In this respect, Madison argues, the incipient United States enjoyed a distinct advantage. As a large if not yet heavily populated country, it could reasonably be expected to develop a wide array of factions based not only on religious and economic, but also cultural and geographic, self-interest. Since no one faction was ever likely to achieve a clear majority, there was little to fear from a "tyranny of the majority."

Adam Smith and James Madison provided remarkably cogent analyses of the economic and political spheres, respectively—so much so that, in the two centuries since they wrote, we seem to have advanced very little beyond their understanding. Moreover, while *The Wealth of Nations* and *The Federalist Papers* are today less widely read than they deserve to be, in the United States at least Smith and Madison are readily cited and their authority appealed to whenever "common sense" in economic or political thought seems in need of defense. Their analyses, not only of economics and politics per se, but also of human motivation have thoroughly permeated the public consciousness. For our present purposes, then, the question that needs to be addressed is: what is the significance for our conception of human dignity that both of these profoundly influential thinkers stressed, not only the inevitability, but even the legitimacy, of self-interest as the primary basis for action in the marketplace and in politics?

After all, the explicit message of *The Wealth of Nations* and the implication of the tenth and fifty-first numbers of *The Federalist Papers* is that, given the right economic and political systems (i.e., a democratic republic dedicated to free enterprise), the public good can be expected to take care of itself, even if the individual citizens in such a society focus almost exclusively upon the satisfaction of their private interests. Indeed, Smith went further and suggested that even well-intentioned interference with the natural operation of the market economy—in the form of wage and price controls, for example—could undermine its efficiency and thus its capacity to serve the public interest. This contention was never intended by Smith to discredit good motives in general, but it obviously could be—and indeed has been—seized upon and put to precisely that use by those who have a vested interest in evading regulation of their business activities by the state.

Madison, in theorizing about politics, never came close to suggesting that the existence of factions rooted in the pursuit of self-interest is in any sense a positive good. Instead, he stressed that their existence is merely a perfectly understandable and unavoidable development in any society in which liberty is enjoyed. The actual business of governing, he hoped, would fall upon those "whose enlightened views and virtuous sentiments render them superior to local prejudices and to schemes of injustice."[17] But by acknowledging the inevitability of factionalism, by drawing attention to the fact that the deepest and most natural cause of factionalism is disparity in wealth, and by—as could hardly fail to be noticed—building into the Constitution of the United States a number of safeguards for the protection of private wealth (in which he himself, as a wealthy Virginian landowner, had a private stake),[18] Madison certainly helped set the stage for a more cynical interpretation of the pursuit of self-interest in politics. Thus today the idea that politics is the art of compromise between factions, and that compromises will be determined on the basis of relative factional strength, is taken by many people to be the most obvious of political truths—a truth adumbrated, moreover, by the "father of the Constitution" himself.

But if the public good will take care of itself even if—and in the marketplace, precisely because—each individual looks almost exclusively to his own affairs, how much of a connection remains between the possession of freedom and dignity? If all we require of an individual is that he use his freedom to pursue his own self-interest, clearly the Kantian conception of dignity has become irrelevant. An individual who exercises self-restraint because duty and justice seem to require it is simply putting himself at a competitive disadvantage with respect to his less scrupulous neighbors, who restrain themselves only when the force of law requires it. Moreover, if the public good really will take care of itself *providing* all individuals look to their own affairs, a Kantian is not only unwise, he is *wrong* to try to adopt the standpoint of objectivity. On this account, after all, justice will be the product of negotiation—of a contest vigorously conducted by the parties concerned—and if one party to the negotiation or contest fails to participate wholeheartedly, the outcome will not be what it should have been. In that case, even some of those who profit by the absenteeism of their competitors may be dissatisfied with the result, given their faith in the correctness of fairly contested outcomes.

Furthermore, if the intention underlying the political guarantee of freedom is simply to ensure that the individual can maximize the satisfaction of his self-interest, there is no room left even for the weaker *inquiry-based* conception of dignity that Mill proposes. Inquiry, in the sense in which the term is being used here, involves the mutual exchange of insights for the sake of coming to a genuine understanding of something which, given the complexity of its nature, is beyond the immediate grasp of a single observer. (Science is the most obvious example of inquiry in this sense, but ethics too is a form of inquiry. And one of the first questions on which we know inquiry to have been focused is that of how best to live one's life.) Given that inquiry is essentially a shared enterprise, in which inquirers reason together in order to arrive *together* at a deeper understanding of their subject matter, the primary virtues required of inquirers are honesty and disinterestedness. That said, it should be obvious that members of different political factions do *not* inquire. Members of each faction already know what they want and why their opponents are wrong. Their opponents are wrong because they want something else. The only thing members of factions have to think about, then, is how to get what they want—and while this is a form of deliberation, it is not inquiry. So too, entrepreneurs do *not* inquire. They seek information in looking for opportunities to exploit but, having uncovered such information, they guard it jealously so that others cannot capitalize on the opportunities first. To the extent that the pursuit of pure self-interest in politics and the marketplace defines our use of freedom, then, inquiry is beside the point. And as inquiry gets shunted aside, so too does the importance of dignity. We may still, if we so choose, take individual dignity to be a matter of one's potential contribution to the exchange of insights that constitutes inquiry. But if no one is listening to what public discussion there still is—if myopia prevails and almost everyone is content that it should prevail—dignity loses its importance.

To say that faction members and entrepreneurs, *as* faction members and entrepreneurs, do not engage in inquiry does not imply, of course, that these individuals are uninformed. It means, rather, that they do not strive to embody in their own reasoning the balanced result that would do justice to all competing arguments and competing perspectives by reconciling them in a larger, presumably truer, vision. Adam Smith and James Madison themselves, in spite of their having offered explanations for the relative harmlessness (at least in a competitive setting) of vigorously prosecuted narrow perspectives, still personally identified with the balanced result.

One should bear in mind, in this respect, the significance of Smith's observation that "people of the same trade seldom meet together, but the conversation ends in a conspiracy against the public, or in some diversion to raise prices." After all, those pursuing self-interest to the exclusion of all else will, where they can, evade the restraints imposed by open competition and gouge to the limit of what society will bear. To prevent injustices of this sort, Smith contends, the public must be prepared to intervene where appropriate—in breaking up monopolies and eliminating collusion, certainly, but in general wherever the rights of the weaker are in danger of being trampled upon. Left to themselves, for example, Victorian-era manufacturers were not above ensuring the diligence of their child laborers by shackling them to the machines that they were tending. And as Robert Heilbroner explains,

> because any act of the government—even such laws as those . . . preventing the shackling of children to machines—could be interpreted as hampering the free operation of the market, *The Wealth of Nations* was liberally quoted to oppose the first humanitarian legislation. Thus by a strange injustice, the man who warned that the grasping eighteenth-century industrialists "generally have an interest to deceive and even to oppress the public" came to be regarded as their patron saint.[19]

So too, James Madison felt that the actual business of governing should remain, as far as possible, in the hands of men who are "superior to local prejudices"—men who can approach questions of national policy with the same disinterestedness that Benjamin Franklin, for example, exhibited in his experiments with electricity. And during George Washington's two terms as president, dignity and disinterestedness in politics seemed to be a more or less attainable ideal. How ironic it was, then, that Madison himself, along with his friend Jefferson, ushered in the age of vicious factional struggle over control of the presidency with their creation of an opposition party to the Federalists.

Both Madison and Smith, as fairly typical Enlightenment thinkers, felt that progress was attainable through the disinterested application of reason to problems of social organization. Thus in spite of how they have been misread, neither of them argued that the single-minded pursuit of self-interest is the best way to operate in the marketplace, or in politics—or, indeed, in life generally; they argued that *usually*, in the marketplace and politics at least, that approach will prove comparatively harmless. In suggesting this, moreover, they were reporting on what—*as inquirers*—they had discovered to be true in the fields of economics and politics. As a result, it is fair to say that, for both Smith and Madison, human dignity continued to matter and continued to be associated with our capacity to be impartial and rational.

So if the seed of corruption—in the form of an explanation of why it does not matter excessively if as individuals we abandon all concern for dignity and embrace instead the unbridled pursuit of self-interest—is already to be found in the Enlightenment, and yet those thinkers who first presented this explanation were quite capable of resisting its corrupting influence, the question arises: why does it seem that especially in the past few decades concern for dignity has gone into eclipse? There are, I think, two reasons for this.

First, it is only since what evolutionary biologists call "the modern synthesis" of the 1940s that Christianity has lost serious credibility. As long as people believed that our lives were part of a divine scheme in which greed and self-centeredness were disapproved of, however natural they might be, it was somewhat easier to think of the dignified individual as a model to be emulated, rather than as a dupe whose "virtues" made him ripe for plucking. (The dignified individual, I will argue below, is and *must be* vulnerable to exploitation.) With the discrediting of revealed faith, it would seem that the temptation to focus entirely on one's own welfare in this, the only life that one will have, would have to have become more powerful.

Second, the consumer culture in which we are constantly inundated with advertisements encouraging us to indulge ourselves with one product or another has fully blossomed only in the past five or six decades. Every conceivable desire, it seems, in that there is someone willing to sell you something with which to satisfy it, is legitimate and natural. Countless times a day we are told, in one context or another, "Buy this. Buy that. *You're worth it!*" The consumer culture undermines human dignity in two ways. On the one hand, in accustoming us to the idea of instant gratification of our desires, it renders us less capable of showing restraint in those situations where patience and forbearance are required. On the other hand, our dignity is directly assaulted when we are treated as a means, rather than an end, by someone hoping to manipulate us into purchasing something. Insofar as we become accustomed to this treatment, we come to expect to be manipulated, and to view manipulation itself as something less objectionable than it actually is. This will seem to many, no doubt, to be a gross exaggeration—a case of making a mountain out of a molehill. But that response, I would contend, is itself evidence of how far the malign influence of consumerism has already gone in undermining our appreciation of the value of dignity.

NOTES

1. See Paul Ricoeur's discussion of this example in *Oneself as Another* (Chicago: University of Chicago Press, 1992), pp. 268–69.

2. John Stuart Mill, *Utilitarianism* (New York: Bobbs-Merrill Co., 1957), p. 6.

3. Immanuel Kant, *Groundwork of the Metaphysics of Morals*, in *The Cambridge Edition of the Works of Immanuel Kant*, trans. Mary J. Gregor (Cambridge: Cambridge University Press, 1996), 4:395–96.

4. As Darwin himself put it, "Natural selection tends only to make each organic being as perfect as, or slightly more perfect than, the other inhabitants of the same country with which it has to struggle for existence." *On the Origin of Species* (London: John Murray. Facs. rpt. Cambridge, Mass.: Harvard University Press, 1964), p. 201.

5. See Fyodor Dostoyevsky, *The Brothers Karamazov*, "Rebellion."

6. Technically, William was the Stadholder only of Holland and Zeeland, since each of the seven Dutch provinces had the right to choose its own Stadholder. For all practical purposes, however, the Stadholder of Holland (traditionally, always a member of the House of Orange) was recognized as the preeminent leader of the United Provinces.

7. Once Shaftesbury's attempt to exclude James from the throne by the Bill of Exclusion had been thwarted, several Protestant leaders began secret preparations for insurrection and perhaps also for the assassination of Charles II. The alleged assassination (or Rye House) plot miscarried, and the key figures in the conspiracy were convicted of treason and executed. In fear for his life because of his own participation in the meetings, Locke fled the country. The following year, while living in Holland, Locke was officially declared a traitor by Charles II and went into hiding for some time.

8. While the United Provinces in the 1680s were not technically a constitutional monarchy, the relationship between the Stadholderate, which was restricted to the House of Orange, and the States General, or representative assembly, probably came closer to embodying the principles of constitutional monarchy than anything to be found elsewhere in Europe at the time.

9. *The Second Treatise*, section 6.

10. *The Second Treatise*, section 61.

11. *The Second Treatise*, section 49.

12. Were the native Americans, for example, engaged in "wrongful war" against the Europeans' encroachment on their lands?

13. The problem, though, goes deeper than this in Locke's case, for he recognized, at times, that the exercise of reason does *not* normally provide us with an infallible guide in matters of morality. Thus he lists as the *first* of the problems associated with living in the state of nature, the fact that "there wants an established, settled, known law, received and allowed by common consent to be the standard of right and wrong, and the common measure to decide all controversies between them." (*The Second Treatise*, section 124.) How he can admit this and *still* ground almost his entire argument in *The Second Treatise* on the assumption that the natural law is perfectly clear

to anyone possessing reason, and thus that our reliance on it is trustworthy, is difficult to understand.

14. We must make an exception here, of course, of the *settlers* of what is now Anglo-America, who arrived not as colonizers but as dispossessors, and who consequently could not afford to entertain such a "charitable" attitude toward the natives.

15. It has been suggested, however, that Anne Robert Turgot may have a better claim to have originated this idea, and Smith was certainly familiar with Turgot's work.

16. Adam Smith, *The Wealth of Nations*, a selected edition (Oxford: Oxford University Press, 1993), p. 292.

17. *The Federalist Papers*, Number 10.

18. As Charles Beard has pointed out, the Constitution contains a strong, and rather obvious, economic agenda.

19. Robert Heilbroner, *The Worldly Philosophers* (New York: Simon & Schuster, 1953), p. 70.

Chapter Two

The Nature of Dignity

A Preliminary Inquiry

In the preceding chapter, I have traced out the foundational structure of our conception of dignity—which is to say, that set of core intellectual commitments without which the cultivation of dignity ceases to be a coherent moral notion. I have examined the key historical sources of our modern conception of dignity and considered to what extent their authority has been undermined by subsequent developments in our understanding of human nature. For if the authority of those sources has been significantly undermined, we must either abandon our traditional conception of dignity—which it appears that we may already, rather unreflectively, be in the process of doing—or discover new and convincing intellectual commitments with which to shore up a notion of dignity that is now in danger of collapsing. Those new intellectual commitments, however, if they are to be of any use in this enterprise, must be capable in fact of supporting *this* conception of dignity that we should be loath to give up. They must be, in other words, closely enough related to the original foundational beliefs—the Christian, Kantian, and Enlightenment beliefs in human dignity—that they too can support this familiar and still welcome way of understanding how we should aspire to live.

How we should *aspire* to live. I am not concerned here with that form of dignity that can be automatically attributed to all human beings—by virtue, for example, of their existence as Kantian rational beings, or of their status as rights-bearing citizens in a democracy. What I am concerned with, instead, is that form of dignity that we find exhibited in the behavior of a certain kind of morally superior individual. I say "a certain kind" because the possession of dignity is not simply to be equated with moral superiority. It is not, for example, the same thing as the possession of a good heart or a kind nature. The possession of dignity is not a matter merely of moral inclination. Rather, it is

a matter of moral intelligence—which is why Kant identifies it with autonomy, rational being, and the capacity to recognize and follow the moral law.
The point, then, is not that all good people possess exceptional dignity, but
that bad and even just morally mediocre people *cannot* possess dignity to any
significant degree.

According to Kant, the dignity to which we should aspire places heavy demands upon us—demands that he refers to as "duties to oneself." These have
"no connection with our well-being or earthly happiness."[1] They are, moreover, more rather than less important than our duties to others. This is because

> only if our worth as human beings is intact can we perform our other duties; for
> it is the foundation stone of all other duties. A man who has destroyed and cast
> away his personality, has no intrinsic worth, and can no longer perform any
> manner of duty.[2]

Kantian duties to oneself and duties to others never conflict because both
stem from the categorical imperative. The duties that one has to oneself are
merely those that derive from the necessity of preserving one's capacity to
obey the categorical imperative. They thus include such things as not drink-
ing oneself into a stupor, not committing suicide, not becoming indigent, and
not providing a temptation for others to violate the moral law.

But Kant's assurance that our duties to ourselves and our duties to others,
and that our duties to *these* others and our duties to *those* others, will always
harmonize is further evidence of his overestimation of the power of reason
and his underestimation of the richness of experience. He seems to have been
incapable of recognizing the existence of those tragic situations in which two
claims, each of them fundamentally justified, cannot be mutually accommodated by any effort of reason and one claim, for all of its legitimacy, must
simply go down before the other. Such situations *are* real; they *do* arise.
Think of the collateral deaths of innocent civilians in the prosecution of a just
war, for example. It is a serious failing of Kant's moral philosophy that he is
unable to acknowledge this.

It would be an even more serious mistake, however, to presume that, because reason cannot always provide unequivocal answers to the question
"How should one act in these circumstances?" we might dispense with it, and
rely instead entirely upon custom or feeling. Social customs typically embody
an enormous amount of unconscious wisdom—the lessons learned by a community over centuries of development. They also, however, typically embody
an enormous amount of ingrained prejudice—the *mistaken* lessons learned by
the community over that time. It has always been, along with self-interest, the
weight of social custom that keeps the disadvantaged disadvantaged. And
challengingly novel situations are almost invariably dealt with badly on the

basis of custom. As for feeling, the problem here is its variability: at one moment our sympathies and nobler sentiments take precedence, at another our selfishness and baser instincts. Forever following our feelings, we may well live intensely, but there will be much that an objective observer would find to criticize in our actions—even if we ourselves refuse to regret our mistreatment of others.

This unreliability of feeling and the blameworthiness of so many actions that stem from our natural sentiments together account for Kant's extreme and exaggerated distrust of inclination. No moral credit whatsoever is to be gained by acting even from worthy inclinations, Kant argues in the *Groundwork of the Metaphysics of Morals*, because inclinations as such are undependable and therefore must not govern our actions in moral situations. The same individual who, merely out of loyalty to his friend, helps him out of financial difficulty today, may tomorrow, on the basis of that same sentiment of loyalty, help him to escape punishment for some crime he has committed in the meantime. Mere loyalty, then, is not to be trusted, according to Kant. Nor is love, nor sympathy, nor devotion, nor kindliness, nor anything but pure practical reason. The consequence of this, even admirers of Kant's thinking agree, is a very *cold* moral philosophy.

SCHILLER ON GRACE AND DIGNITY

The great German poet and dramatist Friedrich Schiller was one such admirer of Kant's thinking, and in his essay, "On Grace and Dignity," he tries to reconcile Kant's insistence on the objectivity of the moral law with his own faith in the fundamental trustworthiness of our aesthetic feelings. In Schiller's estimation, Kant is too hard on our inclinations. There is a species of beauty, Schiller argues—the beauty of free movement, or grace—that can exist only where worthy inclinations achieve spontaneous expression. If, for example, we sense deliberation in the movement of a dancer or the witty conversation of a raconteur, we may approve of *what* is done, but we cannot help but feel disappointment at *how* it is done. What delights us in the graceful expression is the naturalness and ease with which what *should* be done *is* done—without so much as a hint of uncertainty or struggle. In the graceful movement we catch a glimpse of the perfection of human nature. And this has less to do with the conquest of the inclinations by reason than it does with the cultivation of a soul in harmony with itself.

Schiller begins his argument by observing that there is no grace to be found in what he refers to as necessary movements. That is to say, one cannot sneeze, or breathe, or swallow, gracefully. Only voluntary movements can be graceful, and yet it is not a voluntary movement as such that is graceful, but rather the manner in which the movement is executed. A voluntary movement—that of raising one's arm, for example—can be done in any number of ways—abruptly, languidly, smoothly, spasmodically, and so on—no one of which may be consciously chosen in preference to the other possibilities, and yet one of which *must* characterize the motion in question. This makes it possible, Schiller explains, for a voluntary movement to express not only the conscious intention governing the motion but also the more general disposition of the agent's mind.

> [T]he manner in which a voluntary movement is executed is not a thing so exactly determined by the intention which is proposed by it that it cannot be executed in several different ways. Well then, that which the will or intention leaves undetermined can be sympathetically determined by the state of moral sensibility in which the person is found to be, and consequently can express this state.[3]

Indeed, the general disposition of the agent's mind, Schiller goes on to contend, is much more reliably indicated by the manner in which the voluntary movement is executed (that is, by its "concomitant movements") than it is by the mere fact that *this* action, as opposed to some other, was consciously chosen.

> The voluntary movement is united but accidentally with the disposition which precedes it; the concomitant movement, on the contrary, is necessarily linked to it. . . . And in consequence we are not authorized to say that the mind is revealed in a voluntary movement; this movement never expresses more than the substance of the will (the aim), and not the form of the will (the disposition). The disposition can only manifest itself to us by concomitant movements.[4]

A person's disposition need not accord with what he actually does. Where they do not accord, however, his actions are liable to betray themselves. The person in question will merely "go through the motions," making it immediately clear that his heart is not in it. On the other hand, where the individual's disposition or inclinations do accord with what he does, this too is something that we can usually recognize—in the relaxed and comfortable manner in which the action is performed.

Only three dominance-relationships can exist between the sensuous or animal part of a person's nature and his rational or conscientious nature.

> Either man enforces silence upon the exigencies of his sensuous nature, to govern himself conformably with the superior exigencies of his reasonable nature; or else, on the contrary, he subjects the reasonable portion of his being to the sensuous part, reducing himself thus to obey only the impulses which the necessity of nature im-

prints upon him. . . ; or lastly, harmony is established between the impulsions of the one and the laws of the other, and man is in perfect accord with himself.[5]

The individual's natural inclinations, in other words, can be forcefully subdued by reason acting in the service of moral duty—in which case, however, there is liable to be in the manner of one's actions some evidence of the *strain* involved in this subjugation of one's impulses. On the other hand, there is the possibility that one's animal impulses will win in the struggle with reason— in which case not only will the individual's actions be morally inappropriate on occasion, but there is also likely to be in the manner of his voluntary actions some telltale evidence of greedy overeagerness. Finally, there is the possibility of the individual's inclinations harmonizing perfectly with his moral reasoning—in which case there will be evidence neither of strain nor of haste in his behavior, but rather an easy economy of motion indicating that he is comfortable both with himself and with what he is doing. This simple and easy manner in which what *should* be done *is* done is what we refer to as *grace*.

It is Schiller's contention that if we understand grace in this way, as the outward manifestation of a rare but genuine inner harmony between the individual's inclinations and his moral reason, we will see that Kant's insistence on the perpetual antagonism existing between reason and the inclinations is unwarranted. Nonetheless, Schiller does not mean to criticize Kant excessively or uncharitably on this point. It is understandable, he thinks, that Kant should have doubted the reliability of the guidance provided by our inclinations. For where our inclinations and our moral reason coincide, there is always the question as to which of them is ultimately responsible for causing us to do what is right. "Thus to be altogether sure that the inclination has not interfered with the demonstrations of the will, we prefer to see it in opposition rather than in accord with the law of reason,"[6] Schiller explains, because insofar as we take pleasure from doing what we should, there is always at least the suspicion that we are doing what we ought to, in this case, only for the sake of the pleasure that it gives us. And in morality, as both Kant and Schiller insist, it is not merely doing what is right, but doing what is right *for the right reason*—which is to say, because reason requires it—that is important.

All the same, there is much to be said for achieving that inner harmony of inclinations and reason that is productive of grace. Where grace exists, the inclinations have not merely been beaten down as the inveterate enemies of reason; they have been refined, and subsequently enlisted as reason's allies. Moreover, the presence of grace in one's conduct—that is, the absence of any evidence of inner struggle—is reassuring. It indicates that one is comfortably in command of one's own nature—that there are no negative inclinations threatening to burst their restraints and overwhelm one's moral reason. As Schiller puts it, we "prejudge nothing good of a man who dares so little trust to the voice of instinct that he is obliged each time to make it appear before the moral law; he is much more estimable who abandons himself with a certain security to inclination, without having to fear being led astray by her."[7] "In fact," Schiller argues,

> the destiny of man is not to accomplish isolated moral acts, but to be a moral being. That which is prescribed to him does not consist of virtues but of virtue, and virtue is not anything else "than an inclination for duty." Whatever then, in the objective sense, may be the opposition which separates the acts suggested by the inclination from those which duty determines, we cannot say it is the same in the subjective sense; and not only is it permitted to man to accord duty with pleasure, but he ought to establish between them this accord, he ought to obey his reason with a sentiment of joy. . . . By the fact that nature has made of him a being both at once reasonable and sensuous, that is to say, a man, it has prescribed to him the obligation not to separate that which she has united; not to sacrifice in him the sensuous being.[8]

Where grace is possible, then, it should be esteemed as evidence of a soul in harmony with itself.

But grace is not possible under all circumstances. Even the individual who exemplifies grace remains a human being, and as a human being cannot help but feel the things that all creatures feel—hunger, cold, and fear of death, for example. Where these are present, the individual's natural inclination must be to remedy or escape them. But because the human being is also—for Schiller as for Kant—a *rational* being, the individual will not always follow his natural inclination. There will be occasions when the dictates of moral reason compel him to endure hardship or accept danger. Thus while "the animal cannot do otherwise than seek to free itself from pain," where there is a legitimate reason for doing so "man can decide to suffer."[9] Deciding to suffer, however, does not render one immune to the fact of suffering. The pain is real even if it is embraced voluntarily, and the outward signs of one's struggle to master this pain and the inclination to escape it will not be those that are identified with grace. "This is why," Schiller explains, "calmness under suffering, in which properly consists dignity, becomes . . . a representation of the pure intelligence which is in man, and an expression of his moral liberty."[10]

We need not accept Schiller's unflattering—and unfair—characterization of animal behavior (which in fact is on occasion self-sacrificing) in order to recognize that he has identified a crucial characteristic of dignity. *Calmness under suffering.* The restraint of those all-too-natural inclinations which, if we abandoned ourselves to them, would cause us to sacrifice morality for the sake of our own satisfaction, comfort, or safety. What Schiller adds to Kant on this point is the acknowledgment that, even as they are being overcome, the natural inclinations continue to exert their power and cost us an effort to subjugate them. If they did not, if our inclinations could always and effortlessly be made to harmonize with the dictates of reason, there would be no call for expressions of dignity, in that each of us would be a paragon of grace.

> Thus in dignity the mind reigns over the body and bears itself as ruler: here it has its independence to defend against imperious impulse, always ready to do without it, to act and shake off its yoke. But in grace, on the contrary, the mind governs with a *liberal* government, for here the mind itself causes sensuous nature to act, and it finds no resistance to overcome. But obedience only merits forbearance, and severity is only justifiable when provoked by opposition.
> Thus grace is nothing else than the liberty of voluntary movements, and dignity consists in mastering involuntary movements. Grace leaves to sensuous nature, where it obeys the orders of the mind, a certain air of independence; dignity, on the contrary, submits the sensuous nature to mind where it would make pretensions to rule; wherever instinct takes the initiative and allows itself to trespass upon the attributes of the will, the will must show it no indulgence, but it must testify to its own independence (autonomy), in opposing to it the most energetic resistance. If, on the contrary, it is the will that commences, and if instinct does but follow it, the free arbitration has no longer to display any rigour, now it must show indulgence. Such is in a few words the law which ought to regulate the relation between the two natures of man [i.e., the sensuous and the rational].[11]

Dignity and grace are thus names for two of the three different dominance relationships that can exist between our inclinations and our moral reason. Where they harmonize we have grace; where the inclinations are too powerful to harmonize with reason, and reason must forcefully assert its authority, we have dignity. The third relationship, in which the inclinations dominate reason, we refer to by any number of names—greed, lechery, cowardice, dissipation—depending upon which of the natural inclinations is most immediately running out of control. Wanton self-indulgence, though, is the characteristic that all of these more particular vices have in common.

Where grace is possible, dignity is in a sense unnecessary. And yet, according to Schiller, neither grace nor dignity is entirely genuine without the other. Where we find dignity alone, devoid of grace, we recognize that the natural impulses are restrained. But the question arises: is this truly an instance of the moderation of desire by reason, or is it perhaps an instance of some *other* desire dominating the one that we anticipated—this *other* desire staging a great masquerade of restraint even as it indulges itself? Is it not possible, for example, that the individual's love of his own good name, of his reputation for exemplary conduct, is itself excessive?[12] Where this is the case it is not reason that restrains the impulses, but rather one impulse, one lust, that takes precedence over the others. These doubts about the genuineness of a person's dignity, however, do not arise when dignity is accompanied by grace. Where grace is present, the impulses are known to have their legitimate forms of expression, and their own rights. Because of this, where grace accompanies dignity, the impulses are restrained only as necessary, and not gratuitously, to cultivate a reputation for virtue. Grace, then, offers some assurance that it is *genuine* dignity and not a mere counterfeit of it that we are encountering.

On the other hand, where we find grace alone, unleavened with dignity, we recognize in the movements of the individual a comfortable rapport with his own natural inclinations. But the question arises: is this acceptance of the impulses still governed by reason, or is their indulgence, which seems so natural and appropriate here, perhaps a prelude to their inappropriate indulgence elsewhere? The mere appearance of grace, in other words, like the mere appearance of dignity, is difficult to distinguish from the genuine article. But just as the presence of grace dispels all doubts concerning the authenticity of dignity, so too the presence of dignity dispels such doubts concerning the authenticity of grace. For where dignity is present as well, the inclinations will be seen to be subject to the governance of reason. As Schiller puts it, the presence of dignity makes it clear that the liberty of voluntary movements is a simple (and impermanent) concession on reason's part, rather than complete freedom from her jurisdiction.

THE QUESTION OF DIGNITY
IN TWO HOLLYWOOD CLASSICS

In shifting our attention from Kant to Schiller for these past few pages, we have by no means lost sight of the *ethical* dimension of dignity; we have simply acknowledged that there is as well an *aesthetic* dimension to the subject. Nor should we be surprised at this. After all, dignity is not something that we merely—or even primarily—philosophize about. Primarily, it is something that we *sense* in another person's bearing. And if we find it difficult to explain, even to ourselves, exactly what dignity consists in, nonetheless we tend to trust our own judgment that such-and-such a person, at least, exhibits it. The status of those judgments is a little more doubtful, I believe, than we tend to realize—precisely because dignity *is* a problematic notion. All the same, in trying to elucidate the nature of dignity and the source of its appeal, it would seem only reasonable to consider some of these touchstones—that is to say, to examine a few generally acknowledged exemplars of dignity to determine, if possible, what it is in their behavior that we are responding to in describing them as dignified.

We need to bear in mind, of course, that this exercise is no more guaranteed to provide us with an entirely adequate grasp of dignity's nature than was the purely theoretical approach to the subject that we took in looking, for example, at Kant. Thus just as we saw grounds for questioning whether Kant ultimately manages to do justice to dignity, so we may discover that our common judgments—or at least some of them—regarding who does, and who does not, possess dignity are also in need of revision. But the theoretical and the "touchstone" approaches should work to supplement each other. For on the one hand, no theoretical account of dignity that simply gets wrong who it is that we in fact tend to think of as exemplifying dignity is at all plausible. On the other hand, in the absence of any conceptual account of what is meant by the claim, no off-the-cuff judgment regarding so-and-so's dignity is likely to carry much weight with someone else. Thus while we trust another person's ability to identify the color of some garment, say, that we have not yet seen for ourselves, another person's judgment of some third party's dignity is something about which we are inclined to remain rather more skeptical. There is both a theoretical (ethical) content and a felt (or aesthetic) quality to dignity, each of which informs and fleshes out the other. If we bear this in mind, and accordingly allow each side of our investigation to inform the other, it should be possible to deepen our understanding of what dignity truly consists in.

In embarking on the "touchstone" approach, however, we are immediately confronted with what appears to be a serious problem. For in order to learn anything from this approach, we must consider as our test cases individuals whose behavior and bearing we are all familiar with (or can readily become familiar with)—and not just in their broad outlines, but in a detailed, almost intimate, fashion. The problem, of course, is that actual human beings are never widely known in this way. Thus the people that I know well enough to describe, with some confidence, as possessing dignity are people the reader is unlikely to have ever met. On the other hand, the real people who are known to us all—politicians, entertainers, historical figures—are known for the most part only at a distance, and by reputation. As a result, judgments about their relative dignity are extremely unreliable.

Fortunately, there is one class of individuals who are widely and yet quite intimately known. This is the class of fictional characters who are brought to life for us on the movie or television screen by the actors who portray them. Through the actor's craft—which is a matter of disappearing into and embodying the character that one plays—we the audience come to know the niceties of gesture, inflection, and body language that define the physical bearing and moral quality of the character in question. There have been, moreover, and happily for our purposes, a few well-known actors who specialized in portraying dignified characters. In what is sometimes referred to as the classic age of Hollywood, the two preeminent specialists in this regard were, I would contend, James Stewart and Gregory Peck.[13] For each of these actors, dignity was so integral a component of his screen persona that it is the exceptional role in which he does *not* impart some measure of dignity to the character that he plays. In Jimmy Stewart's case, some of the films in which his characters clearly exhibit an exceptional degree of dignity are *Mr. Smith Goes to Washington*, *It's a Wonderful Life*, *Rope*, *Anatomy of a Murder*, and *The Man who Shot Liberty Valance*. Especially in Jimmy Stewart's case, moreover, we can see that dignity in a young man—that is, the Stewart characters of the Frank Capra films—looks rather different from dignity in a more mature man—say, the Stewart character of Otto Preminger's *Anatomy of a Murder*. In Gregory Peck's case, the particularly relevant films include *Twelve O'Clock High*, *The Big Country*, *Cape Fear*, *The Man in the Gray Flannel Suit*, and *To Kill a Mockingbird*.

In this section I propose to consider how the question of dignity—what it is and how it can be maintained—is dealt with in two films: one starring James Stewart, *The Philadelphia Story*, and one starring Gregory Peck, *The Man in the Gray Flannel Suit*. Ironically, though, in focusing on *The Philadelphia Story*, I will be considering one of Jimmy Stewart's rather less dignified characters—the likable but *young* fashion-magazine reporter, Macaulay ("Mike") Connor. And in moving from a discussion of Schiller's "On Grace and Dignity" to *The Philadelphia Story*, there is another interesting irony to note. For if Stewart's screen persona is normally the very embodiment of dignity, then Cary Grant's screen persona must be considered the preeminent embodiment of grace in American film history. And *The Philadelphia Story* is the one film in which "grace" and "dignity"—in the forms of Grant and Stewart—appeared together on the screen. The character who matters most in the film, however, the character whose fixation on dignity establishes the film's theme, is neither Grant's C. K. Dexter Haven nor Stewart's Macaulay Connor, but Katharine Hepburn's Tracy Samantha Lord. What the film reveals, moreover, is a variety of ways in which it is possible to fall short of achieving dignity—even when, as in the case of Tracy, dignity is one's preoccupation.

The Philadelphia Story

As the film opens, Tracy Lord, eldest daughter of a fabulously wealthy Philadelphia family and former wife of C. K. Dexter Haven, is about to get married again, this time to the politically ambitious and self-made George

Kittredge. The impending nuptials attract the attention of Sidney Kidd, the unscrupulous editor of the faintly disreputable *Spy* magazine, who believes that an inside story on the wedding will nicely bump circulation. Kidd arranges, by threatening to publish a story on Tracy's philandering father, Seth Lord, to get one of his reporters, Connor, and a photographer, Liz Imbrie, invited to the wedding, ostensibly as friends of Tracy's absent brother, Junius.

As the plot unfolds, we quickly learn of Tracy's own intense disapproval of both invasions of privacy—of the sort that *Spy* magazine specializes in—and her father's philandering. Indeed, Tracy has been personally responsible for persuading her mother to take a stand by ordering her husband out of the house. She has also made a point of not inviting her father to the wedding, a fact which early in the film leads to the following exchange between Tracy's younger sister, Dinah, and her mother, Margaret:

Dinah: "Mother, why won't Tracy ask her own father to the wedding?"

Margaret: "Your sister has very definite opinions about certain things."

Dinah: "She's sort of . . . well, you know, hard, isn't she?"

Margaret: "Certainly not. Tracy sets exceptionally high standards for herself, that's all. And other people aren't always apt to live up to them."

With this, Tracy's credentials as (loosely speaking) a Kantian moralist are firmly established. But this is by no means the only indication that Tracy's tendency to insist on the letter of the law has alienated her from the people around her. Almost the first words out of Seth Lord's mouth when he encounters her are, "Oh, still Justice with her shining sword, eh daughter?" And even Haven, who clearly wants her back, announces in Tracy's presence, with intent to sting, that "Strength is her religion, Mr. Connor."

Tracy is not irremediably haughty, however. She has simply been too sheltered in life. The very real problems of ordinary human beings have made no impact upon her, not because she is unfeeling especially, but because she has had so little exposure to them. This is made clear in her long conversation with Macaulay Connor after she has discovered that, in addition to being a petty journalist, he is also a very talented writer of "almost poetic" short stories.

Tracy: "Tell me something, will you? When you can do a thing like that book, how can you possibly do anything else?"

Mike: "Well, you may not believe this, but there are people in this world that must earn their living."

Tracy: "Of course, but people buy books, don't they?"

Mike: "Not as long as there's a library around. . . . You know, that book of mine represents two solid years' work, and it netted Connor something under six hundred dollars."

Tracy: "But that shouldn't be!"

The conversation then turns to Liz Imbrie's comparable situation—for Liz, while having to make her living as a *paparazza*, in her spare time is an accomplished painter. "And might be a very important one," Connor remarks, "but Miss Imbrie must eat, and she also prefers a roof over her head to being constantly out in the rain and snow." "Food and a roof. . . ," Tracy muses, and then, a few moments later, naively hits upon the "obvious" solution. She remembers that she has a private hunting lodge, which she seldom visits, and offers to let Connor use it. When Connor declines the charity, with the observation that "The idea of artists depending on a patron Lady Bountiful has more or less gone out," Tracy is hurt, showing that she, too, to borrow Liz's later remark about Connor, "still has a lot to learn."

No sooner does this conversation establishing the nature of Tracy's personal failing come to an end with the sudden appearance of Dexter Haven at the poolside, than the point is driven home.

Tracy: "Oh, we're going to talk about *me*, are we? Goody!"

Dexter: "It's astonishing what money can do for people. Don't you agree, Mr. Connor? Not too much, you know, just more than enough. Now take Tracy, for example. Never a blow that hasn't been softened for her. Never a blow that won't be softened. As a matter of fact, they've even changed her shape. She was a dumpy little thing at one time."

Tracy: "Only as it happens, I'm not interested in myself for the moment."

Dexter: "Not interested in yourself? You're fascinated, Red. You're far and away your favorite person in the world."

Tracy: "Dexter, in case you don't know . . ."

Dexter (interrupting): "Of course, Mr. Connor, she's a girl who is generous to a fault."

Tracy: "To a fault, Mr. Connor."

Dexter: "Except to other people's faults. For instance, she never had any understanding of my deep and gorgeous thirst."

Tracy: "That was *your* problem."

Dexter: "Granted. But you took on that problem with me when you took me, Red. You were no helpmeet there. You were a scold."

Tracy: "It was disgusting. It made you so unattractive."

Dexter: "A weakness, sure. And strength is her religion, Mr. Connor. She finds human imperfection unforgivable. When I gradually discovered that my relationship to her was supposed to be not that of a loving husband and a good companion. . . . Oh, never mind."

Tracy: "Say it."

Dexter: "But that of a kind of high priest to a virgin goddess, then my drinks grew deeper and more frequent, that's all."

Here we find that Tracy's blindness to the problems faced by others is not entirely a product of her unfamiliarity with their situations. She has shown herself unable to identify even with her own husband, when his problem proved sufficiently "unattractive." Life, it seems, must not present itself to "the unapproachable Miss Lord" unless it conforms to a certain minimum standard of refined elegance. And if it must appear ill-kempt, it had best prove readily susceptible to cosmetic rearrangement—as Kittredge does, for example, when Tracy trips him in order to rub dirt into his too-pristine-for-good-taste jodhpurs. In contrast, no sooner does the problem of impoverished artists prove rather too intractable to be solved by means of a single act of charity than Tracy loses all interest in it.

In spite of this, Tracy does possess the virtue of being able to listen to, and register, eventually, what others are saying. As a result, even the fairly brutal lecture that Dexter delivers makes an impression upon her.

Tracy: "You seem quite contemptuous of me all of a sudden."

Dexter: "No, Red. Not of you. Never of you. Red, you could be the finest woman on this earth. I'm contemptuous of something inside of you that you either can't help or make no attempt to. Your so-called strength. Your prejudice against weakness. Your blank intolerance."

Tracy: "Is that all?"

Dexter: "That's the gist of it. Because you'll never be a first-class human being or a first-class woman until you've learned to have some regard for human frailty. It's a pity your own foot can't slip a little sometime. But your sense of inner divinity wouldn't allow that."

Less than twelve hours later, Tracy is vehemently repeating the conclusion of that lecture almost verbatim for the benefit of Macaulay Connor, quite unaware—until she hears herself—of the implications of what she is doing.

And Tracy's foot does slip. For the second time in her life, she gets so drunk that she later has no recollection of what she may have done. One might comment on the irony that, given her contempt for Dexter's alcohol problem, it is Tracy who has demonstrated a propensity to drink herself into oblivion. One might also suspect, though, that a subconscious awareness of this danger on her part is precisely what causes her to be so critical of alcoholism. It is worth recalling at this point that self-control in the consumption of alcohol is one of the duties to oneself that Kant specifically addresses. We have a responsibility, Kant contends in *The Lectures on Ethics*, not to deprive ourselves in any way of the capacity to recognize and act in accordance with the moral law—and this implies, of course, that we must not drink ourselves into a condition of stupidity. Now, as was mentioned earlier, it is Tracy, with her "definite opinions," her "exceptionally high standards," and her "shining sword" of Justice, who is (admittedly, rather loosely speaking) the resident Kantian here. But the combined effects of Haven's lecture and too much champagne at the prewedding party have Tracy in the mood to reject the creed of righteous self-control by which she has lived. After fighting with her fiancé just hours before the wedding, she flirts outrageously with Connor, first drawing him into a profession of love, and then taunting him when he stops, on realizing the inappropriateness of his behavior, with "Has your *mind* taken hold again, dear professor?" Only when Connor responds to this provocation by seizing and kissing her does she recognize that it is time to douse the fire with which she has been playing—and the two of them race off hand-in-hand for a dip in the pool.

But the dip in the pool, while in fact constituting the very much needed at this moment cold water, not only brings a sudden end to their flirtations ("Seems the minute she hit the water, the wine hit her," Connor explains to Haven and Kittredge), it is also suggestive, to suspicious minds at least, of more libidinous doings. Those suspicious minds include Tracy's own the next morning, given that she awakens with no clear memory of her time with Connor, and evidence rapidly accumulates to the effect that something improper may have gone on between them. Like Kittredge, she is inclined to suspect the worst of her behavior, and the discovery of her lapse is positively devastating to her self-image. "Oh Dext," she blurts out in her misery, "I'm such an unholy mess of a girl." As is soon made clear, nothing more serious than a pair of kisses were exchanged—not, however, because of Tracy's vaunted sense of propriety, but rather because of Connor's more comfortably low-key but ultimately more meaningful appreciation that Tracy was "a little the worse, or better, for wine, and there are rules about that." Tracy, of course, is immensely relieved to discover that nothing more untoward has happened, but her relief is not merely for the sake of her own honor. What she has discovered as well is the truth of Schiller's claim that a more relaxed and comfortable, and in that sense a more *gracious*, approach to life is still capable of conforming to the requirements of virtue. Recognizing this, she now turns down the opportunity to return to her earlier "made out of bronze" existence, with its decisively pronounced moral judgments, by rejecting Kittredge as a future husband in the process of rejecting his request that she promise him "never to touch the stuff again." In doing so, she embraces instead Liz Imbrie's consoling observation that "We all go a little haywire at times, and if we don't, maybe we ought to."

Her "eyes have been opened," Tracy declares in the course of the morning's revelations, and this eye-opening process has been largely a matter of having her former overblown sense of certainty undermined. Virtually everyone in the film except Tracy herself recognizes right from the start that she and Kittredge are ill-matched. Dexter even tells her straight out, in their poolside conversation, that "Kittredge is not for you." To this, Tracy replies, "You bet he's for me. He's a great man and a good man. Already he's of national importance." (As if this could possibly be to the point.) Having failed to make an impression, Dexter now warns her, "Whatever he is, toots, you'll have to stick. He'll give you no out, as I did." To which Tracy replies, with sublime assurance, "I won't require one." A few hours later, when Connor too tells her that "You can't marry that guy," her total confidence in what she is doing remains unshaken: "Come around about noon tomorrow." But in the morning, of course, with her life seemingly in a shambles, things look rather different.

Tracy: "Oh, I don't know. I don't know anything anymore."

Dexter: "That sounds very hopeful, Red. That sounds just fine."

And by the film's end, as Dexter smoothly insinuates himself into the position of bridegroom lately vacated by Kittredge, the language of certitudes has given way to that of probabilities, and the recognition that life does not come with guarantees. When Tracy asks him, "Dext, are you sure?" Haven replies, "Not in the least. But I'll risk it."

So which of the characters in this film, which is so centrally concerned with the question of what it is to behave both well and naturally, best exemplifies genuine dignity? Not George Kittredge. Everyone is a trifle contemptuous of his stiffness and his excessive concern for his public image. But more damning by far is his willingness to think the worst of Tracy's interlude with Connor, for jealousy is entirely incompatible with dignity. Not Connor, and not Tracy. While both are fine people and show signs of growing into dignity, they are still at this point in their lives rather naive and self-absorbed. That self-absorption is broken down a little by the events just described, but their education is by no means finished for either of them at the movie's end.

Not Dexter. Stanley Cavell, in *Pursuits of Happiness*, is quite right to describe Dexter as a kind of magus within the film. He seems to have the power to orchestrate events, or at least to influence the way in which others interpret events. "He is a true therapist of some sort," Cavell concludes. And in that the therapist *as* therapist has in some sense transcended both suffering and desire, he has no inclinations to hold in check, and thus dignity is extraneous to his role. But Dexter, of course, is not simply a therapist (or a magus, for that matter); he is also a former husband who continues to love his ex-wife. Desire and suffering are thus not entirely alien to him, and there are at least two moments in which he clearly does exhibit considerable dignity. The first occurs in Sidney Kidd's office when Connor misrepresents Dexter's motives in helping to place Liz and himself inside the Lord household, accusing Dexter of wanting to get back at his ex-wife. Dexter says nothing, but gives Connor a sharp look, before taking his leave of Kidd and walking out the door, prompting Liz to offer Connor her handkerchief, saying, "Here, Mike. There's a little spit in your eye. It shows." The second moment occurs at the wedding hall when Connor urges Tracy to marry *him*—a moment of some danger, for Dexter recognizes that Connor is a far more credible match for Tracy than Kittredge ever was. Again, his moment of dignity takes the form of a pregnant silence. For this is a decision that is Tracy's alone to make, and if there is to be any hope at all of her making the correct choice, Dexter must not lift a finger to influence it. Dexter, then, is certainly not devoid of dignity; but given his somewhat more than humanly powerful role within the film, it is not what he primarily exemplifies.

My own vote goes to Ruth Hussey's Liz Imbrie. Liz and Connor are themselves lovers, although Connor is prone to forget this at times, which provides Liz with numerous opportunities to practice self-restraint. She, too, faces the moment of danger in silence as Tracy considers Connor's proposal of marriage. And unlike Kittredge, she manages to keep in perspective Connor's two-kiss affair with Tracy. Liz is the person whose rightful claim to equal consideration everyone—except for Dexter—keeps overlooking. This is the price, perhaps, of associating with so many self-absorbed, even if vibrantly attractive, individuals. But Liz bears up under the neglect remarkably well. As she observes, in response to the manicurist's unwittingly meaningful "A little rough?" as Connor, completely forgetting her, walks away with Tracy, "A little, but I'm used to it." Liz, however, is far from being a mere victim of other people's neglect. She is the one person in the film who can meet the magus in Dexter on an equal footing, as is shown in their discussion on the staircase when she explains why she is not quite ready to marry Connor. Like Dexter and Connor, moreover, Liz is always ready to play if the occasion is right, but she does so with a surer judgment of which inclinations are actually harmless than does Connor. Thus when she and Connor are left to themselves for a while after first arriving at the Lord mansion, she keeps up her end of the banter with Mike, but tries to stop him when he begins horsing around with the intercom. Liz is also too experienced and too wise to be swept, as Tracy is, from one extreme attitude to its opposite. Thinking that she has disgraced herself with Connor the night before, Tracy is despondent. When she then discovers that Connor refused to take advantage of her inebriated condition, her expression of relief takes the form of "I think men are wonderful!"—a gaseous sentiment that Liz quite rightly punctures with "The little dears."

For it was only one particular man who demonstrated on this particular occasion that he knew how a gentleman should behave. And there is another "gentleman" waiting in the wings at this point—the head of the household, prevailing upon the minister and assembled wedding guests to remain patient while his daughter resolves things with her fiancé. Seth Lord too has a claim to dignity that must be considered, if only to see why, in spite of his possessing all the advantages of age, wealth, power, intelligence, good looks, refined manners, and the natural authority of the father figure, he so thoroughly *lacks* dignity. The reason is not merely because he has cheated on his wife, although this in itself is a major failing. For if dignity is a matter of restraining those inclinations that reason cannot approve, then adultery must surely count against one's possession of dignity. But far more damning than the mere commission of adultery is Seth Lord's inability to acknowledge that he has behaved abominably. Unlike Tracy, whose redeeming feature is her willingness to listen to others and learn even painful lessons about her shortcomings, Seth Lord is a smooth and eloquent rationalizer of his own transgressions. Throughout the film he remains convinced of the proposition that he has done nothing wrong and that "most wives fail to realize . . . that their husbands' philandering has nothing whatever to do with them."

As Kant explains, the habitual rationalizer is beyond the pale.

> There is nothing worse, nothing more abominable than the artifice that invents a false law to enable us, under the shelter of the true law, to do evil. A man who has transgressed against the moral law, but still recognizes it in its purity, can be improved because he still has a pure law before his eyes; but a man who has invented for himself a favorable and false law has a principle in his wickedness, and in his case we can hope for no improvement.[14]

One need not accept Kant's contention that the true moral law is readily discernible in order to agree with his condemnation of rationalizing. If the

requirements of morality are more complex and problematic than Kant realized, then it is all the more important that they be sought for honestly.

This goes a long way toward explaining why *The Philadelphia Story*, for
all of its witty dialogue, engaging characters, and genuinely important theme,
is ultimately a far from fully satisfying film. It is a film about (and also an exercise in) moral education. But in the end it delivers far too simple a message.
It quite properly calls into doubt the legitimacy of the dogmatic moral certainty. But ultimately all it has to offer in its place is Tracy's "insight" (as she
bounces from one extreme attitude to its polar opposite) that "The time to
make up your mind about people is *never*." This newfound "wisdom" allows
her, as the plot hastens to its conclusion, to follow her mother's earlier lead
and welcome back her defiantly unrepentant father. But this is no reconciliation. Tracy and her father have had no meeting of the minds; they have not
even agreed to continue disagreeing about the moral status of Seth Lord's in-
fidelities (which we have no reason to believe will cease). Tracy, like her
mother before her, has simply surrendered the right to "make up her mind"
about her father. And the film, ending on that note, does not end altogether
happily.

The Man in the Gray Flannel Suit

Infidelity is a crucial issue as well in *The Man in the Gray Flannel Suit*, and
the issue is dealt with more honestly here. This is, however, in one sense at
least, a much simpler film than *The Philadelphia Story*—in that it involves no
serious attempt to portray significant character *growth*. All it does instead is
show us how a number of fine people try to cope with the complexities of real
life in hard times. There is also a far more obviously and conventionally dignified character at the center of it—Tom Rath.

The year is 1955. Tom and Betsy Rath (played by Gregory Peck and Jen-
nifer Jones) have been married for about thirteen years, have three young
children, and are finding it difficult to make ends meet. Tom, in spite of the
financial difficulties, is reasonably content with his life; Betsy, on the other
hand, is not. Early in the film we see them at home together at the end of a
long day, wrestling with the everyday burdens of a sick child, jealous siblings,
and a broken washing machine. A phone call brings news of yet another financial disappointment. There is nothing left in the estate of Tom's recently
deceased mother except an "old rookery" of a house that will bring only a pit-
tance if sold. In discussing how best to make use of the inheritance, Betsy
suggests that they hang onto the house for a while, at least until they can find
some way to get more for it than they have already been offered. Tom dis-

agrees. He points out that the house will cost more to maintain than they can afford, given his seven-thousand-dollar a year salary at the Foundation.

Betsy: "But you're not always going to be making seven thousand."

Tom: "That's what I mean. I could be making less."

Betsy: "But you can't look at things like that, Tommy. You've got to believe that things are going to get better—promotions, opportunities, some good breaks. That's what life is—hope, and the breaks. You can't just accept the way things are now."

Tom: "I think we ought to sell and put the money in the bank as some insurance. Did you ever stop to think what would happen to you if I should drop dead some morning?"

Betsy: "I'd drop dead right there by you."

Tom: "What about the children?"

Betsy: "I don't even want to think about that. What I want to know is, you don't expect to be with the Foundation forever, do you?"

Tom: "Well of course not, but you've got to admit it's an absolutely safe spot."

Betsy: "Alright then. What about this? We sell grandma's house and this house too, and we get us a nice house in a nice neighborhood."

The idea of moving is, evidently, a longstanding source of disagreement between them, and Tom is ready to dismiss it out of hand in favor of his more cautious approach. But Betsy will not let go of the idea.

Betsy: "I'm sorry, Tommy. You know I hate this house, but you don't know how much I hate it. Its ugliness. Its depression. But most of all, its defeat. . . . It's a graveyard of everything we used to talk about."

Tom refuses to be persuaded. He reminds Betsy that "There are a lot of people in this world doing a lot worse than we are." At this, Betsy begins to get desperate. "Oh no, they aren't," she replies. "They may look like it, but they aren't."

Betsy: "Ever since the war. . . ."

Tom (interrupting): "Will you stop harping on the war. It's been over for ten years. It's gone and forgotten."

Betsy: "I don't believe it. Not for you anyway. Whether you know it or not. . . ."

Tom (interrupting again): "All I know is that I don't think this is any time to be taking chances."

Betsy: "Then if it wasn't the war, what *has* happened to you?"

Tom: "What do you mean, 'What's happened to me'?"

Betsy: "I don't know, except that you've lost your guts and all of a sudden I'm ashamed of you."

This last remark ends the conversation. Betsy, fully aware of how she has stung her husband, turns her attention to the stove, in order to avoid further eye contact. After a few moments, Tom asks her quietly if she would like another drink. "No, thank you," she says. Tom pours himself a second, leaves the room, and heads upstairs. There he comes across his six-year-old son, Petey, who is upset because his sick sister has been getting a disproportionate share of attention, and he has been prevented from taking the family dog to bed with him. Tom goes back downstairs to fetch the dog, which he then carries up to Petey's bedroom. Having put things right with his young son, Tom checks on his daughters.

In allowing Petey to sleep with his dog, it might be thought that Tom is setting the stage for yet another quarrel with Betsy, since it was she who made the initial decision that Petey's bed was no place for the pet, and in overturning her decision, Tom walks right past her in the kitchen with the dog in his arms. But in fact Betsy says nothing about Tom's action, and it is worth taking a moment to consider why. It might be suggested that, having received her rebuke so calmly, Tom has gained "the moral high ground" and is thus, temporarily at least, in a position to overturn Betsy's decision with impunity. This answer would get the whole tenor of the scene wrong, for it fails to recognize the profound respect, as well as love, that Tom and Betsy have for each other. They do not trump each other's moves, because they are clearly in this relationship together. They trust each other's judgment—even when they disagree. Tom's indulgence of Petey at this moment, moreover, is of a piece with the gentle dignity with which he received Betsy's criticism. Letting Petey sleep with the dog tonight is *not* spoiling him. The circumstances *are* special today, and Petey needs some extra consideration. Tom trusts Betsy to recognize this as he walks past her with the dog in his arms, and her acquiescence in his action is thus not compelled by her temporary moral "disadvantage." Rather, it is an indication that she too understands that good parenting does not take place "by the book."

If all of this is not yet entirely clear at this early point in the film, two later scenes revealing how sensitive Tom and Betsy are to each other's needs and perspectives establish it beyond doubt. The following afternoon, when Betsy picks up Tom at the commuter station, he mentions that he has just applied for a higher paying job at UBC (The United Broadcasting Corporation). Before he can go any further, Betsy apologizes profusely for her harsh words of the night before, to which Tom quietly replies that perhaps he had them coming. When she goes on to ask him, "What's the matter with us, Tommy? Is it me?" he denies that there is anything wrong. And when Betsy begins to list their blessings, Tom adds, "Must be the house." With the unresolved tensions of the night before cleared away, they begin to discuss the possibility of taking a trip, should Tom be hired at UBC, which raises Betsy's spirits immeasurably.

The second of these later scenes occurs the following night—after Tom has been interviewed by the head of UBC, Ralph Hopkins (played by Fredric March), and his two senior assistants. Tom discusses the details of the interview with Betsy, who is now laid up in bed with a fever, having caught the chickenpox from her daughter. In the course of their conversation, Betsy shows herself to have in some respects a sharper sense of how things work in the business world than Tom does. First she explains to him the advantage of moving into his mother's house. If, but only if, they do so, it will be possible for them to get the local zoning laws changed, allowing them to subdivide, and build houses on, the twenty-three acres of land attached to the old home. Then she goes on to explain why, on the basis of what Tom has told her about his interview, not only will he be hired at UBC, but he will be able to get himself a handsome raise as well, if he wants it.

Tom: "What do you mean, 'if I want it'?"

Betsy: "You can get a raise because those two fellows wouldn't have been talking about salary if Mr. Hopkins hadn't said he wanted you. And if Mr. Hopkins said he wanted you, Mr. Hopkins is going to get you. And for ten thousand dollars if you have the" (she pauses) "the nerve to hold out for it."

She almost says "guts" here, but she catches herself in time. All the same, Tom is a bit flustered, not only by this brushing of a sore spot between them, but by Betsy's acumen and determination to see them improve their lot. He heads downstairs, for a glass of milk, he remarks, but equally for an opportunity to mull over what Betsy has just said. A few minutes later, he is back in the bedroom.

Tom: "Nothing ever scares you, does it?"

Betsy: "Only you."

Tom: "*Me?*"

Betsy: "You *have* changed, since the war."

Tom: "I suppose I have in a way. I was what we have to have in our country—what they call a 'citizen soldier.' One day a man's catching the 8:26 and then suddenly he's killing people. And a few weeks later, he's catching the 8:26 again. It would be a miracle if it didn't change him in some way."

Betsy: "The way I mean is—sometimes now you seem so far away from me."

Tom: "I'm not darling—ever."

Betsy: "The way I think about marriage, it ought to be a kind of secret between two people—just between them and nobody else in the world. Sometimes now, I get the feeling that I'm not sharing all of ours."

Tom denies this, but by this point in the film we have been let in on his private secret.

By means of a series of three flashbacks, we have been shown that the war is still very much on Tom's mind, as well as something of what the war involved for him. One of the things it involved was inadvertently killing his own best friend with a grenade, and temporarily losing his reason as a result. Something else it involved was a six-week-long affair in Rome after the fighting had ended in Europe while Tom was waiting to be shipped to the Pacific. There was nothing tawdry about Tom's relationship with Maria, though. In the depths of war weariness and unable to credit the possibility of his surviving the war and going home, Tom encountered another lost soul, a young woman whose entire family had been killed. They were drawn to each other by the qualities and situation they shared—by their gentleness and extreme vulnerability—and for what both realized could only be a short while, they fell in love as if they were entering a haven to escape a storm. On their last night together before Tom was shipped out to the Pacific, Maria told Tom that she thought she was pregnant. She did this not to hold onto him, but to let him know that she believed she would no longer be alone.

In due time, Betsy's predictions that Tom will be offered the job at UBC, and for ten thousand dollars, are borne out. Tom finds, however, that his new job involves him in some complicated office politics. He becomes an instant favorite of Ralph Hopkins, because he reminds Hopkins of his own son, who was killed in the war. But in doing so he alienates Bill Ogden, his immediate superior in the public relations department at UBC. Tom's first assignment is to write a speech that Hopkins will deliver at a convention of doctors—a speech intended both to jump-start a national campaign for mental health, and to ensure that Hopkins himself will be asked to head the campaign. But Ogden, seemingly out of spite, refuses to pass any of Tom's drafts of the speech on to Hopkins to read. Frustrated at having his fifth draft rejected by Ogden without anything useful in the way of criticism or explanation being offered, Tom complains and Ogden peremptorily removes him from the project altogether, leaving Tom uncertain for a time as to whether or not he has been fired. It soon becomes clear, though, that Ogden would not presume to fire Tom without Hopkins's approval, and that Hopkins has no idea yet of the tensions developing among his assistants — no idea even that Tom has been taken off the project. At a private meeting in his apartment, Hopkins presents Tom with a draft of the mental health speech — a draft that he himself has been working on along with Ogden. He asks Tom to take it home, read it, and then give him his opinion about it. This sets the stage for the film's pivotal scene.

That evening Tom discusses with Betsy what he will say about the draft, which both of them think is dreadful. Betsy wants him to provide his honest opinion, but Tom has doubts about the wisdom of such an approach.

Tom: "One thing I've learned already is that you've got to protect yourself in the clinches. The thing to do is sort of feel your way along. I mean when they call you in to give a report like this, you begin with a lot of highly qualified contradictory statements and watch your man's face to see which one pleases him. For instance, you can begin, 'I think there are some wonderful things in this speech.' Then you pause for a second or two. If that seems to make him happy, then you go on, 'And I have only a few minor alterations to suggest.' But if he looks a little startled on the word 'wonderful,' then you switch and say, 'But on the whole, I don't think it quite comes off.' If you've been smart enough about it, you can wind up telling him exactly what he wants to hear."

Betsy: "But that's *not* what you're going to do, is it?"

Tom: "I don't know."

Betsy: "*You don't know?*"

Tom: "Well, I've got to protect myself, haven't I?"

Betsy: "Well, I'll tell you what *I* think about it. I think the whole idea is sickening."

At this, Betsy gets up from the kitchen table and heads into the living room, where she begins agitatedly straightening things up. "Now just a minute," Tom says, following her. "What's the matter with you?"

Betsy: "It's not what's the matter with *me*. It's what's the matter with *you*. Even thinking of such a slimy trick!"

Tom: "Well, what do you think I should do? Go in there and tell the man his speech is a farce, and get thrown out on my ear?"

Betsy: "How do you know you'd get thrown out on your ear? Is he that much against honesty?"

Tom: "Look, Betsy. You don't know this business."

Betsy: "Is he dishonest himself?"

Tom: "How do I know whether he's dishonest? That's exactly the point. I haven't the faintest idea who's honest in there and who's not. All I know is that he helped write this speech, and it's his own personal baby."

Betsy: "I don't care whose baby it is. This is a speech that could make or break a very important health campaign for this country, isn't it?"

Tom: "It could."

Betsy: "Then are you going to tell him the truth about it or not?"

Tom: "But how do you *know* that that's the truth? How do you know that this isn't precisely the way to appeal to those people?"

Betsy: "Oh, Tommy! You don't even believe that yourself."

Tom: "It's exactly the sort of appeal that sells a billion dollars' worth of cars in this country every year."

Betsy: "That's entirely different. That's some sort of mass nonsense. These are very intelligent men you'll be talking to. They'll throw up at that muck."

Tom: "You don't know anything about it one way or the other."

Betsy: "All I know is that he's asked you for an honest opinion in a very important matter, and I'd like awfully to know if he's going to get it or not."

Tom: "Well, I could have told you that at the beginning. . . . He is."

Betsy: "You mean you're going to tell him?"

Tom: "I'm going to tell him exactly what I've told you—that I honestly don't know. But that this sort of approach has been successful in other sales campaigns, and that I see no reason why it can't work in this one."

Betsy: "Are you trying to kid me?"

Tom: "But that *is* the truth—the exact truth, as a matter of fact."

Is Tom rationalizing here? Betsy clearly thinks so. But then Betsy has a tendency to feel things passionately and to see things in black-and-white terms. This is not a simple failing on her part (as it is, for example, with Tracy Lord), because Betsy *is* remarkably insightful. As we have already seen, Tom recognizes this and to a great extent trusts Betsy's judgment, but he himself—especially through his wartime experiences—has been exposed more immediately to the moral complexities and ambiguities of life. His own judgment, then, is also not without weight. The truth often *is* difficult to determine, and his argument that the commercial advertiser's approach might work is legitimate. Moreover, Tom knows that survival is never an unimportant value. (At one point during the war, in order to keep from freezing, he had to stab to death a young German sentry, who could not have been more than sixteen, for possession of his overcoat.) And survival *seems* to be at stake here.

Tom: "I've told you that this is a loaded situation, and with all kinds of angles to it. But there's another side to it which I think you must have overlooked. It just so happens that I've landed one of the neatest positions in the whole organization, right next to Hopkins himself. It's a spot that three quarters of the people at UBC would give their right arms for. And he likes me, I know it. Now will you try to remember what that could mean to us, if I handle it carefully?"

Betsy: "If you handle it carefully and honestly—yes."

Tom: "Weren't you the one who wanted more money, a new house, no more worries every week?"

Betsy: "I still do. But that wasn't the real idea. The real idea was that I wanted you to go out and fight for something again—like the fellow I married. Not to turn into a cheap slippery yes-man."

Tom: "That's wonderful. But would you think about this for a minute or two? When a man's got plenty of security, money in the bank, other jobs waiting for him, it's a cinch to be fearless and full of integrity. But when he's got a wife and three children to support, and his job's all he's got, what do you think he ought to do about it then?"

Betsy: "I know what *I'd* do."

Tom: "And while we're about it, there's another little thing I think you ought to think about. We may not even own this house."

The house being referred to here is the "old rookery," into which they have recently moved, having sold the place that Betsy was so desperate to escape. The elder Mrs. Rath had a personal attendant, Edward, who now claims that, before she died, Tom's mother had promised the house to him in return for his years of service to her. The matter of ownership is one that a court will have to decide.

Tom: "Meanwhile I think you ought to keep that little situation in mind, while you're giving me this lecture on nobility."

Betsy: "Alright. You can try it. But I don't think it will work."

Tom: "Well, you just leave that to me. I never wanted to get into this rat-race, but now that I'm in it, I think I'd be an idiot not to play it the way everybody else plays it."

Betsy: "No, I mean with you. Because for a decent man there's never any peace of mind without honesty. And I've always thought of you as a decent man. Right

now it just makes me wonder how long it will be before you decide that it will
be simpler and safer not to tell *me* the truth."

With that closing line, the full significance of which she herself is not yet in
a position to appreciate, Betsy wins the argument. Tom resolves to be honest
with Hopkins.

It is revealing, however, that Tom has announced that he has no idea
whether or not Hopkins himself is honest. It is revealing as well that what is
wrong with the speech that Hopkins has set the tone for is, precisely, its tone,
which is insincere in places and obviously manipulative. Ralph Hopkins, we
are to understand, as the founder and president of a major broadcasting corporation, is a master of the skills needed to achieve extraordinary success in
the corporate world. But now he is faced with an unfamiliar situation. He is
not negotiating a business deal; he is hoping to be permitted to play the lead
role in a major public service campaign. That he desires, intensely, to see a
meaningful campaign for mental health launched speaks well of his moral
sensibilities. That he desires, just as intensely, to lead the campaign, and does
not know quite how to persuade those who must follow to accept his leader-
ship indicates that there is also some question about his fitness for the role.
What he needs in this situation is the kind of insight that only someone not
yet thoroughly immersed in the "slippery" ways of the corporate world—
someone like Tom Rath—can offer him. Tom tells him, in effect, that he *does*
have a legitimate claim to lead the campaign, given his possession of the machinery that will make such a campaign successful, but that he can only expect this claim to be recognized by the physicians whose support he requires
if he deals with them honestly and straightforwardly. It is to Hopkins's credit
that he immediately sees the value of Tom's advice.

In *The Man in the Gray Flannel Suit*, Ralph Hopkins represents, just as much
as do Tom's flashbacks about the war, the moral complexity of real life. The
Hopkins we see in the film is a man with good impulses as well as considerable
talents and achievements, and we understand why Tom both likes and respects
him. For one thing, Hopkins is genuinely dedicated to a worthy cause. For another, he treats other people, including his subordinates, with consideration and
obviously cares deeply about the welfare of his wife and daughter. On the other
hand, however, neither his wife nor his daughter wants anything to do with him
now because he has neglected them so egregiously in the past. With respect to
his family, Hopkins has made choices in his life that he now regrets—at least
partially. Having received Tom's advice about his speech, and almost simultaneously having received word that his willful young daughter has eloped with a
gigolo twice her age, Hopkins's carefully preserved charm cracks for a moment,
and he brutally justifies his own life-choices while disparaging Tom's.

Hopkins: "I know where I made my mistake. . . . And yet, somebody's got to do it." (growing agitated) "Somebody's got to dedicate himself to it. Big successful businesses just aren't built by men like you—nine-to-five and home-and-family. You live on them, but you never build one. Big successful businesses are built by men like me. You give everything you've got to it. You live it, body and soul. You lift it up regardless of anybody or anything else. And without men like me there wouldn't be any big successful businesses. . . . My mistake was in *being* one of those men."

Self-pity and self-congratulation are almost equally mixed here. But on a superficial reading of this passage we might think that, nonetheless, Hopkins has a point. Big successful businesses *are* necessary, aren't they? And if so, *somebody* has to build them. (Let us not forget, after all, that to a large extent it was America's economic might that made victory in Tom's war possible.) Ralph Hopkins and Tom Rath, it would seem, have simply chosen different paths in life. Hopkins, by implication, has nothing to apologize for. On the contrary, he has done much for which others—such as Tom Rath—should be thankful. The film, in other words, might be thought to be advocating a kind of value pluralism.

But this reading will not survive more careful scrutiny. For one thing, Hopkins genuinely does regret having neglected his family. In fact, just prior to his outburst he had been encouraging Tom to spend a lot of time with his own children and to "kick in and stomp on" the television set if it is taking up too much of their time. If we remember that television *is* Hopkins's "big successful business," we can see that this piece of advice does not square with his single-minded dedication to work. In fact, notwithstanding the vehemence of his contention that, for men like him, when it comes to their business, they "lift it up regardless of anybody or anything else," Hopkins has a troubled conscience precisely because he recognizes that in life we are called upon to balance conflicting obligations that arise from conflicting loyalties and involvements, and that he himself has failed to achieve the proper balance among those obligations. Even the successful entrepreneur is never just a successful entrepreneur and nothing else. Instead, one is always simultaneously a number of different things—a father and husband perhaps, a member of the workplace, a citizen of one's country, and one human being among others. Each of these roles imposes its requirements, and no one of them can simply be sacrificed to another. By implication, then, one can never morally adopt "regardless of anybody or anything else" as a working principle. Tom Rath implicitly understands this, and the film is essentially a chronicle of how he meets the conflicting obligations in his own life (work and family, humanity and country) and manages to balance them so that each is given its due.

Ralph Hopkins, in contrast, has come to appreciate this need to balance conflicting obligations only late in life, and even then has not fully understood its implications. He takes great pride, for example, in his son's having decided during the war to enlist rather than use his father's connections to secure an officer's commission. But in the very act of praising his son's uprightness, Hopkins betrays himself. "Oh, he'd cut a little corner now and then on little things. Who doesn't? But when it came to the big ones, there was only one way to play it for him—*straight*." But which are the big and which the little things in life? No doubt each of the many nights that Hopkins did not spend at home with his family, each birthday or school event missed, seemed like a "little" thing at the time. Only collectively did they amount to a "big" failure as a father and husband. What makes Tom Rath so much more admirable a person is that he appreciates the importance of "little" things— such as letting Petey sleep with the dog for one night.

Yet Tom often *seems* about to lose his moral compass. In what I referred to earlier as the film's pivotal scene, Betsy expresses her fear that Tom is turning into a "slippery yes-man." And indeed he does sound like one when he explains, so earnestly and convincingly, what the expedient thing to do would be. Later in the film, when he learns that shortly after the war Maria had a son and that the two of them are now in serious financial need, Tom has two immediate reactions: first, "I'm going to do something about it," and second, "I'll have to keep my wife from knowing, of course." The point is, however, that these questionable impulses of Tom's are not only *not* followed when the crunch arrives, but also that the impulses do have some legitimacy. Tom knows that finding out about his wartime affair will hurt Betsy terribly and to no good purpose—were it not for the need now to help Maria and her son. So too, Tom's obligations as a husband and father mean that he cannot take lightly the possibility of losing his job by being too forthright with his opinion. Thus his questionable impulses—on the one hand, to tell Hopkins what he wants to hear and, on the other, to continue keeping his long-ago affair secret—deserve to be taken seriously and weighed in the process of deciding what it would be best for him to do. This does not mean that those impulses should carry the day. It means only that Tom is right to weigh collateral harms as well as obligations—that he should not live his life as if it could be governed through the fixed application of some rulebook.

Once put to the test, it takes him only a few hours to recognize that Betsy must be told of his affair if he is to provide at all effectively for Maria and his son. Again Tom does the right thing, but the cost of doing so is considerable. Betsy is devastated. She reacts bitterly, hysterically. She leaps into their car and drives off into the night, not to be heard from again until she is located at a police station the next morning, having run out of gas on the road. Betsy is a remarkable woman, but as a housewife in 1950s America she has been nowhere near as directly exposed to the struggle of conflicting obligations as Tom has. She wants it all—more money, a nice home, a happy family life, *and* a principled husband. When challenged regarding the difficulty of reconciling the competing demands of family and workplace, country and humanity, it is easy for her to reply, all too glibly, "I know what *I'd* do." Thus the film's final crisis over Tom's infidelity can be seen as *Betsy's* education in the moral complexities of life. For one thing that Tom will *not* do is accept that his affair with Maria represented a betrayal of Betsy simply because it *feels* that way to her. Betsy's feelings are legitimate, of course, and Tom had anticipated them. But against those feelings one must also weigh the realities of Tom's wartime experiences. These he finally tries to explain to Betsy in order to make her understand that his affair was not a rejection of her, but an embracing of comfort and support at a time of truly desperate need. As the film ends, we see Tom and Betsy making the legal arrangements to have support payments sent on a monthly basis to Maria and her son. In setting up these arrangements Betsy is no sullen bystander but a self-possessed and full participant. She has heard and understood Tom's explanation; she has asserted control over her impulses and shown herself to be Tom's match in dignity.

The Man in the Gray Flannel Suit, the reader will have surmised by now, is in my opinion a very fine film. It moralizes, but gently, and with due respect for the complexity of its themes. Moreover, in the postwar economic boom of the 1950s, with its enormous increase in the proportion of white collar workers, the question of how to maintain one's integrity while functioning as a team player within the corporate structure was on the minds of a great many people. It should not be surprising, then, to learn that when Sloan Wilson's novel, upon which the film was based, was first published it was widely considered to be an important comment on the state of American society. Despite its producers' hopes for it, the film did not achieve the same degree of success that the book enjoyed, although it was well received by the critics and generally considered to be one of the major films of its year. Today, in contrast, while a great many other films of the 1940s and 1950s are widely known and not infrequently replayed on television and in the repertory cinemas, *The Man in the Gray Flannel Suit* languishes in comparative obscurity. But if, as I have suggested, today we have to a large extent lost our appreciation of personal dignity as a moral achievement, the film's present obscurity might be considered unsurprising.

SOME IMPLICATIONS

So what can be said about the nature of dignity on the basis of an examination of these two films? First, it is clear that much of what Kant has to say on the subject is essentially correct. As Tom Rath's character in particular illustrates, one's dignity flows from one's willingness to restrain inappropriate impulses—which is to say, from one's determination to establish what morality or justice requires and to see this done. On occasion, it will not be immediately obvious what morality requires, and one will have to think hard before acting—as Tom does, for example, the night before giving Hopkins his opinion of the mental health speech. More often, the need for restraint will be instantly apparent, and dignity will require simply that one not react as one might be initially inclined to. (Think of Dexter silently accepting Connor's insult in Sidney Kidd's office, for example, or of Tom silently accepting Betsy's accusation that he has lost his guts.) Moreover, as our distaste for Seth Lord's character should make clear, dignity is not to be confused with the possession of intelligence, fine manners, power, and authority. These may be the accoutrements, but they are not the substance of dignity; they *tend* to accompany an appreciation of the necessity of self-restraint, but they are no substitute for its absence. On the contrary, precisely because they arouse in us an expectation of moral worthiness, where intelligence, fine manners, and authority are present but self-restraint is not, we feel an indignation that goes beyond our normal disapproval of harmful behavior—rather as if we detected an element of hypocrisy in the person enjoying those advantages. The reason for this, of course, is that fine manners in themselves already constitute a (minor) restraint on natural impulses, intelligence *should* recognize where self-restraint is needed, and authority, we feel, should only be possessed by those who are prepared to place the general welfare before their own.

Seth Lord might be taken, then, as an illustration of a particular variety of what should be called "false dignity." There are, moreover, considerably cruder varieties of this false dignity to be noticed. Seth Lord *is*, after all, intelligent, finely mannered, and entirely comfortable in the exercise of authority. There are those who lack some or all of these qualities and who yet put on, portentously, the outward show of dignity. Consider, for example, the adolescent who wishes to be taken more seriously than he deserves and who moons about as if he were personally carrying the burdens of the world, or the small-minded judge who, gavel ever at the ready, insists on the "dignity of his office" even as he hands down biased and careless decisions, or the callow self-indulgent political aspirant who has been laboriously coached on how to look "presidential" by his handlers. In none of these instances is the individual's "dignity" grounded, as genuine dignity must be, in the morally appropriate exercise of self-restraint.

The films show us as well, however, that Schiller's correction of Kant's moral philosophy is also justified. An individual's natural impulses are not always harmful, and where they are consistent with the dictates of moral reason there is no reason not to indulge them. This harmless indulgence of one's impulses is nowhere more obvious than in play, and both films show us that dignity is perfectly compatible with moments of innocent playfulness. In *The Philadelphia Story* virtually everyone, except for George Kittredge and Seth Lord, is shown to have a playful side, and their playfulness in no way undermines the inherent dignity of, for example, Liz Imbrie and Dexter Haven. It does undermine Macaulay Connor's to some small extent, but this is because Mike's playfulness is not always entirely innocent. In *The Man in the Gray Flannel Suit*, Tom Rath has one moment of exuberant playfulness. On his last day with Maria, he gets a jeep and takes her on a picnic—in the rain. Letting her drive, he pulls out a mandolin and begins to sing, rather raucously and to Maria's evident delight, the fight song of his alma mater. The moment makes us appreciate Tom's fineness of character all the more.

But if playfulness is compatible with dignity, why are public exhibitions of pleasure, humor, or self-deprecation sometimes condemned as instances of undignified behavior? There are times when serious affairs are being conducted and any form of levity would show a lack of respect for the significance of the occasion and would thus be considered, not undignified, but rude or offensive. When levity is condemned as undignified what is usually meant is that one person's expectation of someone else that the latter will present a dignified demeanor—thereby assuring the first person of the second's possession of some special moral quality—has been frustrated by the latter's refusal to comply. The presentation of a "public face"—on the part of politicians, clergymen, doctors, and members of many other professions—is a familiar enough phenomenon and there is nothing intrinsically deceitful involved in this. Indeed, there are times when the public face is sorely needed—by relatives of a cancer patient, or by a nation going to war—and too casual a demeanor on the part of the reporting physician or president would be undignified in the sense that it would be unsatisfying for those seeking reassurance that the gravity of the situation is understood by those entrusted to handle it. Given that dignity is a matter of restraining inappropriate impulses, when others have a legitimate right to receive reassurance, one's indulgence of impulses that undermine that reassurance is quite properly called undignified behavior. At the same time, however, it is possible for people to become too demanding of the public face—to wish to see it even on comparatively unimportant occasions. Then, of course, the person upon whom the expectations have been projected may justifiably feel that he has no obligation to play along—that he too is entitled to enjoy the full range of emotions and to behave naturally when this is harmless. Everything depends on the occasion.[15]

Another conclusion that can be drawn from the films is that dignity and cynicism are incompatible. Cynicism is a matter of expecting the worst from other people, and this represents in each case a judgment that the cynic has (prematurely) passed on the other person's character. Those who are cynics themselves tend to think of their state of mind as worldly wisdom, but in this they are mistaken. For one thing, it often constitutes the first step toward adopting a pattern of selfish behavior oneself—so as to avoid being disadvantaged by the anticipated selfishness of others. We see Tom Rath flirting with this option when he tells Betsy, "I never wanted to get into this rat-race, but now that I'm in it, I think I'd be an idiot not to play it the way everybody else plays it." Of course, if competitive success were the only thing that mattered, and if everyone else invariably acted selfishly, then refusing to behave selfishly oneself would place one at an enormous competitive disadvantage, and would thus be both a foolish and a strategically mistaken thing to do. But what Betsy reminds Tom is that competitive success is not the only thing that matters—that he might become a great success in the business world and still lose what really matters, by losing his right to her good opinion of him.

But is Betsy perhaps being naive here? Is she simply hobbling her husband, by requiring that he behave in a principled fashion even though, in the larger scheme of things, there are no good reasons for doing so? For clearly Betsy would want Tom to behave honorably even if this did not win him (as it in fact does) the affectionate respect of Ralph Hopkins. She wants Tom to behave well, not for the sake of cultivating another's good opinion (not even her own, ultimately), but simply because behaving honorably is the right thing to do in and of itself. Are there good grounds for believing this—for believing that even if *everyone* else were selfish to the core, and *every* good deed one performed were repaid with scorn and material disadvantage, that nonetheless one should still behave in a moral fashion? This is a crucial question, and one that I will spend considerable time discussing in the final chapter. For the moment, then, I will restrict myself to the following observations. First, experience teaches us that others may behave badly, and thus the wise person is not shocked when they do. Second, insofar as wisdom involves as well an appreciation of the value of behaving morally *regardless of how others behave* (assuming for the moment that there *is* some such value), then the wise person will anticipate that others too will be able to appreciate this value, and that they may well act morally as a consequence of this. Thus if there *are* such grounds for behaving morally, and some people at least choose to act morally in recognition of those grounds, the genuinely wise person will not expect others to behave badly. For on the one hand, as a purely pragmatic matter, this cynical expectation itself discourages good behavior, at least on the part of those who do not yet fully appreciate the deeper reasons for behaving well. And on the other hand, as a matter of moral principle, this cynical expectation in itself constitutes an injury to certain others, in that it *misjudges* them.

Finally, my examination of the films suggests that dignity is not only compatible with, but actually *requires* one's acknowledgment of, a certain measure of uncertainty regarding precisely what constitutes moral versus immoral behavior or appropriate versus inappropriate impulses. To say that the dignified individual must acknowledge *a certain measure* of uncertainty on these matters is not to imply that he has no firm convictions or is often at a loss as to how to behave. Far from it. It means simply that he is sensitive to the limitations of his own experience, sensitive to the relevance of changing circumstances, and extremely sensitive to the relevance of viewpoints other than his own. All of this makes him reluctant to declare too quickly or too dogmatically what morality requires in novel or unexpected situations.

At first glance, though, this claim that dignity requires an acknowledgment of uncertainty may seem to be contradicted by the observation that, if dignity is about self-restraint, this is always self-restraint *in the pursuit of an ideal*. Dignity, after all, is not the same thing as prudence. In prudent behavior one exercises self-restraint as well, but here one's momentary inclinations are sacrificed for the sake of one's own private long-term satisfactions. (Thus the student who forgoes a party in order to study for an exam exhibits prudence, without gaining—through *this* act—any measure of dignity. In contrast, the student who forgoes both the party and the studying in order to participate in a political rally for some worthy cause may gain a measure of dignity even as she perhaps exhibits a lack of prudence.) Dignity, then, given that it is not prudence, is tied to idealism. But surely insofar as one *is* committed to an ideal, one must be *wholeheartedly* committed to it. This is made especially clear by the fact that dignity often accrues to an individual by virtue of his demonstrated willingness to fight for the ideal to which he is committed.

If we consider for a moment some of the other films in which James Stewart and Gregory Peck have starred, we can find any number of illustrations of this last point. Think, for example, of Jefferson Smith's dogged one-man filibuster on the floor of the U.S. Senate to prevent a corrupt bill from becoming law, in *Mr. Smith Goes to Washington*. Think of the eminently civilized Rance Stoddard, so seemingly out of place in the brawling frontier town of Shinbone, and his willingness to confront, gun quite inexpertly in hand, the armed and brutal leader of the local outlaw gang, in *The Man Who Shot Liberty Valance*. Think of Atticus Finch's courageous defiance of his hometown's bigotry when he represents a black defendant against spurious rape charges, in *To Kill a Mockingbird*. Finally, think of Frank Savage's readiness to lead his men by example, and to give of himself to the point of emotional collapse to ensure the success of an air campaign that must not be allowed to fail, in *Twelve O'Clock High*. In each of these films the main character's dignity is confirmed by his willingness to risk his life or his reputation for the sake of doing what is right, and in each case this involves vigorously putting down an opponent who is in the wrong.

Clearly one cannot fight a battle successfully unless one is prepared to be wholehearted in one's efforts. Just as clearly, though, not every individual's willingness to fight contributes to his possession of dignity. On the contrary, the person who fights for selfish or immoral ends, for this very reason *loses* whatever dignity he may have possessed. So given that dignity can require one to fight on behalf of justice—and on occasion on behalf of truth[16]—even though the precise shape of justice, and so too that of truth, is something that at best we can only imperfectly discern, the question is: how can one be wholeheartedly committed to an ideal—such as justice or truth—and acknowledge at the same time that one is to some extent uncertain as to what it involves? Unless this question can be satisfactorily answered, I would seem to have run into a contradiction in claiming that dignity involves an unshakable commitment to what are only imperfectly knowable ideals.

In starting to address this objection, it is important to observe that not all idealists acquire, by virtue of their idealism, a heightened measure of dignity. There are some ideals that are so wrongheaded—the promotion of racial purity, for example—that no matter how deep one's commitment might be, self-restraint in the service of such an ideal can in no way enhance one's dignity. With respect to the specific ideal of racial purity, there are two reasons for this. First, expressions of selfishness are incompatible with dignity, and anyone dedicated to racial purity as an ideal could hardly escape the suspicion that his motivation, if unpacked, would prove to be profoundly selfish. Second, foolishness and culpable ignorance[17] are destructive of dignity, and today the ideal of racial purity can look compelling only to someone who remains willfully ignorant of biology.[18]

Thus there are, on the one hand, bad ideals, and a commitment to one of these does not produce dignity. On the other hand, even commitment to a worthy ideal, if the ideal is blindly pursued, will not enhance one's dignity. We distinguish, after all, between praiseworthy idealists and fanatics—a fanatic being an idealist who has ceased to have any doubts, who is thus prepared to embrace any line of action that seems to contribute to the achievement of the ideal *as it is currently understood*. A fanatic, in other words, is a person many of whose initial impulses now originate in his idealistic commitment, and who does not check and restrain those impulses by means of reason. But given that dignity is precisely a matter of reason's governing and restraining our inclinations, an individual who has ceased to employ his reason in these respects, even though he be deeply committed to a worthy ideal, *cannot* exhibit dignity. Worthy as his ideal may in fact be, the manner of his commitment to it, which is by definition blind, is incompatible with dignity, because it is not the approach that reason will adopt.

In the realm of experience reason does not achieve certainty, but struggles always with the evaluation of relative plausibilities. The plausibility of any one belief is always a function not only of direct perceptual evidence in support of it (where this is available), but also of how much corroborative and countervailing evidence is provided by all of the various other relatively plausible beliefs that reason entertains at a given moment. This is to say—what is now a commonplace in epistemology—that reason is concerned, primarily, not with the plausibility of individual isolated beliefs, but with the relative coherence of an all-encompassing "web of belief," and that any reasonably complex individual belief is plausible only to the extent that it is supported by this web. Because of this, a genuinely rational commitment to an ideal will always be tentative in two respects: first, regarding what the ideal actually involves; and second, regarding the justifiability of the commitment in the light of other considerations.

The objection I am now considering is based upon the somewhat ambiguous assumption that insofar as one is committed to an ideal, one must be wholeheartedly committed to it. Everything depends, however, on what "wholeheartedly" is taken to mean here. It certainly can and should imply a preparedness to act—even to fight—on the basis of one's commitment. So long as one's commitment to the ideal is to be understood as a rational commitment, however, to be wholeheartedly committed cannot mean to be committed blindly or without qualification. Because our knowledge and understanding are always incomplete, there will be a steady stream of new circumstances and new insights, the relevance of which to our rational commitment to the ideal will have to be considered as they arrive.

This very brief (and preliminary) detour that we have just taken into the realm of epistemology brings to light another important fact about the nature of dignity. If dignity is a matter of the rational restraint of our inclinations exercised in the service of some ideal, the integrative character of reason goes a long way toward explaining why the relevant ideal here is, preeminently, the ideal of morality. There are other worthy ideals to which one might be committed, of course—the pursuit of beauty, of truth, of distributive justice, of charity, to name just a few. And the restraint of one's inclinations in the service of any of these ideals does provide one with a measure of dignity that goes beyond that attributable as a matter of principle to all human beings. For example, a scientist, just by virtue of his honest dedication to the pursuit of truth, acquires an extra measure of dignity. So too does an artist, a judge, and a volunteer social worker, by virtue of their honest dedication to the ideals governing their respective enterprises. The crucial point, however, is that a scientist can be a good scientist, sincerely dedicated to the pursuit of truth within his field, and yet on the whole be a relatively undignified human being. And the same could be said about the artist, the judge, and the volunteer social worker. The same thing could not be said, however, about the individual who is sincerely dedicated to the pursuit of morality generally. The explanation for this is that morality encompasses the entire range of rationally approved values.

If the scientist, for example, is sincerely committed to the pursuit of truth in his field and yet in spite of this is on the whole an undignified human being, this can only be because he has failed to recognize or acknowledge the need to restrain his natural impulses in the service of some *other* value than the pursuit of truth in his field—a value that the rational individual *should* recognize and approve. The scientist in question is no doubt rationally committed to the pursuit of truth within his field—in that he can provide a sound explanation of why this pursuit is valuable and important, not just for him, but for humanity generally. The problem is that he is not also rationally committed to all of the *other* values that are important for humanity generally. In this sense, his commitment to the values approved by reason is incomplete, and in some dimensions of his life—in his willingness to cheat on his income tax, perhaps, which is to say, in his lack of concern for distributive justice—it is clear that he does not allow reason to call into question, or restrain, his natural impulses.

By contrast, the individual whose dignity is grounded in his commitment to morality as a whole cannot compartmentalize his reliance upon reason. He cannot listen attentively to what it declares with regard to one worthy but partial ideal, and then ignore what it has to say about other equally worthy ideals. He cannot, that is, like Ralph Hopkins, dedicate himself exclusively to the achievement of one narrow goal, pursuing it "regardless of anybody or anything else." Instead, like Tom Rath, he will struggle to resolve conflicting values and commitments—doing justice, insofar as this is possible, to all of them simultaneously. There is no guarantee that he will be successful in this. In fact, it is virtually certain that to some extent he must fail, because the tensions and conflicts existing among the various values that we can rationally approve are enormously complex. Nonetheless, the cognitive thrust of morality is toward the reconciliation of conflicting values. The implicit expectation is that, in the perspective that our moral reasoning ultimately arrives at, each of the various values that such reasoning finally can approve will be given its due.[19] The implicit expectation is also that this perspective ultimately arrived at by our moral reasoning will be *objectively correct*—in the sense that it will be recognized to give each legitimate value precisely its due by all who honestly and dispassionately examine the matter.[20]

Kant too believes that moral reason adopts the universal or objective perspective. But he contends that reason itself, independently of the ways in which it is actually employed by flesh-and-blood human beings, has its *own* perspective and that *this* perspective is universal and objective. Thus the categorical imperative is dictated by reason itself, and not by any particular rational human being (whether Confucius, Moses, Hammurabi, or Kant himself) even though all human beings, given their possession of the faculty of reason, are equally capable of recognizing those dictates. As a consequence, morality is not something that needs to be—or even could be—negotiated about by different human beings with different interests and different ranges of experience. It is dictated, and the same way for everyone, by the principle of universalizing the maxim. But in all of this Kant is mistaken, for he overstates the degree to which reason is invariant among rational beings and grossly exaggerates the degree to which it is capable of arriving at meaningful conclusions independently of the provision of factual detail.

Today, in the light of what we know about evolution, we need to understand reasoning as a natural (rather than a noumenal) process. Then the fact that virtually all human beings reason in much the same way will not surprise us—no more so than does the fact that all human beings digest their food, or walk, in much the same way. The fact that we all reason in fundamentally the same way and the fact that we all walk in fundamentally the same way is in each case a function of our possessing similar physiological structures and of our having to cope with the same real-world constraints. But the fact that human beings possess in large measure the same musculature and skeletal structure does not prevent them from differing considerably in the finer details of shape and size. Nor does it prevent those differences in detail from finding stylistic expression in what is fundamentally the same mode of walking. So too there are noticeable stylistic differences in the way that various human beings engage in what is, at least in its general features, fundamentally the same process of rational thought. (Although here, of course, the stylistic differences have more to do with the differences in our ranges of experience and our acquired thought habits than they do with any physical differences.) And just as, when we compare these stylistic differences, we have to conclude that there is no definitively correct way of walking for two-legged creatures, but rather only a relatively normal way that is more or less closely approximated by any given individual, so too, when we compare the stylistic differences in the way people reason, we have to conclude that there is no definitively correct way of thinking, but only a relatively typical way to which we all more or less closely approximate.

The implication of all of this, for our physical activities at least, has been the development of ergonomics—which is to say, the recognition that our furniture, our homes, our workplaces, and so on need to be designed to suit not just the statistically average individual, but as broad a range of different human physical types as possible. The aim here is still, notice, to produce one size that fits all; but now the size in question is not one *fixed* size chosen because it will fit more, and frustrate fewer, individuals than any other fixed size would, but rather one maximally *flexible*, and thus maximally appropriate, size. The challenge of moral reasoning is analogous to this. The different legitimate interests and values that human beings pursue need to be maximally accommodated. But no more than in the ergonomic design of furniture or homes does this imply that "anything goes." On the contrary, the task of maximally accommodating legitimate human values, like the task of maximally accommodating actual human shapes, is much more demanding than is choosing one fixed size and declaring arbitrarily that, henceforth, as far as accommodating human variation goes, this is all that is on offer. The task, indeed, is so much more demanding that it is always an open question whether or not it can be successfully accomplished. But the difficulty of the problem, and the uncertainty of its solution, do not constitute grounds for declaring that the task is unimportant, and that we can therefore afford to take the easy way out.

In an important sense, then, it is still correct to say that moral reasoning at least *strives* to adopt the universal or objective perspective. What this means is that moral reasoning prevents an individual from pursuing *all* and *only* those things that appear to be good as seen exclusively from his personal perspective, by compelling him to consider as well how things look from the viewpoints of others. But this objective perspective is not something that can reliably be reached by means of a shortcut—such as Kant's principle of universalizing the maxim—any more than simply declaring that one fixed size fits all will make this true. If we genuinely desire to know how things look from the viewpoints of others, we must allow those others to tell us, and not presume that we can anticipate everything of importance that they may have to say. To the extent that we take this necessity of consultation seriously, however, a personal dedication to morality becomes a somewhat more costly enterprise than it has traditionally been thought to be.

Even where morality has been understood as a matter simply of following some code, such as the Ten Commandments, it has been widely recognized that moral behavior in the real world has its price. For behaving morally is a matter of not taking advantage of the vulnerability of others in order to improve one's own situation. And insofar as others do *not* feel bound by this same constraint, one is liable to come out, in one's interpersonal exchanges, somewhat the worse on balance. (In that one will occasionally be cheated by others, and one will never offset those losses by taking the opportunity to cheat in one's own turn. Whether those losses will in due time be fully offset by the increased benefits of the cooperation that one's exceptional trustworthiness invites is an open question and one that I will postpone considering until chapter 5.)

But an individual who seriously strives to achieve the objective perspective of morality, and who recognizes that this requires that one listen to what others have to say about what *they* value, is vulnerable in another respect as well. The openness and sincerity that are a precondition of genuinely *hearing* what someone else has to say is itself a form of vulnerability. After all, the struggle to achieve the objective perspective amounts, in practical terms, to a refusal to push one's own claims and desires beyond their due. But given his awareness of the limitations of human understanding—and more importantly, of his *own* understanding—a moral individual will not infrequently experience some measure of uncertainty about the legitimacy of his personal claims and desires. And given this uncertainty, he will feel a certain reticence about pushing them vigorously, and therefore effectively. Thus once again, in his interpersonal exchanges with others who are *not* similarly hampered, in this case with uncertainty and reticence regarding the legitimacy of their own desires, an individual struggling to achieve the objective perspective will typically come away having received somewhat *less* than his due. For while single-mindedness of purpose is *not* the frame of mind in which to seek that reconciliation of all conflicting values and commitments that is the ultimate goal of morality properly understood, nonetheless single-mindedness of purpose undeniably *is* conducive to getting what one wants in some immediate and narrow sense. Insofar as dignity is bound up with the pursuit of morality, then, it is indissolubly bound up as well with a heightened measure of vulnerability.

NOTES

1. Immanuel Kant, *Lectures on Ethics*, trans. Louis Infield (Indianapolis: Hackett, 1963), p. 117.

2. Kant, *Lectures on Ethics*, p. 121.

3. Friedrich Schiller, "On Grace and Dignity," in *Essays Aesthetical and Philosophical* (London: George Bell & Sons, 1916), p. 184.

4. Schiller, "On Grace and Dignity," p. 185.

5. Schiller, "On Grace and Dignity," p. 195.

6. Schiller, "On Grace and Dignity," p. 198.

7. Schiller, "On Grace and Dignity," p. 202.

8. Schiller, "On Grace and Dignity," p. 199.

9. Schiller, "On Grace and Dignity," p. 206.

10. Schiller, "On Grace and Dignity," p. 212.

11. Schiller, "On Grace and Dignity," pp. 212–13.

12. In the *Lectures on Ethics* (see p. 125), Kant declares that concern for approbation is a precondition of dignity. This concern, however, can easily get out of hand.

13. A case could be made, I think, that in contemporary American film, Denzel Washington is another actor in the Peck-Stewart mold. And it is interesting to contrast Denzel Washington's comparatively relaxed form of dignity (highly reminiscent of Peck's) with the far more defiant dignity of, say, Sidney Poitier. Forty or fifty years ago, one might surmise, so many (white) people would have considered it presumptuous for a black man to exhibit extraordinary dignity, that if a black actor of Poitier's generation exemplified dignity, it had to be defiant dignity. In this sense, the very possibility of a Denzel Washington or a Morgan Freeman exhibiting exceptional dignity *quietly* would seem to be a small but telling indication that race relations have improved significantly in America.

14. Kant, *Lectures on Ethics*, p. 137.

15. There is another related form of undignified behavior that deserves a few words at this point—the pratfall. The pratfall is a momentarily humbling experience, but the individual who makes no pretense of always being in comfortable control of his circumstances is *prepared* to be humbled on occasion. It is only the individual who is guilty of acting as if he were above the misfortunes that affect the rest of us whose "dignity" is undercut by being dumped on his hindquarters. But such a person's "dignity" is not the genuine article. If we bear in mind that true dignity is a matter of the individual's willingness to restrain his own inappropriate impulses, it becomes clear that accidents are not the sort of thing that *can* threaten one's dignity.

16. Truth is significantly at issue in two of the four films just mentioned. In *To Kill a Mockingbird*, it is the falseness of the accusation of rape against Tom Robinson, as well as the injustice of deciding his guilt on the basis of race, that Atticus Finch must expose and overcome. In *Mr. Smith Goes to Washington*, it is the fraud involved in the Willard Creek Dam bill that Jefferson Smith must resist.

17. Not *all* ignorance is destructive of dignity because, given the limitations of human understanding, each of us is inevitably ignorant of a great many things, and there are an even greater number of things of which all of us collectively remain ignorant. There are things, then, for which one cannot be faulted for not knowing.

18. NB: Of biology, *not* of history or sociology. These latter disciplines have shown us the damage that doctrines of racial purity have done in the past, and continue to do today, but they cannot show, as biology does, why the doctrine of racial purity is in principle misguided.

19. Not all values that at one point or another seemed rationally defensible will ultimately prove to be so, of course. Slaveowners have usually been of the opinion that their right to own other human beings is a rationally defensible value. They have been wrong in this belief.

20. Given that we are referring here to the perspective *ultimately arrived* at by moral reasoning, it is important to understand that those who will recognize its legitimacy (on the basis of their "honest and dispassionate" examination) will also be *ideal* moral reasoners. Any actual flesh-and-blood inquirers will be constrained by a constellation of preconceptions, not all of which they will be capable of overcoming no matter how diligently they pursue Gadamer's injunction to "place one's prejudices at risk."

Chapter Three

Implications of Human Finitude

AUTONOMY AND VULNERABILITY

On somewhat different grounds from those just given in the last chapter, the suggestion that dignity is inextricably bound up with vulnerability has recently been developed in some detail by George W. Harris, who sees this connection as something the significance of which not only Kant, but also the classical Stoics, and even certain Christian sects, have failed to appreciate. Harris's basic contention is that "fragility of character is essential to many of the qualities of character we value most," and thus that it is simply not true, as Kant and the Stoics imply, "that inadequate strength of character is always inadequate virtue."[1]

According to Kant, the essence of morality is autonomy—or an individual's capacity to recognize and impose upon him*self* (thus *autos*) the *law* (in Greek, *nomos*) of pure practical reason. Insofar as he is capable of doing this, an individual asserts mastery over his own natural impulses and avoids heteronomy—or the condition of being governed by something *other* (*heteros*) than his own rational essence. Now what the claim that human beings *can* be autonomous in this sense suggests, of course, is that human beings can in principle at least always resist the temptations and afflictions directed our way by the natural world. Desires, in other words—whether for things we have never had or for things we once had and now lack—are to be schooled by reason. Kant makes it clear, however, that in actual practice human beings—given that we are *both* natural creatures as well as rational beings—will always fall somewhat short of that perfect command of our impulses that is required by pure practical reason. But this is merely to say that, as creatures of nature, we are never quite as good as we might conceivably be, as rational beings. And our failures to be fully autonomous are things that, if only we had been morally stronger, would have been made right. Thus our failures to be all that we should rationally have willed ourselves to be are things either to be *regretted*, if we have fallen significantly short of what one could reasonably expect of a human being, or at best *excused*, on the grounds that we are as well, after all, creatures of nature and thus inevitably less than perfect.

But this Kantian view of morality pits reason, as that which should rule, inexorably against inclination, as that which is to be distrusted, given its origin in nature. And we have already seen Schiller argue that this opposition between reason and inclination needs to be relaxed—that some at least of our inclinations are to be applauded, and that these inclinations would *not* be improved by being brought under the conscious direction of reason. Harris launches his own rather more penetrating criticism of Kantian morality from this same point.

In order to explain his objection, however, I must first say one or two more things about autonomy. For autonomy does not only mean self-government; it also involves, as the sine qua non of self-government, the power to function effectively in the world. (This is the reason that Kant offers for suggesting that drunkenness constitutes a violation of one's duty to oneself—i.e., to one's autonomy.) Harris speaks, though, not so much of incapacitation as of "integral breakdown," which is what occurs when "the limitation threshold that measures fragility" of one sort or another is reached.[2] An individual human being experiencing integral breakdown, however, *is* significantly incapacitated, and thus his autonomy is forfeit to at least some degree. Harris's objection against Kant is that there are certain virtues—the *caring* virtues—that themselves *increase* the likelihood of integral breakdown for their possessor, and which thus have the potential to undermine autonomy.

Harris is quite prepared to admit that some virtues—such as courage and honesty, which he refers to as the *heroic* virtues—will never contribute to integral breakdown. These are virtues that, while they will always actually be possessed to only some limited degree, could in principle be strengthened indefinitely and would, in the process, continually increase the degree of autonomy exhibited by their possessors. Thus, for example, if a soldier succumbs to fear and flees from the battlefield, the loss of autonomy connected with this integral breakdown could have been avoided if only he had had more courage. Nor would an increase in his courage ever give rise to a different sort of integral breakdown—for courage is not recklessness, and does not become recklessness through being increased.[3]

In contrast with the heroic virtues, Harris argues, the virtues of care all

> have a point of integral breakdown internal to them; they cannot be conceived
> as indefinitely strong; and they can be the source of self-destruction for an agent.

Unlike heroic virtues, they do not always deal with stress but sometimes generate it. Moreover, when stress is traceable to such a virtue, "more" of the virtue only increases the stress. Yet these virtues are among those in terms of which we find persons most admirable.[4]

Think, for example, of a loving mother weakened by grief over the death of her child. One would hardly be inclined to suggest that somehow she is *less good* in her grief-induced infirmity. It is, after all, the very qualities that made her a good mother and a good person when her child was alive that have now taken their toll. If, then, in her grief she is unable to fulfill her obligations— if the quality of her work drops off, if she becomes distant, or unable to withstand the ordinary small frictions of social interaction without snapping—this loss of autonomy is not something for which she is to be *blamed*. But neither is it simply an understandable *failing* for which she is to be *excused*. For in fact, if there were *no* such infirmity, an interested observer would begin to question the depth of her feeling for the lost child—and thus the degree to which she possesses the virtue of being a caring individual. In other words, the reduction of her autonomy is a consequence of one facet of the woman's own moral *excellence*. If she had cared still more, her incapacity to deal with everyday life, we presume, might have been even greater. In this sense, then, the reduction of autonomy can be thought of almost as a gauge of the mother's virtue.

Almost, because the strength of the woman's love for her child is not the only factor determining how much her autonomy will be reduced under these circumstances. Her religious faith, if she has any, may be of some assistance to her. And most certainly her sense of obligation—which is to say, her reluctance to let her own misfortune become a misfortune as well to others— will also weigh in the balance. In that regard, her dignity will be the product of her struggle not to succumb entirely to her grief. For as Harris observes, an individual who has no capacity at all to cope with situations of what should be manageable grief—a person thrown into inconsolable despair by the loss of a pet, say—is someone we tend to pity rather than respect.[5] Self-restraint is still the essence of dignity, and grief must be wrestled with. But Harris's point again is that sometimes the failure to succeed in restraining one's impulses—in this case, one's grief—may itself be a sign not of moral weakness, but rather of the depth of one's capacity to care.

Few people would suggest that as a life strategy one should protect one's autonomy against this sort of breakdown by simply *refusing* to care—about anything or anyone—and thus evading the danger of ever losing that which one cares about. After all, not to care about anything is to have no reason for living. Of course, not everything about which one cares should constitute an autonomy-threatening vulnerability. The loss of some portion of one's material possessions, for example, should not be debilitating. Perhaps even the long-anticipated death of an elderly parent is something one should be able to negotiate without too great a personal crisis. But there are certain things (people primarily) about which we *should* care intensely, and if the sudden and premature loss of a child, parent, spouse, or very close friend does not to some extent impair one's capacity to function effectively, this would seem to be clear evidence that one simply has not cared enough about someone who deserved more of one's involvement in his or her fate. (There is a superb poem by Robert Frost, "Home Burial," in which precisely this point is developed as the central theme. It is not, as some critics seem to think, Amy's inability to bounce back from the death of her infant that is morbid. Rather, it is her husband's capacity to take his customary pride in a job well done—even when that job is the digging of his child's grave—that is morbid, and that costs him his wife.)

Harris makes the important point as well that there is a limit, not so much to the number of people that one can love intensely, but to the number of times that one can *lose* such people and recover one's capacity to love again. As he puts it,

> [t]he capacity to replace loved ones in one's life can only be limited. For at some point such a capacity slides into a kind of promiscuity incompatible with intimacy. This is a fact about human love and its phenomenal features. Love attaches to particular individuals and is incompatible with a disposition that allows either instant or endless substitution.[6]

"In this regard," he points out,

> love is like a fuel in limited supply; it can be burned off, and one can die in the flames. We cannot change this about love; all we can do is either take our chances in this regard or abandon our commitment to being loving people.[7]

But this is hardly a choice between legitimate options. For as Harris argues, a person who does *not* love others cannot possess dignity to any great extent, because this capacity to care deeply is part of what we value most in human beings. Thus "to survive by being unloving is to survive by the lack of virtue."[8] And yet, important as it is, this private dedication to the welfare of some specific others that is love is not a condition that we enter into *rationally*. It privileges some people over others on no better grounds than that these first are close to us—close to us, initially at least, in the sense of physical proximity, and then close to us *emotionally*—and in this sense it constitutes a denial of the objective or universal perspective to which reason aspires. Pure practical reason can certainly acknowledge the fact that, as finite human beings, we are in a position to invest in the welfare of only *some* others, that these will naturally be those closest to us, and that, as a universal principle, such specific investment in the welfare of certain others is to be approved. But such a rational justification of the value of love is not itself love. Nor can it lead us to love anyone in particular.[9] For that, reason must stand aside and allow inclination to make its choice.

Harris's criticism of Kantian morality is thus essentially an extension of Schiller's criticism. The inclination to love, at least when it is welcomed by the other, is just the sort of inclination that Schiller spoke of in "On Grace and Dignity"—the inclination that reason can approve, and which therefore should be allowed free expression. Reason may guide, but it does not initiate love. And the grief that love may lead us into can easily reach "unreasonable" proportions. In all of this it is love rather than reason that, in human terms, "gets it right."

In illustrating how dignity differs from grace and yet is intertwined with it, Schiller attempts to humanize Kantian morality somewhat. Acting well, in Schiller's estimation, is not just or always a matter of an incursion into the natural realm (in which inclination dominates) of a force—the force of reason—that belongs essentially to another, non-natural (that is, the intelligible) realm, and which, simply by virtue of that fact, should always rule our natural inclinations. Without wishing to deny the otherworldliness of reason (for he remains a Kantian), Schiller insists that the natural realm too has its intrinsic values—values that are not merely *borrowed* from the rational/intelligible realm (even if they are *compatible* with those of this other realm). Chief among these values is love. And it is important to understand why love fits so poorly into the Kantian moral scheme.

When Kant speaks about love in *The Metaphysics of Morals*,[10] he distinguishes between love as benevolence, love as beneficence, and love as delight in another. Only the last of these, however, captures what we normally have in mind when we refer to human love. The first, benevolence, is merely a matter of taking satisfaction in the well-being of others. And given that this costs us nothing at all, it is an attitude that in principle can be adopted toward everyone. Indeed, according to Kant, it is part of the moral imperative that we should adopt this attitude of good will toward *all* rational beings. In contrast, the second form of love, beneficence, involves making the promotion of someone else's happiness one's own purpose. But because this involves an investment of time, energy, and material resources on one's part, beneficence is not an attitude that one can practically adopt toward all others. We do have a moral obligation to practice beneficence, Kant contends, but this is a limited obligation. ("How far should one expend one's resources in practicing beneficence?" he asks. "Surely not to the extent that he himself would finally come to need the beneficence of others.")[11] Because of the limited character of the obligation, contingent considerations determine in each case whether one practices beneficence toward *this* as opposed to *that* person. And clearly one such consideration could be the fact that one *loves* (i.e., takes delight in) *this* rather than *that* person. But charity is also beneficence, and offering charity is not the same thing as loving those that one helps. Thus neither of the two forms of love that Kant feels we have a moral obligation to engage in as practical activities is really what we have in mind as *human love*—as the love that binds together parents and children, or lovers, or close friends.

This *binding* form of love is what Kant calls "love as delight in another," and it is significant that he denies that there can ever be a moral obligation to feel this kind of love. *Human love*, we have already observed, is not rational: first, in the sense that it does not attend upon a rational choice of *whom* we are to love, but second, and perhaps more importantly, in the sense that it is not readily constrained by considerations of justice. For human love is essentially *partiality*; it is the *preferring* of this person to that person because one happens to delight in this one. And *as* partiality and preferment, love does not weigh individuals equally, as justice and reason require. On the contrary, it is always eager to excuse and forgive the beloved, and thus is always ready to violate, in particular, the strict requirements of retribution.

Kant does not explore this issue, but it is clear that from his perspective this necessarily constitutes a significant failing on the part of love—for according to Kant, without retribution there can be no justice. Where the rights of an individual have been violated, only retribution can make right the imbalance established by the crime. Why this should be the case is not made entirely clear, but it seems to be related, as Kant sees it, to the fact that the appropriate punishment for a crime is always implicit in the nature of the crime itself. The criminal, in other words, is to be thought of as doing to himself whatever he has done to someone else. If he murders another, he murders himself; if he steals from another, he steals from himself (imprisonment amounting in this case to the theft of his freedom). In this way, the principle that justice is a matter of universalizing the maxim is extended even to punishment. As rational beings, Kant contends, we recognize the necessity and appropriateness of retribution, regardless of how we may feel about the matter when, as imperfect creatures of nature guilty of some offense, we are subjected to punishment.

It follows that a criminal's attitude toward receiving his punishment is indicative of the degree to which he has recovered his status as a rational being. Insofar as a criminal both recognizes his guilt and *welcomes* his punishment as a way of demonstrating this, he shows himself to be fit to reenter human society and associate once again with other rational beings. For this reason, those who genuinely understand what is at stake in the matter will not wish to see a criminal deprived (either through clemency or forgiveness) of the opportunity to reestablish, through his willing acceptance of just punishment, his credentials as a rational being. Thus, according to Kant, the natural inclination of love to indulge in forgiveness and clemency is a *mistake*. On the one hand, it violates the fundamental principle of retributive justice that offenses must be redressed; on the other, in excusing and thus infantilizing the guilty party, it deprives him of any opportunity to reestablish his dignity as a rational being.

This line of reasoning has significant theological implications. As a good Christian, Kant must and does declare that God is loving. But a God who loves us in the way that a *father* loves his children—*preferentially* and not merely benevolently—cannot at the same time be the utterly impartial guarantor of ultimate justice as Kant understands it. This tension between divine mercy and divine justice has always been present in the Christian conception of God. But for Kant, given his position on clemency, the tension is especially troublesome, amounting virtually to an inconsistency. This is especially the case given that, of these two divine properties, justice is the more crucial to Kant's way of thinking. Our only legitimate ground for believing in God's existence is, according to Kant, the dissatisfaction that we feel in the prospect of permanent and unresolved injustice. Thus God as the implacable guarantor of justice takes priority for Kant. But how we are to reconcile this conception of God with the idea of a loving *God the father* is impossible to imagine—as Kant himself confesses when, at the end of *The Metaphysics of Morals*, he declares that

> only the moral relations of *human beings to human beings* are comprehensible by us. The question of what sort of moral relation holds between God and human beings goes completely beyond the bounds of ethics and is altogether incomprehensible for us.[12]

This dodge simply makes a virtue of necessity and calls into question the cogency of Kant's initial understanding of (the Christian) God as the guarantor of ultimate justice.

It *is* possible, however, to offer a justification of love's clement and forgiving approach to moral offenses, but only if we first free ourselves of Kant's rigoristic conception of justice and the mistaken assumptions upon which it is based. We will be far less prone to insist on retribution, after all, if we acknowledge the limitations of human knowledge—the limitations of *both* our knowledge of facts *and* our knowledge of general principles. Let us consider our knowledge of facts first. Kant never suggests that we are entitled to any extraordinary confidence in our empirical knowledge. But in practice, an exaggerated conception of how much certainty we are entitled to regarding general principles (such as moral laws) is likely to go hand-in-hand with an exaggerated confidence in the adequacy of our factual knowledge. This is because general principles are typically abstractions of tendencies observed across a range of empirical events, and only if we are confident about *what* we have actually observed will we also be confident about what principles are to be abstracted from those observations. In practice, too hasty a tendency toward generalization is evidence of a lack of appreciation of the possible significance of subtle differences across the range of those things that are judged to be *the same*, and this lack of appreciation of their possible significance can easily follow from a failure to have noticed those differences in the first place. This is one reason for supposing that ethical rigorism, such as Kant's, relies upon an inflated estimation of our powers to determine the facts of a given case. But there is a second and more important reason. An exaggerated confidence in what we feel we know the facts to be is almost always necessary if we are to overcome that lingering suspicion (that "reasonable doubt") which undermines our willingness to exact retribution—the suspicion that we may not after all have correctly identified the guilty party. Those who are prone to a heavy-handed exaction of retribution have a difficult time admitting the existence of legitimate grounds for doubt. Thus, for example, George W. Bush's astonishingly glib insistence, when challenged during his first presidential campaign concerning the one hundred and fifty-two men and women convicted of capital offenses and sent to their deaths while he was governor of Texas, that "they were all guilty."[13]

Our doubts concerning the actual guilt of some person accused of wrongdoing do not undermine the principle of retribution itself. At best, they indicate the need to be very cautious in determining who is to be punished for a crime. In contrast, our not-so-occasional blindness to the significance—and even the presence—of subtle differences among things that are too readily judged to be *the same* (or of subtle similarities in things that are too readily judged to be *different*) does suggest that justice cannot be simply a matter of retribution. When the circumstances surrounding some moral decision are more complicated than usual, an individual is called upon to exercise what Aristotle calls "practical wisdom" (*phronēsis*)—that is, to act not "by the book" but in a way that is appropriate to the circumstances in question. When the individual in such a situation fails to recognize the relevant nuances, he will get things wrong—inflicting harm, but unintentionally. Clearly, moreover, harms inflicted on others as a result of such moral misunderstandings are not the same as willfully committed wrongs. The former can and should be thought of as excusable errors committed in a learning process—although these are errors with damaging consequences, and which it is therefore crucial that the individual come to recognize *as* errors, in order to avoid repeating them.

To put the matter like this, however, is to exaggerate somewhat the distinction between instances of moral misunderstanding and willful wrongs. Our entire moral life is—or at least should be—a learning process, and thus moral misunderstanding and willful wrong should not be thought of as mutually exclusive, but rather as two extremes in a continuum. We have to *learn* that hurting others is wrong in the first place. And having learned this, we still have to learn all the various ways in which this can be (more or less unwittingly) done—by deception, by breaking promises, by cheating, by selfishness, by exploitation, and on and on (as well as the many subtle variations on each of these). Even obvious moral offenses begin as things the unacceptability of which has to be discovered. On the other hand, at a certain point moral obtuseness becomes culpable—deserving of blame and punishment rather than further patient efforts to clarify its mistakenness. Thus today a racial bigot, for example, receives no leniency in the courts. We demonstrate our recognition of this continuity between moral misunderstanding and willful wrong in a number of ways. Not only do we lose patience with those whose moral obtuseness itself begins to look like a moral wrong, but with respect even to "obvious" crimes we treat those whose capacity for moral discrimination is understandably reduced (the mentally handicapped, for example) more leniently than a strictly retributive "eye-for-an-eye" accounting would require.

All of this indicates that justice involves not the straightforward exaction of retribution wherever a wrong has been committed, but a subtle balancing of the rightful claims of clemency (wherever, and to the extent that, this is warranted by understandable error) and the rightful claims of retribution (wherever, and to the extent that, wrong has been willfully done). It must be admitted that clemency flowing from love *does not guarantee* justice. But where love makes us more inclined to extend clemency in situations in which clemency can be justified as more appropriate than straight retribution, love does in fact serve justice. In other words, insofar as love is *partial* it cannot be counted upon, but insofar as love is a matter of *caring* intensely, it can help to correct the excesses of a purely retributive approach to justice. For what justice requires is *impartial care*: care for the facts, care for the nuances of the situation in question, and care for all the parties concerned—victim and wrongdoer alike.

It is significant that Harris calls the potentially autonomy-threatening virtues *caring* virtues, for we see things more clearly when we care. In contrast, the willingness to ignore subtleties and nuances, the willingness to take an eye for an eye no matter what the circumstances, is a matter of *not caring*. But how, precisely, does care relate to dignity? A few pages ago I asserted, following Harris's lead, that the individual who does not care deeply cannot possess dignity to any great extent, because the capacity to care is part of what we value most in human beings. That cannot be the whole explanation if, as Schiller contends, dignity is fundamentally a matter of exercising self-restraint. If that is so—and there are good reasons for believing that Schiller is correct about this—then we need to consider how care is related to the sort of self-restraint that constitutes dignity. In order to clarify this connection, it will be useful to consider another of Harris's illustrations of how caring intensely can undermine one's autonomy.

At one point, Harris considers the hypothetical case of

> a young American male in the mid-1940s who very much loved his country and fellow citizens, who was both sympathetic with and respectful of the victims of Nazi oppression yet lacked the capacity for exceptional physical courage. Add to this that he believed in the war effort, that he underwent military training designed to reinforce his resolve, and that he subsequently found himself thrust ashore at Normandy. Faced with actual combat of the most horrifying sort, however, he utterly breaks down psychologically in the midst of battle, directly causing avoidable casualties.[14]

Harris then poses the question, "How are we to imagine his [subsequent, reflective] response to this episode in his life if he is as we have described him?" Clearly the soldier could not lightly dismiss the significance of his response on the battlefield—not if he is to be thought of as genuinely concerned for the well-being of his country and comrades. According to Harris, the only response that we could consistently expect of the soldier even after he has returned home would be a severe and extended emotional breakdown. The honest recognition of the magnitude and the consequences of his failure would allow for nothing else.

This hypothetical soldier, then, undergoes *two* discrete instances of integral breakdown: first on the battlefield, when his courage fails him, and then subsequently in the private despair brought on by his reflecting upon the significance of his collapse in combat. It is important to notice, however, that only the first of these two breakdowns is at all blameworthy. That the hypothetical young man found himself being put to the test in serious combat is a matter of what ethicists sometimes refer to as moral luck. That is to say, had the young man been born a generation earlier, or perhaps even just a few years later, he might have been able to live his entire life without ever having the precise limits of his courage so publicly and painfully demonstrated to him. In this regard, he has been unfortunate; many another individual with no more courage than he has will have been able to live a comfortable and unobjectionable life, with no significant moral failures for which to atone. For this reason, the soldier's cowardice can and perhaps should be excused to some extent by all dispassionate observers—*but not by the soldier himself*. For while it may have been a matter of bad luck that he was put to the test, nonetheless he *was* put to a legitimate and important moral test, and he *was* found wanting. Other men—many of them—rose to the occasion in combat. And given what was at stake, it mattered enormously that this soldier could not.

But what about his second breakdown? To begin with, why should one be so confident that it would occur? Would it not be reasonable to presume that the soldier, confronted with the almost unbearable implications of what he has done, will save himself agony by slipping into denial? This is at least theoretically a possibility, but Harris argues that *if* the hypothetical soldier truly is as genuinely concerned about his country, about his comrades, and about the evils of Nazism as has been stipulated, then escaping the hard truths about his own conduct by indulging in self-deception will not be an option for him. If he cares deeply about these things, he will recognize the significance of his own failure. Furthermore, even though this recognition leads directly to his second integral breakdown, this recognition is a *good* thing—something for which he is to be admired rather than either blamed or pitied. For the temptation to indulge in self-deception in these circumstances is the soldier's *second* moral test—and *this* test he passes. But not everyone, perhaps, will immediately see it this way.

> One might object that . . . being self-deceived in this case or in similar cases [could] have the effect of relieving the agent of needless suffering without bringing with it some vice. Here the thought might be that the capacity for truthfulness with oneself is [an heroic virtue] in the same sense in which courage is. Just as not having courage at full strength is not a vice, neither is [not] having the capacity for truthfulness with oneself at full strength a vice. . . .
>
> The problem with this response is that a person who does not have courage at full strength but has it at adequate strength is still courageous. There is no analogue to this in this kind of case of self-deception, though there might be in others. To be sure, we can have the virtue of truthfulness with ourselves and not have it at full strength, but [this] . . . cannot have the result of a fundamentally flawed view of who we are at our core. Lacking the ability to see ourselves for what we are at the core can hardly be consistent with possessing the virtue of truthfulness with ourselves. This is why this kind of truthfulness is such a demanding virtue.[15]

The soldier cannot rationalize his way out of seeing the implications of what he has done precisely because he does care deeply about those things that have been damaged by his failure. Again, one sees certain things more clearly when one cares. This in turn explains how care is related to that form of self-restraint that constitutes dignity. Some of the things that one sees clearly because one cares will be difficult to bear the sight of. But given that one cares, one will resist the temptation to slip away or to close one's eyes. One will, as Schiller puts it, *choose to suffer* rather than betray that which one cares about through an act of desertion. Thus whereas Seth Lord, for example, can be said to compound his desertion of his wife with his dismissive comments about the insignificance of infidelity, this hypothetical soldier, guilty in a sense of desertion on the battlefield, at least refuses to augment that failure by denying its importance.

Harris's central claim in *Dignity and Vulnerability* is that human dignity (and by this he means that dignity of the more demanding sort to which we should aspire) is not and cannot be, as Kant understood it, something one possesses *only* by virtue of one's having achieved *autonomy* to some significant degree. The reason for this, again, is that as human beings our autonomy can be undermined, not only by our succumbing to creaturely temptations (in other words, by our proving to be insufficiently virtuous), but also by our own most worthy inclinations. Caring deeply renders us vulnerable, and if we are unlucky, the intensity of our dedication may cripple us. In spite of this, Harris contends, we must accept the risks to which caring exposes us—for we quite rightly consider our capacity to care to be among the finest of human characteristics. Two implications follow from this. First, dignity does not *always* flow from Kantian autonomy, for an autonomy purchased at the price of not *really* caring one way or the other what happens around one is too cheaply purchased to be of any great value. (There is nothing in Kant's conception of autonomy that positively precludes the possibility of the autonomous individual's caring deeply about things. Harris's point is merely that there is likewise nothing in Kant's conception of autonomy that *requires* it—and this, in his estimation, is a serious shortcoming. Benevolence or wishing others well, it must be stressed, is by no means the same thing as *really* caring about them.) Second, dignity can be exhibited to some extent even by individuals whose autonomy has been undermined—by the hypothetical soldier, for example, insofar as he refuses to rationalize concerning his cowardice. Thus dignity is not just a matter of restraining impulses, although it is that. It also requires that one embrace life's risks rather than attempt to isolate oneself from them. As Harris puts it,

> dignity requires an environment in which an agent anticipates real dangers to significant commitments and stands ready to face those dangers without abandoning those commitments. The life of utter safety regarding all but one's minor interests is not an environment in which this is possible or one in which dignity can have a place.[16]

This indicates yet again why dignity is incompatible with cynicism—for cynicism involves a kind of anesthetizing of the self through a show of indifference. A cynic, in refusing to take up cudgels in order to defend that which he *should* value, refuses to come honestly to terms with the risk of failure.

In all of this Harris seems to be correct. But he is content, in his analysis of the vulnerability that caring introduces into our situation, merely to point out that achieving Kantian autonomy cannot be, given the importance we place on care, the unqualifiedly ultimate aim of moral behavior. The step that Harris does not quite take, but which seems legitimate in light of the relationship between caring and seeing things clearly, would be to argue that *even the pursuit of autonomy* as Kant understands it, insofar as autonomy is a matter of treating others always as ends rather than as means—which is the second of his three ways of formulating the categorical imperative—*requires* that in some sense we *care* about those others. We do not genuinely treat others as ends, after all, if we resolve merely to stay out of their way—or *even* if we offer them assistance ("charity" in Kant's sense), but insist on relying entirely on our own (a priori) judgment about what this should involve.

CARE AND JUSTICE

This is a point that Paul Ricoeur develops at some length in *Oneself as Another*. There is an irresolvable tension, he argues there,[17] between two key Kantian notions—the idea of *humanity* and the idea of *individual persons as ends in themselves*. The distinction, and the tension, are important because they emerge at precisely that place in Kant's thinking where he comes closest to confronting the inadequacy of a purely formal and rationalist approach to ethics. According to Kant's argument in the *Groundwork*, humanity becomes an object of moral respect by virtue of its being a locus (the primary locus that we are aware of) of pure practical reason. Thus when Kant makes the transition from his first formulation of the categorical imperative, which captures the purely *formal* character of the moral law, to his second formulation, which is intended to represent the substantial *content* of the moral law, it is the concept of *humanity* that serves as the link between them. Regardless of whether we *act only on that maxim that we can will to see universalized* or, alternatively, we *treat humanity only as an end and never merely as a means*, our sense of what we must do in a given situation will always be the same, Kant contends, because these are two different formulations of one and the same moral law.

But is that obvious? Our respect for reason, and thus for the possibility of "giving oneself the law," which is what we are doing when we act only on universalizable maxims, implies as well respect for rational beings, since these alone are capable of "giving themselves the law," and this is, in Kant's estimation, the very *purpose* of reason. However, what is crucial to the first formulation of the categorical imperative (*Act only on that maxim* . . .) is reason's universalized perspective—the fact that it views its subject matter from everywhere and nowhere. The emphasis on that universalized perspective is maintained, as Kant moves from the first formulation to the second (*Treat humanity only* . . .), through his contention that it is *rational nature* or *humanity* (suitably abstract terms) that must always be treated as an end rather than as a means. No sooner is the transition to the second formulation effected, however, than a clear inadequacy of the abstract term "humanity" requires Kant to amend the second formulation—since in actual experience it is almost always *individual* human beings that we interact with and treat either well or badly, either as ends or as means, and seldom if ever humanity as a whole. Thus the more practically applicable form of the law that Kant immediately slips into using is that we must always treat *persons* as ends in themselves and never as means. To what extent, however, *can* one treat a given person as an end in himself without coming to appreciate his *specificity* and, most particularly, his *otherness* from oneself? If I am genuinely concerned, for example, to treat *you* as an end in yourself, surely I must make a serious effort to come to know who *you* really are—which is to say, how *you* understand and think of yourself, what *your* values and interests are. And just as surely, it would seem, I cannot genuinely treat you as an end in yourself if I insist on imposing my own entirely *rational* expectations on you—on the grounds that you are, after all, just as I am, a *rational being*.

In his second discussion of charity in the *Groundwork*, Kant comes close to recognizing this. He remarks there that "the ends of a subject who is an end in itself must as far as possible be also *my* ends, if that representation is to have its *full* effect in me."[18] In other words, in one's dealings with someone else, one ought to respect not only the person in question, but also that person's goals, and do what is possible (at least sometimes, since Kant sees this after all as an *imperfect* duty) to contribute to the achievement of those goals. But common sense suggests that this is not possible unless one first discovers, by getting to know this other person as the unique individual that he or she is, *what* those goals actually are. And of course, if one needs to get to know *this* person's goals, then presumably one should also get to know *that* person's goals, and the goals of that other person over there, and so on. A strictly consistent *Kantian* reading of this claim, however, cannot afford to head in that direction. For if it did, the requirements of morality would quickly cease to be discernible by pure reason alone, and Kant's triumphant announcement that a perfect understanding of them is within everyone's grasp would become nonsensical. In no time at all, one would find oneself in need of, and relying upon, Aristotelian *phronēsis* or practical wisdom—in order to determine, for example, whether one's parents' need for security in their old age or one's nephew's need for an education has the greater moral claim upon one's (limited) capacity for charity.

This, then, is the sense in which Kant's first and second formulations of the categorical imperative fail to be congruent in their implications. For it is one thing to say, as in the first formulation, that one must never make an exception in favor of *oneself*. It is quite another to say that one must also never make an exception in favor of *someone else*—since until one is prepared to acknowledge that the other person *is* in an important sense an exception, is *not* exactly like oneself or anyone else, one cannot genuinely treat others with the respect that they deserve as ends in themselves. One's own goals are, after all, if not entirely, at least largely transparent to oneself, and thus with respect to these the danger is that one may make too close an identification of what is right or permitted with one's own preferences. In contrast, the other person's goals are largely (although of course not entirely) opaque to oneself, and thus here the danger is rather that one may feel too much indifference toward the preferences of others. As a result, in moving from a self-oriented formulation of the moral law to an other-oriented formulation, the value of imposing the discipline of universalization is significantly reduced. For ordinarily we do not have to be on guard against the danger of treating the other person *unfairly well*; rather the danger tends to be that of our not treating the other person fairly enough.

But even if, in moving to the other-oriented second formulation of Kant's moral law, we recognize that the value of imposing the discipline of universalization is reduced, it is still not entirely eliminated. Justice, after all, *is* impartial. And in some circumstances, at least, we must take care not to favor those persons whom we happen to know over those whom we have not yet met. For this reason, even though Ricoeur agrees with Aristotle that determining how we can live well together should be thought of as the ultimate aim of ethics, and stresses as well (somewhat in opposition to Aristotle) that we cannot determine what constitutes "the good life" without attending carefully to one another's specific and varying viewpoints, experiences, needs, and desires, Ricoeur also insists upon the necessity of filtering our private, and even our shared, conceptions of the good life through the "sieve" of justice.[19] In other words, even if the question of what constitutes "the good" ultimately takes priority over the question of what constitutes "the just," the latter question too must be satisfactorily addressed. Whatever conception of the good life we work our way toward, that conception must accommodate our demand for justice as well as our aspirations for fulfillment. As Ricoeur puts it, our desire, finally, is to live well "with and for others in just institutions."[20]

We want, then, both the good life and justice; but still, it is important to recognize that the question of goodness takes priority over the question of justice. To see why this is the case, one need only consider the unsatisfactory nature of social contract conceptions of justice, which reverse the priority. In a social contract framework, justice is always a matter of *equality*—since as partners to the contract, as individuals who freely choose to bind ourselves by the social conventions (laws, etc.) which constitute the terms of the contract, we begin (hypothetically at least) *as equals*. As Amartya Sen observes,[21] however, any time we conceive of justice as a matter of establishing or preserving equality, there is a further and more problematic question waiting to be addressed—specifically, what *sort* of equality are we interested in?

There are, after all, many different and—distressingly for egalitarians—mutually incompatible ways in which the situations of different individuals can be equalized. We can at least imagine providing different individuals with perfect equality of opportunity (to get a first-rate education or to land a particular job, say), or perfect equality of resources (at some specific moment in time), or a perfect equality of outcome (as when all participants in a game are declared winners and are awarded identical prizes). We can also *imagine*, although if we are genuinely concerned for justice, we would never consider insisting on the establishment of, a perfect equality of talents across different individuals, since such an equality could only be brought about by hobbling those born with greater natural gifts. The obvious problem, though, is that we cannot simultaneously achieve all of these important forms of equality. If we forgo hobbling the gifted, on the grounds that such interference in a person's life would itself constitute a serious breach of justice, then even if we take steps to ensure equality of opportunity, the varied distribution of natural gifts will ensure that nothing like an equality of outcome will follow from the exercise of those gifts. And insofar as resources tend, in a competitive world, to be distributed as rewards for success, it follows that if at some point we were to impose an equality of resources, such an equality would quickly be upended by the subsequent decisions and efforts of individuals of varying gifts who were, we must suppose, still free to follow their own inclinations in investing their resources. (On this point, at least, libertarians like Robert Nozick[22] are clearly right.)

In practice, then, at least in what is often referred to as "the developed world," this leaves equality before the law as *the* form of equality that is considered by most to capture the essence of justice. And yet, as a principle, equality *before* the law gives us no guidance at all in *creating* substantive law. Should we write a flat, a progressive, or no income tax into law? Are we to embrace affirmative action or reject it? How are we to define fraud, libel, and assault exactly? Which, if any, recreational drugs and sexual practices are to be outlawed? The principle of equality *before* the law—regardless of what the law may be—is conspicuously silent on all of these questions. And wherever there is a significant *in*equality of resources, of course, equality before the law is compromised, in much the same way that equality of opportunity (to which it is related) must be, by the power of wealth to secure more and better assistance than is to be had by the majority.

None of these caveats implies that justice is *not* in some important sense ultimately a matter of equality. The point is rather that, in order to determine what it is precisely that needs to be equalized if justice is to be achieved, we must appeal to some particular conception of the good life—a version of the good life that *this* form of equality (which defines justice) helps to promote. Strict social contract theorists, however, deny that such an appeal is either necessary or possible. They stress the fact that different people understand what constitutes the good life in significantly different ways. And in their opinion, if a consensus had to be established on the question of what the good life in fact *is* before justice could be defined with reference to it, all attempts to achieve justice would be hamstrung from the start. The whole point of justice, they argue, echoing Mill's *On Liberty*, is to protect the freedom of individuals so that they can severally pursue their varied conceptions of the good life without undue interference from others who happen to be committed to a *different* conception of the good life.

While there is clearly an element of truth in this line of reasoning, there is also a serious flaw. The central assumption of the strict social contract theorist,[23] after all, is that ultimately our main desire (and thus a crucial component of the "good life" however else one might understand it) is to be left alone to pursue our own interests in peace. And the point of the social contract—which, in practical terms, amounts to nothing more nor less than the law—is to make possible the satisfaction of this desire. The law can accomplish this, however, only if we know *precisely* what it requires of us in the way of conduct, and precisely what activities it protects. On the basis of this knowledge, we can then confidently pursue our own goals *whatever* they may be. In other words, the law, providing it possesses this pristine clarity with respect to what is and is not permitted, allows us to take steps that, in a more confused environment, might seem too risky to embark upon. Here one finds an echo of Hobbes's contention that only where the social contract has been established—and thus peace and order have replaced the state of war in which each person is opposed to everyone else—can culture and commerce emerge.[24] There is also, however, a less noble-sounding yet equally germane way to understand this claim. If one's personal safety, for example, depended upon not offending one's neighbor's sensibilities, one would think twice about pursuing one's own pecuniary interest to his immediate disadvantage.

But where the law exists to protect private property and commercial transactions that have at least the appearance of being mutually agreed upon, one can freely (and safely) gouge one's customers and employees when the opportunity arises, foreclose mortgages in the aftermath of private catastrophe, and blithely drive one's competitors out of business.

In jurisprudential discussions there is a name for this "benefit" that clear and explicit laws make available to the vigorous pursuer of his own self-interest. It is called "walking the line," and it means staying just on the right side of legality while ignoring the ethical implications of one's actions. The classic example of "walking the line" is tax "avoision." (To *evade* taxes is illegal; to *avoid* them using whatever means are legally permissible, on the other hand, is considered by many to be a sign of intelligence. And where legally permissible avoidance becomes especially inventive, where the line that is being walked is extraordinarily fine, we have something so close to evasion without yet becoming illegal as to warrant its own name—"avoision.")[25] Successful tax "avoision" obviously depends upon one's knowing exactly which tax "dodges" will be challenged by the IRS and which tax "shelters" will not. The crucial thing, then, for would-be line-walkers is not that any particular tax shelter be available or, more generally, that any particular law be in effect, but rather that what *is* legal should be perfectly clear.

But insofar as *justice* is identified with the existence of *clear and specific* law rather than *appropriate* law, justice clearly can no longer be sensitive to the possible relevance of exceptional circumstances. There is no place left for a judge or a jury to consider mitigating circumstances and to set aside the verdict that a literal-minded application of the law would dictate. For it is not *fair* outcomes that "justice" is concerned with in this case; it is *predictability* of outcomes, and the exercise of judicial discretion clearly tends to reduce the predictability of legal outcomes. But in this sense "justice" becomes mere formalism, ensuring a "level playing field" in one privileged sense— that is, in the sense that everyone has, theoretically at least, been given fair and equal warning of the rules—while ignoring countless other "irrelevant" inequalities (such as whether one is rich or poor, healthy or handicapped, the perpetrator or the victim of past discrimination). This is not, of course, the way in which the law (or justice) actually works—at least not entirely. But it is nonetheless the way in which strict social contract theorists tend to believe it should work. For how can there be a meaningful contract between individuals unless the agreement into which they have entered has explicit and enforceable terms? The very point of a contract, after all, is to keep unpleasant surprises to a minimum.

This is why, for example, marriage is poorly understood if it is represented as involving some kind of contract. The terms of such a "contract"—what each partner will be obliged to do in all conceivable future circumstances ("for better, for worse, in sickness and in health")—cannot possibly be specified in advance and thus be mutually and explicitly agreed upon. Marriage, rather, is a matter of two people recognizing and acting upon their mutual desire to, as Ricoeur would put it, "live well with and for each other." The partners to a marriage cannot live well together, of course, if there is no justice between them—if one partner is constantly and selfishly taking advantage of the other's good will. But neither can they live well together if they are obsessed with the question of whether justice has been achieved between them in a strict contractual sense—if every menial task and minor sacrifice by one partner calls for and must be offset by an equal and compensatory sacrifice on the part of the other.[26] Love could hardly take root, much less flourish, in such circumstances.

Is it possible, nonetheless, to represent relations between those who love each other as establishing the model or paradigm, not only for morality, but also for justice? The strict social contract theorist would balk at this suggestion, given his commitment to the idea that justice is simply a matter of delivering on agreements—agreements that are to be presumed fair whenever they are the products of free (that is, not directly coerced) negotiations. All the same, the idea has an old and respectable pedigree—in the moral sentiment school of ethical theory. David Hume, for example, in his *Enquiry Concerning the Principles of Morals*, contends that Hobbes's social contract theory can look plausible only if one begins with an unrealistic conception of human nature—only, that is, if one thinks of individual human beings as solitary and self-sufficient pursuers of their private goals. "But suppose the conjunction of the sexes to be established in nature," Hume continues. In that case, "a family immediately arises; and particular rules being found requisite for its subsistence, these are immediately embraced; though without comprehending the rest of mankind within their prescriptions." *Within* the family, that is to say, problems of sibling rivalry will arise. And the parents, loving all of their children equally, must learn to distribute goods so that each child feels that he or she has been fairly treated. And now "suppose that several families unite together into one society, which is totally disjoined from all others." If this were to happen, then of course "the rules, that preserve peace and order, enlarge themselves to the utmost extent of that society; but becoming then entirely useless, lose their force when carried one step farther." A group of families, in other words, deciding to cooperate and bind their futures together, do not have to work out from scratch the rules that will allow them to get along. The lessons that family life has already taught them about how to deal with jealousy and rivalries can be adapted fairly readily to a community of friends. *Beyond* the boundaries of that community, however, the rules will not apply—for the simple reason that no one expects them to. "But again suppose, that several distinct societies maintain a kind of intercourse for mutual convenience and advantage, the boundaries of justice still grow larger, in proportion to the largeness of men's views, and the force of their mutual connexions. History, experience, reason sufficiently instruct us in this natural progress of human sentiments, and in the gradual enlargement of our regards to justice, in proportion as we become acquainted with the extensive utility of that virtue."[27]

Given that family life is the crucible in which almost all of us acquired our early social skills, Hume's is an eminently plausible account of how ideas of justice first emerge and then are refined and extended in human society. Of course, our notion of justice, as it is refined, will come in time to embrace such technical and "artificial" (as Hume calls them) devices as formal contracts and legal rights. These, though, are mere extrapolations from our informal schooling within the family in the importance of such things as respecting one another's feelings and keeping one's promises. But even if justice begins as a family affair, and is then extended to surrogate family members (our friends), there nonetheless comes a time in our personal moral education when we recognize that justice must be extended not only to those whom we know but to strangers as well. Someone who accepts Hume's account of the origin of justice, however, will understand the nature of justice as it applies to strangers quite differently than will a social contract theorist. For while strangers, by definition, are not known in the close sympathetic manner that friends and family members are, this does not imply, for Hume, that they are to be viewed as individuals toward whom we are appropriately indifferent. (Or worse, that they can be viewed as sheep to be sheared,[28] as long as the shearing is legal.) On the contrary, given that Hume sees the extension of justice (in circles emanating outward from the family) as being driven by our progressively wider "intercourse" and "mutual connexions" with other people, there is a presumption at work in his theory of increasing intimacy with others. Thus the newly encountered stranger, toward whom we are considering extending justice, is to be viewed as someone whom it is conceivable that we might get to know and then find ourselves liking and wishing to associate with more closely. The extension of justice to the stranger makes such increasing intimacy possible, just as the denial of justice to the stranger almost certainly makes it *impossible*. On Hume's more humane account of justice, then, it makes sense that anticipatory sympathy or the expectation of friendly involvement should govern our relations even with those whom we do not yet know at all well.

One of the strengths of Hume's account is that it readily explains a characteristic of justice with which we are all familiar—specifically, the fact that we have a far clearer idea of what constitutes *injustice* than we do of what justice itself consists in. Ricoeur too notes this peculiarity of our understanding:

> [W]hat we are first aware of is injustice. "Unjust! What injustice!" we cry. And indeed it is in the mode of complaint that we penetrate the field of the just and the unjust. And even on the plane of justice as an institution, before courts of justice, we continue to behave as "plaintiffs" and to "lodge a complaint against someone." The sense of injustice is not simply more poignant but more perspicacious than the sense of justice, for . . . people have a clearer vision of what is missing in human relations than of the right way to organize them. This is why, even for philosophers, it is injustice that first sets thought in motion.[29]

Now if justice *were* merely a matter of adhering to the terms of any contract into which one has freely entered, none of this would be true, and the tendency of those who have been manipulated and taken advantage of to complain about this treatment would actually *be* as incomprehensible as strict social contract theorists claim it to be. But the phenomenon that Ricoeur is describing is well known, and Hume provides the explanation. Our sense of injustice, he argues, is based on our sympathetic identification with other people. This is not to suggest that our tendency to identify with others, and thus to sympathize even with our victim's pain, cannot be overpowered by our own selfish desires. Hume has no illusions about our capacity for evil. But where there is no personal interest of our own at stake—especially where one stranger is dealing in some way with another stranger—our sympathetic responses tend to determine how we feel about this interaction, and thus to decide whether or not we feel that an injustice has been perpetrated. In other words, because of our natural tendency to suffer one another's pains vicariously, at some incipient level we *care* about what happens even to strangers.

Sympathetic identification must begin with a recognition of similarity between oneself and the object of one's sympathy, since it is only if the other's reactions can be trusted to be much like one's own that one can reasonably presume to feel the other's pains and pleasures. But actually *caring* about someone else, which is the condition that sympathy, given time and encouragement, gradually moves us toward, involves recognizing not only the other's similarity to oneself but, even more importantly, the other's difference from oneself. Indeed, we can truly be said to *care* about someone else only if, and to the extent that, we show a genuine interest in coming to know that other person's story, situation, perspective on things, and tastes—all of which will be in important respects different from our own. Where this interest in the other person deepens into the love that one feels for a close friend, care itself becomes something stronger—something that Ricoeur refers to as *solicitude*. And solicitude, Ricoeur explains, is bound up with our recognition that our friend, precisely *as* the unique person that he or she is, "is irreplaceable in our affection and our esteem."[30]

Although neither Hume nor Ricoeur develops the following line of argument, it is possible to build upon this notion of the irreplaceability of those whom we love a naturalistic explanation for our recognition of that form of human dignity that is felt to be universal. Those whom I love, as the particular and unique individuals they are, are irreplaceable *for me*. Analogously, those whom I personally do not love are nonetheless loved by, and irreplaceable for, *others*. Love, which is directed always to particular and unique individuals, binds us into a network of solicitude encompassing the whole of humanity. (In the sense that each of those whom I love, in his or her turn loves others, each of whom loves still others, and so on, until at length, if we continued tracing these bonds of affection, virtually every single human being would be accounted for.) Our appreciation in principle, then, of the importance and value of each and every human being is derivable from this fact, of which we are all aware—that each of us is valuable and important to some *other* human being who is (or was) valuable and important in her turn. Insofar as it is love and affection that sustains this network of solicitude, it is in each instance the *uniqueness* of the individual—his or her particular sets of memories and experiences, character traits, desires and hopes—precisely, in other words, the things that the individual could be expected to value as well—that accounts for the individual's importance and value, and thus his or her dignity in the universally applicable sense.

It might be argued, however, that some few individuals may in fact *not* be loved or valued by *anyone el*se—and not only *are no*t loved, but *cannot* be genuinely loved, given the depravity of their characters. Such individuals, this naturalistic account of dignity might seem to suggest, are undeserving of the attribution to them of *any* degree of dignity, unless the mere fact that these monsters love themselves suffices to establish their value and importance. (And if that were the case, then obviously there would be no need to make this detour through the "network of solicitude.") There are two responses to this objection. First, on the basis of the argument just developed, we will always wish presumptively to attribute dignity to unknown individuals, since the mere fact that *we* do not happen to love them does not imply that no one else does. And if, as a matter of principle, we initially at least attribute dignity to *everyone* we encounter, on the presumption that they are capable and deserving of being loved, then at least occasionally we may attribute dignity to someone who in fact is *undeserving* of this recognition. Clearly, though, it is far better to err in this respect by overinclusion than by underinclusion.

The second point, which is even more important, is that the possession of dignity (especially of the universally applicable sort) must be understood to be in one sense an *interpersonal* matter. One's possession or nonpossession of dignity is manifested, after all, in how others treat one—as we can see, for example, in any racially or ethnically motivated abuse of one group by another. Dignity is vulnerable, in other words, even where its recognition is warranted. Those who flatly refuse to acknowledge one's value strip one of one's dignity. But if the possession of dignity is in this sense an interpersonal matter, then presumably the value and importance that one must have in order to warrant the attribution of dignity must also be *interpersonal* importance and value. It is not enough that one be irreplaceable *for oneself*. If I am to attribute dignity to you, your value and importance must be real for me, even if I do not yet personally *feel* it. In that regard, the fact that others love and hold you in affection establishes, in my mind as well, the possibility of your being valued for the sake of the *unique* individual that you are. On the basis of this affection in which others hold you, it would appear that there is at least *something* objectively worthy about you, and *that* is what I acknowledge in attributing dignity to you.

But the importance of an individual *as* someone capable of being loved *for* the unique person that he or she is accounts not only for our presumptive attribution of dignity; it explains as well why Ricoeur is right to think that, even if our concern for the good life ultimately takes priority over our concern for justice (in the sense that what constitutes justice can be determined, in the final analysis, only with reference to the good life), justice nonetheless has its own *independent* claim to make upon us. To see why this is the case, it may be useful to consider for a moment how Aristotle's and Ricoeur's discussions of the good life differ in what they emphasize. Aristotle is as conscious as Ricoeur of the fact that individual human beings differ from one another in tastes, interests, talents, and importantly, as their lives unfold, in luck. Nonetheless, according to Aristotle, human flourishing is largely one and the same thing for *all* human beings, for the simple reason that human nature is in large part defined by its *telos* or intrinsic aim. This is why he declares unequivocally that flourishing requires, for example, that one have children, long life, and at least a modicum of wealth, and that the life of intellectual reflection is the highest and most suitable kind of life for a human being to live. In other words, Aristotle tends to represent those things that *almost all* human beings in fact desire and recognize to be sources of happiness (children, long life, wealth, etc.) as *universal* goods *even as* he acknowledges the significant differences existing between individual human beings. He holds this view because he believes that human nature has an essence[31] (defined by our *telos*) in which we all partake regardless of our individual particularities.

Given what modern biology tells us about human nature, Aristotle's ethics stands up rather better today than does Kant's ethical theory, but even so in one important respect it comes in for damning criticism. If we take seriously the scientific evidence that humanity, like every other species of life, arrived on the scene through evolution, Aristotle's idea that there is a *telos* or aim governing human nature is not credible. This does not imply that it is no longer legitimate to generalize about the sorts of things that in fact do tend to make human beings happy; it simply means that we must be wary about taking such generalizations as statements that are *universally* true with respect to humans. In the light of modern biology, it is clear that human nature has no essence. Instead, we must think of human nature as a kind of statistical average or mean. With respect to physiology, for example, it is where most of us tend to be found. But the mere fact that most of us congregate around the mean does not imply that there is anything *wrong* with being a physiological outlier. What is true of our physiology is true as well of our (harmless) inclinations. For example, the fact that most people are fairly gregarious does not make the inclinations of the comparative loner inappropriate. Each individual has his own natural character just as he has his own natural physique, into both of which he will naturally grow if he is given opportunity, reasonable sustenance, and exercise. With respect to both his physique and his character the challenge facing an individual is to discover how to achieve the good life *for himself* given his particularities.

Most of Aristotle's observations on ethics—his contention, for example, that virtue is always a mean between two vicious excesses, his claim that justice is a matter of proportional equality, and his comments on the importance of practical wisdom and the cultivation of sound habits, all of which exhibit considerable sensitivity to the significance of particularities—can still be embraced in the light of modern biology as long as we acknowledge that there is no *telos* defining human nature, and thus that the search for *eudaimonia* or happiness is one that each individual must pursue for himself to an even greater degree than Aristotle appreciated. In the absence of a human *telos*, the advice of others, even of the comparatively wise, is liable to be less immediately relevant than Aristotle expected it to be. The pursuit of the good life, in other words, is not only a pursuit of those things that contribute to the good life, but is also a search for clarification of what the good life actually consists in *for the particular individual who is now inquiring*. This is why the shift in emphasis that Ricoeur effects within the Aristotelian framework in *Oneself as Another* is a welcome refinement. In contrast to Aristotle, Ricoeur stresses the personal dimension of the search for the good life. What prompts Ricoeur to shift the emphasis as he does, however, is not evolutionary biology and its implications, but his analysis of the role played by our lifelong engagement with historical and fictional narratives in the development of our self-understanding.

There is a strong connection between character and plot, not only in fiction and history, but also in our own lives. To a considerable degree, we *are* what we *do*. But *what* we do, of course, can be properly understood only if our actions are viewed not as isolated incidents, but as events that must be contextualized. To provide a context for events, to explain what led up to them, what they were intended to accomplish, and what actually followed from them, is always to bind them into a particular story. For this reason, understanding human beings—ourselves as well as others—is invariably a matter of telling ourselves the various stories that *can* plausibly be told about what has been done and why. One sees this most clearly in a court of law, where the prosecutor and the defense attorney are each concerned to tell a plausible story about the defendant's actions, and the role of the jury, in passing its verdict, is to declare how convincingly the prosecution has succeeded in establishing a definitive narrative account of the events in question. But even to understand oneself or others in what appear to be static terms—to think of oneself as a doctor, say, or a father—requires that one know what sort of stories doctors and fathers typically figure in. For unless one knows what a doctor or a father *does* (and again, this cannot be grasped in terms of isolated actions), one does not really know what a doctor or a father *is*.

Understanding, whether we have in mind the scientific understanding of the natural world or the historical understanding of human actions, has essentially two components. On the one hand, it is a matter of drawing connections between related (usually *causally* related) events. On the other, it is a matter of distinguishing what is important and revealing from what is insignificant and misleading—a matter of separating the message from the surrounding noise. There is thus no reason to balk at the suggestion that human behavior can be understood only through the imposition upon it of a narrative structure simply because a narrative account of events inevitably involves a *selecting* of details that are deemed to be relevant and the *emphasizing* of some at the expense of others. If the chaotic richness of actual experience were never simplified and schematized in this fashion, it could never be rendered meaningful at all. But this is not to suggest that whatever hinders the straightforward unfolding of a plotline is irrelevant to the narrative account. On the contrary, because human intentions are pursued on a stage crowded with chance occurrences and other actors independently pursuing *their* goals, it is virtually a given that the hero of a story will have to cope with changing circumstances, unforeseen developments, and reversals of fortune. Indeed, the bringing of intentions to some kind of resolution (although not necessarily the one anticipated) in spite of the resistance of contingent circumstance is precisely what we tend to mean by a dramatic plotline. It is the presence of a dramatic plotline that defines a *story* and distinguishes it from a mere "uninterpreted" chronicle of events.[32] Ricoeur describes the narrative structure in which such a resolution is reached as one that exhibits "discordant concordance" or a "synthesis of the heterogeneous."[33] And one of the benefits of coming to understand the course of human action in terms of the "discordant concordance" that is exemplified in narrative accounts is that it enables us to make sense of (and thus to cope more effectively with) both frustration and success.

Useful as our engagement with narrative accounts may be in providing us with the meaning-structures that allow us to make sense of our own pasts, the really important value of narrative for us is *prospective*. Our lives are short and our choices are fraught with consequence. Literature, history, film, and even the play of children (which often has a free-floating narrative structure)[34] allow us to engage in *imaginative variations*—allow us to project ourselves into alternative "realities" and thus to gain some of the benefits of experience without having to pay the costs (in terms of invested time and energy, and closed alternative opportunities) that are invariably associated with actual lived experience. As Ricoeur puts it, literature (in the broadest sense, which includes history and film) "consists in a vast laboratory for thought experiments."[35] In this laboratory we can sharpen our awareness of our own values, both moral and personal, by sympathetically identifying with a far wider range of other human beings (pursuing a far more extensive array of personal projects under a far greater variety of circumstances) than we would ever be likely to encounter in actual experience.

Whether we actually do so, of course, depends upon the use that we make of literature. For narratives can be used not only to sharpen and broaden the individual's appreciation of values, but also to impose upon society as a whole a *conformity* of values. One can do this simply by restricting the range of narrative-types available and insisting that, even with regard to those few narrative-types that are approved, a privileged interpretation is to be adhered to. This is the use of literature as propaganda, and almost any creed can be the beneficiary of such an approach. Thus when Ricoeur invokes the development of self-understanding through our engagement with narratives as grounds for stressing the *personal* dimension of the search for the good life, this cannot be because exposure to literature always broadens and liberalizes our values. Rather, the explanation is that in a society such as our own in which narrative-types are numerous and varied and their interpretation is left to the audience, we discover both that a wide diversity of human values are presented and explored, and that the development of the individual's self-understanding through engagement with narrative turns out to be an intensely *personal* process.

Given the uniqueness of the individual—the particularity of his hopes, talents, inclinations, and circumstances—the question of what constitutes the good life *for him* is one to which there can never be given a definitive answer. This is the case not only because no one *else* can speak definitively for the individual in question, but also because he discovers that his own circumstances, capacities, inclinations, and hopes are in a process of constant change. New possibilities are constantly emerging, and old possibilities are constantly being closed off, and all the while (it is to be hoped) the richness and depth of his understanding are increasing. For these reasons, if we take it as fundamental that each individual has a right to pursue his own happiness, it follows that he must have a right as well to protection against illegitimate intrusions into, or illegitimate constrictions upon, his ongoing quest first to *discover* what happiness and the good life consist in, and then to *realize* as much of the good life as he can manage. This right to protection from interference, moreover, is in a sense *all* that is referred to when one speaks of *justice*.

This at least is Mill's contention in *On Liberty*, where he insists on the individual's right not to be interfered with, provided one very important condition is satisfied. As he puts it, "the only purpose for which power can be rightfully exercised over any member of a civilized community, against his will, is to prevent harm to others."[36] But not only *can* power be rightfully exercised over a person against his will in these circumstances; the logic of Mill's position requires that, if someone is harming others, power *should be* exercised over him, for the sake of redressing that harm. For the point of the harm proviso in *On Liberty* is to guarantee reciprocity in the exercise of freedom—to guarantee that, in exercising *my* freedom, I do not, by harming you in some way, impair *your* exercise of freedom. This reciprocity of freedom matters, ultimately, for two reasons: first, because each of us is presumptively equally deserving of respect; and second, because such reciprocity improves the open exchange of ideas, which is in turn a precondition for the effective pursuit of truth—in which all of us have a stake.

But given the significance of the harm proviso in *On Liberty*, Mill's authority cannot be invoked convincingly by social contract theorists who presume that, as long as a freely entered contract is adhered to, by definition no harm has been done. For ironically, the effect of fetishizing the contract (which, it has to be admitted, in *some sense* is clearly a paradigmatic reciprocal relationship) is, potentially at least, to *undermine* this reciprocity that Mill insists upon. In the actual world, access to information, the capacity to analyze that information, and the freedom to take or leave a particular offer seldom if ever are equally distributed between the two parties entering into a given contract. And any significant inequality favoring one of those parties puts that individual in a position to harm the other without the latter being immediately aware of this. If we recognize this—if we understand that there is indeed a *harm* involved when, for example, an adult and a child *freely* enter into a sexual relationship—we will reject the social contract theorist's contention that the terms of an agreement, once accepted by both parties, are never subsequently to be subjected to the test of *fairness*.

One concession, however, must be made to the social contract theorist before we leave this subject, since it is only *intentional* harm committed by means of a contract that should alarm us. In applying the test of fairness to a contract, in other words, what matters is not those consequences absolutely unforeseeable to both parties that might, as things work out, leave one party significantly worse off than the other. (Thus if a football player under contract sustains a paralyzing injury in the course of a cleanly played game, he can hardly accuse the team's owner, after the fact, of having taken advantage of him.) For we are all equally vulnerable to the unknown. What is to be condemned, then, is "walking the line"—that is, taking advantage of the other's inexperience, inattentiveness, or gullibility to squeeze out advantages for oneself, with no regard for the fully foreseeable corresponding *dis*advantages imposed upon the other party. And whether one can be said to be guilty of this, of course, will always depend upon what one knew (relative to what the other party knew) about the possibilities of harm flowing from the agreement. It follows that insofar as we are interested in seeing justice done, we must be constantly prepared to probe where the social contract theorist would like— on purely formal grounds—to prevent us from probing. We must be prepared to inquire into what forms of harm actually exist or might emerge, and to inquire into what each party knew about potential harms at the time of entering into their agreement without presuming that simply because one party did not know something relevant to the agreement in question, this ignorance was automatically his own fault. In engaging in these inquiries, we are driven both by our concern for the particular individual *in his uniqueness* and also by our *equal* concern for the welfare of all other individuals.

JUSTICE AND TRUTH AS REGULATIVE IDEALS

According to Aristotle[37] (whose basic insight I mean to borrow here without being committed to all of the details of his position), justice is a matter of giving to each person what he or she is due. This holds, in somewhat different senses, for both distributive and retributive[38] justice, since not only wealth, powers, and honors are to be distributed to those to whom they are due, but punishments as well. The idea of *dueness*, however, needs to be unpacked somewhat. Specifically, the kind of dueness that Aristotle associates with justice is *proportional equality*. In other words, the individuals in a just community are to be treated equally *even as* their individual talents, characters, accomplishments, and crimes are registered and taken into account in the distribution of goods and punishments. Thus the pursuit of justice, in its most elementary instance, involves the analysis of a proportional relation with four terms: two persons, with their respective merits and demerits, and the two shares that they are to be assigned on the basis of those merits. The analysis of proportional equality does not end there, but proceeding from that first step, moves on to an analysis of the appropriateness of *all* the shares that are distributed within and by the community that has set itself the goal of achieving justice.

This continues to be, I would argue, the fundamental conception of justice with which we all operate. Even defenders of unfettered capitalism, who balk at the idea of permitting any central authority to decide who is due what, argue that we should allow the impersonal forces of the market to distribute income on the ground that the market will do a fairer job of this—that is, produce a distribution that accords *better* with individual merits—than would any human being, or group of human beings, given the limitations of their capacity for the sort of analysis required and given everyone's all-too-human tendency to succumb to greed. (At the same time, of course, it has to be acknowledged that defenders of unfettered capitalism are proposing that we abdicate the pursuit of at least *distributive* justice as a deliberative enterprise. The shrillness of the libertarians' insistence on the reliability of markets must be understood as a symptom of this refusal to deliberate themselves, or to accept the deliberation of others, about what would constitute proportionally equal shares in their community. The market is thus embraced as a *surrogate* for deliberation about distributive justice.)

For my purpose, the first thing to notice about this conception of justice is that (as the libertarian quite correctly observes) it presents us with an in-principle-unfinishable task of analysis. But this holds even for that part of justice—that is, *retributive* justice—from which the libertarian does *not* want to exclude deliberation. The analysis of how proportional equality should be achieved in the distribution of criminal punishments may be a *smaller* unfinishable task than would be the analysis of what proportional equality requires in the distribution of wealth, powers, and honors in a given community, but it is unfinishable all the same—for human nature and the circumstances of human action are incalculably complex. The range of factors that could enter into our evaluation of someone's merit and the range of considerations that may come to have a bearing on how we weigh those factors are potentially infinite. The point is that in spite of the unfinishability in principle[39] of the task of deliberation, the pursuit of justice continues to be a crucial enterprise for us—one that we are not about to abandon.

The second thing to notice is that we cannot give one person what he or she is due without coordinating this with an account or analysis of what others are due. Again, this holds with respect to both distributive and retributive justice. With regard to distributive justice, what one is due depends not only on one's personal merit, but also on what is *available* for distribution. Thus whether a particular young woman, for example, *deserves* to be given a college education by her parents depends not only on whether she has the intelligence and maturity to profit from going to college, but also on whether or not her parents can afford to pay for such an education. The family's socioeconomic status has a bearing on what the individual family member has a right to expect. (This becomes still more obvious when we consider how unjust it would seem for the well-to-do parents of two equally talented sons to pay for one son's college education and refuse to do so for the other.) Even John Locke, the patron saint of libertarians, recognized this principle that what a person is entitled to depends to some extent upon what is available for distribution—as we can see in his proviso that, after one has mixed one's labor with the re- sources to be found in nature and thereby made some portion of them one's own, "enough and as good" must still be left over for the benefit of others who will be arriving on the scene later. The crucial question in all delibera- tions about distributive justice, however, would seem to be not only "*How much* is available for distribution?" but also "Available for distribution *among whom?*" In other words, who does and who does not have a claim on the available resources? Who belongs to, and who is excluded from, the group to which these resources collectively belong? But here again, of course, even if we accept that *not everyone* has a claim on some particular set of resources, a justifying account must be given. If in fact there is nothing objectionable, nothing wrong, with a few people enjoying enormous wealth while others around them starve, this must nonetheless be explained—and explained in such a way as to make clear what the relevant *difference* between these peo- ple is that gives some of them a claim to extraordinary wealth while giving others no claim at all.

With respect to retributive justice, this coordinating analysis of what each individual is due has two entirely distinct dimensions. First, we wish to see that the punishments applied are *commensurable* both to the crimes for which they are meant to atone, and to each other. Thus today we would not wish to see anyone sentenced to death for stealing a loaf of bread, or a first-time petty thief sentenced to twenty years in prison while a violent first-time rapist was sentenced to two years' probation. But in addition to this coordination of pun- ishments, we also insist—and even more stringently—on the coordination of the stories[40] offered up in court by the defendant, the plaintiff, and the vari- ous witnesses to the events in question. By the time a trial is finished, there must be in the minds of the jury one coherent (and one hopes, relatively true) account of what has happened. The reason for this is that there is a significant difference between being the victim of bad luck and being the victim of a crime. While the former would appreciate *assistance*, the latter feels he has a right to *redress*. But only if there is a *perpetrator* of the crime, can one be the victim of a crime as opposed to bad luck. Thus if a victim's claim to redress is to be satisfied, the court must find its way to a *single* account of events that places both victim and perpetrator in their proper relation to each other—thus establishing the perpetrator's degree and type of guilt. We cannot, that is, do justice to everyone concerned by accepting at face value each party's separate account of what happened, even though doing justice to everyone concerned may require that we acknowledge that each party's version *seems* correct to him or her. While the world is experienced subjectively by individuals, it is nonetheless a shared world that we live in. We play our parts, as a result, in shared stories, and justice is never determined simply by what we feel we deserve.

Thus the identification of what justice requires is of necessity an ongoing endeavor in which we attempt to synthesize a *whole* out of disparate parts— those parts consisting, on the one hand, of the rival accounts of accuser and accused, and, on the other, of the rival claims of individuals desiring in each case to be given his or her due. Another way to put this is to say that the identification of justice is bound up with the discovery of truth more generally— in the sense that, in order to establish what justice requires, we must determine not only what has happened in particular cases, but also what the world is like (what there *is* to be distributed, for example, and also what forms of merit, demerit, and need there *are* to be taken into account). And a major part of the reason why the pursuit of justice is an in-principle unfinishable task is that the pursuit of truth is also, and even more obviously, an in-principle unfinishable task. Like the identification of justice, moreover, the identification of truth is also an ongoing endeavor in which we attempt to synthesize a whole out of disparate parts. In the case of truth, those disparate parts are the countless bits of information that we are inclined to accept as worthy of belief. For only to the extent that these bits of information can be woven into a logically coherent whole are we entitled to have any confidence in their individual truth. Because it would be useful to have a term to describe this characteristic that both truth and justice exhibit of involving us in an in-principle unfinishable task of discovery and analysis, I propose to describe them both, when they are understood in this fashion, as *regulative ideals*.

What it means to say that truth is a regulative ideal, however, is not merely that the boundaries of what is known are constantly being expanded. At the present moment in human affairs, this ongoing expansion of what is known is something that we tend to take for granted. But if not only the *breadth* of our beliefs but also their *coherence* matters, if in fact the coherence of our beliefs is the hallmark by which we recognize their (relative) truth, then the most important feature of truth, understood as a regulative ideal, is that each and every claim that we *take to be true* at some moment must be conceived of as being, in principle at least, revisable. For the extension of the boundaries of what is known always has the potential of requiring the restructuring of beliefs to which we may have been long committed. As we *learn more* we often discover that we in fact *knew less* than we thought we did. Thus for example, the explorations of the great European seafarers of the Renaissance not only revealed to us the existence of new continents; they established that what we had long taken to be an obvious truth—that the earth was flat—was actually false, and always had been. So too, discoveries in the twentieth century on the part of geneticists, paleontologists, and evolutionary biologists have made it clear that the distinction theologians in particular have always drawn between animals and humans is untenable. Indeed, in the last century even our formerly bedrock faith in the (Newtonian) constancies of space and time came to be shaken and recast in the light of Einstein's work on relativity.

It is relatively easy, of course, to recognize this essential characteristic of knowledge—its perpetual revisability—retrospectively, by comparing what we once believed with what we later came to understand. The challenge is to bear in mind that *all* empirical knowledge, including our *current* beliefs, is provisional. For truth—which is best understood as *the ideal coherence of our beliefs with each other and with our actual and possible experiences*—is on this definition the sort of destination at which it is quite impossible to arrive. If truth is understood in this Peircean fashion, moreover, as the web of belief in which *all possible* experience would be *perfectly* synthesized, we will want to make a distinction between it and *knowledge*, which as I propose to use the term is always a matter of sound current understanding, and thus is to be identified with the web of belief in which *past* experience is *best* synthesized. This distinction, I am prepared to admit, is entirely stipulative. In loose everyday parlance we tend to speak of truth and knowledge as if they were almost interchangeable. Analytic philosophers too tend almost to conflate the notions—for example, when they define knowledge as "justified true belief." But there is an excellent reason for observing the distinction that I have just laid down. For we do not wish the unattainability of truth (in the strong sense of a regulative ideal) to be used as a justification for suggesting that any belief is as good as any other, simply because both have adherents and neither is positively known to be true.

It matters whether one believes, for example, that witches actually exist, and thus that it is a sensible precaution to identify and eliminate them from one's company, or whether one believes instead that a witch hunt is merely a search for scapegoats upon whom to pin the blame for whatever unpleasant events one is unable to explain (or worse, a handy way of targeting personal enemies). It is thus disturbing to see a contemporary sociologist of science, Bruno Latour, suggest that there was actually little to choose between the methodology of Galileo, as an investigator of the heavens, and that of Jean Bodin, as an inquisitor who employed torture to extract confessions of witch-craft from elderly women, on the grounds that each of them made use of elaborate "laboratory conditions"(!), and in the comfortable conviction that "everyone on earth is as logical or as illogical as everyone else."[41] Most of us (I would dare say, all of us) are not equally logical from one moment to the next. The circumstances in which we find ourselves and the consequent state of our emotions have a lot to do with how coherent our thinking is at any given moment.[42] Some individuals, moreover, seem prone to emotional up-heaval and distraction while others without too much difficulty manage to maintain their focus and negotiate life on a comparatively even keel. It is thus obvious nonsense to make the sweeping claim that everyone on earth is equally logical, and to draw from this the implication that everyone's beliefs are pretty much equally respectable.

Nonsense that it is, however, it is far from being an unusual claim. A con-siderable number of social scientists and more than the occasional philoso-pher, on coming to appreciate that absolutely certain knowledge is not to be had given the limitations of human understanding, have concluded that, as the philosopher of science Paul Feyerabend notoriously put it a few decades ago, "anything goes."[43] This catholicity of taste in matters of belief seems to be bound up with a particular form of political correctness—that which enjoins "respect" for the opinions of others. But in actuality to contend that all beliefs are pretty much equally respectable is not really a show of respect at all. For in extending an easy tolerance to *all* beliefs—even when, as will frequently happen, they contradict each other—it refuses to take *any* of them seriously. Respect is only properly shown for an idea when it is considered a genuine candidate for belief, and when it is appreciated that committing to *this* belief requires that one renounce other possible beliefs. Because such a commit-ment has serious implications for how we subsequently behave in the world, it is crucial that our beliefs be subjected to serious critical scrutiny.

What *constitutes* serious critical scrutiny is a relative matter—relative, that is, to what is known about the world at the time that the belief in question is being critically examined. We must not be too eager, in other words, to con-demn our ancestors for their cognitive errors, since some measure of cogni-tive error is permanently inescapable, and inevitably a certain number of the things that are taken to be true by one age will seem to a later and somewhat better informed age to be clearly mistaken. But it must not be concluded on the basis of *this* argument that it is a sign of intellectual sophistication to "acknowledge" that in Jean Bodin's day (the mid-1500s) it was reasonable to have confidence in the employment of torture to identify witches. For by the time of the Renaissance it had already occurred to many people that confessions extracted under torture were suspect. After all, it takes no great insight (then or now) to recognize that in extremis people will tend to say whatever might seem likely to gain them even temporary relief. Thus while it would be anachronistic to criticize Galileo for having used *crude* telescopes to study the moon's surface (as if the Hubble were an available alternative), there is nothing anachronistic about criticizing Bodin's use of torture to acquire information on the basis of which individuals were subsequently put to death. The fact that the practice was widespread in no way establishes that it constituted *good* practice, even by the epistemic standards of the day.

Honoring the epistemic standards of one's own day is the indispensable virtue of anyone who genuinely seeks to know. Those standards, of course, are not only fallible; from the vantage point of truth itself, they are *wrong* in significant respects. Nonetheless, they constitute the best grounds that can be offered for accepting a given belief at a given moment in time.

Truth, as the ideal coherence of our beliefs with each other and with all of our actual and possible experience, is unattainable. But the fact that we can never expect to arrive at a state of perfect knowledge does not imply that we are unable to make progress toward such a state. What does such progress consist in? And how would we recognize that it is being made? Clearly we cannot judge our progress by measuring our present beliefs and our past beliefs against the yardstick established by the *content* of truth itself—for the content of truth is precisely what we can never expect to know. Nor does the mere fact of *change* in our beliefs signify that we have progressed. For a culture, just as much as an individual, can lose sight of knowledge that it once possessed—can become, that is to say, not better but *worse* informed. Progress with respect to knowledge must be identified instead by appealing to the criteria in terms of which truth is defined. If truth is the ideal coherence of our beliefs as these relate to all possible experience, then it follows that the more logical consistency we can establish among our beliefs, while simultaneously extending the range of our experience that can be accounted for by those beliefs, the closer we have come to holding true beliefs. The epistemic standards of a given day are merely the salient facts that must be borne in mind (given what is known *at that time*) as we struggle to maximize the logical coherence and explanatory scope of our belief structure.

But to contend that we can approach the truth is not to imply that each and every step taken for the sake of bringing our experience and our beliefs into harmony will produce beliefs that are in some measure more like the actual content of truth itself (whatever that may happen to be). The history of science, and of inquiry generally, meanders. Not infrequently an early but substantially correct model (by our current lights) has been abandoned because of inadequacies in the model that a subsequent age found both disturbing and insurmountable. Then, after a period of struggling to make do with an apparently promising but in fact even less adequate alternative, some crucial insight has been gained that cleared the way for a "return" to something like the original view.

Thus Ernst Mayr points out, for example, that Aristotle's notion that a species-specific *eidos* (or immaterial "form") governs the physiological development of organisms was rejected in the nineteenth century by all physicalist biologists, who insisted instead that physiological development, just as much as an organism's capacity for locomotion, is to be accounted for in terms of the "movement of atoms" and the "balance of potential and kinetic energy." Yet in hindsight, and with the benefit of our subsequently acquired understanding of genetics, it seems clear that Aristotle's conjecture came substantially closer to the mark than did that of the physicalists. For while we cannot understand how the chromosomes function without engaging in molecular analysis, the crucial point is that the genotype of a species, just as much as Aristotle's *eidos*, is a means of conveying highly specific information about what a given organism is to become—and the cybernetic dimension of embryology is something that physicalists completely failed to appreciate.[44] Modern genetic theory represents a huge improvement on Aristotle's conjectures and an improvement that could be made only *after* the physicalists had firmly established the expectation that even physiological development was to be explained entirely in terms of material processes. Thus biology's detour through physicalism was necessary, and did represent progress, even though today physicalist theories in embryology seem significantly less apropos than do Aristotle's references to a species-specific *eidos*.

To contend that we approach the truth by improving the coherence and expanding the scope of our belief structure does not imply, then, that this carries us on a straight-line path through a series of progressively more correct depictions of our subject matter. What it implies, instead, is that, as we are exposed over time to the workings of the natural world, and the changes that our experience suggests are incorporated into our web of belief, we get progressively closer to the truth in the limited sense that there remain ever fewer corrections needing to be made. But this is perfectly compatible with the idea that the changes made in our belief structure might at certain points carry us *away* from the actual content of truth. For the truth does not shine forth beaconlike, drawing us toward it. It is approached only laboriously and indirectly, through the progressive elimination of anomalies from our belief structure and through our efforts to make that belief structure as broad in scope as possible.

This, then, is the situation confronting us in the realms of science and of law: we *can* make progress (indeed, we *have* made considerable progress), but the key to doing so over the long term is an abiding commitment on our part to the pursuit of an ideal (truth or justice) that we can only ever expect to know approximately and imperfectly—an ideal, moreover, to which we *cease* to be truly committed the moment we presume to have a perfect grasp of it. This sort of commitment, it should be clear, is extraordinarily difficult to maintain. Human beings seem naturally to have a deep desire for the comfortable assurances of certain knowledge. We like to know what we can count on. Unfortunately, the price of intellectual maturity is the growing disquietude that comes over us as we recognize, in one field of inquiry after another, that certainty is not to be had. Intellectual maturity has been achieved, one might add, only when this unavailability of certainty ceases to be disquieting. And this occurs precisely when we come to understand that our capacity to distinguish between degrees of plausibility never depended upon our prior possession of absolute knowledge, and thus that this capacity is still available to us and is all that we need to be able to carry on with the work of *improving* the quality of our knowledge and of our social relations.

As was mentioned above, the pursuit of justice is inexorably bound up with the pursuit of truth. For justice is a matter of granting to each and every member of the just community his or her due—and determining the specifics of what "dueness" amounts to requires that we establish the merits, needs, capacities, and so on of each and every interested party as well as agree upon a principled basis for assessing rival claims. A true understanding of the relative merits of individuals and actions is thus a precondition of achieving justice, and this understanding can be acquired only through the pursuit of truth itself—in the broadest sense and not merely with respect to individuals and actions. For since the criterion of truth is the ideal coherence of *all* of our beliefs, the true merits of individuals cannot be known independently of a comprehensive understanding of all things that might bear upon those merits—and that means, in principle at least, *everything*.

By the same token, in an important sense the pursuit of truth cannot occur independently of the pursuit of justice. For truth can be arrived at only as a result of granting each (possible) belief its (ideal) due. That is to say that the ideal coherence of beliefs can emerge only when beliefs are given exactly what they merit in the way of credence and in the acknowledgment of their implications. Justice is the analogous principle applied to the potential holders of beliefs. There is, moreover, a practical sense in which justice cannot be done to beliefs unless justice is also done to the holders of beliefs, as a precondition for their beliefs becoming adequately known. The pursuit of truth, after all, is necessarily a collective enterprise, in that in principle it commits us to a consideration of *all actual and possible experiences*. The experience of each of us, in other words, is prima facie equally relevant to the enterprise. And given that no one can be counted upon (independently of corroboration) to accurately represent another's experience, those genuinely dedicated to the pursuit of truth will wish to see everyone empowered both to openly express what their experience has been and to reflect upon the meaning of that experience. If this is our goal, however, all of those forms of injustice that tend to silence individuals (and are there any that do not?) must be corrected. Thus if the pursuit of justice necessitates our thorough immersion in the pursuit of truth, in an important sense the pursuit of truth also demands our thoroughgoing commitment to the pursuit of justice. This does not constitute any sort of vicious circle, but is rather a dialectical interrelationship or hermeneutic circle.

THE QUEST FOR INTEGRITY

The pursuit of justice and of truth involves in each case the effort to integrate the disparate parts of our experience into a coherent whole. But this crucial process of integration can be undertaken, of course, not only with respect to the totality of our experience, but also with respect to what is for each of us perhaps the single most important *element* of our experience—which is to say, one's sense of oneself. And the more than usually successful effort to integrate all of the various aspects of one's sense of oneself—without having to deny or avert one's gaze from any of the true characteristics of one's nature—is what we refer to when we speak of personal *integrity*. The connection between integrity and integration can be seen etymologically, when we consider their common derivation from the Latin word *integer*, meaning whole. But so too it can be recognized when we contrast integrity with its opposite number—hypocrisy. For hypocrisy is fundamentally a matter of duplicity—of an inconsistency arising between what one says and what one does. And for basically the same reason that it was argued earlier that rationalization—or the refusal to face up to inconsistencies in one's behavior—is incompatible with the possession of dignity, so too is self-aware and unapologetic hypocrisy incompatible with dignity. Integrity, it would seem, is thus related to, even if it is not exactly the same thing as, dignity.

Dignity implies something more than integrity for the simple reason that integrity, like autonomy, can be cheaply purchased. Achieving consistency in one's sense of self, after all, is not always a difficult thing to do. Other animals, for the most part (as well as some morally unambitious humans), seem to achieve this condition almost effortlessly. When they are hungry, they eat; when they are in heat, they mate; when they are tired, they sleep; and that's the end of it. If conditions permit, they satisfy their urges. They are never troubled by a guilty conscience for doing what comes naturally. And the reason for this, of course, is that many animals seem to be aware of no other imperative than that of their immediate natural drives. There is, in other words, no self-restraint here; there is merely the satisfaction of desires, if possible, in the order of declining urgency. This is not to suggest that other animals are entirely unresponsive to social constraints. We know that complicated patterns of social interaction have evolved among most higher organisms (especially birds and mammals). But one of the most powerful of the natural drives is fear, and the prudent restraint of one's impulses in order to avoid the disapproval (and potentially violent outbursts) of others is not quite the same thing as *self*-restraint.

Integrity becomes problematic, then, only for those creatures (human and otherwise) that are capable of entertaining *commitments* and of betraying those commitments. Now a commitment still clearly involves a desire of some sort, but the converse of this is not true: not all desires involve commitments. For example, we should probably be prepared to call a sparrow's determination to raise its young, come rain or shine, high winds or marauding starlings, a commitment. The reason this characterization seems appropriate is that the satisfaction of this particular desire on the sparrow's part requires that it devote some significant portion of its energies toward furthering the welfare of something *other* than itself. If we were to take this example as establishing a general principle, we could readily find exceptions, of course. A struggling student, for example, may be described as being committed to mastering calculus or German, and yet there does not seem to be any way in which his commitment "furthers the welfare" of anything other than himself. (Clearly the calculus itself or the German language is not affected by his efforts.) Here too, though, we must admit that immediate desires (to close his books and go see a film, perhaps) are being resisted. And what these immediate desires are being resisted *for* is the achievement of some distant state (in which he will be fluently conversant in German or capable of solving highly sophisticated math problems) the precise nature and significance of which the student is not at this moment even able to imagine. The student is committed, in other words, to some meaningful goal—and the relevant sense of "goal" here cannot be extended to include the satisfaction of immediate desires (not even if these take some effort to satisfy) or the prudent avoidance of suffering (which is why we would not describe the student who is at this moment cramming for an exam, but who is otherwise negligent of his studies, as being "committed" to the mastery of his subject).

We might ask at this point what the sparrow's commitment to its young amounts to. When it abandons them to a predator that it cannot drive off, does it feel conscience-stricken? Or does it merely blame the predator? Does it, as some biologists seem to suggest, simply assess the situation and "cut its losses," knowing that there will be other nestlings in future years? This, of course, is something that we can in all likelihood never expect to know. But bearing in mind both the developmental continuity of life (through evolution) as well as the danger of our anthropomorphizing here, it might be worthwhile to consult the evidence provided by human parents who lose a child to an accidental death. Often, no matter how blameless they may have been in the matter, parents suffer excruciating pangs of conscience. (If only they had done *this*, rather than *that*, their child would still be alive.) To the outsider, this may look counterproductive, even irrational. Why blame oneself for what one could not reasonably have anticipated, and therefore could not have prevented? To the grieving parent, though, the eminently rational suggestion that there is no point in flaying her conscience—in regretting the abandonment of her commitment (for that, of course, is how it feels—like an *abandonment* and not merely a loss)—is almost obscene. Is she, like the sparrow, supposed to "cut her losses?"

So too the young soldier we considered a while back, whose courage broke on Omaha Beach, causing the deaths of a number of his comrades-in-arms, might be told by some well-meaning outsider to "snap out of" his subsequent self-inflicted mental breakdown. There is no need to rationalize about the matter, it might be suggested. He should simply face the fact that his courage broke under horrifying circumstances—circumstances that would have broken (and did break) the courage of many other men—acknowledge that this directly led to the deaths of his comrades (a result that he never intended, of course), and move on with his life. He too, in other words, should "cut his losses," since nothing is served by his breaking down yet again. As was argued earlier, however, too ready a willingness to cut one's losses (by refusing to indulge in regret) probably implies too shallow a commitment in the first place.

Human beings, after all, are not mechanical calculators. As the products of a three-billion-year-long process of natural selection, we are endowed with a complex system of emotional responses that are rooted deep in our physiological structure. And we possess these responses because, as they evolved, they demonstrated clear adaptive value. In other words, in a changeable environment—one filled with both nourishing fruits and poisonous shoots, with predators and prey, with potential mates and potential rivals for mates, with siblings and strangers—in short, with both dangers and opportunities—the creature equipped with highly tuned reactions of desire, aversion, fear, anger, lust, sympathy, and anticipatory excitement was better prepared to survive (and even more importantly, to procreate) than was the (same) creature in whom such responses were less well developed. Life has always been a struggle, and (on balance) the emotions equip us to cope with that struggle effectively. It is because the emotions enabled our ancestors to cope with that struggle in the past, and to survive long enough to pass on their characteristics to their offspring, that we possess those same emotions now.

Nor should we wish to overcome or root out those emotions today on the mistaken grounds that they are no longer needed. For on the one hand, life is *still* a struggle in which the emotions play a valuable role.[45] And on the other hand, given their physiological basis, the idea that we might successfully "root out" our emotions is about as problematic as the idea that we might be able to "root out" our hearts or livers. There is no question that our emotions—like our organs—can become diseased if neglected or, alternatively, can become highly disciplined if properly attended to. But they cannot be done away with—in order to be replaced with pure reason. Even Kant, of course, never went quite so far as to suggest that this would be possible. But he did come close to implying that, were it possible, it would be desirable, and this is what made Schiller uneasy.

It was David Hume, however, who best explained why reason could never replace the emotions. For, as he memorably put it in his *Treatise of Human Nature*, "Reason is, and ought only to be the slave of the passions, and can never pretend to any other office than to serve and obey them."[46] What he meant by this is that without the passions—without desires, inclinations, emotions—there are no *ends* to be achieved and no goals to be pursued through human action. Clearly it *is* possible for reason to prefer one line of action as opposed to another; but only on the grounds of efficacy, Hume contends. In other words, given a prior desire to see some end achieved, reason can evaluate and criticize our choice of means in achieving that end. Reason can tell us, for example, that there are easier ways to get what we want, or that, given the circumstances, our proposed line of action will not succeed at all. But reason cannot tell us *what* we should want. To quote Hume again:

> Where a passion is neither founded on false suppositions, nor chooses means insufficient for the end, the understanding can neither justify nor condemn it. 'Tis not contrary to reason to prefer the destruction of the whole world to the scratching of my little finger. 'Tis not contrary to reason for me to choose my total ruin, to prevent the least uneasiness of an *Indian* or person wholly unknown to me.[47]

No doubt anyone who preferred the destruction of the world to being mildly scratched could be accused of having his preferences out of alignment. But that is merely to say that his ordering of preferences would not coincide with the ordering of preferences to which the rest of us would have subscribed. Once that is admitted, there is nothing that *reason* can offer in an effort to get the person in question to change his preferences (always providing, of course, that he is being honest with himself as to what his preferences truly are).

If Hume is right, though, why does it nonetheless seem that reason can (and should) school the passions? For even if we acknowledge that a purely rational derivation of ethical norms through the process of universalizing the maxim looks entirely implausible, most of us, I suspect, are still prone to agree with Kant's insistence that reason should govern our natural inclinations. After all, when in some disturbing situation we still manage to restrain ourselves, it certainly *feels* as if reason is in control and our passions are being held in check. It is important to understand, however, that reason's correction of our emotional assessments in such a situation is not a matter of its substituting itself for them. For we learn to restrain our immediate emotional reactions only through experience—and that means the experience, primarily, of having reacted emotionally *in the wrong way*—not, however, as judged by reason, but rather as judged by our own subsequent and *better-informed* emotional reaction. This will take some clarification.

In the first appendix to the *Enquiry Concerning the Principles of Morals*, Hume observes that in situations calling for moral judgment it is crucial that we know *all* of the relevant circumstances. (In this respect, he contends, moral judgment differs decidedly from purely rational deliberation.)

> A mere speculative reasoner concerning triangles or circles considers the several known and given relations of the parts of these figures, and thence infers some unknown relation, which is dependent on the former. But in moral deliberations we must be acquainted beforehand with all the objects, and all their relations to each other; and from a comparison of the whole, fix our choice or approbation. . . . All the circumstances of the case are supposed to be laid before us, ere we can fix any sentence of blame or approbation. If any material circumstance be yet unknown or doubtful, we must first employ our inquiry or intellectual faculties to assure us of it; and must suspend for a time all moral decision or sentiment. While we are ignorant whether a man were aggressor or not, how can we determine whether the person who killed him be criminal or innocent? But after every circumstance, every relation is known, the understanding has no further room to operate, nor any object on which it could employ itself. The approbation or blame which then ensues, cannot be the work of the judgment, but of the heart; and is not a speculative proposition or affirmation, but an active feeling or sentiment. In the disquisitions of the understanding, from known circumstances and relations, we infer some new and

unknown. In moral decisions, all the circumstances and relations must be previously known; and the mind, from the contemplation of the whole, feels some new impression of affection or disgust, esteem or contempt, approbation or blame.

Granting the correctness of Hume's point here, it is easy to see that, when we react emotionally in the wrong way, this is because our emotional reaction expresses itself prematurely—before all of the circumstances of the situation are known to us. In due time, as the relevant but previously unknown circumstances are discovered, our subsequent and more appropriate emotional reaction constitutes not only a new judgment on the situation in question, but also a negative judgment on our own earlier and premature reaction. (What another person happens to think of one's value judgments may be a matter of comparative indifference; but one's *own* assessment of one's premature value judgments is always telling. This is why it is safe to describe the earlier reaction as having been *wrong*[48]—as seen from one's current perspective.)

But finding oneself having reacted in the wrong way is unpleasant, which is why, as our first impulses are corrected time and again, we learn to be less precipitate. We develop a new desire, in other words—a desire *not* to have our initial emotional reactions painfully shown to have been inappropriate. And in order to avoid this, we learn to delay giving them expression until we have become reasonably sure that we know all the circumstances that should have a bearing on some particular emotional assessment (or value judgment) on our part.[49]

This, it turns out, is all that we really mean by "self-restraint." It is not a matter of "pure reason" holding our passions in check; it is a matter of one comparatively quiet but nonetheless powerful desire—the desire *not to be wrong* when it comes to judging a person, an action, or a situation—that holds our other more impulsive passions in check. The circumspection we resort to in trying to avoid error *is* rational. Reason tells us that circumspection is appropriate, as a means, if we wish to avoid finding ourselves having reacted in the wrong way. Reason tells us as well what sorts of circumstances we should be looking for, as liable to affect our evaluation of the situation in question. But our willingness to be circumspect is ultimately grounded in this quiet inclination on our part *not to be wrong* in our reactions, if possible.

At one point in the *Treatise*, Hume makes almost exactly this point. "What we call strength of mind," he announces, "implies the prevalence of the calm passions above the violent." It is because reason "exerts itself without producing any sensible emotion," he observes, that

every action of the mind, which operates with the same calmness and tranquillity, is confounded with reason by all those, who judge of things from the first view and appearance. Now 'tis certain, there are certain calm desires and tendencies, which, tho' they be real passions, produce little emotion in the mind, and are more known by their effects than by the immediate feeling or sensation.[50]

Among these "calm passions," Hume lists benevolence, the love of life, and "the general appetite to good, and aversion to evil, considered merely as such." But surely in any such list of "calm passions" the desire to avoid error where possible should figure prominently. If we grant this, then we have all the explanation needed to account for our reluctance to part company with Kant when he insists that morality is a matter of reason's controlling the passions. For in a sense, reason—at least in the form of circumspection—does restrain the passions. Hume's point, however, is that reason, in restraining the *impulsive* passions, always acts at the behest of one or another of the *calm* passions. Thus it is they, rather than reason, that are ultimately responsible for human morality.

Before proceeding further with the argument, it may be worthwhile to pause for a moment in order to address a couple of questions that might have occurred to the reader. First, if self-restraint is, as I have just argued, grounded in our desire not to find ourselves having reacted in the wrong way, but "wrong" here always means wrong in the light of our own subsequent and revisionary value judgment, what are we to say about the individual who avoids ever finding himself having reacted in the wrong way by the simple expedient of never revisiting his own reactions? Does he achieve self-restraint and acquire dignity (as well as integrity) on the cheap, as it were? The answer, of course, is no. The possibility of finding oneself in error must be seriously entertained before its avoidance can become a motivating factor in one's conduct. One does not achieve self-restraint, in other words, simply by never feeling the need for it.

The other question/objection that I suspect may have occurred to the reader has to do with my lumping together of passions, inclinations, desires, emotions, and (raw) value judgments.[51] Is it not possible, even likely perhaps, that some important distinctions are being obscured here? That there *are* distinctions to be drawn between, for example, what we normally mean by "emotions" and what we mean by "inclinations" I will readily admit—although it is by no means easy to separate their meanings too precisely. So too a passion, such as anger, is not exactly the same thing as the desire (to harm or eliminate the object of one's anger) that can be thought of as corresponding to it, and yet they are obviously closely related. In general, we might say that emotions and passions are the immediate feelings that incline us to act one way or another on the basis of a value (either positive or negative) manifested within the feeling.

The point, however, is that reason is not a matter of feeling in this sense at all. It is concerned, instead, with the recognition of abstract relations. And the "coolness" that we associate with reason follows directly from this. For the relations under consideration may pertain to objects that are not at the moment physically present to the reasoner—to entirely hypothetical entities even. And the crucial thing about reason is that the presence or absence or hypothetical nature of the entities being referred to makes no difference whatsoever to the rational process. As far as reason is concerned, in other words, *all relations* might just as well be relations between hypothetical entities. Now the question that we have been concerned with in the past few paragraphs is whether morality is determined, as Kant contends, entirely by the dictates of reason or whether, as Hume contends, regardless of whatever role reason may play in illuminating the details of morality, our moral impulses are ultimately and inescapably grounded in *feelings*—feelings (like care) that are prompted by the presence of things. This question, I think, is one that we can settle in Hume's favor without having to inquire too closely into the precise differences existing between the various kinds of feeling that might be relevant.

Having said this, however, it is worth noting that there is a continuity existing between our immediate inclinations, our short-term projects, our long-term commitments, and our dedication to unattainable ideals. By this, I mean to say that underlying all of them are desires of various kinds. (There is, in other words, no radical split in our sources of motivation, such as Kant imagined, between reason on the one side and desire on the other.) Our desires, moreover, can readily conflict in ways that threaten to overwhelm our ability to achieve consistency among the various commitments that we adopt in the process of defining ourselves—in ways that threaten our integrity, in other words. For if we are careless, our long-term commitments can be irrecoverably sacrificed to our immediate inclinations. And more tragically, sometimes our various projects and commitments simply prove to be irreconcilable.

Think again of Ralph Hopkins's attempt to justify his failure to make good on his commitment to his family by stressing his dedication to the creation of his "big successful business," and contrast this with Tom Rath's insistence on balancing the various commitments in his life—on doing justice, if possible, to each of them. Hopkins, we realize, was less attentive to his family responsibilities than he should have been, and Rath is clearly more admirable in this respect. But we must not lose sight of how close Rath came to seriously damaging his *own* family. Given the complexities of his life, moreover, this was a risk that he could not avoid taking—*not*, that is, without destroying his own integrity. Hopkins, then, can be described as lacking a certain measure of integrity because he embarked upon family life and made a hash of it. Rath, in contrast, manages to keep his integrity intact precisely because he is prepared, in certain circumstances, to run the risk of ruining his family. (And the fact that his family is saved in the end, which is entirely his wife's doing, neither adds to nor diminishes Rath's integrity one jot.)

The explanation of the ironic contrast here, of course, is that integrity is not a matter of *succeeding* with respect to each of the specific commitments that one happens to make. It is a matter of achieving harmony and consistency among one's commitments by *doing justice* to each of them. It is a matter of negotiating the struggle of conflicting obligations. And unless one forgoes making commitments altogether (thus gaining for oneself a brutish sort of integrity), one can only expect to negotiate one's conflicting obligations if one has an overarching commitment to justice and truth in general. But as we have seen in this chapter, justice and truth must be understood as the objects of an ongoing (and never to be completed) investigation.

What does it mean, then, to be committed to justice and truth when these are properly understood—that is, understood as *regulative ideals*? Given that the regulative ideal can never be reached in any event, it would be easy, of course, merely to pay lip service to its pursuit, while carrying on self-insistently with the satisfaction of one's immediate inclinations. For if truth and justice are unattainable, who would even notice when one falls short of them? And if error is inevitable, who could possibly fault one for slipping into it? But as we saw earlier, the fact that truth itself is not available as a standard against which to measure the adequacy of our beliefs does not mean that we are unable to distinguish even now between better and worse beliefs— between those that represent steps in the direction of truth and those that represent the inertia of self-satisfaction.

Thus to be genuinely committed to truth and justice requires that one walk a very fine line. For on the one hand, one must be seriously committed to the recognition, not only by oneself, but also by others, of the merits of what are, at present, the best beliefs available. Similarly, one must be firmly committed to the actualization within our social relations of the most convincing principles of justice currently available. For only if the progress that is currently discernible as a mere theoretical possibility is converted into actuality can we position ourselves to recognize the forms of still further progress that are currently invisible.[52] And yet, on the other hand, precisely because our current best beliefs do not represent the final word, one must avoid becoming dogmatically and closed-mindedly committed to *any* position.

There is no way to hide the fact that the needs of action and of reason are in serious tension here. To bring about the results that constitute progress in the face of opposition—opposition in the form of inertia and lack of interest, but also in the form of individual selfishness—requires that people be brought to feel the pressing need for change. But a tentative and circumspect commitment to one's principles is hardly likely to galvanize others into joining one's crusade. (And "crusade" is not too strong a term here. The abolitionists and civil rights marchers, for example, most certainly *were* crusaders. The point is that, given the opposition that improved understanding often encounters, and social progress almost invariably faces, it *takes* a crusade.) The challenge, then, is to be appropriately insistent without becoming *self*-insistent—to be firm without becoming blind.

Where the shortcomings of prevailing beliefs and social arrangements are seen clearly (and these *can* be seen clearly only when they are compared to other less inadequate possible beliefs and social arrangements) there is normally a powerful urge to correct them. Rising to an appropriate level of insistence, in this case, is not difficult. Resisting the tendency to rise beyond the appropriate level—which is to say, avoiding *self*-insistence—is the difficulty. For it is all too easy for our awareness of the perpetual possibility that our beliefs may have to be changed to remain an awareness of a mere theoretical possibility rather than of a practical reality—especially when we are already struggling to bring about change in the beliefs and attitudes of others. What is indispensable, then, is a continuing willingness to learn—that is, to be shown our errors. This, moreover, must be a willingness that is neither eager nor grudging. It must be a willingness to change that is neither a chasing after novelty for its entertainment value nor a foot-dragging apprehensiveness about what the implications of the new idea might cost us personally. The mere novelty of an idea, after all, is no endorsement of its adequacy. And so too the fact that an idea, if taken seriously, might require restructuring our lives in some respect is in itself no evidence of the idea's *in*adequacy.

Here again that quiet but potentially powerful desire *not to be wrong*, which was described a few pages ago as the drive-spring of self-restraint, comes into play. For it is the careful evaluation of the merits of the idea in question which gives us, not a guarantee that we will avoid error, but our best chance of doing so. There is, of course, only an apparent inconsistency between saying that our willingness to be shown our errors goes hand-in-hand with our desire to avoid being wrong—since, given that we all inevitably make mistakes, the best way to avoid being wrong is to correct our errors as quickly as possible. But this is the case only if it is genuinely *error itself* that we wish to avoid. If, instead, it is our own recognition of being wrong that we wish to avoid, we can accomplish this by simply refusing to reconsider our original stand on the matter in question. And if it is being thought of as wrong by others that we wish to avoid, we can accomplish this by taking on no new beliefs and postponing our reactions until we have polled general opinion.

But if one is committed to the pursuit of truth and justice, it is error itself that one wishes to avoid. When truth is understood as a regulative ideal rather than as something that can be settled here and now, however, avoiding error means avoiding error *as one comes to understand it oneself.* (There may be others, of course, who understand *now* what one has not yet understood. One will come to recognize that these others understood better than one did oneself, however, only *after* one has come to see the matter in question as these others already did.) What this implies, then, is that a commitment to the pursuit of truth (or alternatively, a genuine desire to avoid error) requires that one be constantly willing to revisit any question, in order to see how one's previous beliefs and reactions will hold up when further information is brought to bear on the issue.

Underlying this dispassionate willingness to be shown one's errors, moreover, there must be a faith in one's own, but also more generally in the human, capacity for growth. For the pursuit of justice in all respects, and the pursuit of truth in a great many respects, is necessarily a collective enterprise. If we are to make progress in this enterprise, we need to pool the benefits of our disparate experience and attend to one another's insights. And we cannot do that with any confidence unless we believe that others too are sincerely trying to understand. Cynicism, one might say, is simply the barbarity of spirit that comes in the absence of such faith in the human capacity and desire for growth.

Dignity, then, is incompatible with either an extensive suspicion of the motivations of others or an indifference to their fate. Insofar as we are engaged in a collective enterprise—one that we are truly committed to and care about—some measure of trust in those others with whom we must cooperate in the pursuit of our goal is indispensable. But human nature being what it is, of course, our motivations *will* often be selfish. Thus dignity, trusting in the sincerity of others, is and must be vulnerable to betrayal. When others dissemble convincingly to further their own ends at the dupe's expense, the dignified individual must simply take what comes as the price to be paid on occasion for extending trust. He must do so, moreover, without allowing resentment at the fact that there *is* a price to be paid to affect his commitment to justice and truth—or he will soon forfeit his dignity.

Dignity, though, is vulnerable not only to intentional betrayal. It is and must be, if anything, even more vulnerable to the disappointment that follows when those with whom we have entered into a cooperative relationship simply show themselves to be unable to handle their side of the responsibilities. All humans, after all, have their limitations—and the limitations of others, upon whom one depends, can readily be the cause of one's personal disaster. Tom Rath, for example, was fortunate indeed that Betsy was capable of rising to the occasion when he found himself honor-bound to confess his wartime affair with Maria. Had Betsy responded by filing for divorce, Tom would still have known that he had done the honorable thing, but this would have provided scant compensation for the loss of his family. (Which is not to say, of course, that he had any choice in the matter. If he was to maintain his decency, the risk was one that he had to take.) The ending of *The Man in the Gray Flannel Suit*, in other words, is a tragedy averted by virtue of Betsy's capacity for growth. And tragedy, of course, is not always averted.

NOTES

1. George W. Harris, *Dignity and Vulnerability* (Berkeley: University of California Press, 1997), p. 3.

2. Harris, *Dignity and Vulnerability*, p. 7.

3. It might be thought that Aristotle's doctrine of the mean implies that in fact recklessness *is* the excessive form of courage. (See *The Nicomachean Ethics* III, p. 7.) But Aristotle himself suggests that there is more than a hint of cowardice to be found in recklessness, and that there is no readily available term to be found for the excess of fearlessness.

4. Harris, *Dignity and Vulnerability*, p. 9.

5. Harris, *Dignity and Vulnerability*, p. 68.

6. Harris, *Dignity and Vulnerability*, p. 32.

7. Harris, *Dignity and Vulnerability*, p. 31.

8. Harris, *Dignity and Vulnerability*, p. 31.

9. This is a point that Kant himself makes in *The Metaphysics of Morals*. See 6:401–2.

10. Immanuel Kant, *Groundwork of the Metaphysics of Morals* (Cambridge: Cambridge University Press, 1996), 6:449–54.

11. Kant, *The Metaphysics of Morals*, 6:454.

12. Kant, *The Metaphysics of Morals*, 6:491.

13. Then-Governor Bush made this assertion, moreover, in the teeth of the American Bar Association's call for a moratorium on capital punishment, given its estimate that as many as one in seven of the inmates on death row in America have been improperly convicted. For a disturbing account of George W. Bush's approach to the issue of clemency while governor of Texas, see Alan Berlow, "The Texas Clemency Memos," *The Atlantic Monthly*, July/August 2003, pp. 91–96.

14. Harris, *Dignity and Vulnerability*, p. 16.

15. Harris, *Dignity and Vulnerability*, pp. 16-17.

16. Harris, *Dignity and Vulnerability*, pp. 64–65.

17. See pages 222–26 of Paul Ricoeur, *Oneself as Another* (Chicago: University of Chicago Press, 1992).

18. *Groundwork of the Metaphysics of Morals*, 4:430.

19. Ricoeur, *Oneself as Another*, p. 170.

20. Ricoeur, *Oneself as Another*, p. 172.

21. See Amartya Sen, *Inequality Reexamined* (Cambridge, Mass.: Harvard University Press, 1992), and in particular, his first chapter, "Equality of What?"

22. See Robert Nozick, *Anarchy, State, and Utopia* (New York: Basic Books, 1974), pp. 161–63. It is interesting to note that Nozick's well-known demonstration in these pages of the impracticability of adopting equality of wealth as a social ideal is anticipated, not by his idol, John Locke, but rather by David Hume in section 3, part 2 of his *Enquiry Concerning the Principles of Morals*. Hume, however, unlike Nozick, draws from this absolutely no implications regarding the inviolability of property rights. For Hume, at least (see section 3, part 1 of the *Enquiry*), public utility trumps individual property rights.

23. In referring to "strict" social contract theorists here, my intention is to eliminate from consideration someone like John Rawls, who would seem to have more in common with Kant than with Hobbes, and who uses the notion of an idealized social contract merely as a device to determine what *reason* requires of us in the way of justice.

24. See Thomas Hobbes, *Leviathan*, chapter 13. Note that, while Hobbes argues that it is crucial for the ruler of a state to establish *clear* laws, so that those laws can be obeyed, he fully expects that the laws will contain as well a certain *arbitrariness*—reflecting the idiosyncratic character of the ruler—and that any such arbitrariness, as long as the ruler's subjects are aware of its details, will in no way undermine the effectiveness of the social contract in promoting peace.

25. See part 1, "Avoidance and Evasion," of Leo Katz, *Ill-Gotten Gains* (Chicago: University of Chicago Press, 1996), and especially pp. 4–6.

26. Central to the legal understanding of a valid contract, after all, is the legal notion of a *consideration*—which states that, whatever A does for B is something that A is contractually *bound* to do only if B in turn is bound to do something for A.

27. David Hume, *An Enquiry Concerning the Principles of Morals*, section 3, part 1.

28. There is more than a slight echo of Thrasymachus's cynical remarks on justice as "the interest of the stronger" (see Book I of Plato's *Republic*) to be found in the strict social contract theorist's insistence on the blamelessness of actions—*any actions*—that comply with uncoerced agreements.

29. Ricoeur, *Oneself as Another*, p. 198.

30. Ricoeur, *Oneself as Another*, p. 193.

31. One gets a sense of how *specific* Aristotle's conception of our human essence is when one comes across a claim like the following: "by nature the right hand is stronger." See *The Nicomachean Ethics*, Book V, section 7 (as translated by David Ross).

32. See Paul Ricoeur, *Time and Narrative*, vol. 1 (Chicago: University of Chicago Press, 1984), pp. 145–48.

33. Ricoeur, *Oneself as Another*, p. 141.

34. Think of such archetypal forms of dramatic child's play as "cops and robbers," "cowboys and Indians," and "house."

35. Ricoeur, *Oneself as Another*, p. 148.

36. John Stuart Mill, *Three Essays* (Oxford: Oxford University Press, 1975), p. 15.

37. See *Nicomachean Ethics*, Aristotle, Book V, section 3.

38. Note that *retributive* justice here does not refer to what Aristotle calls *rectificatory* justice. The difference between the two corresponds roughly to the difference between criminal law and the combination of tort and contract law.

39. But not in practice. The realities of the human condition demand that at a certain point deliberation is broken off and a decision is arrived at—in courts of law as in all other spheres of human action.

40. Here "coordinating" stories does not imply, of course, anything like splitting the differences between them. One person's story may be declared by the court to be a complete fabrication. In that case, "coordinating" the lie with the true description of events is simply a matter of understanding why the lie was offered, and why it may have seemed plausible.

41. Bruno Latour, *Science in Action* (Cambridge, Mass.: Harvard University Press, 1987), p. 195.

42. As does one's natural talent for rational thought. Anyone who would deny that this talent is unequally distributed has clearly never been a logic *teacher*.

43. Paul Feyerabend, *Against Method* (London: Verso, 1988), p. 14.

44. See Ernst Mayr, *This Is Biology* (Cambridge, Mass.: Harvard University Press, 1997), pp. 5–8, 153–54.

45. In recent years a number of works have appeared that focus on the cognitive dimension of emotions. Some of the more interesting of these are Ronald de Sousa's *The Rationality of Emotions*, Antonio R. Damasio's *Descartes' Error: Emotion, Reason, and the Human Brain*, Martha Nussbaum's *Upheavals of Thought*, and *Passion and Reason: Making Sense of Our Emotions* by Richard S. Lazarus and Bernice N. Lazarus.

46. David Hume, *A Treatise of Human Nature*, 2.3.3.

47. Hume, *A Treatise of Human Nature*, 2.3.3.

48. On the same principle, whenever we describe another person's emotional reaction as having been wrong—unless we presume that our own emotional reactions set the standard for all other people as well—we can only mean by this that we expect that, on fuller acquaintance with the relevant circumstances, this other person would react differently than he has.

49. Learning to suspend one's value judgments in this way is not an easy thing to do, however, which probably explains why so many young people, knowing full well how untrustworthy their initial impulses often are, end up overplaying the suspension—by refusing to pass value judgments at all (except, of course, in situations that touch them personally). But this is a matter of having avoided one error by falling into another. And as these young people mature and acquire more self-assurance, they usually have another change of heart. As they come to understand the world somewhat better, they find themselves condemning certain kinds of people and certain kinds of activities that they had formerly tolerated, or scrupulously avoided judging. Typically, this happens because, with increasing experience, they come to recognize consequences of those activities that they had not appreciated before, and with increasing confidence, they come to trust their own negative assessments of such activities.

50. Hume, *A Treatise of Human Nature*, 2.3.3.

51. In this regard, I have more or less followed Hume's practice, although it must be admitted that Hume introduces a few broad distinctions—between direct and indirect passions, for example.

52. In other words, if what we are capable of seeing is determined by our vantage point, which is itself a product of the achievements of past generations—if, like Newton, we see further by standing on the shoulders of those who have come before us—then our commitment to the pursuit of truth and justice—which is to say, to the attainment of a still wider perspective than that which is currently available to us—requires that we do our part to raise and improve the vantage point from which the next generation will take *its* bearings.

Chapter Four

Tragedy and Sacrifice

THE CONFLICT OF PERSPECTIVES

Philosophers have long been fascinated by tragedy as a literary genre because of what it has to show us about the potentially disastrous consequences of human finitude. In particular, there are two dimensions of human vulnerability that the great tragedians have explored. First, there is the radical insecurity of the human condition—the possibility of our being suddenly brought to destruction despite our best efforts and regardless of our personal merits. The tragic hero (think of Oedipus, Lear, Othello) is typically subjected to a fate the dreadfulness of which is out of all proportion to whatever mistakes he may have committed or whatever character flaws he may possess. In this respect, moreover, the tragic hero's fate is representative of what might happen to any one of us. Our recognition that we share with the tragic hero this possibility of being suddenly brought to destruction is what gives rise to the emotional catharsis on the part of the audience that Aristotle saw as the definitive response to tragic drama.[1]

The second dimension of human vulnerability that tragedians in particular have explored has to do with the intransigent conflict of perspectives—which is to say, with the possibility of two individuals or groups finding themselves locked in a death struggle (either figuratively or literally) by virtue of their inability to appreciate each other's values, and thus by virtue of their inability to compromise regarding those values. It was Hegel who first recognized that in the greatest tragedies of Aeschylus (the *Oresteia*, *Prometheus Bound*) and Sophocles (most especially in *Antigone*) we witness a conflict "not between good and evil but between one-sided positions, each of which embodies some good."[2] This kind of conflict, Walter Kaufmann observes,[3] does not *define* the genre of tragedy to anything like the same degree that the focus on the radical insecurity of the human condition does, since many works of tragedy do not exhibit such a conflict of perspectives at all. Nonetheless, it does constitute an important component of human vulnerability, and one that takes on particular interest as soon as we acknowledge that a sincere pursuit of truth requires that we do justice to the beliefs and perspectives of others.

A conflict of *perspectives*, it should be understood, is a far more serious thing, and thus is far more likely to generate tragedy, than is a conflict of beliefs. On many if not most issues, after all, one can change a belief without feeling especially threatened by the need to do so. ("Basel is *not* the capital of Switzerland? I could have sworn that it was.") But one's perspective is not a mere belief; it is a reasonably coherent way of seeing things—a predisposition to fit one's beliefs together in a particular pattern. To say that one's perspective is a patterning predisposition implies, of course, that it is not simply the sum total of the beliefs that one holds. For even where two people know almost all of the same facts, and share almost all of the same experiences— spouses or siblings, say—they may nevertheless possess significantly different perspectives. What makes this possible is the fact that one's perspective is primarily a function of the relative importance that one attaches to one's various beliefs. Some of those beliefs *mean* more to one than do the rest of one's beliefs, and to some degree at least those more meaningful beliefs determine how one understands the relevance of the remaining beliefs. One's perspective, in other words, is an expression not only of one's knowledge but also of one's values.[4] And for this reason one's perspective tends to be far more vigorously defended when someone calls it into question than are one's commitments to mere individual beliefs.

Now because perspectives are reasonably coherent and integrated wholes, susceptible to painless change for the most part only at their peripheries— which is to say, regarding what is felt to be rather unimportant factual detail— when two perspectives collide it is not surprising that they should conflict. In everyday life we tend to avoid such conflict by, whenever possible, declining to challenge our neighbors' perspectives. Where we sense the likelihood of serious disagreement, good manners dictate that we should change the subject. But now and then politely "agreeing to disagree" is not an option, because a line of action with serious consequences is at stake. (Abortion clinics either will or will not be permitted in one's community; the wealthy either will or will not be expected to pay proportionally higher taxes; blacks either will or will not be permitted to share public facilities with whites.) On those occasions, the fact that rival perspectives mutually exclude each other's central beliefs, at least *as* those beliefs are understood in the light of each perspective's value structure, makes the conflict between them highly threatening. The conflict becomes, in effect, a matter of "life and death"—if not for the human antagonists involved, then certainly for the rival perspectives. For insofar as a winner emerges from the conflict, the value structure of the defeated perspective is publicly declared to be inadequate and unworthy of determining social policy. Anyone who continues to identify with the discredited perspective must learn to cope with the cognitive dissonance that is generated by his having to tolerate in public what he finds intolerable in the structure of his private beliefs. And in the long run— which is to say, across successive generations—such cognitive dissonance tends to prove fatal to the perspective in question.

Today, for example, no reasonably well-informed American would even think of suggesting that segregation, much less racial slavery, is justified in light of the "fact" that blacks are not human in quite the same sense that whites are. In the first half of the nineteenth century, on the other hand, this was considered by many respectable Americans (including congressmen and senators, and at least one vice president—John C. Calhoun—as well as some of the leading scientists of the day, such as Louis Agassiz) to be an absolutely compelling argument.[5] To consider another example, this tendency of cognitive dissonance to prove lethal to a perspective is obviously one reason why opponents of *Roe v. Wade* are so determined to see that decision overturned, and soon. They recognize the danger that, if *Roe v. Wade* continues to stand, in due course their children and grandchildren will become comfortable with the idea of abortion, and in the process will have abandoned the value structure of their parents.

But if it is possible for the value structures entertained within a family to change across generations (often much to the dismay of the older members of the family), why does there tend to be so much inertia in the value structures entertained by individuals? Why, that is to say, is it such a rare occurrence to see really significant revision of basic values within the thinking of a given person? (Anyone who doubts that this is the case should consider how vigorously Christian fundamentalists continue to resist the implications of Darwinism, in spite of the enormously high—if somewhat uninformed—regard in which most modern science is held by the general populace. A truly astonishing number of Americans do not wish to know the facts of evolutionary biology themselves, and do not wish their children to be informed of them either.) An important part of the explanation is a simple matter of the conservation of energy. Because the values to which one is committed establish the pattern of relevance for one's beliefs, determining how one should act in various circumstances, it is time-consuming and difficult to think through the implications of a serious change in one's values. One's belief structure, after all, is a more or less coherent and integrated whole, and thus a change in any reasonably central belief—such as a belief concerning what sorts of things are *important*—will have wide-ranging implications. As a result, one's conduct will ordinarily have to change not in one or two easily identifiable ways, but in many subtle ways.

Think, for example, of all of the implications that flowed from the simple claim that women really should be treated as men's equals. It was not as if this claim could be satisfied simply by extending to women the right to vote, and then, somewhat later, the right to work. For the right to work had implications for family life and for male-female interaction, both inside and outside of the workplace. Suddenly people found themselves embroiled in complicated discussions about the meaning and appropriateness of equal pay, equal opportunity, affirmative action, childcare, paternalism, sexual harassment, and courtship roles. Thus granting in principle the fundamental correctness of the claim that women should be treated as the equals of men was one thing; thinking through the implications of that claim and adjusting our conduct accordingly was something else again. And the resistance that men, in particular, tended to exhibit toward feminism throughout the 1970s can probably best be understood as the manifestation of a deep reluctance on their part to make the effort of adjustment that they implicitly recognized would be required if they accepted in full seriousness this fundamental claim of feminism—that women should be treated as the equals of men.

Nor was this concern for the time and effort involved in having to adjust their values entirely unreasonable on the part of men—in spite of the obvious importance and correctness of the feminist claim (which is easier for men to see in retrospect) and therefore of the clear necessity that the effort to restructure gender roles be undertaken. After all, as finite creatures we have only limited resources available, and we must use those resources wisely and effectively. Not every change, in other words, not even every change for the better, is worth the cost in time and effort that achieving it would require. There is, moreover, even with respect to changes that should be made, always an appropriate moment for undertaking the effort. There comes a point, as there did with feminism, at which the cost (in cognitive dissonance and frustration) of *not* making the effort outweighs the cost involved in making it. But what almost invariably makes social change a matter of political struggle is that the costs that are to be weighed against each other seldom if ever fall upon the same people. Here it was a matter of primarily female frustration having to be balanced against the cost of a social restructuring in which most men—viewing the issue rather selfishly—could not see that they had much to gain for their efforts.

That there is an appropriate moment for the restructuring of values, and that this moment is determined by the availability of resources as well as felt need, can also be seen if we consider how our attitudes toward our values tend to change across the course of our lifetimes. Young children, having to as-similate an enormous amount of information, having to work it into a coher-ent whole, and having to determine what its implications should be for their personal action, naturally adopt the shortcut of taking their values and beliefs pretty much ready-made from their parents and teachers. Given the size of the task facing them, and the necessity of getting a working belief-and-value structure into place as quickly as possible, this is clearly the most efficient way in which to proceed. By the time children reach adolescence, however, much of this early pressure is off. Adolescents have a reasonable understand-ing of how the world works and know as well what their parents approve and disapprove of. Importantly, they also have time and energy to spare, given that they have not yet taken on the responsibilities of adulthood. It is not sur-prising, then, to find that adolescents typically go through a period of exper-imenting with their values—which should be understood as a matter of ad-justing those values to more closely suit their personal temperaments and experience. They are not clones of their parents, after all, and growing up a generation later than their parents, the potentially quite different circum-stances that they find themselves having to deal with may also necessitate some reworking of the values that they inherited. Moreover, given that their most important job at this stage in their lives is to extend and fine-tune their education, this process of value revision during adolescence is not only toler-ated, it tends to be encouraged—by their teachers, if not always by their par-ents.

But once the years dedicated to education come to a close and adulthood arrives somewhere in the mid-twenties, people get down to the "serious" business of earning their livings and raising their families. The time and en-ergy needed for major value revision is no longer readily available, and thus for the most part neither is the inclination to engage in it even where it might seem to be called for. When adults are challenged by a change of circum-stances that implies the need for a change in their values, it tends to be easier (that is, more cost-effective) simply to deny the need for change for as long as this seems feasible. After all, given the individual's propensity to interpret his experience in the light of his current values, it is seldom obvious to the in-dividual concerned that those values are in fact inadequate. At most, the cru-cial change in circumstances will leave him having to cope with a signifi-cantly greater amount of cognitive dissonance than he previously had to face. And such cognitive dissonance, while uncomfortable, does not *compel* him to change his values—not as long as it can be dealt with instead by denying cer-tain aspects of his experience.

If someone comes along, moreover, who insists that his cognitive dissonance problem can and should be solved by altering his values, the individual whose perspective is being challenged has two reasonably legitimate concerns that may cause him to resist this advice. First, there is the question of whether this other finite human being who *claims* to possess greater insight has in fact correctly assessed the situation. Perhaps she too is in error—perhaps even more serious error than he is, and her exhortations to him to change his values are simply part of her way of coping with the cognitive dissonance generated by the flaws in her *own* perspective. (Doubts about the correctness of one's beliefs, after all, tend to be reduced to the degree that one finds other people willing to subscribe to those beliefs as well.) On the other hand, it may be that her motives are not even this benign; perhaps she is quite consciously hoping to manipulate his belief structure for her personal benefit. These considerations, while they will tend to be seized upon a little too eagerly as reasons for remaining committed to his current values, have at least some measure of legitimacy. There is, however, yet another consideration, which possesses no legitimacy whatsoever and which nonetheless often contributes enormously to the inertia of our values, for there is also the mounting psychic cost to be counted. Significantly changing his values, after all, may involve the individual in the unwelcome task of having to admit to himself that his past actions were inappropriate, perhaps even unjust. And clearly the later in life he comes to this change in values, the more there will likely be to regret—assuming that he makes the change at all. But for this very reason his reluctance to engage in serious value revision will be all the stronger.

The reluctance to reconsider one's values is thus a natural consequence of human finitude—a consequence, that is, of our possessing only limited time and energy with which to attend to those things that clamor for our attention—and it follows that everyone, to a greater or lesser degree, is prone to such reluctance. But if, as was argued in the previous chapter, that rarer form of dignity to which we should aspire accrues to an individual by virtue of his dedication to the pursuits of truth and of justice—if the individual's dignity is, in effect, an expression of his honest willingness to be shown his own errors, and to correct them— it should be clear that this all too human reluctance to reconsider one's values is directly at odds with dignity. And insofar as one succumbs to it, it undermines one's dignity. It is never possible, of course, to be wholly indifferent to the costs involved in value revision, since it is always taxing and our resources are limited. But the dignified individual is one who is relatively more willing to accept the challenge of reconsidering his values. Dignity, it follows, is not something that one either possesses or does not possess; it is invariably something possessed in some measure—and the degree to which one possesses it will vary as one's willingness to meet the challenge of value revision varies.[6]

Thus when perspectives conflict, it is not a foregone conclusion that they must conflict irreconcilably. In principle at least, the value structures underlying those perspectives always can be changed in such a way as to bring them into harmony. But even where change would be appropriate, whether value structures will be modified in a given instance will depend upon two factors: first, the willingness of the individuals whose value structures are being challenged to acknowledge that they may in fact be wrong in their estimations of what is important; and second, the cost in time and effort that changing those values would require. This cost, moreover, can be prohibitive. For the time required for a necessary change in one's value structure may simply not be available, given the need to act not eventually but now.

When values *are* revised, they are revised in the light of what experience shows us about the relation between those questionable values and our deeper bedrock values. And Aristotle was almost certainly correct in suggesting that, of all of our values, the most fundamental is that of living well.[7] Everything else that we might consider important and worth pursuing, Aristotle argues, is important only by virtue of its contributing to a well-lived life. Money, power, health, and friendship are all clearly important, but only because life cannot possibly be lived well in the utter absence of these things. Given that they are important *constitutively*—that is, as contributing to *eudaimonia* or the good life—the degree to which and the manner in which they are important must be determined by reflecting upon our own experience and the experience of others. And that, of course, takes time—time that may not be available or, given our natural reluctance to engage in value revision, time that may have been available but which was squandered. When there is either insufficient time or insufficient willingness to affect a pressing and necessary revision of one's values, the result is often an implacable and tragic conflict of perspectives.

We can find a ready illustration of this in perhaps the greatest of American tragedies—the sectional dispute over slavery that tore the country apart in 1861. In principle at least, it would have been possible for slavery to be eliminated peacefully in the United States, as it was in Great Britain. That it would eventually be eliminated through legislation was the fervent hope of many of the nation's founding fathers (even many of its Virginian founding fathers). But the investment that the South had in the "peculiar institution" of slavery and the safeguards that had been built into the Constitution to protect that investment meant that in practical terms this was highly unlikely to occur. As it turned out, the Southern slave-holding class had plenty of time—three generations from the Constitution's ratification to the breakup of the country following Lincoln's election—in which to recognize that slavery was incompatible with living well, in which to recognize that the comforts and leisure that slavery purchased for them were incapable of compensating for the moral inconsistencies that slavery introduced into their lives. But the natural human reluctance to engage in value revision kicked in early and effectively to shut down any possibility of a voluntary renunciation of slavery on the part of the South.

In the first four decades of the Republic's existence, the South, confident of its constitutional right to slavery and coming in for only marginal criticism from Pennsylvania Quakers and a few freethinking New Englanders, largely contented itself with rationalization. Blacks were either not human at all, or were so obviously a poorer form of humanity that slavery was actually a blessing to them. While such claims did nothing to silence the critics of slavery, Southerners themselves found them consoling and by means of them managed to avoid having to face the challenge of restructuring both their values and their economic system. By the early 1830s, however, the political climate in America was beginning to change dramatically. The newspaperman William Lloyd Garrison introduced a new vigor and uncompromising tone into the expanding abolitionist movement. Increasing numbers of Northerners were becoming familiar with, and disturbed by, the implications of the Fugitive Slave Act. And Nat Turner's Rebellion, the suicidal uprising of a few dozen slaves in August 1831, aroused in Southerners fears of being slaughtered in their beds in the dead of night, and made the growing Northern protests against the injustice of slavery sound to Southern ears like life-threatening incitements to insurrection.

As the pressure to abandon its reliance upon slave labor steadily increased, the South responded by growing increasingly defensive—aggressively so. When abolitionist pamphlets began to arrive through the mails in Southern cities, post offices in the South introduced a policy of censorship, publicly burning the abolitionist literature instead of distributing it. When petitions from Northern citizen groups began to appear in Congress, asking that slavery be expunged at least from the nation's capital,[8] Southern politicians were incensed and introduced the notorious Gag Rule, which prevented not only official notice being taken of the petitions, but even any mention of the petitions by sympathetic senators or congressmen (thereby violating the First Amendment rights of Northern congressmen, as John Quincy Adams was quick to point out).[9] As the westward expansion of the country led inevitably to the admission of new states to the Union, the South, determined to maintain its advantageous balance of power in Congress so as to be able to protect the constitutional safeguards on slavery against amendment, insisted on the matching of free-state with slave-state admissions, and found itself embroiled in a seemingly interminable power struggle with the North over this crucial issue. Finally, with the election as president of a man who was on record[10] as believing that at some point slavery must be abolished, given its incompatibility with the principles to which the country had dedicated itself in the Declaration of Independence, most of the South immediately seceded and began preparing for war.

Nor did four years' worth of vicious and devastating warfare change men's minds much. Even in defeat, most Southerners continued to cling to their old value system. Rather than acknowledge that the war had been brought on by an increasingly profound disagreement between North and South over the moral permissibility of slavery,[11] Southern apologists insisted that the "War of Northern Aggression" had constituted nothing more than a violation of *their* rights to self-determination. (As if the idea of *instituting* rights to self-determination for blacks could not possibly be understood as taking priority here.) And in the meantime the Ku Klux Klan emerged to take up the important work of terrorizing and lynching "uppity negroes."

The point of this illustration has not been to castigate "evil" nineteenth-century Southerners (although there is also no intention here to deny that morally, they were profoundly wrong). The blindness of which slave-holding Southerners were guilty is a blindness to which all human beings are susceptible. By nature we are all (even the political liberals among us) deeply *conservative* once we have established our values. It takes a heroic effort to remain open to the possible need to significantly revise one's value structure, and most humans (although perfectly prepared to fight vigorously *for* their current values, whatever they may be) are not heroes in this sense. That is why the conflict of perspectives is such a breeding ground for tragedy.

For this reason as well the genre of tragedy has its almost paradoxical double message to offer us. On the one hand, there is the need for flexibility—a need that is sometimes quite explicitly invoked. Martha Nussbaum points out, for example, that near the end of *Antigone*

> Tiresias . . . urges Creon to heal himself from a sickness of reason that is "common to all human beings." This sickness is, presumably the rage for control, with its attendant impieties. . . . But how does Tiresias propose to "heal" this sickness without falling into the opposite trap of immobility? . . .
> Tiresias says that good deliberation is connected with "yielding," with renouncing self-willed stubbornness, with being flexible.[12]

On the other hand, there is the fact, insisted upon in the genre of tragedy, that often no measure of flexibility will prove to be enough—that catastrophe will sometimes strike regardless of our efforts. For renouncing self-willed stubbornness is not a panacea. Flexibility is a virtue that may *sometimes* enable us to escape the destructive consequences of a conflict of perspectives. But tragedy comes in a variety of forms,[13] and even where it does turn on a conflict of perspectives, there is seldom if ever a pat solution to such conflicts—a solution on which the flexible individual can simply alight.

To be "yielding" is all well and good, but one cannot go on yielding indefinitely and regardless of what one's opposite number is doing. And sometimes, of course, yielding is (at least temporarily) out of the question because one is *so much more in the right* than is one's antagonist. This possibility—that one side in a conflict of perspectives really is almost entirely right and the other almost entirely wrong—is one that philosophers commenting on tragedy since Hegel have tended not to dwell upon, given their fascination with his dialectical vision of mutual one-sidedness giving way—or *not* giving way—to a more all-encompassing truth for *both* parties. But that such situations do occasionally occur cannot be denied. Had the North, for example, shown a willingness to yield in 1861, as it had in 1787 with the drafting of the Constitution, and repeatedly in crises throughout the first half of the nineteenth century, while the tragedy of the Civil War might have been averted, the ongoing tragedy of racial slavery in the South would have dragged on for generations to come. The willingness to yield cannot come entirely from one side without domination resulting. But neither is it necessarily enough that there be movement on both sides, since both sides must move *appropriate* distances, and there will often be residual disagreement on what constitutes an appropriate compromise of concerns.[14] Repeated *failed* attempts at compromise, moreover, can probably generate almost as much tragedy as can a blunt refusal to compromise at all.

We can acknowledge, then, the need for flexibility in situations involving fundamental disagreement. And if we understand by "flexibility" not means-end expediency but rather a willingness to be shown one's errors and to adjust one's commitments accordingly, we can go further and say that this same flexibility is what gives rise to dignity on the part of the individual. But we must recognize as well that the press of circumstances, in combination with the natural inertia that all human beings exhibit to a greater or lesser degree in the matter of value revision, will not infrequently bring about catastrophes that can only be suffered through—the moment for averting them having been missed. And often, if the catastrophe in question has been produced by an unresolved conflict of perspectives between advocates of legitimate values, it is quite impossible for anyone caught in the midst of the catastrophe to know where the point of compromise, where the balance of conflicting legitimate claims, should have been found. Thus the question to which this lengthy preamble has been leading is: what does dignity amount to in a situation combining tragedy with uncertainty? How does the individual who possesses dignity comport himself when the opportunities for compromise and mutual understanding have been missed—as they all too often are?

WAR AND THE PAUCITY OF OPTIONS

Clearly war represents the most destructive form of tragedy resulting from the unresolved conflict of perspectives. Moreover, the individuals whose fates are affected must ordinarily decide how they will respond to the challenge that war represents on the basis of disturbingly fragmentary and one-sided information. For typically the reasons that nations go to war are so enormously complex that determining with any objectivity *why* a war was fought (and thus which side was, in the scheme of things, more in the right) can be accomplished only after the fighting is over, when scores of historians have the leisure and opportunity to spend decades poring over the relevant documentation and teasing out its implications. When events are still breaking upon each other, even policy-makers can form only a rough idea of what is at stake. And once arms have been seized and each side's propaganda machinery kicks in, any hope of achieving mutual understanding and compromise is lost—at least until one side lies prostrate before the other and the new terms upon which peace is to be reestablished can be dictated.

Disturbing as this situation is, however, pacifism (or the determination as a matter of principle that *nothing* is worth fighting for) constitutes an easy and unsatisfactory escape from the moral complexities involved in war. No doubt, judged in retrospect, the pacifist's refusal to fight will often prove to have been justified in particular instances—since most wars represent morally unwarranted descents into mass violence. But occasionally there are just wars that, on one side at least, deserve to be fought. World War II perhaps can serve as an example, and most certainly the American Civil War could.[15] There are also wars of resistance against genuinely unprovoked aggression.[16] Thus the individual who is concerned to do what is right in each particular instance must decide, when war breaks out, whether or not to fight—recognizing all the while that his decision must be made, in all probability, on the basis of seriously inadequate information, and that each option entails enormous costs. For to take up arms is to sacrifice comfort, security, and quite possibly his life, while to reject his nation's call to arms is to sacrifice his status as a citizen in good standing, and perhaps even his right to continue living in his homeland.

While all wars are tragic in nature, perhaps no recent war has been more tragic than World War I. Only the comparatively just Second World War exceeded it in destructiveness, after all, and the First World War, historians tend to agree, was in a curious sense both "inevitable" and utterly unnecessary. While there was no truly compelling issue over which to fight in 1914, the major European powers had nonetheless jockeyed themselves and each other into a position in which it seemed crucial to be the first off the mark with mobilization and a "preemptive" strike. Thus in 1914 Europe in effect jumped at its own shadow, and a generation of young men tumbled into the trenches. Four years later, what came out of the trenches, along with the survivors, was a harvest of remarkable literature—the war poetry and personal memoirs of such authors as Wilfred Owen, Robert Graves, Siegfried Sassoon, Edmund Blunden, Guillaume Apollinaire, Erich Maria Remarque, and Carl Zuckmeyer. This literature, as Niall Ferguson makes clear in *The Pity of War*,[17] is on the whole less unambiguously antiwar in tone than it is often represented as being. The best of it, however, provides us with honest, intelligent, and reflective accounts of the tedium and horror of modern warfare as well as the attitudes of the men subjected to that tedium and horror. In the pages to follow, I focus upon one small, little-known (and slightly flawed) gem in this body of literature—a work that probes more searchingly than any other that I know of into the question of what morality requires of one in such a situation.

The Love of an Unknown Soldier

The book in question was published simultaneously in London and Toronto just a few months before the end of the war. It was not in fact a "book" in the normal sense of the word at all. It was a collection of letters that had been written—but never sent—by a British subaltern (or second lieutenant) to an American Red Cross nurse, confessing his love for her, and explaining to himself why he would not tell her of his love until he had survived the war—*if* he survived the war. The subaltern, as it turned out, was killed in a rearguard action. He was an artillery spotter, and when the Germans pushed forward (presumably in their spring 1918 offensive), he and his men were left behind as a sacrifice battery. (We know this, and everything else that it seems possible to know about the author's story, from the letters themselves.) Later, when the lost ground was recaptured, his letters, which had been wedged behind a support post in his dugout, were discovered by a Canadian officer, who thought at first that, given the care with which they had been hidden, they might be papers of some military significance. On discovering what the letters actually were, the Canadian officer was somewhat uncertain about how to deal with them. Because the ground in question had been occupied at various times by many different British units, there seemed to be no possibility of discovering who their author had been. The thought occurred to the Canadian that perhaps the author's privacy should be respected and the letters destroyed (which would in fact have been in keeping with the author's own expressed wish at one point in the letters). Finally, however, the Canadian decided that they ought to be given to the nurse to whom they had been notionally addressed. (This too can be thought of as in keeping with the author's intention, for it was clear that, had he survived the war, he was planning to give the letters to the nurse all at once.) Since she, like the author, was nowhere mentioned by name, though, it appeared that the only way to bring them to her attention would be to make the letters public. And so they came to be published, under the title *The Love of an Unknown Soldier*.

This is how the "unknown soldier" came to fall in love. Early in 1917 he was mildly wounded and during his convalescence he was sent as part of the British Mission to America, which had just entered the war, in order to speak at various public meetings on behalf of the war effort. At one of these he was introduced to a young socialite who mentioned that she was about to leave for France in order to join a Red Cross unit that was tending to children in the devastated districts. He was taken by her immediately, and tried to contact her the next day, but she had already sailed. Soon he too was back in France, and by luck received a week's leave to spend in Paris long before he had any right to expect one. As he put it,

> I came to Paris thinking, "There's just a chance that I may see her." I went to call on the only girl I knew and found you [that is, the American nurse] staying with her. Perhaps it was fate; I prefer to think that it was something else.
>
> That first day I did not see you, but the next you called me up. I took it as an omen of good fortune that you should have gone to that trouble; it seemed to prove to me that to you also that hurried introduction had been more than an incident; that you, too, had been intrigued and made a trifle curious.[18]

The two spent virtually every evening of the subaltern's leave together and, insofar as it is possible to judge such a question on the basis of an entirely one-sided recollection of events, it seems clear that the young American nurse reciprocated the subaltern's feelings—or at least *would* have reciprocated them, had he only confessed those feelings.

But he did not confess them, and not because of shyness, but for the weightiest of reasons.

> I wonder if you have guessed. Surely I could not have loved you so much without your knowing. And yet—yes, I am glad that I said nothing. What right have I, who may be dead within a month, to speak to you of love? To have done so would have been the act of a coward.
>
> I want to put the case to myself so that I may act strongly. If I had spoken and you had loved me in return, what would have resulted? Only suffering—until the war is ended, we could never have been together—and you, all the time you would have been lonely. All the time you would have been worrying about my safety. If I were wounded again, you would think me dead. Though I were badly wounded, you would not be able to come to me, for you too have your duty up

there behind the Front at J—-, you and the other American girls who take care
of the French babies. And then I might have been mutilated. With the French a
man's wounds are like decorations, they are tokens of the new religion of sacrifice. With us they are still horrible. I would not have you held to your bargain
with a mutilated man, for I might have to live to see you shudder. And then I
may die in this war—who can tell? If I had married you, I should have stolen
your happiness and left you deserted. No, I am glad I did not speak of love.[19]

In deciding *not* to declare his feelings, however, the subaltern was fully
aware that many others in his situation had done differently—had hurriedly
become engaged to, or even married, girls they barely knew. "I don't believe
in these war-engagements and war-marriages," he wrote. "Still—the heart
cries out; it is difficult to say 'No' to self when one is young. I will not think
of these things; they make me distracted."[20] But in spite of his resolution not
to think of these things, at the front he could think of little else, when he was
not immediately involved in the business of fighting.

Perhaps I did not do right by keeping silent; perhaps my silence was false pride.
I was talking to one of your friends the other day about soldiers getting married,
arguing that such conduct was selfish. She had been quiet—hardly interested.
Suddenly, with an unexpected violence, she turned. "I wish I had married my
man," she said. I learnt her story afterwards. She had been engaged to a French
officer and he had been killed. She had joined the Red Cross and ever since has
been working her way grimly nearer and nearer to the Front. Did they smile as
quietly as we smiled when last they parted?[21]

The thought that he may have been overscrupulous—the thought that his refusing to confess his feelings might have been an effort to control a situation
that he should not presume to control, and that in so doing he might have
missed out on the one opportunity for love that life had provided him so far, perhaps the only opportunity for love that he would be given—tormented him. And
yet, tormented as he was by doubts that could never be wholly silenced, whenever he thought the matter through he came to the same conclusion.

If I had only met you earlier, in the days before war started, I could have made
love to you honourably. But not now. I turn my head and look out into the passage across my shoulder; I see the boots, the form beneath the blanket, the
stretcher. He was a man once; in a second of time what lies there was all that
was left. Perhaps he too loved a girl. Perhaps he told her. How much better if he
had kept silent. And yet . . ."I wish I had married my man," your friend said. It's
a problem. Self-interest dictates that I should tell you. That choice might be
more righteous than silence; it depends on you. But because the choice would
be selfish I distrust it.[22]

There is a tremendous *earnestness* implicit in the subaltern's refusal to confess his feelings to the American nurse, but who can suggest that his earnestness was unwarranted, knowing as we do that he *was* killed in action, and that consequently he *did* miss his chance to experience requited love? Notice as well that his behavior in this matter exhibits all of the key features that Schiller identified with dignity. First, there is the powerful natural inclination which, in other circumstances, it would be perfectly appropriate to indulge. Second, there is reason's subduing of that inclination in *these* circumstances, because here it cannot be indulged harmlessly. And finally, there is the evidence of struggle, for the natural inclination is by no means easily subdued. In this case, though, the struggle is made even more difficult in that the subaltern cannot be all that sure that the principle that he discerns and acts upon is correct. He does not enjoy the confidence of a Kant that righteousness is easily recognized in all circumstances. The situation in which he finds himself in France in 1917 is fraught, not only with danger and significance, but with ambivalence and confusion. As a result, he must find his way through it without the comfort of certainty.

For there is, of course, no clear and unchallengeable rule to invoke here — no categorical imperative prohibiting wartime romance. But this hardly means that the subaltern is faced with nothing more than what Kant would call a prudential calculation, in which only his own happiness is at stake. The nurse's future happiness too is, potentially at least, very much at stake, and thus the question of whether or not to confess his love in these circumstances is most definitely, as the subaltern himself realizes, a *moral* one. But he must approach that question as a consequentialist, weighing the goods and harms that are likely to follow (for all affected parties) on his either confessing or not confessing his love. And he must weigh them, moreover, in a condition of considerable uncertainty about events that would make a huge difference to his calculations—"I might be mutilated, I might be killed." It is possible, of course, for us to conclude, on the basis of our own assessments of his situation, that the subaltern was somewhat overscrupulous—that he should have confessed his feelings, and permitted the nurse to take her chances with him, if she was so inclined. The very fact that she was in France voluntarily shows, after all, that she was a young woman prepared to accept risks for the sake of things that really mattered to her. But whether we agree or disagree with the answer at which the subaltern arrives, it should be clear that the distrust of self-interest that ultimately settles the issue for him ("Because the choice would be selfish I distrust it") is fully Kantian in spirit, and wholly admirable.

It is important to recognize, however, the significance of that consideration's coming last rather than first in his deliberations. Self-interested decisions, after all, are not in principle always improper or immoral. It is only because here the possibility of harm to someone else is very real, even if far from certain, that the subaltern is on guard against the danger of rationalizing his own desire—that is, of finding spurious reasons to justify indulging his natural inclination. Given the complexity of the situation in which he finds himself, he realizes that he must weigh potential consequences in order to determine the morally correct thing to do. But conscious as he is of his own self-interestedness (which is to say, of the fact that he is human), he is very much aware that the balance that he is employing in weighing these consequences against each other is skewed. That does not mean, of course, that he can abandon the process of weighing and comparing consequences—for there is no *other* means available of determining what is morally right here. What it means, rather, is that he must factor into his calculations the probable skewing effect of the balance itself—which is to say, of his self-interestedness. This becomes the deciding factor for him, in this decision, only because the consequences on each side of the question appear to be so evenly balanced *before* he asks himself what the likely effect of his own private desires has been on his assessment of those consequences.

The subaltern is also intelligent enough to recognize that it is not only *his* judgment that is susceptible to skewing, and to incorporate this recognition into his calculation of consequences.

> Why didn't I propose to you? Because I was afraid of trading on your sentiment. It's a difficult thing for a girl to refuse a man who is going back into the line. She may easily be deceived into a belief that she loves him, whereas her only feeling may be pity for him.[23]

Since sentimentality is so much less blameworthy than selfishness, it is not difficult to imagine how a good person—and especially how a fine young idealistic person—might succumb to it. What the subaltern hopes for from his American nurse, though, is true love, not a sentimental counterfeit of it. He can hardly be accused of paternalism, then, in reminding himself of the risk of being accepted for the wrong reason.

As the book progresses, yet another consideration gradually emerges into view for the subaltern. He slowly becomes aware that his hopes for the future—specifically, his hopes for a future with her—might undermine his performance as a soldier. Early on, as he begins his correspondence with the nurse—one set of friendly letters that he actually sends to her, and to which she chummily responds, and another set of secret letters in which he confesses his true feelings—he hopes that the latter might actually function as a source of strength for him.

> I am glad I met you. I am glad of the pain I shall carry back with me. My great loneliness before was that no woman had come into my life. Now I shall be able

to think, "I am doing this for her." I shall be able to say, "Perhaps she knew why I did not speak. Perhaps she too is remembering." I shall tell myself stories about you, just as if you were really mine. Your face will be with me, the sound of your voice and the memory of your gentleness. I shall be a better soldier because we have met.[24]

Since I can't forget you, I must make your memory a help. Who was it said— Epictetus, wasn't it?—that every burden has two handles: one by which it can be carried, and one by which it cannot? The wise man finds the handle by which he can carry his burdens. Here's the way in which I'm going to make my love for you help. At the end of the war, if I survive, I'll seek you out; that promise shall be my goal.[25]

But as these unsent letters accumulate and become more meaningful to him, he begins to recognize the potential danger they pose. "To hope too much is to court cowardice. To be brave one should live a day at a time."

I don't think I will write to you any more, my dear. These unposted letters, written out of loneliness, are becoming a luxury which is dangerous. They make the future seem too valuable. I begin to realize how sweet life is—how glorious we could make it. I would rather be at rest within myself if I am called upon to say "Good-bye." You ran up the stairs without turning your head when we parted. That's the way I would prefer to go out of life.[26]

Even the vague hopes that he entertains at this point, amounting to little more than a resolution to seek her out at war's end, have begun to prey upon his mind. But if there is any need to be reminded of his own vulnerability at the front, and consequently of the tenuousness of his hold on the future, he needs only to consider the situation of his friend, Jack Holt, a fellow officer who happens to be married and a first-time father.

Since [Jack] has come back [after the birth of his daughter] and I've seen how life can clutch at a man through a woman's love and children, I'm glad that I did not tell you. I don't want to feel bound up with life too much; I see every day what a tremendous lot this new reason for living is costing Jack. Those two, in England, are never out of his thoughts.[27]

And before the letters run out, we learn of Jack Holt's death. He too is part of the sacrifice battery that is left behind to slow up the German advance.

Jack is dead. A shell struck our mess, wounding him and myself and killing the major. That happened three days ago. Jack stayed on to help me run the battery, but this morning I insisted that he should go out. He had walked about a hundred yards towards freedom when a shell fell right on top of him. There is something damnably vindictive about all this after the way we have tried to shield him. Four days ago the transfer came through to the Flying Corps, which would have given him six months in England with the woman and kiddy whom he loved. He ought to have gone away at once, but he was too much of a sportsman. He knew that we needed him. So Steven's dream has been fulfilled.[28]

It is disturbing, of course, to think that even just entertaining hopes for the future—hopes that one might be granted the opportunity to love and perhaps have a family of one's own in due time—might in some circumstances be a luxury one can ill afford. But that was simply the measure of the sacrifice demanded of men in the trenches. The subaltern knows what is required of him, and he faces it unflinchingly.

> I must externalize myself—see myself as I am—a mere unimportant cog in a vast machine which is struggling for the world's redemption. Someone who, without altering the course of nations, may be dead tomorrow. A man muddy, unwashed, unpleasing, sitting in the chaos of an old battlefield and doing his infinitesimal share. *My share!* That's what I must remember. If you stop me from doing my share, you must be forgotten.[29]

It would be easy to misread this passage—to think that the subaltern is noble, yes, but also a bit of a dupe, surely. "A vast machine struggling for the world's redemption?!" A Billy Yank at Gettysburg or a Tommy hitting the beach at Normandy might be excused for thinking of himself as part of such an enterprise. But what was the great cause for which so much blood was spilled at Verdun and the Somme? In what sense was the world even *improved*, let alone *redeemed*? The defeat of Russia sent that country careening into revolution, civil war, destitution, and appalling tyranny. The defeat of Germany led fairly directly to unbearable reparations, hyperinflation, economic collapse, the rise of fascism, and a second even more destructive world war. The great tragedy of World War I, everyone recognizes, with the benefit of hindsight, is that it was so utterly unnecessary—indeed, more than unnecessary. For the world that emerged in 1918 seemed a far more dangerous and brutal place than the world (at least as Europeans knew it) that had existed prior to 1914.

But all of this misses the point, since the subaltern was in no position to know—as we know—that his sacrifice was wasted. He knew full well that it *might* be. (He writes at one point, "You may call war damnable, a vile misuse of courage—there is nothing too bad that can be said about it.")[30] But once having decided to answer his country's call to arms, the subaltern was irrevocably committed to an enterprise the full moral and historical significance of which lay far beyond his control. Statesmen *might* be able to determine, to some degree at least, whether the war would unfold as an endeavor to preserve and promote international justice or instead as an endeavor to increase national power at the expense of someone else. Mere soldiers, however, had no such influence. Having cast their lot with the struggle, all they were subsequently in a position to do was determine how they would conduct themselves under fire. Thus the subaltern demonstrated his personal concern for justice, and his readiness to exercise self-restraint in its service, with respect to everything over which he continued to have some control—in his relations with the American nurse, in his relations with his fellow officers and the troops under his command, in his determination to fight well and, most revealingly, in his attitude toward the enemy (to which we will be turning in a moment). But with respect to that which he could not affect at all—which is to say, with respect to the ultimate significance of the war—all he could do was *hope* that the sacrifice that he and his comrades in arms were being called upon to make would prove to be justified. When he describes himself, then, as an unimportant cog in a vast machine struggling for the world's redemption, we should understand this as the subaltern's expression of his own fervent hope that this would indeed prove to be the meaning of his efforts in a war that was too horrible to contemplate in any other terms.

Nor can one reasonably fault the subaltern for his initial decision to enlist. In the fall of 1914 the sheer pointlessness of the coming war was by no means obvious. The major European powers had been preparing for it for decades. All the powers except Britain had instituted mandatory military service for young men some time earlier and had built up the arsenals required to provision their modern citizen-armies. In order to justify doing so, they had had to persuade their citizenry that war was a serious possibility, and to reassure them that of course they would be called upon to fight only for the noblest of causes—to defend the motherland. And Britain, while it had no huge standing army, had certainly been building up its arsenal as well—specifically in the form of the massive and enormously expensive dreadnoughts—and thus also had needed to publicly justify the expenditure with frequent references to the threat that German power represented. The upshot was a widespread sense in Europe of the eventual inevitability of war. At some point, it seemed, the Central Powers and the Entente nations would have to face the showdown for which they had so long been preparing. Everyone was ready and willing to defend the homeland, and in their readiness to fight a *defensive* war, they were prepared to strike first if need be. None of this implies that the war, when it finally came, was in fact justified. But it does explain to some extent why the prescient few—such as Bertrand Russell—who could see the folly of it all were *quite* few.

As it happened, Germany was the first of the major powers actually to enter enemy soil, and was also the first to violate another country's neutrality in the pursuit of its own war aims. In doing so (in accordance with the long-laid plans of the military technocrat, Field Marshal Alfred von Schlieffen) Germany immediately forfeited such moral high ground as the Central Powers possessed after the assassination of Archduke Franz Ferdinand. While the Germans themselves could rationalize this as a necessary evil forced upon them by the exigency of having to fight on two fronts simultaneously, the French and English press were quick to seize the propaganda benefits that Germany's invasion of Belgium made available. Thus the young men of Britain were called upon not only to protect British soil (which was far less obviously imperiled than was French soil) but also, in the interests of fair play, to punish the Teutonic bullies of Europe. In this regard, the reports of atrocities coming out of Belgium had enormous propaganda value. Jittery and inexperienced German soldiers, marching through the territory of a still-resistant nation, territory that they erroneously believed was crawling with *francs-tireurs* ("free shooters" or resistance fighters, as we would call them), were quick to take and execute hostages whenever they found themselves fired upon by unknown assailants. In the confusion of battlefield conditions, however, those unknown assailants frequently were Belgian regulars, who had every military right to resist the Germans. And on more than one occasion, reprisals were taken against Belgian civilians in response to what later proved to have been instances of German troops mistakenly firing upon other Germans.[31] The British and French press played up these incidents to such a degree that, after the war was over, a reaction set in and embarrassed Western intellectuals began to deny that there had been any significant German outrages in Belgium. As we now know, the crimes were real, and while these were minor by comparison with the atrocities of World War II, it was not difficult for idealists in 1914 to conclude that, in opposing the callous invaders and despoilers of Belgium, they were opposing the march of barbarism across the face of Europe.

The unknown subaltern certainly felt that he was fighting for principle—for the ideals of justice and fair play, which Germany had violated. But once he had arrived at the front, he soon came to recognize that a distinction had to be drawn between the enemy as a political entity, which was pursuing a barbarous and aggressive policy, and the enemy as so many discrete individuals who, like himself, cowered in their trenches under artillery barrages, dispassionately took their opportunities to kill when these arose and, between encounters, coped as best they could with the mud, the lice, and the rats. At the front there were only two attitudes that one could adopt toward the enemy as individuals. One could hate them for the deaths and the misery they caused—an attitude which probably made it easier to kill them in one's turn, but an attitude as well which threatened to become increasingly demented as the horror of war dragged on and the list of one's grievances lengthened. Alternatively, one could recognize their similarities to oneself and on this basis achieve a kind of "amused tolerance" of their efforts. A perfect example of this attitude is to be found in Coningsby Dawson's *Living Bayonets*.

Our chaps are as philosophical and cheery as ever. "Good old Fritz," they say, "so he's taken another fifteen miles! Well, it'll be our turn next." Through defeat and success we carry on quite normally and unperturbed, confident of ultimate victory. The general opinion is that the Hun by his advances is only causing himself a lot of unnecessary trouble, as he'll have a longer distance to run back to Germany![32]

This tolerance, though, on the part of a thoughtful soldier, could easily grow into profound respect as one came to acknowledge that one's enemies too were fighting nobly and sacrificing greatly, and presumably because they too believed that there were principles involved worth fighting for.

Such respect for the enemy, it might seem to the politicians and generals responsible for conducting the war, comes perilously close to the kind of fellow-feeling that must be guarded against if soldiers are to be effective at fighting. They prefer their soldiers to think of the enemy, if at all, in dehumanized terms—as beasts. And this is why, after outright desertion, just about the worst thing that a soldier can stand accused of is fraternizing with the enemy. For it is difficult to dehumanize an enemy that one gets to know in friendly circumstances—an enemy with whom one is exchanging tobacco and food and ideas. Fortunately, at least from the viewpoint of generals, the conditions of combat ordinarily preclude much in the way of fraternizing. But now and then, even across the killing zone of a battlefield, a meeting of the minds can occur and one's enemy can be seen as the fellow human being that he is.

In *The Love of an Unknown Soldier*, there is one anecdote that illustrates this superbly—an anecdote that is apt to strike the reader as too good to be true, as something that one would expect to find in a novel rather than in a factual account. As an artillery spotter, the subaltern periodically had to venture out into no man's land in order to direct fire. On one such occasion, he and his telephonist found themselves exploring a gun pit with its connecting tunnels and dugouts, control of which had passed back and forth between the British and the Germans several times.

I suppose we must have gone twenty yards when we came to a second chamber. The air was foul with decay and damp. There was a glimmer of light far up above us, which evidently came from a caved-in exit. I turned on my flash-light. What I saw was startling.

A big Prussian was sitting on the edge of his bunk. He must have been dead three weeks; but he looked life-like. On the floor was a book which had fallen from his hand. I picked it up. Incongruously enough its binding was preserved by a newspaper cover. I glanced at the title: "The Research Magnificent," by H. G. Wells. I glanced through the pages; the first thing I struck was a marked passage with some comment scrawled against it in German. The passage read, "Like all of us he had been prepared to take life in a certain way and life had taken him, as it takes all of us, in an entirely different way. He had been ready for noble deeds. . . ." At that point the marking ended. I looked at this philosopher, his mouth was open, his head lolled in an imbecile fashion. Across his temple was a wide gash where the fragment of a bomb had struck him. . . . I felt sick with a kind of physical sorrow—not for him in particular, but for all the world. After that, the crawl back across the hills and dales of the pitch-black tunnel was horrible.

I sat on the topmost stairs at the entrance and turned the pages. I kept on wondering how the Prussian had come by a novel that had only been published since hostilities commenced. Then I discovered. Other passages were marked; beside the markings were pencilled comments, some of them in English, some in German, but in different hands. As I studied the passages I found that most of them had reference to fear and its conquest.[33]

In the margins of this book, German and British soldiers had met each other and engaged in a conversation on the subject of most immediate importance to all of them—the nature of courage. Here, in a temporary suspension of hostilities, the sometime enemies had been able to have their say, to challenge one another's ideas, and come to some agreement about what ultimately mattered.

"Like all of us he had been prepared to take life in a certain way and life had taken him, as it takes all of us, in an entirely different way. He had been ready for noble deeds. . . ." As I sat there hiding in No Man's Land, I reflected on these words. The Prussian had pondered them before he died, and the Englishman who had possessed the book before that. They both had been ready to do noble deeds; they both had tried, and they were enemies. In the old days I would have puzzled over this inconsistency, striving vainly to find a reconciling argument. Now, in the larger kindness which I have gained, I forgot the motive in remembering the sacrifice. I wanted the Prussian to know that I felt like that.[34]

On both sides men had marched to war thinking themselves justified in doing so. As a matter of simple logic, however, not everyone could be. The subaltern himself had enlisted in order to protect his homeland against the aggression of an enemy that saw nothing wrong in its unprovoked invasion of Belgium. But increasingly, he found himself fighting simply because others were doing so, and because the sacrifice in life that had already been called for could apparently only be redeemed by further sacrifice. To simply walk away from the horrors of the front, to declare that the entire conflict had been a huge mistake, was utterly unthinkable. And not just because deserters were shot. It was emotionally unthinkable to betray one's comrades in this way. ("They did not die in vain!" the World War I memorials declare in the same spirit, and in flat denial of what common sense tells us.) Increasingly, as the price of the war became clear, and steadily rose, soldiers like the unknown subaltern found themselves fighting even more to redeem what had happened during the war than to correct any injustices that might have caused it. ("I forgot the motive in remembering the sacrifice.") The task of the soldiers, Allied and German alike, was simply to endure—to accept their suffering, however much suffering it might take, in order to purge mankind of the desire for war. They fought in order to make war itself unthinkable. They fought, they told themselves, "the war to end all wars." Only such a result could justify the magnitude of the suffering inflicted—the nine million dead and the several million more crippled and mutilated.

Only the redemption of the world from war itself could constitute a suitable backdrop for the religion of sacrifice that the subaltern gradually elaborated for himself.

> That I, so poor and human and puny, should be capable of this largeness of spirit, gives me confidence that God's scheme for us must be greater than we have guessed. He cannot be smaller than the souls He has created. . . . those [Germans] whom I saw piled high in trenches so loved their ideal that they could die for it. There is something god-like in such self-abnegation."God so loved the world that He gave His only begotten Son"; these men so loved the world that they gave themselves. Though the ideal for which they die may be mistaken, whether they be English, French, or Germans, they seem somehow to strive up towards God's level. To do that is religion.[35]

Of course, the idea that this might somehow constitute the *final* sacrifice required—the idea that war itself might become unthinkable because of the sheer horrific magnitude of *this* war—proved to be little more than a fond hope. A mere twenty years later Germans, Frenchmen, Englishmen, and Russians were squaring off again. The world was not to be so easily redeemed. The subaltern's own uncertainty about the world's redemption (his uncertainty even about what exactly the phrase might mean) explains perhaps why there is so much more confidence in his voice when he speaks, not of the future, but of the lessons that he and his comrades were learning in the murderous present—in the vale of soul-making that the front represented.

This perpetual murder is damnable and splendid. Our men's courage leaves me breathless. It is only the undiscussed nobility of their purposes that keeps them going. It isn't orders; it isn't pay; it isn't the hope of decorations. It doesn't matter who or what our men were in civilian life, they all show the same capacity for sacrifice when in danger. . . . War has taught me, as nothing else could have done, how to love and respect my brother-man.[36]

What is splendid here, obviously, is the capacity for idealism and sacrifice that men were discovering that they possessed. What is damnable, in contrast, is the purpose upon which that capacity was being wasted—mutual slaughter. And what is disheartening is the realization that perhaps only the call to mutual slaughter could awaken that capacity for idealism and sacrifice in ordinary men. As the subaltern observed in an earlier letter, "it's the immense chance for sacrifice that intrigues one. I suppose even in peace-times the chance was always there, only one's eyes were blinded. Perhaps the sacrifice demanded wasn't large enough."[37]

It should be clear by now that, ultimately, and in spite of his best efforts to do so, the subaltern does not manage to make coherent sense of his position. His intense desire to see justice done by his fallen comrades leads him to the conviction that still further sacrifice—his own—is necessary. At the same time, his fair-mindedness leads him to recognize that the Germans too are sacrificing nobly and that justice demands that their sacrifice as well should somehow be made meaningful. But the irony, of course, is that the sacrifices of his comrades and of the Germans are inflicted upon each by the other. How, then, does one do justice to both sacrifices simultaneously? Here things get vague, of necessity. Only an enterprise that requires both sacrifices—the "world's redemption"—seems capable of reconciling the contradiction. But if, as the subaltern anticipates that it probably will, the world goes back to normal once peace is declared—if the purity of spirit and readiness for sacrifice evaporate in the ordinary daylight of getting and spending—what will have been gained by the mutual slaughter? And could it possibly justify the price?

Near the end of the previous chapter, I spoke of the tension that exists between the needs of action and the needs of reason. In order to act effectively, one must proceed as if one is certain about the correctness of what one is doing. (Confidence alone has won many a victory.) But in order to improve the quality of one's understanding, one must proceed tentatively—as if one were even less certain about the matter under investigation than one probably feels. Nowhere is this tension between the needs of action and the needs of reason more obvious or more pronounced than in war. For entertaining doubts about the legitimacy of one's cause is no way to win a battle. (And yet one's cause *might* be less than legitimate.) It is the soldier's task, once war has arrived, to execute the actions demanded of him by his "superiors." It is not his job, once he has enlisted, to consider disinterestedly the question of which side in the conflict is more fully justified in moral terms. And indeed, once the fight is on, he, like everyone else, will be denied the information that might enable him to consider dispassionately the other side's view of what is at stake. In other words, for the duration of the struggle, and for the sake of the struggle, the pursuit of truth regarding the ultimate justifiability of the struggle is suspended. But then, the pursuit of truth does not enjoy absolute pride of place; the pursuit of justice is equally important. And sometimes, in order to achieve justice, war—and the temporary suspension of open moral inquiry that it calls for—is required. But that is no small concession. For justice, as was argued in the previous chapter, cannot be pursued independently of the pursuit of truth for very long. (With one's eyes closed a moving target is sure to be missed.) Moreover, the state's decision to embark upon a war involves transforming its citizens—citizens who, in a democracy, are believed to possess a right to make their own informed moral judgments—at least temporarily into *tools* to be employed and expended in achieving a goal that the state has decided is worth pursuing.

Not everyone takes equally well to this transformation from an independent moral agent into an implement of war—into a "living bayonet," as Coningsby Dawson expressed it. For some, having to examine the permissibility and merits of their inclinations each time a novel situation arises is felt to be a burden, and for them the freedom to follow orders and thus avoid responsibility is entirely welcome. (These are the men whom one hopes to avoid encountering in the guise of "conquering heroes." They are also the sort of men to whom it is quite safe to turn over the operation of an extermination camp.) For others, like the subaltern whose letters we have been considering for these past few pages, the habit of independent moral thought is more deeply ingrained and more difficult to set aside. These men cannot entirely forget or ignore the fact that their enemies are also human, and that this should entitle them to moral consideration. The necessity of killing is something to which they never become entirely reconciled. While they are willing to fight for what they believe in, and recognize the necessity of accepting and following orders, they persist in trying to determine *why* what they are doing is justified as well as *the degree to which* what they are doing is justified. Even as soldiers, in other words, these men continue to function as rational agents, assuming responsibility for their own actions. This makes them potentially somewhat less malleable and useful weapons in the hands of the state than they might be. But their continued exercise of *self*-restraint, even in the midst of war—their refusal, for example, to indulge in hatred of the enemy, and their alertness to situations in which they must take care not to add unnecessarily to the measure of suffering that war

inevitably entails—is also what accounts for their possession of that exceptional form of dignity to which we should aspire.

In first introducing *The Love of an Unknown Soldier*, I referred to it as a
"slightly flawed" gem. What I was alluding to is the fact that the book is not
quite what it purports to be. In fact, it is something of a literary hoax, although
I did not discover this until most of the preceding discussion of *The Love of
an Unknown Soldier* had been written.[38] The Canadian officer who "found"
the manuscript was in fact its author, Coningsby Dawson, and the publisher
of the book, John Lane of the Bodley Head Press, knew this. For Coningsby
Dawson, in addition to being a subaltern in the artillery corps of the Canadian
army, was also an author whose work John Lane regularly published. So how
does one justify using the product of a literary hoax to illustrate an important
dimension of dignity when it has already been argued that dignity is inexorably bound up with a dedication to the pursuit of truth? Does that not constitute an inconsistency of such magnitude that I should have looked elsewhere for an illustration of dignity in tragic circumstances? I confess that,
when I first discovered the deception, that was precisely my initial reaction.
But in reading Dawson's *Living Bayonets*, which is one of two collections of
his personal letters from the front written to his family,[39] it became clear to
me that *The Love of an Unknown Soldier* was not a hoax in the ordinary
sense—for in a curious way it seems to have been written to assuage Dawson's sense of guilt at still being alive in 1918.

Dawson was born and raised in England. After his graduation from Oxford,
he moved to the United States with the intention of pursuing a degree at the
Union Theological Seminary. Not long after beginning his studies, however,
he had a change of heart concerning his vocation and set out to become a nov-
elist instead. At about this time his parents and sister emigrated from England
to America and Dawson moved back into the family home (now in Taunton,
Massachusetts) so he could concentrate on writing. Just as his literary efforts
were beginning to bear fruit, the war broke out. Dawson felt compelled to get
involved, but since America was not yet committed to the conflict, he headed
north and enlisted in the Canadian army. His first stint at the front lasted from
September 1916 until June 1917, when he was wounded at Vimy. During his
convalescence in England he was asked, because of his literary talents and his
familiarity with America, to engage in public relations work for a time—explaining to Americans what the war in Europe was about, and to the English
what difference America's recent entry into the war would make. Because he
could see the importance of such work in cementing the new alliance between
England and the United States, Dawson agreed to postpone his return to the

front, but somewhat reluctantly, given his sincere and intense desire to be back among his comrades.

Together, his convalescence and his public relations work, which resulted in the publication of his *Out to Win*, kept him out of the front lines for ten months. While he was away, word came to him one day of the death of a close friend.

> My major walked in today. . . . He got concussion of the brain eight weeks ago through a shell bursting in his dug-out. S. was wounded at the same time, but didn't go out till next day. He had got 100 yards from the battery when he and his batman were killed instantly by the same shell. [November 11, 1917]
>
> This hanging round London seems a very poor way to help win a war. I couldn't stand very much of it, however invaluable they pretended I was, when my pals are dying out there. Poor old S.! He's in my thoughts every hour of the day. He was always getting new photos of his little daughter. He longed for a Blighty that he might see her again. He was wounded, but stopped on duty for two days. At last, only one hundred yards down the trench on his way to the dressing-station a shell caught him. He was dead in an instant. Before the Vimy show two of our chaps in the mess had peculiar dreams: one saw D's grave and the other S's. Both S. and D. are dead. The effect that all this has on me is not what might be expected—makes me the more anxious to get back. I hate to think that others are going sleepless and cold and are in danger, and that I am not there. [November 15, 1917][40]

The reader will no doubt recognize the detailed similarity in the fates of Charlie S. (Dawson's close friend) and Jack Holt.

These remarks to his family were written in November 1917. From then until Dawson's return to the front in April 1918,[41] his letters were filled with explanations of his desire to return to the fighting—explanations that he felt his family might need, since they knew that he had been asked to continue with his public relations work, which would have kept him safely in London, and that he had refused the request. Most revealingly, in his letter of December 10, 1917, Dawson wrote to his father:

> I wonder if you've reached the point yet where you don't think that dying matters? I suspect you have. You remember what [Teddy] Roosevelt said after seeing his last son off, "If he comes back he'll have to explain to me the why and how." That's the Japanese spirit—honour demands when a man returns from battle that he can give good reasons why he is not dead. Others, his friends and comrades, are dead; how does he happen to be living? In that connection I think of Charlie S., lying somewhere in the mud of Ypres, with an insignificant cross above his head. He won a dozen decorations which were not given him. He had a baby whom he had only seen once. He was my pal. Why should I live, while he is dead?[42]

Given that *The Love of an Unknown Soldier* must have gone to press just a few months after this letter had been written, it is not difficult to believe that, consciously or not, Dawson's motivation for writing it was to produce an alternative autobiography for himself—one in which he shared his friend's fate.

There can be no denying, of course, that our emotional reaction to *The Love of an Unknown Soldier* is intensified by our belief that the subaltern has died at the end of it. And that belief is misleadingly instilled in us. In this sense the work is untrue. But in another more important sense the work is thoroughly truthful. For the sentiments expressed in *The Love of an Unknown Soldier* are the same sentiments that we find expressed in Dawson's letters home. The only difference is that, because the letters in *Carry On* and *Living Bayonets* were addressed to his family, they assume a context of intimate familiarity into which we cannot entirely enter. Passing unexplained references to the details of his homelife occasionally intrude. In contrast, the letters of *The Love of an Unknown Soldier* are entirely self-contained and are addressed, moreover, to the best part of Dawson himself. They reveal him as he would wish to be seen by an adored woman whose love is—temporarily at least— unattainable. In this respect, in *The Love of an Unknown Soldier* we get the truth about Dawson's motivation for fighting and his attitudes toward his comrades and enemies presented in a compressed and purified form. And for the sake of our philosophical discussion, this is what primarily matters—the possible ways of confronting tragic circumstances. As a final consideration, we should recall as well that the difference between dying and not dying at the front turned on trivialities. More often than not it was a matter of where one happened to be standing—here or two yards to the left, say—at a crucial moment. When the prospects of annihilation were that arbitrary, one had best accept the likelihood of one's own death going in. This no doubt is what Dawson meant in suggesting that, ultimately, dying or not dying did not matter. What mattered was making the decision to accept the risk of death and the certainty of suffering for the sake of the Allied cause, and then "playing the game" nobly and generously to the end.

ON AGGRESSION

Dawson felt that the readiness of both Germans and Englishmen to sacrifice themselves for their ideals—ideals that pitted them against each other—constituted an "inconsistency" in need of a resolution that he was unable to discover. But today we need not, and should not, see the matter in this way. For the most part, it was the *very same* impulse that sent Germans on the one hand and Englishmen on the other into war in 1914. Each was defending "his own" against "the outsider." And once war had been declared, that impulse to protect one's own was more than powerful enough to guarantee that the fighting would continue until one or both sides lay exhausted from the effort. To say this, however, is not to deny that there were any ideals at all in play; it is simply to observe that not all—perhaps even not many—of the ideals that motivate men are embraced primarily on the basis of rational deliberation. Consequently, we should not be surprised when groups locked in a death struggle are discovered to be deeply and equally "idealistic" in their motivations.

Ideals of national power and glory, for example, insofar as such power and glory is to be purchased at the expense of other nations, whose subjugation constitutes the pedestal upon which one's own nation is to be exalted, cannot be considered *rational*. For reason is utterly impartial. It entertains no preference at all for the exaltation of *this* nation as opposed to *that* nation. It is only insofar as we emotionally identify with a given nation—and usually for no better reason than that it happens to be where we were born—that we wish to see it exalted above others.

So too the ideal that Dawson himself held in highest regard—the ideal of self-sacrifice—is grounded ultimately, not in reason, but in our emotional attachment to our homes, family, and friends. Ordinarily we have good reason to approve of that emotional attachment, which causes us to care for the welfare of those around us, especially in times of need. But the value of this emotional attachment is questionable when it finds expression in one's willingness to defend one's homeland against all comers—especially if this extends to a willingness to engage even in "forward defense" (as in "the best defense is a good offense"). We understand this inclination to rally to our country's defense and we tend to view it, moreover, as a fundamentally noble impulse. But it is not *reason*'s endorsement that the inclination to defend one's homeland is receiving here; it is *instinct*'s endorsement. For to anyone willing to think the matter through, it should be clear that there is nothing noble in the sentiment "My country, right or wrong." That way lies the willingness of hardscrabble-farmers-turned-Confederate-soldiers to shed their blood for the preservation of a plantation system grounded upon black slavery. That way too lies the willingness of young German soldiers to lay down their lives in defense of a fatherland that is busily herding Jews, gypsies, and other "undesirables" into technologically sophisticated extermination camps. One's homeland, in other words, may be fully deserving of defeat and reform. Insofar as one rallies to its defense nonetheless, one has unwittingly become a tool for the promotion of evil. Yet the inclination to rally round the flag is enormously powerful. Instincts are.

Most of us tend to think that, in contrast to "animal" behavior, human behavior is not significantly governed by instincts. But this quite erroneous presumption is based on a serious misunderstanding of the nature of instinct. As Konrad Lorenz explains,

> The terms often used for various instinctual motivations are frequently tainted by the unfortunate heritage of "finalistic" thinking. A "finalist," in this bad sense of the word, is someone who confuses the question "What for?" with the question "Why?" and thus believes that by demonstrating the species-preserving reason for a certain function he has solved the problem of its causation. As the determinant of a concrete function whose survival value is obvious, such as feeding, copulation or flight, it is tempting to postulate a special impulse or instinct. We are all familiar with the term "reproductive instinct." However, we should not imagine . . . that the invention of such a term provides the explanation of the process in question. . . .
>
> A definite and self-contained function of an organism, such as feeding, copulation, or self-preservation, is never the result of a single cause or of a single drive. The explanatory value of a concept such as "reproductive instinct" or "instinct of self-preservation" is as null as the concept of an "automobile force," which I could use just as legitimately to explain the fact that my ancient car still goes. . . .
>
> A functionally uniform behavior pattern such as feeding or reproduction is always achieved by a very complicated interaction of many physiological causes, whose systematic function has been "invented" and thoroughly tested by the two constructors of evolution, mutation and selection. . . .
>
> In the realm of behavior the hereditary co-ordinations or instinct movements are independent building stones. As unchangeable in their form as the hardest skeletal component, each one cracks its own whip over the organism as a whole.[43]

Instincts, that is to say, are not to be identified with the major drives of feeding, reproduction, and self-preservation, which govern the lives of virtually all animals—even though they do often serve such drives. Instead, instincts are motor reflexes—reflexes that are prompted in each case by quite specific stimuli—reflexes, moreover, that are almost universal within a given species, but which vary remarkably from one species to another. In our own species such reflexes include, for example, the impulse to return a smile, to laugh, to keep time to music, to scratch an itch, and to dodge. One could also describe as instinctive our impulse to blush when embarrassed, and even our sneezing, blinking, and swallowing reflexes.[44] It should be clear, then, that human beings often do act instinctively. William James, moreover, in *The Principles of Psychology*, even goes so far as to suggest that "man has a far greater variety of impulses than any lower animal; and any one of these impulses, taken in itself, is as 'blind' as the lowest instinct can be."[45] The reason that it nonetheless seems to us that we are free of instincts for the most part is that we are conscious of what most of these motor reflexes are good for.

[O]wing to man's memory, power of reflection, and power of inference, they come each one to be felt by him, after he has once yielded to them and experienced their results, in connection with a foresight of those results. In this condition an impulse acted out may be said to be acted out, in part at least, for the sake of its results. It is obvious that every instinctive act, in an animal with memory, must cease to be 'blind' after being once repeated, and must be accompanied with foresight of its 'end' just so far as that end may have fallen under the animal's cognizance.[46]

Thus because we *approve* of the results of scratching, laughing, dodging, swallowing, and so forth, we tend not to think of them as "blind" impulses—even though when we react instinctively we almost always do so without giving it a moment's thought. And our approval of our own instincts, James observes, could hardly be less surprising. For "to the animal which obeys it, every impulse and every step of every instinct shines with its own sufficient light, and seems at the moment the only eternally right and proper thing to do. It is done for its own sake exclusively."[47]

James also explains, however, how reason and instinct can coexist in a species, such as our own, in which both are very highly developed.

[S]ince any entirely unknown object may be fraught with weal or woe, Nature implants contrary impulses to act on many classes of things,[48] and leaves it to slight alterations in the conditions of the individual case to decide which impulse shall carry the day. Thus, greediness and suspicion, curiosity and timidity, coyness and desire, bashfulness and vanity, sociability and pugnacity, seem to shoot over into each other as quickly, and to remain in as unstable equilibrium, in the higher birds and mammals as in man. They are all impulses, congenital, blind at first, and productive of motor reactions of a vigorously determinate sort. *Each one of them is an instinct*, as instincts are commonly defined. But they contradict each other—"experience" in each particular opportunity of application usually deciding the issue. The animal that exhibits them loses the "instinctive" demeanor and appears to lead a life of hesitation and choice, an intellectual life; *not, however, because he has no instincts—rather because he has so many that they block each other's path.*

. . . In other words, there is no material antagonism between instinct and reason. Reason, *per se*, can inhibit no impulses; the only thing that can neutralize an impulse is an impulse the other way. Reason may, however, make an inference which will excite the imagination so as to set loose the impulse the other way; and thus, though the animal richest in reason might also be the animal richest in instinctive impulses too, he would never seem the fatal automaton which a merely instinctive animal would be.[49]

Having established that human beings *are* very much subject to instinctive reactions—reactions, moreover, that "shine with their own sufficient light"—in the context of our discussion of warfare, it is worth turning for a moment to consider the significance of one such instinctive reaction in particular. For although reason and instinct, both highly developed in our species, are able to coexist, they are by no means necessarily in harmony. There are times when a "blind" instinct, aroused by the appropriate stimuli, is sufficiently powerful to sweep reason (and all counterimpulses) out of its path. We will let Konrad Lorenz describe the particular instinctive reaction of interest to us here.

Militant enthusiasm is particularly suited for the paradigmatic illustration of the manner in which a phylogenetically evolved [that is, instinctive] pattern of behavior . . . is prone to miscarry most tragically if not strictly controlled by rational responsibility based on causal insight. The Greek word *enthousiasmos* implies that a person is possessed by a god, the German word *Begeisterung* means that he is controlled by a spirit, a *Geist*, more or less holy.

In reality, militant enthusiasm is a specialized form of communal aggression, clearly distinct from and yet functionally related to the more primitive forms of petty individual aggression. Every man of normally strong emotions knows, from his own experience, the subjective phenomena that go hand in hand with the response of militant enthusiasm. A shiver runs down the back, and, as more exact observation shows, along the outside of both arms. One soars elated above all the ties of everyday life, one is ready to abandon all for the call of what, in the moment of this specific emotion, seems to be a sacred duty. All obstacles in its path become unimportant, the instinctive inhibitions against hurting or killing one's fellows lose, unfortunately, much of their power. Rational considerations, criticism, and all reasonable arguments against the behaviour dictated by militant enthusiasm are silenced by an amazing reversal of all values, making them appear not only untenable but base and dishonourable. Men may enjoy the feeling of absolute righteousness even while they commit atrocities. Conceptual thought and moral responsibility are at their lowest ebb. . . .

The subjective experiences just described are correlated with the following, objectively demonstrable phenomena. The tone of the entire striated musculature is raised, the carriage is stiffened, the arms are raised from the sides and slightly rotated inwards so that the elbows point outwards. The head is proudly raised, the chin stuck out, and the facial muscles mime the "hero face" familiar from the films. Down the back and along the outer surface of the arms the hair stands on end. This is the objectively observed aspect of the shiver!

Anybody who has ever seen the corresponding behaviour of the male chimpanzee defending his band or family with self-sacrificing courage, will doubt the purely spiritual character of human enthusiasm. The chimp, too, sticks out his chin, stiffens his body, and raises his elbows; his hair stands on end producing a terrifying magnification of his body contours as seen from the front. . . . The whole combination of body attitude and hair-raising constitutes a bluff. . . . Our shiver which, in German poetry, is called a *heiliger Schauer*, which means a "holy shiver," turns out to be the vestige of a pre-human vegetative response of causing to bristle a fur which we no longer have.

To the humble seeker of biological truth there cannot be the slightest doubt that militant enthusiasm evolved out of a communal defence response of our pre-human ancestors.[50]

But to say that militant enthusiasm is an instinctive response that all men "of normally strong emotions" feel in the presence of certain stimuli (martial music, for example) is not simply to disparage the response. After all, the strong feeling of solidarity with one's own group, which also characterizes militant enthusiasm, is by and large a useful impulse. It facilitates cooperation, even in trying and dangerous circumstances, and reinforces our determination to succeed—for the sake of the group as a whole. In this sense, militant enthusiasm can be seen to follow the pattern of *all* instincts, which evolve precisely because they offer an edge in reproductive fitness to those who possess them.

In paleolithic times, when small bands of hunters living on the savannas had to cooperate to bring down big game and to fend off the attacks of predators, the readiness to confront danger side by side with one's friends and brothers would have had an enormous survival value—since a single human being, armed only with the most primitive weapons, could expect neither to outrun nor to outfight the other predators that shared its environment. Only through cooperation could humans expect to survive, much less thrive. And thus the instinct to face danger together and head-on, which early humans presumably had *already inherited* from their prehuman primate ancestors (the same prehuman primate ancestors from whom our cousins, the chimpanzees, inherited *their* instinct to face danger together), would have *continued* to be strongly selected for in these circumstances.

But as Lorenz points out, there would have come a time when that instinct to stand side by side and fight as a team against lions, bears, and wolves would shift its focus.

[I]t is more than probable that the destructive intensity of the aggression drive . . . is the consequence of a process of intra-specific selection which worked on our forefathers for roughly forty thousand years, that is, throughout the early Stone Age. When man had reached the stage of having weapons, clothing and social organization, so overcoming the dangers of starving, freezing, and being eaten by wild animals, and these dangers ceased to be the essential factors influencing selection, an evil intra-specific selection must have set in. The factor influencing selection was now the wars waged between hostile neighboring tribes. These must have evolved into an extreme form of all those so-called "warrior virtues" which unfortunately many people still regard as desirable ideals.[51]

Once the harshness of our environment had been reasonably tamed, in other words, the willingness to face danger side by side increasingly found expression on the battlefield rather than in the hunt. It seems plausible as well that, with this shift in focus, the aggression drive would have increased in intensity, since fierceness and brutality had a tendency to pay off in battle in a way that had no parallel in the hunt. We know from history that, as long as battle involved primarily hand-to-hand fighting, the fiercer the combatants were, the greater their likelihood of success, even against superior numbers. (Think, for example, of the terror struck in the hearts of their enemies by the Assyrians, the Vikings, and the Mongols—a terror which meant that many of their battles were won virtually before they had started.) Since the fiercest combatants tended to emerge victorious, and since to the conquerors went the spoils of war—chief among which were the women of the conquered tribes— any hereditary disposition to fierceness would tend to have been more widely propagated in our species.

One can accept the basic correctness of Lorenz's contention that human militant enthusiasm evolved primarily out of a comparatively benign "communal defense response," which grew stronger and fiercer as a result of intertribal warfare, without having to reject other plausible accounts of how the inclination toward violence against other members of our own species evolved in human beings. In evolutionary biology there is often more than one influence supporting the development of a particular trait. Recently, for example, Richard Wrangham and Dale Peterson (in *Demonic Males: Apes and the Origins of Human Violence*) have argued that some measure of violence among young human males—especially that involved in the killing of heavily outnumbered victims by a gang of their enemies—can be attributed to the reproductive benefits that eliminating sexual rivals would have bestowed in the distant past, when our current instincts were largely shaped. This theory, though, should be thought of as complementary, rather than opposed, to Lorenz's account of human aggression, since the intertribal warfare that Lorenz suggests intensified human fierceness no doubt had many different specific causes. Sometimes the seizure of land or other scarce resources (including women) belonging to one tribe by another tribe would be the casus belli. Sometimes the ambush and murder of an isolated male or small group would set off the fighting.

The point of the past few pages, I trust the reader will understand, has not been either to condemn or to applaud militant enthusiasm and the battle-fierceness of our paleolithic ancestors. To say that there are fairly obvious explanations of how this instinct arose in human beings is to acknowledge that it has served a purpose, but it is not to endorse the instinct in question—especially if one recognizes that the circumstances in which human beings find themselves living today are substantially different from those that favored the evolution of the instinct in the distant past. It may be that we can no longer afford to indulge our aggressive instincts in the traditional fashion (that is, in war), given the enormously more powerful weapons that are now available, and the far more indiscriminate forms of slaughter that these make possible. But this is merely the most readily apparent aspect of a much wider problem that now confronts us. According to Lorenz, today the greatest dangers facing our species arise, not from our environment any longer, but from the fact that our instincts, which evolve at a snail's pace across tens of millennia, are seriously "out of sync" and unable to cope with the changing conditions brought about by human cultural evolution, which has been significantly accelerating of late.

Cultural evolution, in our species, has long been bound up with developments in technology, and the pace of technological innovation that has been noticeably increasing in the past few centuries. The more important of our technological innovations—gunpowder, the printing press, plumbing and sewage systems, electric lighting, pesticides, refrigeration, radio and television, computers, improvements in transportation, in fuels, in construction methods, and in medicine—have utterly transformed our environment. On average, we now live much longer and infinitely more convenient lives than did our primitive ancestors. There are also, of course, far more of us living in much closer proximity than ever before. But most problematically, our instinctive inclinations, which were incorporated into the genotype of our species ages ago, when the comparatively stable environment with which we had to contend for thousands of generations was both more natural and more hostile than it is today, are in many respects inappropriate to our changed circumstances. We are not without resources with which to address this growing discrepancy, Lorenz contends, but in order to address it, we must first understand our situation correctly.

> Among the many phylogenetically adapted norms of human social behaviour there is hardly one that does not need to be controlled and kept in leash by responsible morality. This indeed is the deep truth contained in all sermons preaching asceticism. Most of the vices and deadly sins condemned today correspond to inclinations that were purely adaptive or at least harmless in primitive man. Paleolithic people hardly ever had enough to eat and if, for once, they had trapped a mammoth, it was biologically correct and moral for every member of the horde to gorge to his utmost capacity; gluttony was not a vice. When, for once, they were fully fed, primitive human beings rested from their strenuous life and were as absolutely lazy as possible, but there was nothing reprehensible in their sloth. Their life was so hard that there was no danger of healthy sensuality degenerating into debauch. A man sorely needed to keep his few

possessions, weapons and tools and a few nuts for tomorrow's meal; there was no danger of his hoarding instinct turning into avarice. . . . In short, man's endowment with phylogenetically adapted patterns of behaviour [that is, with instincts] met the requirements well enough to make the task of responsible morality very easy indeed. Its only commandment at the time was: Thou shalt not strike thy neighbour with a hand-axe even if he angers thee.

Clearly, the task of compensation devolving on responsible morality increases at the same rate at which the ecological and sociological conditions created by culture deviate from those to which human instinctive behaviour is phylogenetically adapted. Not only does this deviation continue to increase, but it does so with an acceleration that is truly frightening.

The fate of humanity hangs on the question of whether or not responsible morality will be able to cope with its rapidly growing burden. We shall not lighten this burden by overestimating the strength of morality, still less by attributing omnipotence to it. We have better chances of supporting moral responsibility in its ever-increasing task if we humbly realize and acknowledge that it is "only" a compensatory mechanism of very limited strength and that . . . it derives what power it has from the same kind of motivational sources as those which it has been created to control.[52]

The last sentence of this quotation should remind the reader of Hume's contention that it is always our *passions* that provide the impetus to our actions, and that *reason* can at best only indicate where and why our passions are likely to miscarry. Reason cannot directly resist the impulse of a passion, according to Hume; only another passion contradicting the first can be expected to do that. But where two passions are in conflict, reason can often tip the balance in favor of the weaker natural impulse by drawing attention to circumstances that will impede the satisfaction of the stronger impulse—and thus make the satisfaction of the weaker seem like a more sensible, because more achievable, goal. As we saw a few pages ago, William James made much the same argument. Human beings have so many instincts, James contends, that these actually tend "to block each other's path." Even so, however, "there is no material antagonism between instinct and reason." If reason "can inhibit no impulses," nonetheless it can "make an inference which will excite the imagination so as to set loose the impulse the other way."[53] It follows, then, that if we are to avoid the dangers implicit in the growing disharmony between our inherited instincts and our current social circumstances, it is on reason's capacity to change the balance of our impulses that we must rely. But if reason is to play this role successfully, it is crucial that we understand aright what our own most powerful impulses actually are, why we possess them, and how they are liable to lead us into trouble.

Reason can and should analyze and compensate for the discrepancies emerging between our instinctive inclinations and the requirements of our social circumstances. But reason cannot possibly penetrate *all the way through* the inner logic of either our instincts or our social practices. This is because our customs for the most part, and our instincts in their entirety, have arisen *blindly*—through the perpetually ongoing process of natural selection. "In both cases," Lorenz observes,

> the great constructor has produced results which may not be the best of all conceivable solutions, but which at least prove their practicability by their very existence. To the biologist who knows the ways in which selection works and who is also aware of its limitations, it is in no way surprising to find, in its constructions, some details which are unnecessary or even detrimental to survival. The human mind, endowed with the power of deduction, can quite often find solutions to problems which natural selection fails to resolve. Selection may produce incomplete adaptation even when it uses the material furnished by mutation and it has huge time periods at its disposal. It is [hardly] more likely to do so when it has to determine, in an incomparably shorter time, which of the randomly arising customs of a culture make it best fitted to survival. Small wonder indeed if, among the social norms and rites of any culture, we find a considerable number which are unnecessary or even clearly inexpedient and which selection nevertheless has failed to eliminate. . . .
>
> However, even if some social norms or rites are quite obviously maladaptive, this does not imply that they may be eliminated without further consideration. The social organization of any culture is a complicated system of universal interaction between a great many divergent traditional norms of behaviour, and it can never be predicted without a very thorough analysis what repercussions the cutting out of even one single part may have for the functioning of the whole.[54]

Thus in order to avoid the disastrous consequences that occasionally follow from the more than occasional maladaptiveness of both our instincts and our social practices, we must intentionally search for better social arrangements and individual responses than those that natural selection has hit upon by chance. If we do not, we can be certain that from time to time our instincts and social customs will, as they repeatedly have in the past, lead us blindly into catastrophe. (Given our penchant for militant enthusiasm, for example, we should expect to find ourselves engaged periodically in episodes of largely pointless mutual slaughter far into the foreseeable future.) At the same time, however, we must recognize the limitations of reason—specifically, that it can never expect to analyze *exhaustively* either the social organization of an entire culture or even just the inner workings of an individual human being's mind. The reason for this is not merely that the culture and the individual human being is each an extraordinarily complex "system of interaction between a great many divergent norms of behavior," although this is clearly true and important. Just as important, however, is the fact that each is an extraordinarily complex system in a more or less constant state of change as a result of its interaction—much of which is utterly haphazardous—with its environment. Contingency, one might say, is the heart of biology. There are principles, of course, chief among which is natural selection. But the single most compelling and recurrent consideration in biology is that, had *these* two individuals not encountered each other—and they could *easily* have missed each other—*this* product of their interaction would not have resulted. This principle applies, it should be clear, just as readily to social interaction and its consequences as it does to predation, or sexual reproduction, or genetic recombination.[55] And the significance of these countless chance encounters, in evolutionary terms, is that (except for instances of predation) each represents the possible emergence of something entirely unprecedented—something which, in its novelty, just might open up a whole new order of values.[56]

Because of this, the urge to engage in social engineering, in the confident assumption that we know all that there is to know about ourselves and about the physical and cultural worlds in which we live, is *never* justified. But between the illegitimate attempt to reconstruct our social world from scratch and the laissez-faire insistence that *nothing* is to be consciously altered in our social arrangements, there is plenty of room for the implementation of carefully considered piecemeal alterations. And indeed, that quiet desire *not to be wrong* to which was attributed, in the previous chapter, our underlying motivation for the pursuit of truth and justice, will strongly incline us to make such alterations wherever our natural impulses seem to be so far out of harmony with our current social circumstances as to pose significant dangers. But the desire *not to be wrong*, insofar as it is really our prevailing desire, will also prevent us (and with the same measure of insistence) from exaggerating the extent or certainty of our knowledge, and will thus preclude the offering of any "final social vision."

⊷

As was explained in the opening chapter of this work, the traditional Kantian conception of dignity has been seriously undermined by two important post-Kantian developments in Western thought. Evolutionary biology, for those who take it seriously, has effectively refuted Kant's assumptions that nature has a purpose, an important part of which is the cultivation of human good will, and that our faculty of reason is ideally suited to determine on a priori grounds the requirements of morality. Equally threatening to the Kantian conception of dignity has been the emergence, in both economic and political thought, of sophisticated theories stressing the benefits of allowing decision-making processes to be governed almost entirely by the pursuit of self-interest. In light of these challenges to Kant's insistence on the clarity, simplicity, and unconditionality of the moral law, in the past three chapters a somewhat different conception of dignity has been offered—one that remains committed to Schiller's (Kantian) view that dignity is self-restraint exercised in the service of morality, but which also stresses the limitations of our understanding, in many instances, of precisely what morality requires of us. This new conception of dignity, however, must itself be tested more rigorously than it has been so far against the challenges posed, on the one hand, by evolutionary biology, with its contention that only the fit survive, and on the other, by the harsh realities of the political economic sphere. Is the cultivation of dignity even a meaningful option, given what evolution and political economics reveal about human nature and the conditions governing our interactions with one another? This will be the focus of the next three chapters.

NOTES

1. As Hans-Georg Gadamer puts it in *Truth and Method* (second revised edition, Crossroad, 132), "What is experienced in such an excess of tragic suffering is something truly common. The spectator recognizes himself and his own finiteness in the face of the power of fate. What happens to the great ones of the earth has an exemplary significance." See also Martha Nussbaum, *The Fragility of Goodness* (Cambridge: Cambridge University Press, 1986), 387–91.

2. Walter Kaufmann, *Tragedy and Philosophy* (Princeton: Princeton University Press, 1968), 235.

3. Kaufmann, *Tragedy and Philosophy*, 213.

4. Antigone, for example, knows full well that Polyneices has proven himself to be a traitor to Thebes and thus in some sense deserves the disgrace of having his corpse left unburied, just as Creon knows full well that his kinsman Polyneices was Antigone's brother and thus has a claim to a proper burial from her. Neither Antigone nor Creon is ignorant of what the other knows; they simply disagree—and irreconcilably so—as to which is the more *important* of the two claims.

5. Today it is difficult for many people even to comprehend how this argument could have seemed convincing a century and a half ago. And that, of course, is precisely the point: that perspectives—and the values that inform them—change across generations. Today the intellectually fashionable, and almost equally erroneous, claim is that "there is no biological basis for racial differentiation." In biological terms, however, races, while not constituting separate species, do constitute separate *subspecies*. The historical irony is that, no sooner did the colonization of the New World and the black slave trade begin, than the process of allopatric speciation, which had been carrying the genotypes of the "red," "white," and "black" races away from each other for thousands of years during the relative isolation of those races, and which inevitably would in fact have led them to become separate species had it been allowed to continue unchecked for long enough, was abruptly reversed, and interracial breeding began to knit the human races more tightly

together. In other words, it was European seafaring and colonization that halted the evolutionary divergence of Caucasians, Amerindians, and Negroes. Such divergence as had already occurred, however, was responsible for the disastrous epidemiological consequences for Amerindians of their first contact with Europeans. See William H. McNeill, *Plagues and Peoples* (Garden City: Doubleday, 1976), chapter 5. (I hasten to add, moreover, that none of this biology was understood by those nineteenth-century polemicists who were convinced that blacks were subhuman.)

For an explanation of the principles of allopatric speciation, see Ernst Mayr, *Toward a New Philosophy of Biology* (Cambridge: Harvard University Press, 1988), especially chapters 19 ("The Species Category") and 21 ("Processes of Speciation in Animals").

6. Just in case there is any danger of misunderstanding, it should be emphasized that here "meeting the challenge of value-revision" does not necessarily imply *changing* one's values; it means instead being genuinely *prepared to change* one's values should it become clear that change is warranted. And that means, of course, being prepared to be *shown* that change is warranted.

7. See Aristotle, *Nicomachean Ethics*, book I.

8. That is, from the District of Columbia, which sits south of the Mason-Dixon Line, and over which Congress exerts the equivalent of state-level political authority.

9. For an exhaustive account of events surrounding the introduction of the Gag Rule and of Adams's struggle to get it overturned, see William Lee Miller's *Arguing about Slavery* (New York: Knopf, 1996).

10. In, among other places, the "House Divided" speech of 1858.

11. To say this does not imply, of course, that all or even most Northerners went to war with the conscious intent of freeing the slaves. What it does imply is that the war would not have occurred *without* the sectional disagreement over slavery, and that those who were directing the Northern war effort saw the emancipation of the slaves as a primary war aim. Of course, preserving the Union was *also* a primary war aim, but one is not compelled to choose between these as explanations of why the war was fought, since had the Union *not* been preserved there could have been no emancipation of the slaves.

12. Nussbaum, *The Fragility of Goodness*, 79.

13. Enormous misery is all that is required, as Kaufmann makes clear. Thus the sack of Troy, for example, was also a favorite theme of tragedians.

14. Thus in the end the various small concessions made by the South — in agreeing to, for example, the termination in 1808 of the importation of new slaves from Africa, and the Missouri Compromise of 1820 — were quite inadequate to produce a lasting resolution of the sectional dispute and prevent civil war. The first of these represented no more than a small concession, of course, because the natural population increase of blacks in the South was generating more than enough new slaves to satisfy the demand for labor in any event.

15. The Civil War, however, was morally justified *only* as a struggle to free the slaves. That imperative in turn justified the preservation of the Union by force. But those soldiers fighting for the Union who had no concern for the freedom of blacks were in fact fighting in a far *better* war than they realized — for aside from the neces-

sity of freeing the slaves, there was no compelling *moral* reason to preserve the Union.

16. But these are rarer than they might seem to be at first, since wars can be provoked by hostile foreign policy as well as by military invasion. Poland in 1939, for example, could claim to be defending itself against unprovoked aggression by Germany. The Soviet Union in 1941 most certainly could not, given its own record of aggression between 1939 and 1941 in Poland, Finland, and the Baltic states, and earlier in the Ukraine.

17. Niall Ferguson, *The Pity of War* (New York: Basic Books, 1999), 448–56.

18. *The Love of an Unknown Soldier* (Toronto: McClelland, Goodchild & Stewart, 1918), 16.

19. *The Love of an Unknown Soldier*, 11–13.

20. *The Love of an Unknown Soldier*, 13.

21. *The Love of an Unknown Soldier*, 25–26. We learn later that this nurse, grimly working her way nearer and nearer to the front, was subsequently killed in a German artillery barrage.

22. *The Love of an Unknown Soldier*, 39.

23. *The Love of an Unknown Soldier*, 52–53.

24. *The Love of an Unknown Soldier*, 27–28.

25. *The Love of an Unknown Soldier*, 62–63.

26. *The Love of an Unknown Soldier*, 46, 47–48.

27. *The Love of an Unknown Soldier*, 151.

28. *The Love of an Unknown Soldier*, 203–4.

29. *The Love of an Unknown Soldier*, 92–93.

30. *The Love of an Unknown Soldier*, 81.

31. See John Horne and Alan Kramer, *German Atrocities, 1914: A History of Denial* (New Haven: Yale University Press, 2001), 28–29, 32–34, 120–22.

32. Coningsby Dawson, *Living Bayonets* (London: John Lane The Bodley Head Press, 1919), 132.

33. *The Love of an Unknown Soldier*, 66–68.

34. *The Love of an Unknown Soldier*, 75.

35. *The Love of an Unknown Soldier*, 187.

36. *The Love of an Unknown Soldier*, 154–55.

37. *The Love of an Unknown Soldier*, 50.

38. For drawing to my attention first the likelihood, and then, somewhat later, the clear proof, that Coningsby Dawson was the author of *The Love of an Unknown Soldier*, I owe thanks to Jim Steel and Malcolm Dawson, both of St. Catharines, Ontario. Jim Steel is a First World War historian, and Malcolm Dawson, to whom Jim Steel introduced me, is the grandson of Coningsby Dawson.

39. *Carry On*, published in 1917 and containing the letters that Dawson wrote between July 1916 and February 1917, was edited by his father. *Living Bayonets*, edited by his sister, contains the letters he wrote home between April 1917 and the end of the war. Both books, like *The Love of an Unknown Soldier*, were published in London by John Lane The Bodley Head Press.

40. Coningsby Dawson, *Living Bayonets* (London: John Lane The Bodley Head-Press, 1919), 49–50.

41. After returning to the front, he was wounded again in September 1918, and spent the remaining two months of the war in convalescence.

42. *Living Bayonets*, 67.

43. Konrad Lorenz, *On Aggression* (London: Methuen, 1966), 72–74.

44. William James, *The Principles of Psychology* (Cambridge, Mass.: Harvard University Press, 1981), 1006.

45. James, *The Principles of Psychology*, 1010.

46. James, *The Principles of Psychology*, 1010.

47. James, *The Principles of Psychology*, 1008.

48. Not intentionally, of course, but through the process of natural selection. James was as staunch an adherent of the theory of evolution as any modern biologist is, but even today one finds biologists occasionally lapsing into this intentionalist mode of speaking about "Nature," and the mode of expression was far more widespread, and thus easy to slip into, in 1890 when *The Principles of Psychology* was first published.

49. James, *The Principles of Psychology*, 1013.

50. Lorenz, *On Aggression*, 231–32.

51. Lorenz, *On Aggression*, 34.

52. Lorenz, *On Aggression*, 218–19.

53. James, *The Principles of Psychology*, 1013.

54. Lorenz, *On Aggression*, 224–25.

55. It might even be said to capture the contingency of induced mutation.

56. Thus Lorenz writes, "That the origin of a higher form of life from a simpler ancestor means an increase in values is a reality as undeniable as that of our own existence. None of our western languages has an intransitive verb to do justice to the increase of values produced by nearly every step in evolution. One cannot possibly call it development when something new and higher arises from an earlier stage which does not contain the constituent properties for the new and higher being." *On Aggression*, 195.

Chapter Five

Dignity and the Struggle for Survival
Evolutionary Biology

Today, almost a century and a half since the publication of Darwin's *On the Origin of Species*, a significant number of *reasonably* well-educated people continue to harbor serious doubts about the fundamental correctness of evolutionary theory—and that, of course, primarily because of their prior commitment to some form of religious dogma that is incompatible with a Darwinian account of human origins.[1] But that life-forms do in fact evolve is as firmly established today as is *anything* in science. Our understanding of the subtler details of that process continues to be refined, but no biologist questions the reality of the process itself. As Ernst Mayr, the last of the great architects of the modern evolutionary synthesis, declared a little over a decade ago,

> One hundred and twenty-five years of unsuccessful refutations have resulted in an immense strengthening of Darwinism. Whatever attacks on Darwinism are made in our age are made by outsiders, jurists, journalists, and so on. The controversies within evolutionary biology . . . all take place within the framework of Darwinism. The claims of certain outsiders that Darwinism is in the process of being refuted are entirely based on ignorance. . . . [T]he basic Darwinian principles are more firmly established than ever.[2]

Those basic Darwinian principles are remarkably simple and by now should be quite familiar, yet their implications remain largely unassimilated, even by philosophers.

Biological evolution is the outcome of the—both literally and figuratively— *mindless* repetition of a two-step process. The first step involves the reproduction of organisms within a given species. There are three characteristics that such reproduction must exhibit in order to set the stage for the second step, which involves natural selection. First, there must be variation among the individual members of a species. Second, at least some of the traits with respect to which these individuals vary must be heritable by their offspring. And third, there must be some difference in reproductive success among the individual members of a given species. (That is to say, some individuals must succeed in producing more offspring than do others.) In 1859, when Darwin published the *Origin*, he was fully confident that all three of these necessary conditions were satisfied, but biology was not yet sufficiently advanced to be able to explain why the first two of these conditions will always hold for the reproduction of organisms. Early in the twentieth century, however, biologists began to unravel the mysteries of genetics. As a consequence, we now understand that the process of meiosis accounts for the heritability of parental traits (in sexually re-producing species), while the processes of mutation, genetic recombination, and (in some cases) sexual reproduction account for the wide range of individual variation that we find in all species.

Given that a species is a collection of organisms that do vary in their physiological (and sometimes also in their instinctive behavioral) traits, and that at least some of these variations are heritable by their offspring, it is both possible and inevitable that the environment will have some impact on the reproductive success of individuals. That is to say, inevitably some individuals will be favored by the possession of traits that tend to increase the number of offspring that they are capable of producing relative to the average member of their species. Those traits may, on the one hand, simply improve their chances of reaching the age at which it is possible for them to reproduce *at all*. Thus the traits in question may give them an advantage in escaping predators, in finding food, or in surviving whatever climate changes they may encounter. On the other hand, the traits in question may provide them with a far more immediate advantage in reproductive success. In a sexually reproducing species, for example, one male may be found to be far more attractive by the females that it encounters than are its immediate rivals. Conversely, one female may be rather more optimally fertile than other females of its kind.

From an evolutionary standpoint, all that matters is that there is some *difference* in reproductive success among the various members of a species. As long as this is the case, then, given the heritability of parental traits, there will be some change from one generation to the next in the *frequency* with which various traits appear within the species. Such a change in frequency can be relatively low, virtually unnoticeable, between two successive generations and yet, if the tendency for certain traits to be favored by natural selection[3] is continued across dozens or hundreds of generations, a significant transformation will occur in the average set of characteristics exhibited by the members of the species in question. The environmentally favored traits will become much more widely possessed and thus far more typical of the species than they had originally been. In this way, what biologists refer to as the *phenotype* of the species—which is to say, the typical combination of genetically and environmentally determined physiological and behavioral traits exhibited by members of the species—is gradually transformed. Given enough time, this gradual transformation of the phenotype of the species may well cause it to become something so different from what it originally was that it makes sense to say, not only that the species we have been considering has changed, but that it has changed into a *new* species.

EVOLUTION AND ETHICS

These basic principles of Darwinism, which seem so obvious once they are known,[4] are tremendously important, because they demand to be applied to the *entire realm of life*. In other words, given these principles, and enough time for them to operate, we can account for the entire three-billion-year-long process of the unfolding of life on Earth. And, as we saw in the opening chapter, the recognition that follows inexorably upon such an account—the recognition that there is no creative work left for God to have done—changes everything in our traditional (that is, theistic) worldview. For if God is *not* the creator of humanity, and thus presumably *not* the ultimate guarantor of justice either, not only do we forfeit the comforting promise of an afterlife, but we must ask as well what becomes of Christian (Judaic, Islamic, etc.) morality—morality that has traditionally been grounded in appeals to *God's will*.

One thing that both could and should happen, of course, is that our new understanding of ourselves as products of evolution should be incorporated into our moral theorizing. But if anything, what is remarkable is the degree to which the implications of evolutionary theory were *excluded* from twentieth-century moral reasoning. There seem to have been two primary reasons for this. On the one hand, there continued to be a great many people who found the implications of evolutionary theory unsettling or unwelcome. These individuals, unsurprisingly, remained committed to some form of either divine command or natural law theory. But on the other hand, even those individuals who would seem to have been comfortable with a naturalistic approach to morality avoided for the most part[5] any explicit references to evolution—almost as if this would have somehow *tainted* their moral reasoning. And that is probably not at all an inappropriate way to put it, since the first attempts to apply the principles of evolution to questions of morality were so crude that they seem to have brought the very idea of linking ethics and evolution into disrepute.

Social Darwinism, the late-nineteenth-century moral theory associated in particular with Herbert Spencer and William Graham Sumner, was predicated on the assumption that natural selection was inherently a *good* thing. Every farmer, after all, knew the practical value of culling his herd or flock—of sending the weakest and least satisfactory calves, lambs, or pullets to the slaughterhouse first and allowing only the best individuals to breed. In the wild, natural selection seemed to accomplish the same useful results. The antelope or zebra herd was kept strong and vigorous by the predation of the lion, given that it was typically the weakest and slowest animals that were taken. By analogy, the struggles of human beings to survive and get ahead could also be seen to favor the "best" individuals. Those who fell behind in work or business were fired or bankrupted, and deservedly so. According to Sumner, moreover (who in this respect advocated a rather more brutal form of Social Darwinism than did Spencer),[6] any and all attempts to alleviate the human suffering caused by this natural "culling" process were misguided.

> Competition . . . is a law of nature. Nature is entirely neutral; she submits to him who most energetically and resolutely assails her. She grants her rewards to the fittest . . . without regard to other considerations of any kind. If, then, there be liberty, men get from her just in proportion to their works, and their having and enjoying are just in proportion to their being and doing. Such is the system of nature. If we do not like it, and if we try to amend it, there is only one way in which we can do it. We can take from the better and give to the worse. . . . We shall thus lessen inequalities. We shall favor the survival of the unfittest, and we shall accomplish this by destroying liberty. Let it be understood that we cannot go outside of this alternative: liberty, inequality, survival of the fittest; not-liberty, equality, survival of the unfittest. The former carries society forward and favors all its best members; the latter carries society downwards and favors all its worst members.[7]

The attentive reader cannot help but sense the equivocation on the word "just" as it is used in this passage. According to Sumner, the individual receives from nature "just [that is, *exactly*] in proportion" to the (worthwhile) effort that he puts in, and consequently his reward is also *just* in the sense of morally appropriate and deserved. But each of these claims is sheer nonsense.

For with respect to the first claim—that individuals are rewarded "just in proportion to their being and doing"—one must never discount the role played by *luck* in the struggle for survival. The principle of natural selection does not imply that in each and every instance the fit survive and the unfit perish. One can be the cleverest, strongest, healthiest, and most attractive member of one's species, and still be struck down by a lightning bolt or a landslide before one has an opportunity to accomplish *anything* in one's life.

By the same token, one can be the most dim-witted, sickly, and ugly speci-men of one's species and nonetheless stumble, by sheer accident, upon the equivalent of a gold deposit. The fit survive and pass on their genes in greater proportion only *for the most part*, as a statistical trend. But that is all that is required to ensure that a species will evolve in the direction of increasing adaptedness to its environment. With respect to the second claim—that *what-ever* one gets by one's own efforts (and one's good luck, let us not forget) is, by definition, exactly what one *deserves* in a moral sense—it should be clear that the question of *justice* has not even been intelligently raised here. Does the invalid, who is too ill to prepare her own food, much less earn her living, obviously *deserve* to starve to death? Is this what *justice* requires simply be-cause, if she were alone with Nature, this is what would happen? Does the blind man *deserve* to be run down in traffic because no one had an obligation to help him cope with his infirmity? (See Sumner on the nonexistence of any rights other than those that one can wrest from society by force.)[8] These ob-jections, though, are almost too easy to point out. Given that Social Darwin-ism is in such thorough disrepute today, taking the trouble to refute its tenets is almost like beating a dead horse. *Almost*. For while the *name* "Social Dar-winism" is in disrepute, most of the movement's central tenets, stripped of their pseudo-biological justifications, are still embraced by libertarians.

Social Darwinism, one might say, takes what most people would identify as selfishness and ruthlessness and attempts to recast these as if they were the virtues of prudence and industriousness. Moreover, it is *almost* possible to do this convincingly—for the simple reason that prudence and industriousness, unchecked by any consideration for the well-being of others, *are* selfishness and ruthlessness. But why, one might ask, does the Social Darwinist even at-tempt to recast our moral language in this way? If *whatever* happens is good simply by virtue of its happening—if whatever *works* in a given situation is good simply by virtue of its working there—surely there is no need to ap-prove of it beyond acknowledging that it has happened to work. This indi-vidual, let us say, has become wealthy; he also *wished* to become wealthy; so surely whatever he did in order to become wealthy must have been the *right* thing to do. It was clearly the right thing to do in an instrumental sense. The Social Darwinist wants us to accept that it was therefore also the right thing to do in a *moral* sense.

The question one might ask, however, is, *why* does he want our agreement on this? Perhaps the Social Darwinist has such a love for the spectacle of un-bridled competition that the sight of some competitors handicapping them-selves with pointless scruples actually *disturbs* him. Knowing (as he pre-sumes) that these must do less well, given their handicap, perhaps he wishes to see how they would fare when competing with the unscrupulous on equal

terms. That *might* be the explanation. It is also possible, of course, that the Social Darwinist secretly worries that, with respect to moral judgments, he
might be missing something. And thus he seeks our agreement with his "hard-
headed" analysis in order to reassure himself that he has not, in fact, overlooked anything really important. But a more cynical explanation also suggests itself. Perhaps the Social Darwinist's motivation for recasting our moral
language is to insulate certain (customarily condemned) actions against moral
censure. Perhaps he wishes that he and his friends[9] might be thought prudent
rather than selfish, industrious rather than ruthless, and so he attempts to persuade us that selfishness *is* prudence, that ruthlessness *is* industriousness. If
he succeeds, then the selfishness and ruthlessness of him and his friends will
encounter fewer social obstructions, and should pay off more handsomely—
at least for a time. (Only for a time, of course, because in the long run, if he
succeeds, he will encourage selfishness and ruthlessness to become more
widespread. When that state is reached, there will be fewer easy pickings for
him and his friends to take advantage of.) Whatever the explanation may be,
it is fairly clear that if the Social Darwinist ever succeeded in bringing about
the transformation of meaning that he seeks, moral language could and would
soon drop away as superfluous. For to say that a man is powerful *and* good
(or powerless *and* bad) would now be redundant.

Moral language, in other words, only has a role to play where a certain
kind of tension exists between what *should* be done and what all too often
is done. The particular kind of tension that is relevant here, moreover, cannot be accounted for in terms of the discrepancy between expedient or
clever action on the one hand and inexpedient or foolish action on the
other. For where a person is engaged in mere foolishness, there is no *tension* at all. The person in question is not torn between conflicting impulses;
he is simply blind to what expediency requires of him in a given situation.
And if his eyes were suddenly to be opened, and the clever action became
clear to him, there would still be no tension experienced. For he would instantly and happily abandon his foolish action for the clever one. Now consider the case of someone who is blind to what should be done on *moral*
grounds. She too, of course, will experience no tension as long as only one
line of action occurs to her. But if her eyes were to be opened and she were
to recognize what morality requires of her, she would suddenly find herself torn between conflicting impulses. That is because her original selfish
inclination, unlike a foolish intention, does not immediately evaporate the
moment she realizes what should be done.

Among the things that even a cursory familiarity with biology will tend to
reinforce in our awareness is the fact that the inclination of self-interestedness
is fundamental—in the sense that almost all organisms spend most of their

time looking to their own welfare. And of course, if they did not, they would perish in short order. We need to distinguish between this basic self-interestedness of the organism, which is morally neutral, and the sort of selfishness that comes in for moral condemnation, and yet at the same time to recognize that a continuity exists between them. In social species, such as our own, it is widely if somewhat roughly understood (by members of the species in question) what the limits of legitimately self-interested behavior are and where the realm of offensively selfish behavior begins. Self-interestedness, in other words, is by no means an absolute in Nature. It is qualified, in some species, by an impulse to associate with others of one's own kind. This social impulse can mitigate the excessively self-interested (or selfish) inclination in a couple of ways. For on the one hand, if the individual is too blatantly self-interested when he is in the company of others, he will offend his companions. That is to say, his companions will come to recognize that their *own* self-interests must necessarily suffer so long as they tolerate the presence of this exceptionally selfish individual, and they will tend to respond to this insight by excluding him from their company. In due course, the excluded individual, recognizing the costs incurred by being overly direct in the pursuit of his self-interest, will learn to rein in those selfish impulses at least to the point at which others are once again prepared to tolerate his presence. On the other hand, one of the great benefits of association is that, in a species exhibiting intelligence, it readily leads on to cooperation. And again, in order to reap the benefits of cooperation, the individual must learn to rein in—even to temporarily suspend—his selfish inclinations, in the expectation, of course, that in so doing he will gain a more than offsetting reward down the road. In both of these cases, then, it is the *intelligent* pursuit of self-interest that softens the rough edges of self-interestedness.[10] In other words, the *expedient* way to be self-interested is often to be less than obviously self-interested. And the implication of this, clearly, is that the social impulse alone does not quite carry us from the realm of expedient considerations into the realm of moral considerations. For that, something more is needed.

What is needed is the altruistic impulse—which is to say, the impulse to invest some of one's energies in furthering the welfare of others *without* the expectation of reward. Where the altruistic impulse exists, excessively self-interested inclinations are not merely softened by considerations of expediency; they are, to a greater or lesser degree, directly *opposed* by unselfish inclinations—inclinations involving some measure of *sacrifice* on one's own part. Morality arises when the expectation of a measure of unselfish behavior in certain circumstances becomes part of a social tradition. And this explains, of course, why the language of morality presumes a tension between conflicting impulses. For even where—as it is expected to—the unselfish inclination wins the day, it must do so by overcoming the omnipresent self-interested inclination, which is not at all well disposed toward personal sacrifice.

That the altruistic impulse exists, in some species at least, is impossible to deny. The altruistic impulse exists, however, in widely varying degrees of intensity. It ranges from a willingness to make sacrifices *only* for the welfare of one's own young (and even then only for a time), which is widespread among mammals, birds, reptiles, and some insects, to a *total* willingness to sacrifice oneself for the benefit of the colony, which we find in the social insects, such as ants. At the one extreme (of minimal altruism), in other words, we might point to any animal—the sea turtle, say—which goes to the trouble of making a nest for its eggs, but which then abandons its offspring to their fate.[11] At the other extreme (of maximal altruism), we might point to the honeybee, which is prepared[12] to disembowel itself in the act of stinging an intruder in defense of the hive. In our own species, the altruistic impulse typically extends well beyond merely caring for one's own young. Most, if not all of us, tend to care as well about the welfare of our parents and siblings, our friends, our coworkers, even our neighbors—and to be willing to make *some* efforts to improve their welfare.

The interesting thing about humans in this regard, however, is the wide variation in both the *intensity* of the altruistic impulse, and the *range* of others toward whom the altruistic impulse is directed. In many other species, the altruistic impulse, if it exists at all, manifests itself in much the same way and to much the same degree in all members of the species that belong to the same caste or gender. (Thus among honeybees, for example, when the hive is threatened, it is not as if some workers held back so that others might do the stinging—and dying—for them. On a human battlefield, in contrast, one will always find a mix of cowards, stalwarts, shirkers, and "berserkers.") The more *personality* the individual members of a species exhibit, of course, the greater the variation they are likely to exhibit with regard to altruism as well. And in no species is personality quite so highly developed as it is in ours. In large part, of course, this is because we have become extraordinarily *cultural* creatures, and culture provides us with resources (such as spoken language) that enormously enhance the expression of individual personality. An acknowledgment of the significance of this cultural factor in influencing the expression of the altruistic impulse should, I hope, forestall any notion on the part of the reader that I might be implying that the altruistic impulse, as it manifests itself in a particular individual human being, is *simply* determined by his genetic inheritance. There are good reasons for believing that genes have *something* to do with one's character—that is, with the constellation of impulses that move one—but there are equally good reasons for believing that one's upbringing and culture are also importantly character-shaping. And at the moment it has to be acknowledged that we are in no position to say with any conviction just how great a role is played by nature as opposed to nurture. What can and should be admitted, however, is that our genes provide the initial disposition, which is then shaped—to a greater or lesser extent—by the influences of culture and upbringing.

Regardless of how, exactly, the altruistic impulse is produced in human beings, it is tempting, and far from implausible, to attribute much of the widespread disagreement about what morality actually requires to the variations that exist in our species with respect to the intensity and objects of our altruistic impulses. One might suggest, in other words, that those who find Social Darwinism convincing are prone to feel only a minimal altruistic impulse. This would account for their placing (what most people would consider to be) inordinate emphasis on the *naturalness* of the parent's desire to see his children prosper, and thus on the naturalness (and supposed appropriateness) of the parent's exploiting others *in order* to see his children prosper as much as possible.[13] The altruistic impulse here is *minimal* in that it is directed almost exclusively toward one's own young. If we now search for an example of *maximal* altruism finding expression in moral theory, we might consider someone like Peter Singer—that is, someone intelligently committed to animal rights—who, it would seem reasonable to suggest, must be moved by more extensive and more intense altruistic impulses than most of us feel. The idea that higher degrees of altruism generate more extensive ranges of moral obligation is well captured, moreover, by the image of the "expanding circle" of moral concern, which Singer borrows from David Hume.

Hume, as we have seen, argues that morality is ultimately grounded in our sympathetic identification with others. That "sympathetic identification" (or "moral sentiment") might be taken as merely another name for the altruistic impulse. This may not be immediately obvious, especially since Hume himself expected our sympathetic identification with others to be only moderately strong, and to manifest itself primarily in our reluctance to take advantage of those with whom we identify. Does this already qualify as altruism in a biological sense? The answer is, yes, it does. For biological altruism can be defined as the willingness to forgo maximizing one's own fitness for the sake of increasing another's fitness.[14] In this sense, the (uncoerced) willingness to share food that is in scarce supply would obviously be altruistic. But so too would be the *refusal to steal* food that one could clearly get away with, if we assume that stealing the food would increase one's own fitness, but at the expense of its current owner's fitness. Self-restraint, then, constitutes a more moderate but far from unimportant form of altruism. And the impulse to engage in self-restraint as a result of one's sympathetic identification with another individual is as much a dimension of the altruistic impulse as is the impulse toward generosity.

Thus if we accept Hume's analysis of morality in its broad outlines, and register as well the implication from evolutionary biology that there will always be some (possibly considerable) variation in the degrees to which individual human beings feel the altruistic impulse, not only can we explain some of the persistent disagreements that have seemingly always divided us on the subject of what morality requires, but we can also see that some disagreements over ethics almost *have to* remain irresolvable. For on the one hand, the individual whose altruistic impulses are significantly *weaker* than average will always be inclined to deny that morality is as stringent in its requirements as the average person takes it to be, and consequently, where he can, he will cut corners with a clear conscience, and expect others to do the same. On the other hand, the individual whose altruistic impulses are significantly *stronger* than average will always be inclined to conclude that morality requires *more* than the average person presumes and, finding that the majority of people exhibit no desire to meet the standards that seem natural to him, some part of him will perpetually lament human frailty.

Finally, if we understand evolutionary biology correctly, it has to be acknowledged that *Nature* does not prefer or privilege either of these perspectives over the other. It is only human beings—and largely by virtue in each case of their particular and personal degree of altruistic inclination—who find one or the other of these viewpoints "obviously" preferable to its rival. We are left, in other words, with the problem of having to negotiate among ourselves—and *for* ourselves—what morality should be understood as requiring. There is, that is to say, *nothing* that can play the role of authoritative source (neither scripture, nor Nature's intent, nor reason, nor human *telos*) to which we can refer and simply "read off" the requirements of morality.

THE PROBLEM OF ALTRUISM

But if we acknowledge that we are, indeed, among the products of evolution, and that human morality is "merely" the codified expression of our own altruistic impulses, an interesting question arises: how did these altruistic impulses ever manage to evolve in the first place? For it would seem that natural selection should resist their development, since on balance altruism must evidently *reduce* individual fitness, and thus be selected *against*. In raising this question, we are not implicitly embracing the notion that was repudiated a few paragraphs back. We are not, in other words, surreptitiously suggesting now that the altruistic impulse in fact *is* determined entirely by genetic inheritance. But it was remarked as well that our genetic inheritance provides the *initial* component of our behavioral disposition, which is then further shaped by the influences of culture and upbringing. And the genetic inheritance of our species as a whole, while constantly changing in small ways, has very ancient roots—roots that stretch back far farther than do the sophisticated forms of human culture that now play such an important role in determining how we live. It is by no means an illegitimate question to pose, then, if we ask how any initial genetically provided inclination toward altruism (an inclination that would subsequently be both reinforced and stifled in various ways by social and cultural influences) could have taken hold in our species and persisted in spite of the obvious pressures arrayed against it.

Natural selection, after all, is a process by which (on average) those members of a species that are *less well* able to cope with their environment are either eliminated or reproductively disadvantaged in favor of those members of the species that are *better* able to cope with their environment. And the upshot of natural selection is that those particular traits that enable individuals to cope well with their environment will gradually become more common within the species as a direct result of the greater reproductive success enjoyed by those who already possess them. Conversely, those traits that disadvantage an individual relative to other members of its own species will gradually become less common as a result of the relatively poorer reproductive success of those already possessing the traits in question. (Taken together, these tendencies are what we refer to as the *adaptation* of a species to its environment.) Now the altruist, who invests some of her own limited resources in improving the welfare and chances for success of someone else, in doing so disadvantages herself to some extent relative to the recipient of her generosity and also relative to those selfish individuals who refuse to extend such generosity. Thus it seems, almost by definition, that altruism must involve the reduction of individual fitness and should be among the things that natural selection tends to stamp out. We may personally approve of the inclination to help others, but the biological mystery remains: how does it survive and spread as a dispositional trait, given that those who are unhampered by this inclination are able to invest more of their initial resources in their own survival and reproductive success?

This mystery is one that Elliott Sober and David Sloan Wilson have recently undertaken to clear up in their book *Unto Others: The Evolution and Psychology of Unselfish Behavior*. Before we consider their rehabilitation of group selection, however, we should take a moment to note that there is no difficulty involved in explaining, in terms of natural selection, why individuals should be "altruists" in the very weak sense of being willing to help their own offspring. The individual who possesses a heritable disposition to care for her young will, all other things being equal, presumably raise more of her offspring to maturity than will others of her species that happen to lack such a disposition. This in itself will ensure that any heritable disposition to care for one's young that might emerge should gradually become more common within a given species (since a percentage of the disproportionately numerous mature offspring of a caring parent will themselves have inherited the caring disposition and will in turn, by virtue of their own exceptional reproductive success, pass that disposition on to a disproportionate share of future members of their species). Thus the problem that we have just identified is not one of accounting for what we have been calling the "minimal altruism" involved in making sacrifices for one's own young. The problem arises only with respect to altruism that is directed toward nonrelated individuals or toward individuals that are only distantly related to the altruist.

There was a time, during the 1950s and early 1960s, when some biologists routinely accounted for this stronger form of altruism by means of poorly thought out explanations appealing to group selection. Their argument ran roughly as follows: since behavior that directly disadvantages the individual engaging in it (the honeybee sacrificing itself for the sake of the hive, say) often has fairly obvious benefits for the *group* to which the individual belongs in *its* competition with rival groups, presumably the process of adaptation *at the group level* would promote the spread of appropriate dispositional traits among the individual members of the group. Using this line of reasoning, V. C. Wynne-Edwards, for example, argued that in a number of species individual organisms voluntarily regulate their reproduction and their consumption of food *so that* the population as whole can avoid crashing to extinction in times of scarcity. (That is, they exercise self-restraint for the sake of the general welfare.) As it happened, Wynne-Edwards's *Animal Dispersion in Relation to Social Behavior* was published at a rather inopportune moment. A backlash against this common but rather slipshod way of accounting for otherwise puzzling adaptations was about to set in, and given the timing of his book's appearance—in 1962—Wynne-Edwards became the favorite whipping-boy for the critics of group selection arguments.

The most important of these critics was George C. Williams, whose *Adaptation and Natural Selection* appeared in 1966. According to Sober and Wilson,

> Williams touched a nerve, and his vigorous rejection of adaptations that exist for the good of the group spread quickly through the community of evolutionary biologists. For the next decade, group selection theory was widely regarded as not just false but as off-limits, as far as serious evolutionary thought was concerned. At best, group adaptation was regarded as a theoretical possibility but as so

enormously unlikely that alternative explanations should be preferred whenever possible.[15]

In *Adaptation and Natural Selection*, Williams offered compelling arguments based on the principle of parsimony for preferring explanations of adaptation that are couched entirely in terms of individual selection. However, at one point in the book he also presented something of a critical test case for group selection.

In certain circumstances, he argued, it would be highly advantageous for a species if it could increase its numbers more quickly than usual. (This is the case, for example, when a species' overall numbers are dangerously low.) So too, in other circumstances, it would be highly advantageous for a species if it could slow down its normal population growth. (This is the case, just as Wynne-Edwards pointed out, if the species is overexploiting the resources of its habitat.) One obvious way in which each of these beneficial results could be achieved would be if the sex ratio of a species changed in response to relative population intensity. Thus when the population was dangerously low, the situation could be improved by having more females produced as a proportion of the overall population. Conversely, when the population was dangerously high, the situation could be improved by having a greater proportion of males produced. (The reason why this would be useful, of course, is that population growth is limited—except in cases of truly extreme gender imbalance—by the number of ova produced rather than the number of sperm.) From these considerations, Williams inferred that, if group selection *were* a significant factor in evolutionary development, there should be *some* evidence of sex ratios varying in accordance with the population trajectory of a species.

On the other hand, if individual selection is *always* the principle that governs evolutionary development, what one should expect, in contrast, is a consistently steady sex ratio of roughly one-to-one.

To see this, imagine a group that is initiated by two fertilized females, S and A, who produce sex ratios of 1:1 and 9:1, respectively. Female S has 5 daughters and 5 sons, while female A has 9 daughters and 1 son, for a total of 14 females and 6 sons in the next generation. When these individuals mate and reproduce, each female will have ten offspring but the average male will have $140/6 = 23$ offspring. Male fitness is higher than female fitness because the average male sires the offspring of more than two females. If we evaluate the fitnesses of the original S and A females by counting their grandchildren, we discover that S has $5(10)+5(23) = 165$ grandoffspring while A has only $9(10)+1(23) = 113$ grandoffspring. In this population males have more offspring than females because they are in the minority, so the female who produced more sons is fitter than the female who produced a preponderance of daughters. Producing an excess of daughters, therefore, is an act of altruism—it benefits the group while decreasing the mother's fitness. In general, any deviation from a 1:1 sex ratio at birth will cause the minority sex to have the higher relative fitness within groups, at which point genes that return the sex ratio to 1:1 will be favored.[16]

The group-selection model and the individual-selection model, in other words, generated clear-cut and quite different predictions about sex ratios—predictions that could be more or less readily tested with empirical data.

Williams then ran the test. He surveyed the information that he could find on sex ratios in the scientific literature and arrived at the following conclusion:

> Despite the difficulty of obtaining precise and reliable data, the general answer should be abundantly clear. In all well-studied animals of obligate sexuality, such as man, the fruit fly, and farm animals, a sex ratio close to one is apparent at most stages of development in most populations. Close conformity with the theory is certainly the rule, and there is no convincing evidence that sex ratios ever behave as a biotic adaptation [that is, evolve by group selection].[17]

In Williams's estimation, this constituted fairly conclusive evidence that group selection was *not* a significant factor in evolutionary development, and most biologists agreed with him. According to Sober and Wilson,

> After *Adaptation and Natural Selection*, group selection was a dead issue for most evolutionary biologists. Dead but not forgotten. On the contrary, the rejection of group selection was celebrated as a scientific advance, comparable to the rejection of Lamarckism, that allowed biologists to close the book on one set of possibilities and concentrate their attention elsewhere.[18]

The irony, however, was that in fact some of the best evidence available *in favor* of group selection related precisely to sex ratios, and that this evidence was about to be supplied by, of all people, W. D. Hamilton, whose theory of inclusive fitness or kin selection (first presented in 1963) was almost as important as Williams's own work in undermining the credibility of group selection accounts of the evolution of altruism.[19]

In 1967 Hamilton published an article entitled "Extraordinary Sex Ratios,"[20] in which he provided a number of examples of female-biased sex ratios that he had come across in the scientific literature, and in which he offered as well a theory to account for their evolution. As Sober and Wilson explain, Hamilton framed his theory in terms of a parasite species that is searching for hosts. Each host is colonized by a certain number of females, whose progeny mate randomly among themselves before dispersing in search of new hosts. All mating takes place within groups prior to dispersal by the females.[21]

In a scenario such as this, the two reproductive strategies we have been considering may *each* enjoy a particular kind of advantage.

Imagine for a moment, as shown in figure 5.1, that we have six such parasites taking advantage of three hosts. Let us suppose the parasites to be a type of wasp. Each of the hosts is parasitized by two of the wasps, which each lay a clutch of four eggs. One of the wasps, however, possesses genes that cause female-biased sex ratios, and thus of her four offspring, only one will be male. When the wasp larvae mature into adults, they will mate among themselves before the females disperse in search of new hosts to parasitize. Notice, however, that, because one of the original females possessed genes causing female-biased sex ratios, there will be five female wasps emerging from the first host, as opposed to the four females emerging from each of the other two hosts. Because of this, a greater number than usual of second-generation offspring will be produced for *both* the original female with the aberrant genes relating to sex ratio *and* the normal original female whose good fortune it was to choose the same host to parasitize. In fact, the female producing the normal (even) distribution of male and female offspring benefits significantly more than does the female producing three daughters and just one son. Together, they will have produced twenty second-generation offspring (four by each of the five females emerging from the first host). But the proportion of their own chromosomes carried by those twenty grandoffspring—given equally successful and fully random mating among their first-generation offspring—will favor the normal original female in the ratio of 8:7. (The ratio is established as follows. The normal female's genetic contribution to the second generation of offspring will be $20 \times \frac{3}{5}$ (males) $+ 20 \times \frac{2}{5}$ (females) as opposed to, for the aberrant female, $20 \times \frac{1}{5}$ (males) $+ 20 \times \frac{3}{5}$ (females). This gives us a proportion of $21\frac{1}{3}$ to $18\frac{2}{3}$ or 8:7.)

Thus the act of producing a disproportionate number of daughters reduces the fitness of the "*altruist*" (in the sense defined four paragraphs ago) relative to the fitness of the normal wasp that laid its eggs in the same host. At the same time, however, relative to the average normal wasp (of which there were five, recall), the altruist has done well. In fact, in terms of reproductive fitness, she has outperformed them by a margin of $9\frac{1}{3}$ (that is, $20 \times \frac{7}{15}$) to $8\frac{9}{15}$ (that is, $[4 \times (16 \times \frac{1}{2}) + 1 \times (20 \times \frac{9}{15})] / 5$). Given *these* particular circumstances, then, we can expect that the altruist's aberrant genes governing sex ratio will—temporarily at least—tend to become more common within the population of wasps. As they do, however, the circumstances favoring their

Altruism in Sex Ratios

Wasp	Mating Swarm	Second Generation Offspring	Original Wasp's Genetic Share
▷ ♀♀♂♂			▬▬▬▬
Host	⇨✴⇨	20	
▶ ♀♀♀♂			▬▬▬▬
Altruist			
▷ ♀♀♂♂			▬▬▬
Host	⇨✴⇨	16	
▷ ♀♀♂♂			▬▬▬
▷ ♀♀♂♂			▬▬▬
Host	⇨✴⇨	16	
▷ ♀♀♂♂			▬▬▬

Figure 5.1. Altruism in Sex Ratios.

spread will gradually disappear. For the reproductively normal wasp that parasitizes the same host as an altruist will always enjoy a significant fitness advantage over the latter, and thus, as the proportion of reproductive altruists increases, and with it the likelihood of a normal wasp having the good fortune of sharing a host with such an altruist, the overall fitness advantages of being an altruist will disappear. At that point, a stable balance in the proportion of reproductive altruists and reproductively "selfish" types within the population as a whole will have been reached. (It should be stressed that "selfish" is being used here merely as a contrast term to "altruist." We will want some other contrast term than "normal" in order to avoid even implicitly prejudging the question of where precisely the stable balance of reproductive strategies will be reached. It is at least conceivable, in other words, that the reproductive altruist might in time become the *normal* type. On the other hand, clearly there is no basis for objecting to the behavioral disposition of the wasp inclined to produce an even sex ratio in its offspring, and thus the quotation marks around "selfish.")

This little model illustrates the key factors that, according to Sober and Wilson, make the evolution of altruism—even in the more customary sense of intentional self-sacrifice—possible. The main point is that, while group selection certainly *can* play a role in shaping evolutionary development, it never simply displaces individual selection—for traits benefiting the individual *alone* will always play their part in improving its fitness. For this reason, group selection actually does shape evolutionary development *only* when it is sufficiently strong to offset the countervailing influence of individual selection.

It is time to define our terms a little more precisely. *Group selection* is the tendency of traits (especially behavioral traits) that promote *group* welfare to increase the relative fitness of the individual possessing such traits (or engaging in such behavior). In our model, for example, the altruist benefits by virtue of the larger number of second-generation offspring produced by those females emerging from the first host, and this is a group-selection benefit because it extends as well to the normal female who parasitized the same host. At the same time, the altruist suffers a disadvantage in terms of individual selection in that she reaps a smaller than average proportion of the group benefits for which she is responsible. *Individual selection*, in contrast to group selection, is the tendency of traits that immediately benefit the individual, as opposed to any of its conspecifics, to increase the relative reproductive fitness of the individual in question. Thus in our model, the normal wasp enjoying the good fortune of sharing a host with an altruist receives an individual-selection benefit by virtue of her disposition to produce an equal number of male and female offspring. Having produced a greater proportion of the minority sex (males, in this case), her chromosomes will be more widely represented among the second-generation offspring than will those of her altruistic neighbor. The point of the model, however, is that, in spite of the individual-selection disadvantage suffered by the altruist, given *these* particular circumstances, individual- and group-selection influences combine to leave her better off in terms of reproductive fitness than her *average* conspecific. Thus, providing that she is not bound to compete directly *only* against free-riding beneficiaries of her own efforts, her altruistic trait can spread, to some extent, and become a reasonably common characteristic of her species.

Here is Sober and Wilson's analysis of the situation we have just been considering.

> What is required to produce this interesting . . . result? First, there must be more than one group; there must be a *population of groups*. Second, the groups must *vary* in their proportion of altruistic types. Third, there must be a direct relationship between the proportion of altruists in the group and the group's output; groups with altruists must be *more fit* (produce more individual offspring) than groups without altruists. Fourth, although the groups are isolated from each

other by definition . . . there must also be a sense in which they are *not* isolated (the progeny of [all] groups must mix or otherwise compete in the formation of new groups). These are the necessary conditions for altruism to evolve in the multigroup model.[22]

The fourth condition mentioned here is extremely important. For as we saw, the altruist, by definition, always does somewhat less well than the "self-ish" types *within* her own group. Let us consider, then, how altruism would fare as a heritable trait within a population of permanently isolated groups, one of which initially contains a number of altruists. In this scenario, even though the presence of altruists within the favored group may cause it to grow more rapidly than comparable-sized groups of conspecifics containing *no* al-truists, the benefits of such exceptional growth will accrue in greater propor-tion to the *non-altruists* within the mixed group (whom we might call "free-riders"). It follows from this that, even if the proportion of altruists in the global population (that is, the population of the entire species) temporarily in-creases because of the more rapid growth of the group to which they belong, eventually the fact that they are relatively less fit than the non-altruists within their own group will lead to their extinction (as a type) within that group — and thus of course also within the species as a whole. Without an opportunity to mix with the population at large, in other words, and thus to escape the dis-advantage of having to compete perpetually with the relatively more fit free-riding type, "the global increase in the frequency of altruists . . . will be a tran-sient phenomenon of little interest."[23]

Another important implication that follows from the fact that an altruist is always (again, by definition) at a reproductive disadvantage relative to a free-rider in the same group was briefly touched on a few paragraphs ago, and is worth elaborating. Even when the four necessary conditions that Sober and Wilson have specified above are satisfied, there is a limit[24] on how large a percentage of the overall population altruists can come to constitute. This is because, as the overall proportion of altruists increases, an increasing propor-tion of non-altruists will reap the benefits of belonging to a mixed group — as opposed to having to associate exclusively with other "selfish" types like themselves. Since the fitness benefits enjoyed by the "selfish" members of a mixed group are greater than the benefits enjoyed by the altruists in the same group, the presence of free-riders constitutes a drag on the spread of altruism as a heritable trait. And since the proportion of free-riders increases along with (and indeed, *because* of) the increase in the proportion of altruists, the spread of altruism must gradually slow down as an equilibrium frequency be-tween "selfish" and altruistic types within the species is approached. As Sober and Wilson point out, "The equilibrium frequency is reached when the advantages of freeloading within groups are exactly counterbalanced by the disadvantages of being in groups that lack altruists."[25]

So far we have been considering the evolutionary implications of a fairly simple model—one in which altruism always generates predictable reproductive benefits and in which altruists and "selfish" types make no special effort to identify each other *as* either altruists or potential free-riders. They neither avoid nor seek each other out, in other words, but simply accept the consequences of their chance associations. Within the parameters of such a model, moreover, we have seen that, if certain rather stringent conditions are satisfied, some measure of altruism as a heritable dispositional trait *can* evolve through natural selection.[26]

But as human beings with moral inclinations, the kind of altruism that primarily interests us (our own) is not at all adequately represented by means of this simple model. It is not that anything the model shows us is inapplicable to our own far more complicated situation. The advantages of free-riding, after all, pose a seemingly perpetual threat to altruistic impulses and pretty much guarantee that the altruist will almost always be under-rewarded for his contributions to group welfare. This holds true for humans just as much as it does for parasitic wasps. Rather, it is that, when we turn to human interaction, there are suddenly so many additional factors to consider. We do, for example, try to determine to what extent our neighbors possess either selfish or generous inclinations. And having determined that someone's natural disposition is unduly self-interested, we try either to change that person's disposition, through social conditioning, or at the very least to avoid being exploited by the potential free-rider. Nor is maximizing reproductive fitness by any means the sole—or even the primary—consideration when it comes to assessing human altruism. (When young people, for example, voluntarily entertain the residents of old folks' homes, they exhibit admirable altruistic impulses in doing so, but impulses that quite clearly do *not* increase the reproductive fitness of the elderly beneficiaries of their visits.) We need to consider, then, how the picture is changed and complicated with the introduction of learned and culturally transmitted patterns of behavior.

CULTURE AND THE PROMOTION OF VALUES

The first thing to notice, as we shift our gaze from the genetic to the cultural transmission of behavioral traits, is that the various conditions that were specified at the beginning of this chapter as being *necessary* for evolution are also, when taken collectively, *sufficient* conditions for evolution. Those conditions, again, are: (1) a variation of traits exhibited across a range of individuals in a species, (2) the heritability of some portion of those traits, and (3) a variation in reproductive success resulting from the advantages and disadvantages associated with the heritable traits relative to a given environment. Given these conditions, there *will be* some form of evolutionary development. But as a number of people have pointed out (E. O. Wilson and Richard Dawkins most prominently, in *Sociobiology* and *The Extended Phenotype*, respectively), all three of these necessary conditions are satisfied by *cultures* as well as by biological organisms.

That there is a variation of traits across cultures should be obvious. The French speak French and tend to prefer wine; the Germans speak German and tend to prefer beer. Americans celebrate their independence on the Fourth of July, Thanksgiving in November, and play four-down football; Canadians celebrate their independence on the first of July, Thanksgiving in October, and play three-down football. On and on we could easily go. It should also be fairly apparent that many of these traits are heritable within a culture. American children are raised to understand that the day on which their nation's independence *should* be celebrated is July fourth, not July first. And thus July Fourth continues to have a stable meaning within American culture for generation after generation. As Sober and Wilson point out,

> the fact that a behavior is transmitted culturally should not be taken to mean that it is nonheritable. Cultural differences between human groups are often stable over long periods of time and are faithfully transmitted to descendant groups. They are heritable in the sense that offspring units resemble parent units, which is all that matters as far as the process of natural selection is concerned.[27]

Finally, it should also be clear that some traits have significantly greater survival value than others. For example, the First Amendment of the American Constitution (guaranteeing the freedom of speech and of religion) is still in effect more than two hundred years after it was introduced. In contrast, the Eighteenth Amendment (prohibiting the sale of liquor) was repealed less than fifteen years after its introduction.

But here a potential ambiguity arises. We need to distinguish between the survival value of cultural traits *themselves* and the survival value that traits confer to the *possessors* of the traits in question. It is the former of these two meanings of "survival value" that we illustrated just now in comparing the First Amendment's longevity to the Eighteenth Amendment's short-livedness. For an illustration of the latter meaning, we might consider the Jonestown agricultural commune established in 1977 in Guyana by the American cult leader Jim Jones and about a thousand of his followers. The willingness of Jones's acolytes to do anything and everything that Jones asked of them can be thought of as a cultural trait conferring very *poor* survival value on the community as a whole—which was vividly demonstrated in November 1978 when Jones ordered his followers to drink punch laced with cyanide, and the vast majority of them quite passively complied. In the space of an hour or two, given one of its more deleterious cultural traits, the Jonestown commune ceased to exist.

The same potential ambiguity regarding the meaning of "survival value" can be found, of course, if we consider organisms rather than cultures. Some traits that certain organisms typically possess are actually *disadvantageous* for the survival of the organism itself. Consider, for example, the peacock's extravagant plumage. Only the male of the species sports the enormously long and iridescent tail feathers, and it should be fairly obvious that, by virtue of her comparative nondescriptness, the peahen has, first, a far better chance of going unnoticed by the bird's predators,[28] and second, a better chance than her heavily burdened male counterpart of escaping such predators as do happen to notice her. What goes for the females applies as well, although to a lesser degree obviously, to those males that are somewhat *less* extravagantly endowed than the average peacock. It would seem, then, that natural selection should have worked against the development of the peacock's tail feathers. And if we distinguish, as Darwin himself did, between *natural* selection on the one hand and *sexual* selection on the other, this would be not only a reasonable but also a largely correct conjecture. If predation were the only—or even the chief—factor in play, peacocks would presumably be as physically unassuming as peahens. The reason why the peacock possesses his astonishing tail feathers nonetheless is that, as it turns out, peahens *like* the extravagant tail feathers—and the more extravagant, lustrous, and symmetrical the tail feathers are, the more the peahens like them, and the more eager they are to mate with the owner of the tail feathers in question. Biologists believe that the peahen finds the gaudiest peacock the most attractive because the luster and symmetry of his tail feathers attest both to the quality of his genes and to his freedom from parasites. Thus the more extravagant the display he can produce, the greater the likelihood that he will provide the peahen with healthy and strong offspring. The upshot of this is that the spectacular tail feathers of the peacock have a high survival value *in themselves*—which is to say that, in spite of whatever additional dangers they may subject their owners to from predators (such as foxes), the extravagant tail feathers continue to make their appearance in generation after generation of peacocks.

Here again we find, just as we did in our discussion of how individual and group selection might combine to guide the evolution of sex ratios in a species of parasitic wasps, two distinct and countervailing forces at work in guiding evolution. In the case of the peacock's tail, it is natural selection and sexual

selection exerting pressures that oppose each other—one in the direction of un-
obtrusiveness and the other in the direction of gaudiness. Fundamentally, of
course, all four of these "forces" that we have identified are variations of the
same process: the increasingly frequent manifestation within a species of particular traits that happen to be *reproductively favorable*, given the characteristics of
the species' environmental niche. Where those characteristics are such that cooperation (either conscious *or* unconscious) pays a reproductive reward, group
selection may exert an influence. Where those characteristics include the presence of potential mates exhibiting highly specific and somewhat surprising
tastes in sexual partners, sexual selection may exert an influence. Even group selection and sexual selection, in other words, are still variations of natural selection, the most basic variant of which, however, is individual selection. Thus the
lesson to be drawn from our discussions of peacocks and parasitic wasps is simply that circumstances can arise and (in the case of sex) biological mechanisms
can emerge that render some of the consequences of natural selection highly surprising. (In other words, even less so than ethics can evolutionary biology be
pursued as an a priori discipline.)

One of the more interesting contentions of *Unto Others* is that, when we
turn to a consideration of the evolutionary dynamics of cultures, we find the
emergence of new reinforcement mechanisms, as powerful in their own way
as sexual selection, for promoting the frequency of traits—such as altruistic
behavior—that might have a difficult time evolving if unbridled individual
competition were the only form of natural selection in play. Sober and Wilson open their discussion of *rewards and punishments* as evolutionary mechanisms by considering the case of a typical hunter-gatherer society. It is common in such societies, they point out, for meat to be shared among all
members of the group, even though only a handful do the actual hunting. The
question, of course, is *why* is it shared, given that meat is valuable, often difficult to come by, and initially comes into the possession of only a few members of the group.

Let's call hunting and sharing the *primary* behavior and the rewards and punishments that others confer on hunters the *secondary* behavior. By itself, the primary behavior increases the fitness of the group and decreases the relative fitness of the hunter within the group. If it evolved without the complications of
rewards and punishments, there should be little controversy about calling it altruistic and saying that it evolved by group selection. That is why it seems so
problematic from the standpoint of individual selection. The evolution of the
secondary behavior (the rewards and punishments) can be analyzed in exactly
the same way as the evolution of the primary behavior. By causing another individual to perform an altruistic primary behavior such as hunting and sharing,
the secondary behavior indirectly increases the fitness of the entire group. At the

same time, the secondary behavior is likely to require at least some time, energy, or risk for the individual who performs it. The secondary behavior therefore requires group selection to evolve, just as the altruistic primary behavior would if it evolved without the secondary behavior being present. Economists call this a second-order public goods problem: Any behavior that promotes a public good is itself a public good.

Although the altruistic primary behavior (by itself) and the secondary behavior both require group selection to evolve, there is an important difference between them. The individual costs of the primary behavior are substantial. There is simply no way to hunt game without investing large amounts of time and effort and perhaps also taking risks. That is why the primary behavior intuitively seems altruistic. The individual cost of the secondary behavior might be substantial, but it might also be very small. It is an important fact of human life that individuals can often greatly increase (reward) or decrease (punish) the fitness of others at trivial costs to themselves. It is the low cost of imposing rewards and punishments and the fact that they elicit benefits that make secondary behaviors appear psychologically egoistic rather than altruistic. From the evolutionary standpoint, however, the fact that the cost is trivial does not alter the level at which the behavior evolves. Secondary behaviors evolve *more easily* by group selection than primary behaviors because they are less strongly opposed by within-group [that is, individual] selection, but they still evolve by group selection. The package of primary and secondary behaviors therefore remains a group-level adaptation.[29]

Often all that is required in order to make the imposition of punishments in particular cost-effective is that the group as a whole come to agreement that certain behavior (hunting and sharing, say) is to be approved and other (selfish) behavior disapproved. For once the community as a whole has decided not to tolerate a certain form of behavior, it usually becomes far more time-consuming and potentially painful for an individual to engage in such behavior surreptitiously than it is for someone else to notice and report the improper conduct. This simple fact can radically transform the equations for computing how best to maximize satisfaction of one's self-interest. Even the individual with virtually no natural inclination to share with others can readily be made to appreciate that, if the community so desires, it is in his own best interest to behave *as if* he were the soul of generosity. "The use of secondary behaviors to promote altruistic primary behaviors can be called *the amplification of altruism*," Sober and Wilson suggest. And while "the population structure of many human groups may not be sufficient for primary behaviors to evolve by themselves, [they] may be sufficient for [altruistic] primary and secondary behaviors to evolve as a package."[30]

Of course, altruism is not the only form of behavior that can be amplified through the imposition of rewards and punishments. Because altruism tends to pay dividends for the community as a whole and these dividends are readily foreseeable, it is easy to understand how a group might choose, on the basis of rational deliberation, to reward altruism and to punish what it now calls selfishness. But not infrequently a culture adopts at least some of its social norms on the basis of *mis*understanding. Sometimes, in other words, in some cultures, given the constraints existing on human wisdom, harmless or even beneficial activities are declared taboo. Similarly, detrimental or dangerous activities are sometimes declared worthwhile—even mandatory. And the punishments and rewards that are imposed to reinforce these behavior patterns are just as effective in altering calculations concerning the satisfaction of self-interest. Thus as Sober and Wilson put it,

> virtually any behavior can become stable within a social group if it is sufficiently buttressed by social norms. The costs and benefits that are naturally associated with the behavior are simply overwhelmed by the rewards and punishments that are attached by the social norms.[31]

But even if, *within* a culture, the (primary) behavior patterns that promise success or failure to the individual can be radically reconfigured by the socially agreed upon (secondary) patterns of punishment and reward, there is no way for a culture to escape permanently the natural selection pressures exerted by its environment.

There is often a certain amount of slack in natural selection. That is to say, the struggle for survival is not always equally intense; circumstances matter. Thus even profoundly dysfunctional communities may scrape along for a time. (Even Jonestown in Guyana, which came into and went out of existence at the whim of the charismatic but criminally unstable Jim Jones, managed to survive for about a year.) This explains why it is possible for various cultures that are far more soundly based than this to adopt significantly different norms and customs and nonetheless continue to thrive, often side-by-side. Evolutionary biologists refer to this kind of situation as one in which "multiple stable equilibria" have been achieved. In this case, what the phrase refers to as being in equilibrium are the "packages" of primary and secondary behavior patterns. When these packages are well balanced, they can persist unchanged within a culture for some time because, given the culture's external circumstances and the secondary behaviors to which it is committed, there is no pressure to substantially change its pattern of primary behaviors, and likewise, given the primary behaviors engaged in, there is no serious pressure to change its pattern of secondary behaviors. Individuals within the culture, in other words, are largely content with the standards of conduct expected of them. It is not clear to them that by changing their patterns of behavior they could satisfy significantly more of their needs and desires.

But external circumstances are never permanently stable. Climates change, problems (such as novel diseases) arise that have never been seen before, and in general human history moves on. Here and there extraordinarily clever individuals begin to entertain and then propound ideas that disturb the complacency of their cultures. Elsewhere cultures that were stable in isolation now encounter each other and begin to interact. All of these changed circumstances constitute potential challenges to the stability of the cultures affected. And not every culture's stability will prove equally robust at resisting the disturbances. Under extreme pressures, a culture, like a species, may go extinct. More frequently, a culture is gradually transformed under the pressures of natural selection. That is to say, because they are favored by the new circumstances, some of a culture's longstanding traits become more prominent than they had been formerly. For the same reason, some entirely new traits may be acquired. And at the same time, of course, other of the culture's longstanding traits, given their maladaptedness to the new circumstances, wither away.

In describing the cultural transformations and extinctions of human history in these sorts of evolutionary terms, we must understand that no ultimate value judgments are implied. It is true that when a species or a culture goes extinct, it has in some sense failed one of the tests to which it was put. But just as it is no comment on the worthiness of a species to mention that it has gone extinct (since the vast majority of species ever to have existed on Earth have already gone extinct, and there are excellent reasons for believing that *all* species will eventually go extinct), so it is no comment on the worthiness of a culture or way of life to remark that it has disappeared. We can make the same point, of course, about physiological and cultural *traits*. Just as the physiological trait that has been gradually extinguished within a particular species is not, by virtue of that fact, shown to have been valueless, so too the cultural trait that has been abandoned by a particular society has not been shown to have been worthless as such and in all circumstances. The value of a cultural trait, like the value of a physiological trait for a species, is always relative to an environment. (This does not imply, of course, that just because a trait is found at a given time and place that it *must* have value there. It is always the case, after all, that some traits are in the process of disappearing precisely *because* they are ill-suited where they happen to be found.) Moreover, the same cultural trait that helps a community to cope with one set of circumstances may, when the circumstances change, undermine its chances for success—or even survival—if the community is unable to change its customs quickly enough. For a cultural trait, like a physiological trait, involves a *commitment*, which carries consequences.

That said, however, it is also clear that, just as some physiological features are more generally useful than others, and consequently appear in many guises and in many species (think of the eye, for example), so too some cultural traits have proven their value to the cultures possessing them again and again, and in a wide variety of circumstances. The encouragement of altruistic behavior toward other members of the group is clearly one such cultural trait that has repeatedly demonstrated its usefulness. Its primary advantage, it would seem, is that it contributes powerfully to group solidarity. Where no individuals in the group are simply abandoned to their misfortunes, but all are cared for and aided through their hard times, everyone within the group (and especially the unfortunates) can see the benefits of belonging. As a consequence, almost everyone is inclined, at least when the need is great and obvious, to contribute what he or she can to maintain the group's overall welfare. And in situations of intergroup conflict, the unity of purpose that follows from this willingness to subordinate one's immediate personal desires to the needs of the group can constitute a telling advantage. Other things being equal, the group that fights or otherwise competes as a cohesive unit is likely to do much better than, and thus to prosper at the expense of, the group of headstrong and selfish individualists. Thus there are important group selection benefits to be gained from the promotion of altruistic behavior *within* groups. (On the other hand, it is far from clear that, as long as the human species remains divided into many often violently competing groups, there is any great fitness advantage to be gained by the promotion of altruistic behavior that extends *beyond* group boundaries. After all, the tribe that is too willing to treat all newcomers as friends, and to forgive even serious breaches of friendship, is likely to be exterminated by organized interlopers that refuse to reciprocate this attitude. One might well surmise, then, that at the same time as *intragroup* altruism has been selected for in most cultures, a certain amount of *intergroup* aggressiveness has been selected for as well—as the natural expression of group assertiveness over available resources.)

Given the tremendous power of the reinforcement mechanisms of punishment and reward to change the calculations relating to the satisfaction of self-interest, and thus to transform a culture's behavioral norms, and given as well the group-selection pressures favoring within-group altruism, it should not surprise us too much to find that in almost all cultures people behave rather more altruistically, at least toward members of their own community, than one might expect them to if their actions were determined entirely by their own private motives. Individual selection, of course, still powerfully promotes self-interestedness. As a consequence, the combination of group-selection and individual-selection pressures establishes a tension between what tends to be culturally approved on the one hand and what is individually desired on the other. And because individuals often behave—under coercion—rather better than they would like to, it is tempting to conclude that there is something phony, or at least suspect, about the "altruism" that they exhibit. How genuinely *good* are people who behave well, after all, primarily because they are afraid not to? Indeed, is it not possible, perhaps even likely, that the good behavior that people occasionally engage in can be *entirely* accounted for in terms of social conditioning—that is, in terms of the reinforcement mechanisms of punishment and reward? It seems, then, that even if, through reference to social conditioning, we have been able to explain how it is possible for self-sacrificing *behavior* to have taken hold and spread within our species, we have still not really managed to explain how the genuinely altruistic *impulse*—that is to say, the private desire to help others— could have overcome the tendency of natural selection to stamp it out.

Before we conclude, however, that the genuinely altruistic impulse must be a mere figment of our self-serving imagination—a notion invoked simply in order to put a pleasing gloss on our own willingness to conform to social norms—we should notice that, when altruistic *behavior* is culturally approved and to some extent even demanded, the fitness disadvantage of possessing genuinely altruistic *impulses* is significantly reduced. In other words, the individual with a genuinely "good heart" would be far less frequently taken advantage of in a "civilized" society than he or she would be in the Hobbesian state of nature. What this implies, of course, is that the tendency of natural selection to stamp out the altruistic impulse, should it arise, will be significantly reduced in a community in which most people from time to time *act as if* they were altruists, regardless of what their true motives might be. In such a community, then, even a not terribly powerful biological mechanism promoting altruism through group selection, when added to social conditioning, might be strong enough to offset the already significantly weakened individual-selection pressure exerted against the altruistic disposition, making it possible for individuals possessing genuinely altruistic impulses to thrive. As it happens, Sober and Wilson have just such a biological mechanism to propose as the decisive factor in the evolution of altruism.

As game theory models imply,[32] the main reason that individual selection is stacked against the evolution of altruism is that, when an altruist and a "selfish" individual interact, by definition the altruist can do no better than break even, and often he or she will lose in the encounter. But on the other hand, given the benefits that frequently flow from cooperation, when altruists interact with other altruists they often do better than do "selfish" individuals interacting with other "selfish" individuals.[33] Thus one powerful way in which altruists could protect themselves against exploitation, and in so doing increase their own fitness, would be to associate as much as possible only with others of their own kind. "The idea that choosing associates favors the evolution of altruism is deeply intuitive," Sober and Wilson observe, but it has received little attention from evolutionary biologists. One reason for this neglect is that initial efforts to model assortative interactions encountered a difficulty that can be called the *problem of origination*. In mathematical models, it is convenient to assume that behaviors exist as discrete traits that arise by mutation and therefore initially exist at a very low frequency in the population. If we model discriminating altruists in this way, we discover that they do poorly at a very low frequency because they seldom encounter other altruists with whom to associate. Altruism can easily evolve after the discriminating altruists exceed a threshold frequency, but a model that requires altruists to exist at a frequency of 20 percent (for example) before they can be favored by natural selection fails to address a fundamental problem about how altruism can evolve.[34]

There is a comparatively simple solution to this problem, however, and that is to forego the simplifying assumption that a given individual is either an altruist through and through or thoroughly selfish. Common sense suggests, after all, that genuine altruism—insofar as we can recognize this among our own motivations at least—is a matter of degree. We are more than willing to make certain sacrifices in certain circumstances on behalf of others, but often we are as self-interested as anyone else. And which sacrifices *I* would be prepared to make might be very different from those that *you* would be prepared to make.

To think of altruism in this way—as a disposition that almost everyone possesses to some extent, but which varies dramatically in its strength from one individual to another—is to think of it as a trait that is continuous rather than discrete. As Sober and Wilson point out,

> Behaviors and other traits tend to be continuous when they are influenced by genes at many loci. . . . [And] when altruism is modeled [more plausibly] as a continuous trait, the problem of origination largely disappears. It may be hard for a mutant altruist to find another altruist to interact with, but it is easy for an individual who is above average to find another individual who is [also] above average. This is true even when the *average* degree of altruism is very low.[35]

In other words, even in a group made up almost exclusively of utterly self-interested types, those rare individuals who possess some slight inclination toward altruism should be able to recognize one another's better than average dispositions and choose to associate with each other. This will ensure that the lion's share of the benefits arising from their shared willingness to make occasional sacrifices on each other's behalf will accrue to themselves, and not be dissipated on free-riders, thus increasing their evolutionary fitness *as a type*—which is to say, increasing the likelihood that their altruistic disposition will become more common in future generations.

Let us assume for the moment that this increase in fitness on the part of the slightly altruistic type is enough to bring about a marginal increase in the frequency of (low-level) altruism in the population as a whole. As this slight inclination toward altruism becomes more widespread, it will, as a consequence of the randomizing process of sexual reproduction, tend to manifest itself, like any other continuous trait (such as height or skin color), in varying degrees of intensity. There will be, that is to say, rare individuals who possess a higher than average degree of even this slight inclination toward altruism. And as before, they will presumably be in a position to recognize one another's exceptional dispositions and choose to associate primarily with each other. If we assume, as must surely often be the case, that the group benefits flowing from altruism tend to increase as the degree of altruism intensifies, these exceptionally altruistic individuals will enjoy a higher level of evolutionary fitness (on group-selection grounds) than the merely slightly altruistic individuals, who in turn will enjoy a higher level of evolutionary fitness than the utterly self-interested types. In this way, genuine altruism—that is, not merely coerced altruistic *behavior* but the altruistic *impulse*—could arise from very humble beginnings and nonetheless gradually gain in intensity as well as become more common.

The process we have described here could not continue indefinitely, of course. For no matter how much sorting by voluntary association takes place, there will always be individuals around who are less altruistic than the norm, and *some* measure of interaction with these comparatively selfish types will be inescapable. There will inevitably be, then, some measure of dissipation on (comparative) free-riders of the benefits arising from altruism. Here again, in other words, we find the individual-selection pressure associated with the benefits of free-riding behavior countering the group-selection pressure associated with the benefits of self-sacrificing cooperation. And precisely *how much* altruism can arise by means of assortation within a given population will be determined by the relative strengths of these group- and individual-selection pressures.

One very important factor in establishing these relative strengths will be the ability of individuals to recognize one another's true dispositions. For obviously the more difficult it is for altruists to identify one another, the less successful will be their efforts to associate primarily, if not exclusively, with others who share their own altruistic disposition. But as Sober and Wilson point out,

Humans have a fantastic ability to acquire information about others based on personal interaction, direct observations, and cultural transmission. This information is often used to seek out trustworthy individuals and avoid cheaters in social interactions. The ability to detect cheaters is likely to select for the ability of cheaters to avoid detection, but deception is unlikely to be completely successful. Even if initial intentions can be disguised, behavioral tendencies can be readily discerned from actual behaviors, whenever the history of past interactions is known. . . . [H]uman evolution took place in small groups whose members had extensive opportunities to observe and talk about each other. Information about a single antisocial act can spread quickly through a social network and spoil a person's reputation, with grave consequences for future social interactions. Human social interactions among unrelated individuals are anything but random, and our ability to learn and to change our behavior according to what we learn provides a powerful mechanism for the evolution of altruism and other group-advantageous behaviors.[36]

This is the good news, which increases the plausibility of explaining how the altruistic impulse could have taken hold in our species by appealing to the combination of, first, social conditioning, and second, voluntary mutual association on the part of comparative altruists. The bad news, however, is that the social conditions—the small-group lifestyles—that for countless generations favored the detection of would-be cheaters among one's acquaintances have in recent years largely disappeared. The large anonymous societies that for the most part we now live in offer superb opportunities for free-riding. It may be, then (and we are speculating here, of course), that the longstanding point of equilibrium between individual- and group-selection pressures, which tended to promote a reasonable degree of genuine altruism in our species, has recently[37] undergone a dramatic shift. The new point of equilibrium, given the increasing prevalence of social interactions between relative strangers and the reduction in group-selection pressure that this implies, seems likely to favor a higher degree of self-interestedness than was previously the norm.

THE QUESTION OF GOODNESS

All of this may constitute a reasonably adequate explanation of how the altruistic impulse could arise as a dispositional trait within a species such as ours through natural selection—as well as why the countervailing self-interested impulse can never be extirpated from the species. In other words, it may explain in very broad strokes *how* morality (or the socially sanctioned expectation of some measure of unselfish behavior) has arisen and why it will always meet a certain amount of resistance. If substantially correct, this explanation of how morality arose also shows why morality is *good*—"good," that is, in the sense of being useful, of tending to augment the evolutionary fitness of those individuals that exhibit moral inclinations (at least in some circumstances). But what this account cannot provide—in fact, what it renders highly problematic—is the idea that moral behavior is correct in some objective and absolute sense. What it cannot provide, in other words, is any justification of the claim that morality involves our recognition of a *categorical* imperative.

What we call moral behavior is, from the perspective of evolutionary biology, merely a fitness-maximizing strategy—and more importantly, merely one possible strategy of several available strategies. Those philosophers who have begun "taking Darwin seriously," as Michael Ruse puts it, contend that today any plausible argument for the correctness of behaving morally has to be grounded in an adequate description of human nature. The strategy of morality, in other words, has to be shown to be in some important sense a *better* strategy for *us* to adopt than would be the alternative strategy of immorality (or the nonstrategy of amorality). But if, for example, honesty *is* the best policy, this can only be because, given what we are (as products of evolution) and the various ways in which the world operates, on balance honesty will provide us more of what we are looking for (more happiness [*eudaimonia*], if Aristotle is right about what we ultimately desire) than would dishonesty. And many philosophers, including Ruse, conclude far too readily that this is obviously the case.

As Ruse sees it, a crucial part of what we *are* is a species in which moral inclinations have been "burned into our souls"[38] by millions of years of natural selection. "The Darwinian's point," Ruse writes, "is that our moral sense is a biological adaptation, just like hands and feet. We think in terms of right and wrong,"[39] and we do so because natural selection has made certain "epigenetic rules"[40]—or instinctive aversions to certain kinds of actions and instinctive approval of certain other kinds of actions—as natural to us as are walking on two legs or handling tools. Once we acknowledge this, however, some important meta-ethical implications follow.

> What then must we conclude about the status of morality, when viewed in this Darwinian light? Many would respond: absolutely nothing! They would argue that a genetic account of the evolution of morality says nothing about the justificatory foundations of morality.

But according to Ruse,

> To argue in this way . . . is to miss what the Darwinian has given us. Once you agree that morality is a biological adaptation, you are directed to a meta-ethical conclusion about its status. . . . We must ask whether, to the Darwinian, morality is . . . something objective, in the sense of having an authority and existence of its own, independent of human beings? Or whether morality is—because of the science,

must be taken as—subjective, being a function of human nature, and reducing ultimately to feelings and sentiments—feelings and sentiments of a type different from wishes and desires, but ultimately emotions of some kind?

. . . [H]aving accepted the natural evolution of morality, the Darwinian is forced to take the second option. The naturalistic approach, locating morality in the dispositions produced by the epigenetic rules, makes our sense of obligation a direct function of human nature. We feel that we ought to help others and to cooperate with them, because of the way that we are. That is the complete answer to the origins and status of morality. . . . Morality has neither meaning nor justification, outside the human context. Morality is subjective.[41]

To contend that morality is subjective, in the sense of ultimately reducing to feelings and sentiments, is not, however, incompatible with arguing that the moral disposition is also universal *within our species*. And this is a claim that Ruse goes on to make.

[T]he Darwinian recognizes that there are indeed differences from society to society, and also within societies, particularly across time. However, these are readily (and surely properly) explained in the way that most moral theorists would explain them, as secondary, modified consequences of shared primary moral imperatives. . . .

When it comes to general shared moral principles, the Darwinian stands firm. Humans share a common moral understanding. This universality is guaranteed by the shared genetic background of every member of *Homo sapiens*. The differences between us are far outweighed by the similarities.[42]

But if morality is in fact "merely" subjectively grounded in our feelings—even if admittedly in some of our *deepest* feelings—why do so many laymen and philosophers alike believe so profoundly in morality's objectivity?[43] According to Ruse, the explanation is

that morality simply does not work (from a biological perspective), unless we believe that it is objective. Darwinian theory shows that, in fact, morality is a function of (subjective) feelings; but it also shows that we have (and must have) the illusion of objectivity.[44]

This might be thought to be a rather disturbing state of affairs. For surely Darwinian theory has now given us the means to see through the illusion of objectivity, and *if* the illusion of objectivity is needed in order to make morality work, are we not now in danger of losing morality altogether? (In that case, we are confronted with "Darwin's *dangerous* idea" indeed!) Ruse concludes, though, that the universality of moral dispositions (within our species) can readily substitute for the illusory objectivity.

You cannot justify "Killing is wrong" in the sense of deducing it from factual premises. What you can do is explain why we hold this belief. This is all that can or need be offered. . . . In the case of morality, we are all part of the game, and even those of us who realize this have no desire to drop out. Thus, literally, we would not speak of "illusion."[45]

Everything that Ruse has said about morality being grounded ultimately in our own instinctive feelings should be recognized as sound by anyone who "takes Darwin seriously." But at the last moment, Ruse shies away from the *full* meta-ethical implications of Darwinism. Even the Darwinian will have "no desire to drop out" of the game of morality? Perhaps not. But Ruse seems to have temporarily forgotten that natural selection has also provided us with vigorous self-interested inclinations. We are all, including the Darwinians among us, periodically tempted to cheat when both the benefits of doing so and the likelihood of our getting away with it seem high. The individual who believes in the objectivity of morality will at least feel conscience-stricken if (and when) she succumbs to these temptations. Thus her commitment to morality will not be damaged by her occasional lapses. The Darwinian, on the other hand, recognizing that his own moral inclinations are no more than one set of instinctive feelings that he, like all other humans, has been provided by the evolutionary process, might readily conclude that his *other* (selfish) instinctive feelings are equally legitimate. In this respect, while the Darwinian will not drop out of the game of morality, he may nonetheless begin to play it far more cynically, given what he understands the game to be. He will continue to praise morality in public, of course, and continue to sincerely approve of moral actions (especially on the part of others), but when those temptations to cheat arise, he may be more than ready to give in to them. After all, morality is simply a fitness-maximizing strategy, just as selfishness is, and which of those strategies will prove *more* fitness-maximizing is very much a matter of circumstances. *Flexibility*, then, would seem to be the byword!

One cannot successfully respond to this somewhat distasteful meta-ethical implication of Darwinism by deciding that morality must be objective after all. That would be to abandon the Darwinian account of the origins of morality altogether, and the evidence in favor of that account is overwhelming — virtually coextensive with the evidence for evolution itself. But neither can one reasonably adopt Ruse's attitude that all is well, given that we all have moral inclinations "burned into our souls" — not as long as excessively self-interested, immoral inclinations are "burned" there as well. No, the only solution is to accept, and move through, this implication. To see what such a move would look like, we might go back to the beginning of the debate concerning the implications of evolutionary theory for ethics and consider what T. H. Huxley — "Darwin's bulldog" — had to say on the matter.

In May 1893, Huxley delivered the Romanes Lecture at Oxford University—a lecture that was published the next year, along with an added prolegomenon, under the title *Evolution and Ethics*. In this work, Huxley recanted a position that he himself had earlier flirted with—the idea that the principles of morality might be derived from the evolutionary process itself. His targets, in other words, were the early Social Darwinists, such as Herbert Spencer. Against those, like Spencer, who argued that the evolutionary process is ultimately benign, or those, like Sumner, who argued that the culling process of natural selection is itself a *good* thing, Huxley offered in rebuttal a simple, obvious, and powerful analogy—that of the garden.

The garden is simultaneously both a *product* of Nature and also a *critique* of Nature, Huxley observed. It is a product of nature in two senses. First, each of the plants that we cultivate in a garden is itself entirely "natural." (These are not, after all, concrete or plastic ornaments; they are biological organisms, most of which can be found growing in the wild somewhere.) Second, our own human impulse to cultivate gardens is also "natural"—natural, that is, to us, given what the evolutionary process has made of us. But the garden is also a critique of Nature in the sense that, where we are content to let a plot of land stand exactly as Nature has left it—and where we are content, moreover, to let it change in future in whatever ways that Nature will cause it to change— we have not yet begun to garden. Gardening begins, that is to say, as an expression of our *dissatisfaction* with what Nature, left to its own devices, will make of our environment. It is an attempt to improve on the natural through art. But given that the artistic impulse is itself natural, it would not be inappropriate to see the garden as an instance of Nature's being in some sense at odds with itself.

> No doubt, it may be properly urged that the operation of human energy and intelligence, which has brought into existence and maintains the garden, by what I have called "the horticultural process," is, strictly speaking, part and parcel of the cosmic process. . . .
>
> But if, following up this admission, it is urged that, such being the case, the cosmic process cannot be in antagonism with that horticultural process which is part of itself—I can only reply, that if the conclusion that the two are antagonistic is logically absurd, I am sorry for logic, because . . . the fact is so. The garden is in the same position as every other work of man's art; it is a result of the cosmic process working through and by human energy and intelligence; and, as is the case with every other artificial thing set up in the state of nature, the influences of the latter are constantly tending to break it down and destroy it.[46]

The garden, in other words, is only preserved in its existence by the gardener's constant (and natural) efforts on its behalf *against* the disruptive influences of Nature. According to Huxley, this possibility of Nature's being at odds with itself should come as no great surprise to us. After all, not only is it the case that

> the cosmic energy, working through man upon a portion of the plant world, opposes the same energy as it works through the state of nature, but a similar antagonism is everywhere manifest between the artificial and the natural. Even in the state of nature itself, what is the struggle for existence but the antagonism of the results of the cosmic process in the region of life, one to another?[47]

The point of Huxley's analogy, it should be clear, is that ethics stands to our natural inclinations as gardening stands to the unchecked processes of Nature. In each case, there is an approving selection of *some* of those inclinations or processes, which are then intentionally promoted in opposition to *other* equally natural inclinations or processes. In gardening, we approve, say, of the peony's tendency to grow and produce blossoms, and we disapprove of that same tendency in the weeds that would choke it out. In ethics, we approve of generosity and do our best to promote it, while we disapprove of that measure of self-interestedness that we designate as selfishness, and do our best to subdue it. What is even more important, though, for the sake of Huxley's criticism of Social Darwinism, is the fact that in gardening the principle of natural selection is rightly repudiated as a guide to action—and thus by implication so should it be in ethics. As Huxley writes,

> the principle of the horticultural process, by which the [garden] is created and maintained, is antithetic to that of the cosmic process. The characteristic feature of the latter is the intense and unceasing competition of the struggle for existence. The characteristic of the former is the elimination of that struggle, by the removal of the conditions which give rise to it. The tendency of the cosmic process is to bring about the adjustment of the forms of plant life to the current conditions; the tendency of the horticultural process is the adjustment of the conditions to the needs of the forms of plant life which the gardener desires to raise.
>
> The cosmic process uses unrestricted multiplication as the means whereby hundreds compete for the place and nourishment adequate for one; it employs frost and drought to cut off the weak and unfortunate; to survive, there is need not only of strength, but of flexibility and of good fortune.
>
> The gardener, on the other hand, restricts multiplication; provides that each plant shall have sufficient space and nourishment; protects from frost and drought; and, in every other way, attempts to modify the conditions, in such a manner as to bring about the survival of those forms which most nearly approach the standard of the useful, or the beautiful, which he has in mind.[48]

In morality—as all but the Social Darwinists understand it—there is a comparable mitigating of the competition for survival. The point of morality is that the weak and disadvantaged are not left to their own devices, but are given some assistance—at the very least are protected against the crueler forms of exploitation. Morality does not require (ordinarily) that one sacrifice oneself unconditionally; it requires only that one restrain the nastier of one's self-interested inclinations, thus allowing others the opportunity to thrive as well as oneself.

But Huxley's analogy, apt as it is, implicitly raises three important questions. First, just as the gardener must ask herself *which* are the plants that she wishes to cultivate and which are the plants to be considered weeds, so with respect to ethics we must ask, *which* are to be the approved impulses among our natural inclinations and which the disapproved. Ruse's point, of course, is that to a considerable degree this question has already been answered by our evolutionary heritage. Given what we are—given what we *all* are as human beings—there are many kinds of action that we inherently dislike and others that we naturally applaud. But while this is true, it is by no means the case that the instinctive aversions with which natural selection has equipped us can be relied upon as a completely adequate guide to morality. For example, even though we all tend to condemn obvious instances of theft, many of us have no strong feelings at all about the subtler refinements of theft, such as embezzlement and shoplifting. So too, our fascination with gossip often more than offsets any sense we may have of the injury involved in libel, and so we continue to read—and thus contribute to the maintenance of— magazines that we know full well are often libelous. In other words, those "secondary, modified consequences of [the] shared primary moral imperatives" that Ruse speaks of are far from unimportant. Decisions must be made about these as well.

This first question, then, leads us directly to a second, which is: *who* is to play the role of gardener when it comes to the "cultivation" of humanity? In other words, who—or what—is to make these finer, secondary discriminations between the approved and disapproved impulses of human nature? There are several obvious, if not entirely plausible, candidates: scripture, cultural tradition, statutory law, "pure practical reason," each and every individual affirming his or her own values. As was just indicated, though, for anyone who accepts the evolutionary account of human origins, the primary role of "gardener" has already been claimed. The evolutionary process itself has determined our basic values—"burning into our souls" aversions to murder, theft, cruelty, selfishness, cowardice, ingratitude, and so on. And for the secondary role of "gardener," whose task it will be to refine those basic values so as to make them accord more closely with the changing circumstances in which we live, there is only one plausible candidate—reason. This is not the "pure practical reason" of Kant and the natural law theorists, however. For human reason is itself a product of the evolutionary process. As a result, it is no more reliable an instrument than the pressures of natural selection could make it; and that means it is *far* from infallible. Among other things, it needs to be schooled by experience and tempered by a constant cross-checking of its results.

There is more, much more, that needs to be said in answer to these first two questions, of course, but the general outlines of the answers at least should be fairly apparent. In contrast, the third question that Huxley's analogy implicitly raises is seriously troublesome. It is a question that Western philosophers have periodically struggled with at least since Plato's writing of *The Republic*, and *most* of those who have thought that they had found the answer to it have deluded themselves. The question is simply: *why* should we be interested in "gardening" at all? Not everyone is, after all—neither in the cultivation of plants, nor in the cultivation of virtues. We cannot hope to answer this third question adequately until such time as we have largely correct answers to the first two questions. For that reason, I plan to postpone considering the question of why we should be moral until the final chapter. In the chapter immediately to come, we will look more closely at the first question—which is to say, at what kinds of inclinations we should approve and disapprove. At this point, though, it would seem appropriate to say a few more things about reason, given the enormously important role that it must play in delineating the finer details of morality.

THE STATUS OF REASON

Human reason is a clear—and for our purposes, important—instance of what Stephen Jay Gould calls an evolutionary *exaptation*. An exaptation is a phenotypic trait that evolves initially as a functional adaptation in one direction and which then, by virtue of the structure that it has acquired during this initial adaptation, is subsequently well suited to be developed in an entirely different direction—that is, to acquire an entirely different function. Classic examples of exaptations include the development of pectoral fins in fish into the legs of amphibians, and the development of feathers, which had initially evolved as thermo-regulating features, into instruments of flight. (Darwin—mistakenly, we now believe—thought that the development of swim bladders into lungs represented another illustration of this principle.)[49] From the viewpoint of evolutionary theory, it is fairly clear that the human mind, during its four million or so years of prehistoric development, transformed from something that was initially capable only of very simple problem-solving of a mechanical sort, but quite good already at registering the meaning of complicated social interactions—in other words, from something roughly comparable to the mind of a modern chimpanzee—into what we currently possess. And that is, of course, a mind capable of mastering tremendously intricate verbal language, capable of developing the calculus, capable of negotiating even the problems of space flight and of reconstructing even its own prehistory. What makes this development an instance of exaptation is that the mind that protohumans possessed some four million years ago was already highly functional and presumably well adapted to the needs of our ancestors. But what that mind has gradually turned into, under the selection pressure exerted initially by a change of environment (from arboreal to savannah) and then in time under the stimulating goad of an increasingly complex cultural life, is a mind possessed of extraordinary reserves of excess reasoning capacity. It is not, after all, as if we *needed*—for survival purposes—to get to the moon or develop the calculus.

That "excess" reasoning capacity has made all the difference in our species. It has allowed us, for example, to question how the world as a whole "works"—approaching it as if it too were a machine, although of rather more complicated construction than those that we ourselves tend to fashion, or alternatively, as if it too were a family, with a stern but caring father (or tender but fickle mother) at its head—and to ponder our place in the scheme of things. It has made possible the development of a collective memory in the form of written and representational records, and as a consequence it has opened up for us the entire realm of culture. That collective memory, which is embodied not only in our literature and art, but also in our technology, our sciences, and the shape of our social institutions, molds our interactions with each other and with the natural world. We behave (at times, at least) in far more sophisticated ways than do any other living creatures—reading newspapers, driving automobiles, earning paychecks, and conducting laboratory experiments, for example. This is in part because our collective memory makes generally available the worthwhile innovations that the creative individuals among us manage to produce. It is also, however, a consequence of the fact that our collective memory, in combination with the continued application of reason, makes possible the *ongoing refinement* of our technology, our sciences, and our social institutions. As long as we attend to them in the right way—which is to say, as long as we allow ourselves and each other to think critically, rationally, and fearlessly about them—we can continue to improve our technology, sciences, and social institutions, and perhaps even our arts. What our "excess" reasoning capacity has in effect opened up for us, then, is a new and highly accelerated form of evolution—a (cultural) form of evolution that *augments*, of course, rather than *replaces* biological evolution. But in that augmentation there also lies a particular danger.

Homo sapiens, after all, for all of its cleverness and *more* than cleverness, is still a species subject to the same biological laws that apply to *all* species. And that includes, in particular, the law of extinction. Across generations, species naturally tend to adapt to their environments—even when, as is often the case, those environments themselves are changing. Broadly speaking, a species goes extinct when its rate of adaptation is too slow to keep pace with environmental change. When that happens, the particular environmental niche without which it cannot survive disappears, and the species with it. Some species, of course, have highly specific environmental needs, and are thus especially vulnerable to the effects of change. When a crucial foodstuff becomes scarce or a new type of predator enters its range, the species in question may be doomed. Humans are, in this respect, one of the robust species, capable of coping with an extraordinarily wide range of environmental types. (In biological terms, *coping with* an environment is one thing, of course, and *adapting to* it is quite another. *Coping* is what a given individual does in adjusting its behavioral patterns so as to make them more suitable to new circumstances. *Adapting* is, in biological terms, exclusively a matter of a species undergoing appropriate phenotypic change across generations.) In spite of the fact that we are clearly one of the robust species, there are limits even to our capacity to cope with (and far more stringent limits to our capacity to adapt to) serious environmental change. An environment heavily poisoned by radioactive fallout, for example, is not one in which we could hope to survive.

The highly accelerated (cultural) form of evolution that our own intelligence has opened up for us poses a danger precisely in that it has tended to generate increasingly rapid, significant, and widespread environmental change. It is not merely the threat of radioactive poisoning that confronts us, after all. We are already contaminating wide portions of the earth's surface in more conventional ways, with chemical toxins; we are destroying the ozone layer; we are driving (and have already driven) countless other species into extinction, with incalculable ecological consequences; and finally, our activities seem to be directly responsible for a process of global warming that is now well underway—a process which, if allowed to continue unchecked, will necessarily have enormous although, again, at this point quite incalculable ecological implications. Given how dramatic have been the economic developments made possible by cultural evolution, there is the very real possibility that we might inadvertently change our environment to such an extent that, in spite of our remarkable ability to cope with change, as a species we can no longer survive. Even if things do not come to this pass, really significant environmental change will inevitably require on our part enormous—and largely unwelcome—adjustments. For while individual human beings may be remarkably flexible in coping with change, social structures quite often are not. When really large numbers of people are on the move, for example (as we can expect will be the case if global warming continues unabated), nations and the infrastructures they support tend to crack and shatter under the strain.

But intelligence, of course, is ultimately all about foresight. We study the past, we identify similarities and produce generalizations, we consider the implications of counterfactual conditionals, all with an eye to anticipating what the future may bring so that we might cope with it more effectively. The highly accelerated (cultural) form of evolution, in other words, differs from the process of biological evolution in one especially important respect: it is not *entirely* blind. Whereas in biological evolution adaptation through natural selection is the entirely unintended consequence of different rates of survival, the process of selection involved in cultural evolution is, quite literally, a matter of *selection*. A change in culture is brought about, typically, through the aggregation of innumerable small expressions of preference on the part of those individual human beings who share the culture in question. Often those expressions of preference will be unconsidered, almost reflexive choices. When the issue in question is important, however, it is at least possible that the individuals involved in determining the direction in which the group will turn will think carefully about the matter. And when deliberation and careful thought is required, of course, this is ordinarily because our natural human inclinations on the matter in question threaten to carry us in the *wrong* direction. In those instances, in other words, our deliberations, if they are effective, will often culminate in a collective exercise of self-restraint on our part. We may decide (or our leaders may decide on our behalf) that it is time to curtail pollution, for example, regardless of the initial inconveniences involved in doing so. Similarly, we may collectively decide to provide more meaningfully for the needs of those who find themselves unemployed or without adequate health care, or for the educational needs of children in our society, in spite of the higher taxes that those decisions will entail. In this respect, cultural evolution is, in contrast to biological evolution,[50] at least potentially *progressive*. It is, in other words, at least potentially directed toward improvements in the general welfare—among which are to be included, importantly, improvements in the measure of social justice achieved and improvements in the degree of genuine understanding that prevails. In fact, of course, cultural evolution is seldom anywhere near as progressive as it seems it could and should be. But regardless of whether or not one's culture as a whole, on the basis of a rational assessment of its situation and prospects, embraces the exercise of self-restraint in the service of justice and truth (and perhaps even just survival), the option is always also available to the *individual*.

The individual human being is provided—by cultural reinforcement, on the one hand, and by the history of natural selection acting upon her forbears, on the other—with a constellation of desires and inclinations. These, of course, are often in conflict with each other in various ways. The great advantage of being a comparatively *rational* animal, however, is that, in contrast to those animals whose instincts are simpler and more implacable, the individual human being finds it possible consciously to choose among her inclinations those that she will pursue *at the expense* of certain others.[51] (To take one obvious and widely familiar example, the individual human being may consciously choose *not* to have children in spite of the biological imperative urging her on in this regard.) Thus the possibility exists, for members of our species, of preferring the inclinations of reason (that is, the pursuits of justice and of truth) to the more straightforwardly self-interested inclinations—never to the utter exclusion of the latter, of course, but as a matter of degree. To some extent, in other words, we can *choose* the measure of our commitment to reason itself. We do so by deciding how seriously we will take reason's insistence that we adopt, as far as possible, the *objective perspective* on all questions. The objective perspective is not, of course, that which comes most naturally to us—which is, rather, our self-interested personal perspective. Nor is the objective perspective something that can be slipped on, like an old and comfortable coat. It has to be striven for—painfully—at all times and will always be less than fully realized. It should hardly be surprising, then, that we find it difficult to forego, in the service of reason, the self-interested pursuits of wealth, status, and pleasure; and even more difficult, if these rewards arrive unbidden, to resist their perverting influence on our nobler intentions. But that is merely to say, again, what Schiller has already made clear: that one's dedication to adopting the objective perspective required of us by reason is very much a matter of learning when and how to exercise self-restraint.

NOTES

1. Thus in the United States at least, it is still necessary to fight—in state after state—against the obscurantism that would (re)introduce "creation science" into the public school curriculum.

2. Ernst Mayr, *Toward a New Philosophy of Biology* (Cambridge, Mass.: Harvard University Press, 1988), 264.

3. For the sake of both brevity and simplicity, I am here considering sexual selection to be merely one form of natural selection—although, of course, an extremely important form. In this sense, an individual's potential mates are taken to be part of its environment (in the same way that its predators and prey are part of its environment).

4. So obvious that T. H. Huxley's immediate reaction is said to have been "How stupid of me not to have thought of *that*!"

5. There have been a few exceptions, of course. See, for example, Mary Midgley's *Beast and Man*, J. L. Mackie's *Ethics: Inventing Right and Wrong*, and Peter Singer's *The Expanding Circle*.

6. Because Herbert Spencer's career as an ethicist began before the publication of the *Origin of Species* and, as a consequence, his conception of evolution in his formative phase was Lamarckian rather than Darwinian, the mercilessness of natural selection never figured as prominently in his thinking as it did in Sumner's. Spencer, following Lamarck, believed that evolution was intrinsically progressive, and that its goal was the production of "higher" forms of life. Thus while Spencer, like Sumner, heartily approved of laissez-faire economics, he also thought that in the human species evolution naturally promoted the growth of charity, honesty, and the other standard Christian virtues.

7. *Essays of William Graham Sumner*, eds. A. G. Keller and M. R. Davie (Archon Books, 1969), vol. II, 95.

8. Keller and Davie, *Essays of William Graham Sumner*, vol. I, 358–62.

9. It is worth recalling, in this regard, that Social Darwinism was a moral theory much favored by the "robber barons"/"captains of industry" of the late nineteenth century.

10. While I have been presenting the strategies of ostracism and cooperation from the point of view of someone calculating their cost-benefit implications, it should be understood as well that in many (but by no means all) cases these strategies will *not* be *consciously* worked out by the individuals involved, but will be, instead, the consequences of natural selection. In other words, an instinctive program for ostracism or for cooperating in specific ways can be bred into a species.

11. It might be suggested, and not without reason, that either the simple production of gametes, or the act of reproduction itself in the absence of any further investment, should be identified as the *most* minimal form of altruism. But to make altruism a universally exhibited character in this way rather seems to dilute its importance. It is worth acknowledging, however, that in evolutionary terms altruism appears on the scene long before any conscious intent to help emerges.

12. To say that the bee is *prepared* to do this implies only that it will not hesitate when the appropriate situation arises. It does *not* imply, of course, that the bee is at all conscious that in stinging the intruder it will kill itself.

13. Sumner takes it for granted, for example, that "The right of property, with marriage and the family, gives the right of bequest. . . . It follows, therefore, from the organization of marriage and the family, under monogamy, that great inequalities must exist in a society based on those institutions" (*Essays of William Graham Sumner*, vol. II, 94). And while one might wish to argue that great inequalities in wealth and power need not be based upon, or lead to, exploitation, given that (as Sumner believes) "competition is a law of nature" and success is the only standard by which one can judge the appropriateness of *how* one has competed, it follows that fully exploiting one's *current* advantage in power to *increase* that advantage in power in the future is simple (expedient) common sense.

14. In a discipline as wide-ranging as biology, of course, altruism has been defined in a number of slightly different ways. What I am presenting here as *the* biological definition is that offered by Elliott Sober and David Sloan Wilson for "evolutionary altruism," which they distinguish from "psychological altruism." According to Sober and Wilson, "individuals who increase the fitness of others at the expense of their own fitness are (evolutionary) altruists." *Unto Others: The Evolution and Psychology of Unselfish Behavior* (Cambridge, Mass.: Harvard University Press, 1998), 6.

15. Sober and Wilson, *Unto Others*, 5.

16. Sober and Wilson, *Unto Others*, 38–39.

17. George C. Williams, *Adaptation and Natural Selection: A Critique of Some Current Evolutionary Thought* (Princeton: Princeton University Press, 1966), 151.

18. Sober and Wilson, *Unto Others*, 40.

19. According to Hamilton's theory of inclusive fitness, a moderate form of sibling-altruism makes perfect sense in terms of *individual* selection, given that siblings share roughly half of their genes. Thus we should rather expect an individual to behave altruistically toward a sister or brother if the benefit to the sibling exceeds twice the cost to the individual himself. See W. D. Hamilton, "The Evolution of Altruistic Behavior," *The American Naturalist* 97: 354–56.

20. W. D. Hamilton, "Extraordinary Sex Ratios," *Science* 156: 477–88.

21. Sober and Wilson, *Unto Others*, 40.

22. Sober and Wilson, *Unto Others*, 26.

23. Sober and Wilson, *Unto Others*, 25.

24. As we shall see, though, the limit is not irrevocably fixed. A change in circumstances can shift the limit either upward or downward. And more than anything else, what can significantly shift the location of the limit is cultural interaction.

25. Sober and Wilson, *Unto Others*, 30.

26. The mere fact that favorable conditions exist does not guarantee that altruism *will* evolve, however. In order for a heritable trait to spread through natural selection, it must *first* make its appearance upon the scene—typically as a result of either mutation or genetic recombination. (Much variation in heritable traits is directly attributable to random mating, of course, but if we assume that a species has existed for some time *without* a particular trait's emerging, a more radical creative factor than random mating may need to be invoked.)

27. Sober and Wilson, *Unto Others*, 114.

28. A fact that is especially important, as Darwin pointed out, during the incubation of her eggs.

29. Sober and Wilson, *Unto Others*, 143–44.

30. Sober and Wilson, *Unto Others*, 146.

31. Sober and Wilson, *Unto Others*, 152.

32. See, for a discussion of these implications, Robert Axelrod, *The Evolution of Cooperation* (New York: Basic Books, 1984).

33. Again, "selfish" is being used here merely as a contrast term to "altruist."

34. Sober and Wilson, *Unto Others*, 135–36.

35. Sober and Wilson, *Unto Others*, 136–37.

36. Sober and Wilson, *Unto Others*, 141–42.

37. That is, with the emergence of mass societies, the very earliest forms of which —the capital cities of the great empires—appeared on the scene thousands of years ago. A trend that began as far back as five thousand years ago, though, is still "recent" when the time frame we are considering is that of the lifespan of our species.

38. Michael Ruse, *Taking Darwin Seriously* (Oxford: Basil Blackwell, 1986), 246.

39. Ruse, *Taking Darwin Seriously*, 222.

40. A term that Ruse borrows from E. O. Wilson. See *Taking Darwin Seriously*, 143–47.

41. Ruse, *Taking Darwin Seriously*, 251, 252.

42. Ruse, *Taking Darwin Seriously*, 255.

43. Note that the kind of *objectivity* that Ruse denies to moral judgments here is not the same as the objectivity of moral judgments that was discussed in the second chapter of this book. There "objectivity" was taken to mean, roughly, "susceptible to universal intersubjective agreement." In other words, what we spoke of as *objectivity* in the second chapter is almost identical to what Ruse is referring to here as *universality*.

44. Ruse, *Taking Darwin Seriously*, 253.

45. Ruse, *Taking Darwin Seriously*, 257.

46. T. H. Huxley, *Evolution and Ethics*, ed. James Paradis and George C. Williams (Princeton: Princeton University Press, 1989), 69–70.

47. Huxley, *Evolution and Ethics*, 70–71.

48. Huxley, *Evolution and Ethics*, 71–72.

49. In this, Darwin did not misunderstand the principle; he simply got the direction of development reversed. See Stephen Jay Gould, *The Structure of Evolutionary Theory* (Cambridge, Mass.: Belknap Harvard, 2002), 1224.

50. Darwin made a point of reminding himself in his notebooks about the inappropriateness of using such terms as "higher" and "lower" with respect to the species that are generated by the process of natural selection. There is no point of view consistent with the principle of natural selection from which homo sapiens can be judged to be a "better" or "more advanced" species than is, say, a species of jellyfish or of flatworms. "More complex"—yes, undeniably. But not "more advanced," for that would imply that evolution is tracing some preordained route and that our species is located at a point closer to the destination implicit in that route than are jellyfish or flatworms. This is rather how Herbert Spencer conceived of evolution, and Darwin was so concerned *not* to be identified with Spencer's view that in the *Origin of Species* he virtually never used the term "evolution," preferring instead to describe his own position as having to do with the branching transmutation of species or "descent with modification."

51. Recall William James's remarks to this effect in *The Principles of Psychology*, which we considered at the end of the previous chapter.

Chapter Six

Dignity and the Struggle for Survival

Political Economics

"POWER CORRUPTS"

As biological organisms, we are all immersed in the struggle for survival. This is true even if, for the privileged few, the object of the struggle—the satisfaction of one's needs—is so easily achieved that little sense of its involving a *struggle* is registered. Nonetheless, it is an inescapable feature of our biological condition that we must have food, water, shelter, rest, and the various other necessities of life in adequate measure. As Hobbes points out, moreover, the possession of many of these necessities is inherently uncertain, because they are consumables existing in limited quantity and each of us, desiring to ensure that our future as well as our present needs will be satisfied, is eager to lay claim to more than we can immediately use. In our efforts to maximize our personal security, by maximizing what we can lay claim to among these limited resources, we come into conflict and struggle with one another. For if the "game" of economics is by no means "zero-sum," there are nonetheless quite clear losers and winners in the competition, and one person's loss is typically brought on by someone else's gain.

Another way of putting this is to say that, as biological organisms, we have a basic interest in the acquisition of power. After all, one good way to define power is as the capacity to control the direction in which resources are expended. It may be, in other words, that not all decision-making is an expression of power—because the exercise of freedom is not quite the same thing as the exercise of power—but when resources are at stake, and they are sent in one direction rather than another, the exercise of power is clearly involved. We are all inevitably interested in power, then, insofar as we wish to see resources adequate to the satisfaction of our needs directed to ourselves. *Some* desire to possess a certain measure of power is simply a consequence of being alive and wishing to remain so.

The unbridled pursuit of power, however, has long been viewed with justifiable suspicion. "Power corrupts," the saying goes. But the kind of power that Lord Acton had in mind in remarking that the exercise of power tends to corrupt was the exercise of power over the lives and destinies of other human beings—*political* power, in other words, although the power exercised by "captains of industry" is obviously comparable in scope and nature. And if we ask why the exercise of political power should tend to be morally corrupting, one possible explanation presents itself immediately.

For if justice is, as I contended in the third chapter, a matter of giving each person what he or she is due in accordance with Aristotle's conception of proportional equality, then the pursuit of justice involves us in an in principle unfinishable task of analysis, given that the range of factors that could enter into our evaluation of someone's merit, and the range of considerations that may come to have a bearing on how we weigh those factors, are potentially infinite. Dignity, I have been arguing, is in large part a matter of acknowledging this inexhaustible complexity of justice understood as a regulative ideal and yet pursuing justice in specific circumstances whenever possible. What that amounts to, in situations that are fraught with consequences, is that one must think long and carefully, with an eye to fairness, and consult perspectives other than one's own—most especially, of course, the perspectives of those who will be most immediately affected by one's decision. But in order to accomplish anything in the world, one must at some point *act*, and the point at which one must act is often rather firmly established—which means that, when it arrives, discussion and reflection for the purpose of determining *how* one should act on this occasion must be terminated, *as if* the correct answer were now known. In moments of crisis, moreover, such discussion and reflection must be terminated almost immediately; one reacts, and hopes that one's reaction was not too inappropriate. In the political realm, it goes without saying, the decisions that our leaders and elected representatives are called upon to make are *always* fraught with consequences and are not infrequently arrived at quickly, given the press of events to which they constitute reactions. But this must inevitably tend to produce a certain callousness on the part of those making political decisions, as they grow accustomed to overriding, ignoring and, if need be, *suppressing* opposition viewpoints in order to act in a timely fashion and with the assurance of public support.

And indeed, we can find evidence of such callousness even in the most highly regarded of our political leaders. Even Abraham Lincoln, widely revered by Americans as virtually a saint among politicians, was willing to suspend the writ of habeas corpus and to see the excessively vocal critics of his Civil War policies thrown into prison without trial. (Lincoln made his feelings clear in the message of support he telegraphed to his subordinate, Ambrose Burnside, for the latter's incarceration of the former congressman Clement Vallandigham, who publicly challenged Burnside's prohibition of "the habit of declaring sympathies for the enemy.")[1] Some sixty years later, the widely admired "Great Dissenter" of the Supreme Court, Oliver Wendell Holmes, showed himself more than willing to follow Lincoln's lead in curtailing free speech, by sentencing the socialist Charles Schenck to a prison term for, in effect, having had the poor judgment to falsely shout "Fire!" in a crowded theater—which is how Holmes characterized the impact of Schenck's having protested against America's entry into World War I and having encouraged Americans to oppose conscription. (It is to the credit of both Lincoln and Holmes that very quickly each had at least a partial change of heart. Lincoln's change of heart was expressed in his subsequent order to have Vallandigham released. Holmes's change of heart was expressed in his dissent in the case of *Abrams v. United States*, which unfortunately did nothing to shorten Schenck's prison term and did not prevent Jacob Abrams from being sent to prison for having protested the American attempt at armed intervention in Russia in 1917.)

The callous exercise of political power, which terminates discussion forcefully—whether this be by means of a prison term or merely the threat of recrimination—is already morally corrupt. For under the guise of a concern for *effective* action and, not infrequently, for *security*, it closes off all possibility of criticizing public policy; and such criticism, of course, is absolutely essential if *bad* or *unjust* public policies are ever to be corrected. The suppression of critical discussion after the fact, in other words, is all too easily conflated—especially by those who might expect to find themselves the targets of criticism—with the legitimate (because unavoidable) termination of discussion *preliminary* to the determination of public policy. Once a political leader starts down this road, moreover, it is difficult to reverse course. For the suppression of critical discussion will naturally arouse increased opposition to his policies in some quarters—increased opposition that will have to be met with even firmer measures if it is to be quelled. And once criticism of government policy in even one field has been deemed unacceptable in principle, there will be a strong temptation to gradually expand the range of what is considered unacceptable criticism. In short order a "bunker" mentality sets in. One's concern is no longer to find the best policies to adopt, but to guarantee that the policies to which one has already committed oneself go unquestioned, and to guarantee that any resentments aroused by one's highhanded decision-making do not threaten one's hold on power. At this point, when power is used for the primary purpose of securing more firmly one's own grip on power, really significant moral corruption has set in. A nation never *needs* any particular leader at the helm, after all; what it needs are enlightened policies, regardless of with whom they may have originated. The leader who loses sight of this has ceased to serve his country, and has begun to demand, instead, that his country must serve his own ambition.

Power must be acquired in order to be used, of course, but the acquisition of power can readily become its own end. There is an important distinction to be drawn, in other words, between pursuing power *for its own sake* and concentrating power for the sake of achieving some specific worthwhile goal.

It often *is* possible to determine, with a considerable degree of certainty, whether a particular goal is genuinely worth achieving — that is, worth achieving for the improvement that it represents in the quality of our collective existence. When we have embraced such a goal, moreover, no one can object to our pursuing the means (that is, concentrating the power) necessary to make the goal a reality — providing that, in doing so, we do not cause harm to others. "Causing harm," though, has to be understood here in a fairly broad sense, since others too will have embraced certain goals, and if, in the pursuit of *our* goal, we undermine or destroy the possibility of those other worthwhile goals coming to fruition, clearly the pursuit of *our* goal has involved some harm to others. In that case, there must be a careful, and as far as possible objective, weighing of the relative goods to be achieved and damages to be sustained. But a notable feature of the pursuit of specific worthwhile goals (such as building a hospital, performing a play, or writing a constitution) is that such goals, insofar as they *are* specific, are probably never *permanently* worthwhile, even if they are felt to be quite worthwhile *for the moment*. For as circumstances change, it may be necessary to replace what once was achieved at considerable cost because of its evident value *when* it was achieved with something that better serves the new circumstances. Even if we can anticipate that *everything* we currently value may in due time be discarded or superseded, however, this in no way speaks against the worthwhileness of what currently stands. It is a fact of our common experience that old buildings are regularly torn down to be replaced by new more appropriate structures that will, in their own turn, grow old and eventually fall before the wrecking ball. In the meantime, though, they are lived and worked in, shelter us from the elements, and define the shape of space for us. What holds true of the construction of buildings in this sense holds true as well, in all likelihood, for the achievement of *all* specific worthwhile goals: their value is both *real* and yet, to a greater or lesser degree, *temporary*.

In contrast to the pursuit of specific worthwhile goals, each of which stakes only a temporary claim to a place in the world, the pursuit of power for its own sake involves one in the perpetual struggle to realize a goal that, in a very unhealthy fashion, *refuses* to go out of style. In other words, the individual who desires power pure and simple—the power to determine outcomes in whatever sphere may momentarily attract his attention—is never in a position to rest with a sense that the goal has been achieved. For the possession of power is always a relative thing. In order to be in a position to determine a given outcome, after all, one's power must overwhelm that of all others who might wish to determine the outcome differently. Thus as long as there is a rival who might threaten one's capacity to have one's way, there is a need to amass more power. And the problem, of course, is that there will always be such a rival. Until such time as one's power is preeminent, one's rivals will be obvious and they will have to be challenged cautiously. But even after one has emerged as the "leader," as the biggest fish in the pond, the need to increase one's power persists—for those that one has outstripped for the moment will be looking for opportunities to reverse the relationship. Nor can one be certain that the natural dynamics of growth will always work in one's own favor—that as the biggest, one will continue to grow the fastest. Often it is the smaller fish and the lesser power that exhibits the greater growth potential. For this reason, the pursuit—which is simultaneously the defense—of power is inevitably preemptive. Even when one enjoys preeminence— indeed, especially when one enjoys preeminence—the power of others from time to time must be struck down or undercut in order to preserve one's relative advantage. And this must be done for no better reason than that these others presumably seek the same thing that one does oneself—unfettered power.

These observations about what it means to pursue power for its own sake will not strike readers with a "hard-headed" or "realistic" attitude toward politics and international affairs as either surprising or objectionable. Those who describe themselves as realists with regard to international affairs would argue, in fact, that "might makes right" is now, and has always been, the only justification that really counts in geopolitics—and thus that of course America has been justified in punishing Cuba and Iraq with economic sanctions maintained for decades, and in waging undeclared war against, for example, the Sandinistas of Nicaragua and the Ba'athists of Iraq, at least in part in order to send a message to other nations that they had better toe the line. This is how great powers behave—how they have always behaved, we will notice, if we study history. And indeed, the evidence of history does for the most part support these apologists for Realpolitik. But to acknowledge this is merely to say that *morality* has never governed international affairs to any significant degree. The *language* of morality is regularly used, of course, as a device for securing favorable public opinion. Thus nations tend to attribute only noble motives to themselves, praise the virtues of their allies, and condemn the crimes and atrocities of their enemies. But wherever the principles of

Realpolitik govern the actual conduct of international affairs, this use of the language of morality is a sham—and is known to be a sham by the propagandists employing it. Geopolitical realists, in other words, exercise and pursue power unencumbered by scruples regarding what is fair or just, and take it for granted that the clear-sighted among their competitors are similarly unencumbered.

Does this mean that geopolitical realists are simply and straightforwardly immoral? Not quite. As Hume pointed out, there is commonly a boundary that separates those toward whom one feels the need to behave fairly from those who receive no such consideration. Thus in one's dealings with those within the circle of one's moral concern one may be honest and scrupulously fair, even as one behaves ruthlessly toward those outside of that circle—toward those, in other words, *who do not count*. The nature of politics, moreover, reinforces this natural human tendency. "The people's representatives," after all, are direct representatives only of certain specific people—their constituents. Thus legislative representatives, it might be argued, have an obligation imposed upon them by their institutional role to put the welfare of their own constituents ahead of the welfare of the residents of other states or electoral districts. To whatever extent this might be true, it clearly is the case that a nation's chief executive is expected by the citizens of his country to put their welfare significantly ahead of the welfare of citizens of other nations. As a matter of political practice, legislative representatives must often show considerably more concern for the welfare of nonconstituents than chief executives must show toward noncitizens, but this is simply a function of the fact that political units tend to be nested inside of one another. In other words, being a stranger—or someone whose welfare does not count—is a property that is manifested by degrees. Americans, for example, have no political bonds in common with Cubans, and thus no one is surprised to see the president maintain a boycott on Cuban goods if it can be argued that doing so in any way benefits Americans. In contrast, Belgians and Danes share a supranational citizenship—that of members of the European Union. As a consequence, there are things that no Danish politician could ever advocate doing to Belgians, such as imposing economic sanctions upon them. Even more absurd, of course, would be the idea of the governor of Idaho suggesting a boycott of goods from California. Politics, in other words, sharpens the distinction between insider and outsider at the same time as it establishes degrees of "insiderness." Moreover, if it requires of us at least the pro forma expression of good will, and occasionally the making of concessions, toward those with whom we share membership in some political unit, and in this very modest sense compels us to extend the boundaries of our circle of moral concern, it also appears to legitimate our indifference to the fate of clear outsiders whenever their welfare comes into competition with our own—a fact that is made most obvious in cases of war.

But if the geopolitical realist is not straightforwardly immoral—by virtue of his concern for those with whom he identifies—is there nonetheless reason to conclude that his commitment to morality is inadequate? Hume argues that the challenge of moral growth is to *expand* our circle of moral concern—which is to say, to treat even strangers in accordance with the principles of fairness. There is always a risk involved in doing so, given that one's exercise of self-restraint may not be reciprocated. The practical reason for running the risk involved in treating the stranger fairly nonetheless is that in this way—and *only* in this way—can one expect to turn the stranger into a friend. But just as the circle of moral concern can expand, so too it can contract, and the cynical attitude of the geopolitical realist encourages such a contraction. For the same principles of Realpolitik that operate in the international arena are also readily applicable in the more intimate setting of one's private life. If one argues, on the geopolitical level, that one cannot trust and need not treat fairly neighboring nations, and even one's allies, what compelling grounds are to be offered for trusting and treating fairly one's business associates or one's next-door neighbors? If geopolitical wisdom is a matter of anticipating that one's rivals will attack, given the chance, and to preempt this by launching an attack of one's own when the moment is favorable, then surely wisdom in dealing with one's business associates and neighbors should be similarly grounded in distrust. To a greater or lesser degree, after all, one is vulnerable on *all* of the levels at which one interacts with others.

Granted, our capacity for sympathetically identifying with those who are both close to and significantly like ourselves will tend to preserve the measure of our moral concern for our neighbors, friends, and family. Even the most unapologetic realist, in other words, does not overnight and as a matter of principle decide to hold *everyone* in suspicion. But the *logic* of the realist's argument, insofar as it diminishes our willingness to trust, works directly against the influence of our sympathetic identification with others. The contraction of the circle of moral concern—a contraction carrying one in the direction of utter selfishness and isolation—represents the decay and corruption of the moral impulse. And the geopolitical realist, dedicated as he is to the expansion of his nation's power at all costs and by any means, is in effect an advocate for this contraction of moral concern. Nor is this simply because he is prepared to exclude from consideration the welfare of citizens of other nations. We should be wary of concluding, for example, that if we too happen to be Americans, the geopolitical realist setting policy in Washington is *on our side*—that America's aggrandizement necessarily benefits even average

Americans. "Insiderness," as we have just seen, is a matter of degrees, and history teaches us nothing so forcefully as it does the fact that a nation exercises its power primarily for the benefit of those comparatively few individuals—the wealthy and well connected—who are in a position to determine national and domestic policy.[2]

The geopolitical realist's actual circle of moral concern, in other words, is by no means coextensive with his nation's boundaries. On the contrary, he applies the same realist logic at the level of national politics that he employs in assessing the international scene. Since government *within* a nation is always government by some particular group—a group which, insofar as it holds the reins of power, excludes from the decision-making process other groups—the principles of Realpolitik that govern competition in the international arena are equally relevant here. It may not be fair or just to win an election by slandering one's opponent, or knowingly misrepresenting his policies, or gerrymandering electoral districts, or bribing voters, or perverting the vote-counting process, but it is undeniably effective. And once having won the election, of course, the authority of one's office will go some ways toward diminishing the public's willingness to condemn one for whatever dirty tricks may have been used in order to gain that office. If the point of one's running for office is simply to win—if one pursues political office as part of one's pursuit of power for its own sake, in other words—then clearly the Machiavellian logic of doing whatever one can get away with in order to win will strike one as utterly compelling. And the same indifference to justice and fairness that gives the political realist his edge in winning an election will have no doubt played its part in allowing him to gain his party's nomination for office in the first place. The realist's ruthlessness—which is to say, his willingness to exclude from moral consideration everyone outside of the group with which he identifies for the moment, and for the specific purpose of furthering his own acquisition of power—can be expected to pervade his approach to politics at every level, from the interpersonal to the international.

Success in politics, of course, requires that one solicit the support of others in order to achieve one's own ends. This holds for the realist, who (in the extreme case) has no goal to pursue beyond the acquisition of power, just as much as it does for the idealist dedicated to the achievement of some social good. The realist, in other words, cannot afford to let his indifference to justice and fairness become too obvious or it will undermine the support that he is counting on receiving from others. The point, however, is that the realist's solicitation of support from others is always in principle *exploitative*. For where the idealist pleads for the importance of some particular just cause, and solicits support for his own election in order to further that cause on the grounds that it is just (a claim about which he may of course be mistaken), the realist pleads for his own election *as an end in itself.* He will disguise that fact, however, by promising some special consideration to those whose support he is soliciting. He will, in other words, *bargain*—with his peers and rivals, with his party's power brokers, and with the electorate. But the realist, by definition, never bargains in good faith. His whole attitude toward politics—which is predicated on seizing whatever opportunities present themselves to increase one's power—indicates his readiness to betray whatever bargains he may have made if there is anything at all to be gained from doing so. When the realist actually delivers on his promises to his supporters, then, this is *calculated.* Calculations, that is to say, have convinced him that either (1) there is nothing sufficiently worthwhile to be gained from abandoning his commitment or (2) he is not in a position to renege—not on *these* supporters.

It should be clear that the realist's commitment to the principle of "might makes right" not only encourages the contraction of the circle of moral concern, it already springs from the narrowest form of selfishness. And yet, of course, there is a reason why this attitude is called "realism." In the political realm it does, indeed, seem to be the prevalent attitude. Consequently, if one judges how politics *really* works by examining how the majority of politicians apparently practice their *trade* (bargaining, after all, being the essence of trade), the Machiavellian attitude would seem entitled to be called "realism." Obviously we cannot expect to determine with any precision just how prevalent the Machiavellian attitude is in the political realm. Anecdotal evidence—such as that offered by William Greider (in *Who Will Tell the People?*) or Elizabeth Drew (in *The Corruption of American Politics*)—can be piled up to suggest that it is quite prevalent. But anecdotal evidence could also no doubt be provided to suggest that politicians are, for the most part, high-minded and dedicated public servants. Given the complexities of the political process, it is quite impossible to conduct an objective scientific study of the sort that might show, for example, that in a given year 63 percent of the votes cast in Congress had been "purchased" in one sense or another, while 15 percent had been cast on the basis of blind personal bias, and the final 22 percent had been cast on the basis of a Congressman's conscientiously considered judgment regarding what was best for the country (if not the world) as a whole. Empirical judgments regarding the prevalence of Machiavellian realism in politics are thus inevitably impressionistic. There are, nonetheless, two important theoretical reasons for believing that politic, because of its very nature, tends to be dominated by individuals with a Machiavellian frame of mind.

THE MARKET AND THE FORUM

In order to understand the first of these, it is necessary to get clear on the distinction between what political philosophers refer to as the *market* and the *forum* models of politics. In the market model, which James Madison adumbrated in his discussion of factions in the tenth number of *The Federalist Papers*, individuals (whether average citizens or elected representatives) are expected to cast their votes on the basis of self-interest. In other words, individuals are expected to approach politics with the same frame of mind with which they enter the market—"paying" with their votes for those particular items (policies, projects, laws, etc.) that they happen to desire. Often, of course, on a given issue they will be outvoted, and thus will find themselves unable to "purchase" what they want directly. But the political process provides repeated opportunities to cast one's vote and this puts one in a position to negotiate with others so as to maximize one's "purchasing power." In order to ensure that one sees at least the particular prospective law or project that one cares most deeply about approved, one offers to exchange support with one's rivals on another issue about which one cares less (and they presumably care more). In this way, the senator from Arizona gets an airbase built in his state, with support from Tennessee, while the senator from Tennessee gets a new hydroelectric dam in his state, with support from Arizona. Obviously, the process of negotiating an exchange of support, by which one maximizes the "purchasing power" of one's votes, works far more effectively within a legislative assembly or cabinet than it does in the electorate at large. For only in the comparatively small group of an assembly acting in accordance with prescribed rules of order can it be clear precisely with whom one needs to negotiate on a particular issue, what exactly is owed in return for one's vote, and whether delivery on the exchange has been forthcoming. From time to time one sees something like an exchange of support negotiated between large interest groups with overlapping concerns—between feminists and black activists, for example—but these political coalitions are fragile, given the uncertainty among the rank and file regarding what each group has promised the other, and the ease with which the rank and file on each side can opt out of the agreement. As a result, all that the market model predicts—and prescribes—regarding the behavior of average citizens is that, on those comparatively infrequent occasions on which their vote is called for, they should, insofar as this is possible, vote their own self-interest.

According to the forum model, in contrast, the political sphere is *not* to be understood as an auction in which those who can pay the highest "price"—that is, amass the greatest number of votes—take away whatever is up for bid. On this model, the point of politics, instead, is to bring together individuals from various backgrounds—and therefore with varying perspectives—and allow them to discover, through reasoned discussion, what policies, projects, and laws should be approved on their merits. Here the governing consideration is assumed to be, not self-interest on the part of individual voters and legislators, but how well justice and the interests of society as a whole are served. Ideally, discussion in the political forum should produce unanimity— since citizens and legislators are all presumed (in an ideal world) to be rational, intelligent, and genuinely dedicated to the discovery of what justice requires. On a more realistic account—one that acknowledges that what even well-intentioned individuals are capable of seeing and understanding is profoundly influenced by their own past experience—it is argued that the process of seeking the best and most just policies, projects, and laws should at least result in each individual voting for what he or she believes, sincerely and in good conscience, is the best option for society as a whole.

Here we have two conflicting models of how the political sphere should function. The presumption of most advocates of the market model is that the compromises arrived at as individual legislators (and through them, individual interest groups) negotiate their various exchanges of support will tend over time to produce livable and reasonably just results for society as a whole. Unfortunately, this presumption is entirely unwarranted. For neither in the market nor in the political assembly is there any guarantee that the benefits gained in a system of free exchange will be distributed equitably. The bargaining power with which one enters the market, after all, is determined—not exclusively, of course, but to no small degree—by the hand that luck has dealt one. If fate has been kind—if one is born, for example, as the healthy and attractive son of a John D. Rockefeller or Joseph P. Kennedy—one's bargaining power from the moment that one enters the market (whether economic or political) is immense. It is callous in the extreme, then, for an individual so favored to use that power resolutely, even ruthlessly, in pursuit of the satisfaction of his own private desires, and then to contend that, if only *everyone*—even the infirm and destitute—behaved in this way, the result would be justice. (Because the argument *is* callous, and because the extremely rich and well-connected cannot advance it themselves without its self-serving character becoming immediately obvious, those of them who think along these lines have acquired the habit of paying others to make the argument on their behalf.)[3]

But it is not only the second- and third-generation ultrarich and well-connected who find themselves, through sheer good luck, enjoying inordinate benefits. Even the average citizen, insofar as she is a member of one or more natural majorities, will find that she does disproportionately well (in some respects) in the political "marketplace." As a heterosexual who feels uncomfortable with the idea of gay marriage, she finds that referenda on the issue readily turn out as she would like them to. As a white mother concerned about her children's career prospects, she finds that her worries about the potential impact of race-based affirmative action programs are shared by most voters in her district, and thus to a considerable degree as well by her congressman. As an American citizen concerned about safety, and especially the safety of her own loved ones, she finds that her inclination to meet the threat of terrorism preemptively and as far from American shores as possible is perfectly reflected in federal policy. But insofar as members of natural *majorities* find that, on issues of concern to those majorities, they almost always get what they want, it follows, of course, that members of natural *minorities* almost never get what *they* want on issues of particular concern to them.

For example, as long as Americans viewed the matter entirely on the basis of self-interest, and did not concern themselves overly much with the question of justice, it was easy to maintain a system of racial segregation and Jim Crow laws in the South. Blacks constituted a minority, a substantial minority, but one that was nonetheless easy to exclude from power — for a full century after the abolition of slavery. If the market model of politics were universally embraced, moreover, there is no reason to believe that blacks would ever have acquired such civil rights as they now enjoy — at least not so long as they remained a natural minority. Like the abolition of slavery in the 1860s, the achievements of the civil rights movement in the 1960s became possible only once a substantial number of (for the most part Northern) whites began to sympathetically identify with blacks in their struggle for freedom and equality in the only nation they could reasonably call "home." In other words, only once the political question occupying the minds of a quite considerable number of people had been changed from "What do the majority *want?*" to "What does justice in the treatment of blacks *require?*" was it possible to achieve a transformation that today almost all Americans are prepared to applaud.

As the political philosopher Jon Elster has observed, the primary objection to be offered against the market model of politics is that

> it embodies a confusion between the kind of behaviour that is appropriate in the marketplace and that which is appropriate in the forum. The notion of consumer sovereignty is acceptable because, and to the extent that, the consumer chooses between courses of action that differ only in the way they affect him. In political choice situations, however, the citizen is asked to express his preference over states that also differ in the way in which they affect other people. . . . [T]he task of politics is not only to eliminate inefficiency, [the primary task and advantage of the market] but also to create justice.[4]

And that is a goal, Elster points out, that cannot be achieved simply by asking people to express their private self-interested desires, and then giving the majority what they want. Not until and unless our private desires have become sufficiently *other-directed*—that is to say, not until and unless the achievement of justice, for others as well as ourselves, becomes for each of us a major personal desire—are our desires to be trusted in the political sphere. This is why, moreover, the rhetoric offered in support of the market model of politics—rhetoric praising democracy as if in itself it guaranteed justice—is dangerous. For it inclines citizens to take whatever comes their way through the electoral process as if it were fully deserved and appropriate. The rhetoric disinclines them, in other words, from reflecting as they should on the question of what rights individual human beings should be able to rely upon—to rely upon even, and especially, when they find themselves in the minority or disenfranchised altogether.

In spite of the fact that the market model of politics is not so much flawed as fundamentally *wrong*, its correctness is taken so much for granted by many politicians that they feel no sense of impropriety whatsoever when they meet to negotiate their exchanges of support. They should feel the impropriety, of course, since these exchanges do not serve justice (except by accident) and will quite often *impede* justice. But negotiating exchanges of support, again, is simply what political realists do. They bargain.

At the end of the preceding section ("Power corrupts"), it was mentioned that there are two good reasons for believing that politics *because of its very nature* tends to be dominated by individuals with a Machiavellian frame of mind. We are now ready to consider the first of those two reasons. When politicians who practice their *trade* in accordance with the market model interact with politicians who pursue their *profession* in accordance with the forum model, the latter will almost invariably find themselves shortchanged in the interaction. This is because politicians committed to the forum model will not be seeking a quid pro quo in such interactions; instead, they will be seeking a just policy. But knowing that they themselves are not omniscient, they will understand that the search for justice demands a careful balancing of rival claims and even a certain amount of compromise between viewpoints that refuse to harmonize. This sort of compromising, while it may seem at first glance to be closely related to the political bargaining that has come in for criticism here, is in fact nothing like it. After all, the person striking a bargain does not ask himself, "Which of my opinions is most likely to be wrong?" and "Which of my interlocutor's dissenting opinions is most likely to be right?" Rather he asks, "Which policy, if adopted, will do me and my supporters the most good?" and "Which of the policies that my opponent wishes to see adopted would I find least disturbing?" He is concerned with maximizing his payoff, not with discovering the truth about what justice requires. Consequently, he focuses on the material gains and losses involved in the various possible bargains that he might strike.

In contrast, the politician seeking a just policy pays careful attention to the plausibility of the various claims being advanced. She is prepared to be persuaded by her colleagues, of course, when their arguments seem sounder than her own. But this is not yet a matter of compromising with respect to her commitments. For insofar as the arguments offered by others have genuinely persuaded her, her commitments have simply changed. The need for compromise arises, in her case, when she recognizes that one of her own beliefs is doubtful, that the opposing belief of one of her colleagues is perhaps no less doubtful, but the colleague in question clearly feels a much stronger degree of confidence on the matter than she herself does. In this situation, the reasonable person will acknowledge that her colleague's confidence is in itself *a kind of argument* in favor of the opposing belief. Her colleague, after all, by virtue of his possessing a different background, sees things somewhat differently than she herself does. It is possible, therefore, that her colleague has noticed something that she has not — something crucially relevant to the plausibility of the belief in question, and which accounts for his confidence. This is possible even though her colleague has not (yet) managed to find the language with which to represent this crucial bit of evidence. (After all, he may have found *a* way to represent the evidence, but a way that has not succeeded in conveying to *her* what he is talking about. Alternatively, he may not be aware yet that she has not already noticed this evidence for herself. Finally, the evidence in question may be something that has made a powerful unconscious impression upon him, and thus he may not himself be fully aware of the grounds for his believing what he does — even if they are sound.) Her colleague's confidence constitutes *only* "a kind of argument" in favor of the opposing belief, however, because, until she knows for herself what evidence underlies this confidence, she is not in a position to evaluate how the evidence supports the belief in question. And of course, it is also quite conceivable that the confidence of her colleague is unwarranted, perhaps even a sham. How powerful an argument her colleague's confidence represents, then, is itself something that she will have to evaluate — and she will do so on the basis of what she knows of his character, his biases, and his material interests. In the absence of any good reasons to doubt the sincerity of her colleague's confidence, however, the reasonable seeker of a just policy will give that confidence *some* weight in her evaluation of rival claims. And this fact is what will cause her to be shortchanged in her interactions with bargaining politicians.

The bargaining politician, after all, plays a duplicitous game. In the backrooms, while negotiating his deals with other *tradesmen* like himself, he will name his price. But on the floor of the legislature, in speaking to the public and to all of his fellow legislators, including those genuinely concerned to arrive at a just policy, he will put an entirely different face on what he is up to. There he will argue, apparently in all sincerity, for the appropriateness and justice of the policy that he is (materially) interested in seeing adopted. Locating the airbase in Arizona,[5] for example, is not only wonderful for the citizens of Arizona (and thus wonderful for his own reelection prospects—but how crass of us even to suppose that this might enter into his thoughts on the matter!), it is ideal for the nation as a whole. And those of his colleagues in the legislature who are genuinely concerned to find the right place to locate the airbase will, quite properly, feel themselves obliged to take his arguments seriously. For while his coming from Arizona raises obvious questions about his objectivity, his coming from Arizona might also put him in a better position to understand why locating the airbase there would have legitimate advantages over any other possible location. Those who are genuinely concerned with arriving at the right answer, then, will have to evaluate the significance of the Arizona senator's confidence. And there will be a natural tendency, moreover, to overestimate its significance—to give it too much importance in arriving at their own conclusions about where the airbase should be located.

Those who are comparatively new to the legislature, and who arrive as idealists, will have no prior personal history of encounters with the Arizona senator to rely upon in evaluating the significance of his confidence. As idealists themselves, they will believe that the pursuit of just policies is supremely important, and will be ready to credit others with an appreciation of this as well. Their natural inclination, then, will be to place some trust in the Arizona senator's motivations until such time as they have been given grounds to withdraw that trust. And so they will be duped for a time. This is part of the inevitable price paid by virtue to vice. But even those idealists who are more seasoned and have acquired an appropriately suspicious attitude toward the motivations of some of their colleagues will from time to time be too generous in their evaluations of the reliability of self-interested arguments for particular policies and projects. Now and then, after all, they will be unaware of the specific deals that have been worked out regarding some bill under consideration. On those occasions, while they may strongly suspect that the arguments being offered by one or another of their colleagues are tainted by self-interest, they will not know this for a fact. And thus, insofar as they are genuinely concerned with being fair, to some small degree they will have to discount their own suspicions about the significance of the confidence with which those (in fact self-interested) arguments have been presented. The price paid by virtue to vice diminishes, in other words, as virtue acquires experience, but it continues to be paid in some measure so long as virtue and vice are bound together in a common game that they play by different rules.[6]

The profound unsatisfactoriness of attempting to reason fair-mindedly with someone who has no interest in reciprocating—someone who will cash in on your concessions offered in the service of justice but make none of his own— has been elegantly and amusingly illustrated by Jon Elster.

> Once upon a time two boys found a cake. One of them said, "Splendid! I will eat the cake." The other one said, "No, that is not fair! We found the cake together, and we should share and share alike, half for you and half for me." The first boy said, "No, I should have the whole cake!" Along came an adult who said, "Gentlemen, you shouldn't fight about this: you should *compromise*. Give him three quarters of the cake."

As Elster goes on to point out,

> What creates the difficulty here is that the first boy's preferences are allowed to count twice in the social choice mechanism suggested by the adult: once in his expression of them and then again in the other boy's internalized ethic of sharing. And one can argue that the outcome is socially inferior to that which would have emerged had they both stuck to their selfish preferences.[7]

Elster offers this illustration in fact as part of his criticism of the forum model of politics. It is not that Elster believes that the forum model is wrong in the same sense that he does quite clearly believe the market model is wrong. Rather, he is disturbed at its various impracticalities—impracticalities to which he feels Jürgen Habermas, the most influential exponent of the forum model, pays insufficient attention. In the little story of the two boys, for example, one might almost be inclined to think, as Elster himself suggests, that the reasonable boy would have been better off behaving unreasonably. Except that in a fight over the cake, the prize might well have been destroyed entirely, or been carried off by some third party while the two boys were preoccupied. And if the reasonable lad had chosen instead simply to give up on the discussion—to walk away in disgust from his selfish companion—he would have ended up, of course, forfeiting the entire cake, which is exactly what his "friend" was demanding should happen in the first place.

We saw in the previous chapter that one of the most effective means by which altruists can hold their own in the evolutionary struggle with wholeheartedly selfish types is by withdrawing, as far as possible, from all interactions with them. This is because, insofar as it is possible to avoid interacting with the wholeheartedly selfish, altruists can avoid being taken advantage of by them, and can reap the undiluted benefits of their own mutual willingness to make sacrifices on behalf of the group. Strategies that make evolutionary sense, moreover, have a tendency to become ingrained as (what Michael Ruse and E. O. Wilson call) "epigenetic rules" or instinctive emotional reactions. This probably explains why, among human beings, the *disgust*—the desire to wash one's hands and turn one's back—that the sincerely moral individual feels for the self-serving hypocrite is so compelling. As it becomes clear that the other is not to be trusted, one wishes nothing more than never again to be in a position of having to rely on that person's (nonexistent) good will.

Given that this reaction *is* compelling and common, especially among idealists, it is hardly surprising that the reaction of many individuals who enter politics with high hopes of being able to effect some good is to quickly develop an abhorrence for politics as it is actually practiced—with its cynical bargaining, its double-crosses, its backstabbing, and most disturbingly, its rampant hypocrisy as legislators and executives driven entirely by self-interest pretend to be concerned with justice and the welfare of all. And so, not infrequently, the idealist leaves politics, having discovered that it is "not for him." There seems to be, in other words, an analogue for Gresham's Law in the political sphere. Just as "bad money drives out good," to some degree at least it seems to be case that *bad politicians drive out good ones*. This will happen, of course, not only as idealists abandon politics in frustration and disgust. The tendency will be reinforced as well by the gradual perversion of those politicians who, initially at least, are reasonably idealistic but who are eager to "learn the ropes" from their more experienced and savvy fellow legislators, and who thus become in due time more "realistic" in their expectations. This, then, is the first reason for believing that politics by its very nature tends to be dominated by those with a Machiavellian frame of mind. Those led into politics by the simple lust for power will tend to drive out (intentionally on occasion, no doubt, but far more frequently with no conscious effort at all—just by *being themselves*) those who sought power only as the means by which to achieve some particular social good.

Not that there will be all that many idealists to drive out of politics in the first place, however. For Plato was in all likelihood more correct than he himself knew when he suggested, in *The Republic*, that those who seek extraordinary power are not to be trusted with it, while those who might be trusted with it will not seek it. Plato felt that the problem with politics, at least as he saw it practiced in the Athenian democracy of his day, was that the men who governed affairs of state were unqualified to do so. The solution, he felt, was in a sense to professionalize politics. What he had in mind, of course, was not merely the creation of a class of individuals who concerned themselves almost exclusively with politics—for such a class of "professional" politicians already existed in Athens, and probably always has existed since humans began moving into cities. What Plato had in mind, rather, was that a state should take as much care with the education and training of its politicians as it does with the education and training of, say, its doctors or architects. (After all, an incompetent doctor kills his patients one at a time, and the buildings of an incompetent architect fall down one at a time, while an incompetent politician can, with one or two sufficiently bad decisions, ruin the lives of *everyone* in the state.) But just as not everyone has the aptitude to become a doctor or an architect, not everyone, Plato felt, has the aptitude to become a statesman. Professionalizing politics thus meant, first, identifying those with the necessary aptitude, second, providing them with the appropriate education and training, and finally, pressing them into service for a specified period of time, after which they would be *allowed* to retire.

Identifying those with the necessary aptitude for statesmanship would mean, obviously, the end of democratic elections for high office. For since the average citizen does not himself possess the aptitude for statesmanship, his judgment can hardly be relied upon in identifying those who do have the necessary aptitude. In this sense, politics truly would be *professionalized* on the model offered in *The Republic*. For only those who were already professional statesmen would be in a position to admit others to their profession—which of course is just how things work in medicine, in law, in academia, and the other professional fields of our own day. But the point that most clearly illustrates how great a gulf separates Plato's conception of what politics might and should be from the reality of politics as it is actually practiced is to be found in his presumption that genuinely professional statesmen would have to be pressed into a service from which they would be eager to retire. The genuinely qualified statesman's reluctance to serve followed, Plato felt, as a rather obvious implication from the fact that he or she would have to be, both by disposition and training, a philosopher or "lover of wisdom." As someone who took delight from contemplating the world[8] and deepening his or her understanding of it, the statesman would only reluctantly—and under considerable moral pressure—agree to suspend that contemplation for a time so as to attend to the practical business of governing on behalf of others.

There are few philosophers today who would be inclined to agree with Plato's contention that philosophers, properly educated, would experience no great difficulty in justly and efficiently administering the affairs of a state. This is because there are very few philosophers today who would accept the theory of knowledge that Plato relies on in *The Republic*—with its metaphysical underpinning of a realm of Forms. For good reason we no longer believe, as Plato did, in the possibility of knowing the principles that govern empirical states of affairs with the same kind of certainty with which it is possible to know the derived analytical propositions of Euclidean geometry. The world and the problems involved in coming to understand it are far more complex than this would imply.

But that is precisely why few people today who possess what Plato regarded as a philosophical disposition—people who are genuinely concerned, that is to say, with the pursuit of truth and justice—will have the temerity to put themselves forward for election to high political office. For in stark contrast to Plato's philosopher-kings, who were supposed to know all there was to know about just and efficient government, anyone today with an ounce of understanding will know that *he does not by any means know* all that might have a bearing on the efficiency and justice of government. Conscious of his own ignorance of much that it would be important to know, and conscious as well of the enormous impact that the mismanagement of government has, the individual with a proper appreciation of the importance of justice, as well as the difficulty of identifying and delivering it, will tend to hold back from politics in the hope that someone better qualified will agree to serve. Unfortunately, the man or woman most likely to step forward instead is someone unconcerned about his or her limitations—someone who will see in political office primarily an opportunity rather than a responsibility.

Consider, in this regard, the significance of the fact that we elect someone to political office not to decide an issue, about which he may be extremely knowledgeable, but rather for a term of years. During his time in office, the elected official will contribute to the decision-making process on whatever comes before him, regardless of whether he happens to be an expert on the issue or has never previously given it a moment's thought. Since almost all of the issues that come before a legislative assembly or political executive are complex and multifaceted, with the power to affect different people in a wide variety of ways, arriving at a thorough and well-considered judgment regarding what justice would seem to require on each and every issue coming before the officeholder will be quite impossible. There simply will not be time to research all of the ramifications of every piece of legislation or every possible line of action. Indeed, viewed in this light, one can hardly avoid being struck by the presumptuousness of anyone who believes that he is *qualified* to comment and vote upon whatever may come before him during his term in office. The responsibility, one suspects, is lightly borne by realist politicians because they do not take it all that seriously. What almost any officeholder can expect to do in each and every case, after all, is determine fairly accurately how an issue needs to be decided in order to maximize (at least in the short run) its benefit for himself and for those supporters upon whom he relies for his reelection. Moreover, insofar as the realist is committed to the market model of politics, according to which his responsibility as officeholder is to speak on behalf of a particular faction—the faction to which he owes his election in the first place—it will seem to him that approaching issues self-interestedly is exactly what he *should* be doing! And that, of course, makes the task of holding elected office considerably easier.

This, then, is the second reason we can cite for believing that politics *by its very nature* will tend to be dominated by Machiavellian realists. For not only will those idealists who enter politics be far more likely than realists to become disillusioned and leave the political arena in disgust, but because of their far more demanding conception of what politics should involve, they will also be much less eager than realists to enter the political arena in the first place. Where the idealist sees daunting responsibility and tends, as a result, to hold back in spite of his profound dissatisfaction with the policies being embraced by his state, the realist, in contrast, as a pursuer of power for its own sake, sees in the political arena nothing but enormous opportunity. For nowhere else, except perhaps in the upper reaches of a business empire, is it possible to exert a comparable influence over the unfolding of events. The lust for power, as was mentioned earlier, is directed toward the pure capacity to determine outcomes—any and all outcomes. Thus the fact that there is no telling for sure *what* will come before a legislative assembly or across an executive officeholder's desk, but that *whatever* is important *will* come before that assembly or across that desk, means that politics, to a greater degree than anything else, captures what the lust for power is all about. The individual driven by such a lust will take delight in the simple fact of being in a position to exercise power, but even more important, being in such a position, he will be able to use that power to amass more power.

In this section I have been using the terms "realist" and "idealist" more or less as if they were mutually exclusive and between them exhausted the kinds of people who might enter the political arena. Obviously, this represents an enormous simplification of what is actually a far more complex situation. It would be more accurate to think of the Machiavellian realist, committed to the proposition that "might makes right," and the idealist, intelligently concerned with the pursuit of truth and justice, as representing opposite extremes on a continuum. The vast majority of politicians, like the vast majority of people generally, are neither entirely one nor the other, but fall somewhere in between—occasionally thinking and acting like a realist, occasionally thinking and acting like an idealist. The degree to which one is either an idealist or a realist, then, will be a matter of how frequently one thinks and acts in one way as opposed to the other. (And a quick guide to one's propensity can be had by determining in which way one thinks and acts when confronted with important issues.) To admit that my discussion of the behavior and motivations of politicians has been a simplification is not to suggest, however, that it has had no explanatory value. The laws of mechanics too, after all, when these are used to explain or predict the behavior of material bodies, are sim-plifications. Their explanatory and predictive power is nonetheless genuine because, and insofar as, they refer to real tendencies belonging to the bodies in question. I would argue that the same holds true regarding the account given here. Given how an idealist (of the kind I have stipulated) thinks and acts, he will be taken advantage of repeatedly in his interactions with realists, given how *they* think and act, and will never repay the unkindness. Given how an idealist thinks, he will appreciate, in a way the realist simply cannot, given how *he* thinks, the enormous responsibility involved in putting oneself for-ward for political office. But when it comes to explaining or predicting the behavior along these lines of any actual flesh-and-blood human being in the political arena, the question that remains to be answered, of course, is, how much of an idealist and how much of a realist is this person?

Still, one might ask at this point, do Machiavellian realists and (dignified) idealists—and their various hybrids—really exhaust the kinds of people that one can expect to encounter in the political arena? There is, I think, clearly a third type of individual that one more than occasionally hears about, but frankly, this kind of person holds no interest for me here. He sees the politi-cal arena neither as a market nor as a forum, but rather as what *should be* an extension of the church (synagogue, mosque, etc.). As he sees it, society has no great need of a forum, for the meaning of justice is clear: it is a matter of doing God's will, which is presumed to be obvious and unmistakable. Insofar as he attempts to turn the political arena into an extension of the church, though, he tends to engage in politics *as if he were a realist*—pressuring op-ponents, cutting deals, and reneging on deals already cut whenever it seems possible to improve on them. To all intents and purposes, then, he *is* a realist— except that he does not embrace the principle of "might makes right."[9] He is not prepared, that is to say, to acknowledge that those who dexterously and successfully oppose his will are "right" by virtue of *their* political "might." Righteousness, instead, is always associated in his mind with his own creed and with any action that improves its public standing. He is, it would seem, a realist who lacks the confidence to be unabashedly selfish—to pit himself against the world. Instead, he seems to feel it necessary to reinforce his sense of himself by immersing himself in something enormously more powerful and important than he is and by basking (if only in his own eyes) in its re-flected glory.

The reason the religious fundamentalist does not interest me here, however, is that I see no serious challenge coming from that direction. That is, I see no serious *intellectual* challenge; for there is quite clearly in the United States, as in the Middle East, a very serious *political* challenge posed by fundamen-talists. The religious fundamentalist is, if not necessarily unintelligent, then grievously uninformed by the standard of what is known today with some confidence. In that sense, the moral challenge posed by the way in which he chooses to live his life does not call for a philosophical response. In contrast, the Machiavellian realist poses a challenge that cannot be dismissed on the grounds that it is uninformed or unintelligent. The question that his way of conducting himself challenges us to answer is made, if anything, even more urgent in light of the overwhelming evidence that, as mere biological organisms, we exist utterly by chance and for no more than a few decades. That question is: why should we *not* be brazenly but also cleverly selfish?

Machiavellian realism, as we have seen, has a natural tendency to dominate in the political arena. And decisions made in the political arena have always had a profound impact on the lives of average human beings, whether they have had any input into those decisions or not. For some time, however, the variety of ways in which decisions made in the political arena have been intruding upon the lives of average people has been multiplying—as society has grown increasingly urbanized and increasingly technologized. In spite of nostalgic calls for "smaller government" and "less bureaucracy," there is no avoiding this development. It is the simple and inevitable consequence of the increasingly complex forms of coordination that highly technological and urbanized life requires. But this development implies as well that the altruist's evolutionary tactic of avoiding interaction with selfish types is increasingly unavailable to our species. Insofar as we are all subject to the laws, regulations, and policies arrived at in the political arena, the selfish motivations that tend to govern those decisions exact a toll from all of us. (To cite just one example, think of the enormous toll—in the hundreds of billions of dollars— exacted of American taxpayers by Washington's decision to bail out the savings and loan industry in the late 1980s.) Thus the individual who chooses to reject Machiavellian realism, or the unabashed pursuit of his own selfish interests in any and all circumstances, if he is at all aware of how the political world works, must do so in the full realization that there will be a price to be paid on his part for this decision. On balance, he will almost certainly lose, in material terms, and possibly quite substantially, as a result of his willingness to subordinate his own interests to those of justice. Why, then, should he choose to do so?

THE PURSUIT OF WEALTH

It is not only in the political arena, of course, that we find this challenge (of selfish realism) posed. If anything, we are probably even more profoundly affected by decisions made in the economic realm than by those made in the political realm. This would seem to be a justifiable claim, even if one hastens to admit that drawing any sort of firm distinction between the political and economic realms is rather more arbitrary than is usually supposed.[10] Moreover, the dominant form of economic organization in the world today—capitalism—is a system in which the pursuit of power for its own sake is taken as the drive spring of economic activity. The drive to accumulate more, always more—what used to be called, in an era of somewhat different sensibilities, *greed*—is the very core of capitalism, a fact that is seldom acknowledged, however. Indeed, given how accustomed we are to hearing capitalism praised as if it were identical with liberty itself, more than a few readers will probably balk at the claim that greed is the core of capitalism. It should be understood, however, that no unusual degree of selfishness is being imputed here to those of us who merely happen to earn our living in a capitalist economic system. Those of us who must *earn* a living, after all, are not ourselves capitalists, regardless of how we may feel about capitalism as a system. For a capitalist is not someone who subscribes to an economic theory, the way a Marxist is someone who subscribes to the economic theory expounded in *Das Kapital* and the *Grundrisse*; rather, he is someone who possesses capital, and the large majority of us do not.

As Robert Heilbroner explains in *The Nature and Logic of Capitalism*, capital is not to be understood as mere money—as the sum available in your bank account, for example. But neither is it to be understood, for that matter, as mere production goods—as the machinery sitting in a textile factory, for example. Instead,

> capital is either of these things when it is used to set into motion a process of continuous transformation of capital-as-money into capital-as-commodities, followed by a retransformation of capital-as-commodities into capital-as-more-money. . . .
>
> *Capital is therefore not a material thing but a process that uses material things as moments in its continuously dynamic existence.* It is, moreover, a social process, not a physical one. Capital can, and indeed must, assume physical form, but its meaning can only be grasped if we perceive these material objects as embodying and symbolizing an expanding totality. A human being cannot exist without flesh and blood, but the essence of humanness is that flesh and blood are in the service of an organizing purpose, a life force. So it is with capital. Without the organizing purpose of expansion, capital dissolves into material building blocks that are necessary but not sufficient to define its life purpose.[11]

This characterization puts capital in a rather favorable light. It is governed by a *purpose* that endows it with *meaning*. But we must recognize that that purpose—its own expansion—is nothing more than one form of the pursuit of power for its own sake. For money—the abstract and fluid element in the process of capital—is one of the purest forms of power, given that it can be translated into so many different things. Any real increase in one's money[12] thus represents a real increase in one's power. And most of what has been said so far about moral corruption and the pursuit of power for its own sake, as we will see, applies as well to the purpose that governs capital.

There is no denying that capitalism generates an expansion of wealth far beyond anything attainable by means of other economic systems. Any modern capitalist society (France, say) is enormously more wealthy than its earlier incarnations in feudal or subsistent agricultural times. That increase in wealth, moreover, at least if we look at "mature" capitalist societies, is widely shared—even if to remarkably varying degrees—among the citizens of the nation in question. Thus the living standard of even comparatively poor wage-earners in France today is *far* superior to that which was enjoyed by the feudal peasants of France six or seven hundred years ago. This is so obvious as to be hardly worth mentioning, and it is extremely tempting to give the credit for this improvement to capitalism as an economic system. In one sense, moreover, the temptation need not be resisted. For had capitalism not generated an enormous increase in wealth, there would have been no increase to be distributed by the market to rich and poor alike. But in another sense, it would be a grave mistake to credit capitalism for this improvement in the living standards of the poor. For that improvement in living standards has been gained only as a result of the concerted struggle of wage-earners *against* the natural tendency of capitalism, which is to concentrate wealth and power in the hands of the few.

As Heilbroner observes,

> The extraction of wealth, as a flow of "surplus" production systematically channeled from the broad working body of society into the hands of a restricted group or class, is by no means peculiar to capitalism. Surplus itself, in all societies, refers to the difference between the volume of production needed to maintain the work force and the volume of production the work force produces.[13]

But if capitalism is hardly unique in extracting wealth from the productive activities of society and concentrating it in the hands of a few (since this occurs as well in any command system of economics), the extraction of wealth, followed by its investment as a preliminary to the extraction of even *more* wealth, is nonetheless "the single most important element in capitalism."[14] What makes possible this perpetual alternating cycle of capital investment and the extraction of wealth (in the form of profit, which then becomes additional capital) is a social relationship that one does not find in precapitalist societies—

a social relationship between the owners of money and goods, the momentary embodiments of capital, and the users of these embodiments, who need them to carry on the activity of production on which their own livelihoods depend. The legal crux of this relationship lies in the right of exclusion: a central, although often ignored, meaning of "property" is that its owners can legally refuse to allow their possessions to be used by others. The critical aspect of money or capital goods as private property does not lie in the right of owners to use them in any way they wish, for such a dangerous social right has never existed, but to withhold them from use if their owners see fit. It is this right that enables the capitalist to dominate the sphere of trade and production in which his authority extends.[15]

The capitalist, by virtue of his right to prevent his production goods from being used—which is to say, by virtue of his right, first, not to hire a given prospective employee, and second, to shut down production altogether—is in a dominant position with respect to those who either wish to, or must, work for him in order to earn their living. This gives him the leverage to extract from the production generated by his workers some portion of it (and if conditions are favorable, quite a considerable portion) as profit or "return on his investment."

But this leverage does not exist, of course, if the capitalist's prospective employees are in a position simply to reject his proffered wages—if they have, in other words, the "sturdy independence" of yeoman farmers or guild craftsmen. Thus before capitalism can really take hold in a society, it is necessary for that independence to be destroyed, because "the domination of capital hinges on the appearance of a class of workers who are dependent for their livelihood on access to the tools and land that can be legally denied to them by their owners."[16] There are two aspects to that domination, the first of which was noticed already by Adam Smith. "Many workmen," Smith pointed out, "could not subsist a week, few could subsist a month, and scarce any a year without employment." Thus while "in the long-run the workman may be as necessary to his master as his master is to him, . . . the necessity is not so immediate."[17] The fact that the capitalist can almost always afford to outwait his prospective employees already gives him considerable leverage in forcing them to come to work on *his* terms. What clinches the deal, however, is something that Smith did not apparently notice, but which did not escape Marx. To quote Heilbroner yet again:

the dependency [of the laborer on the capitalist] also presupposed the dissolution of previous social relationships in which the peasant was entitled by law and custom to retain some portion of the crops he directly raised, and in which the urban worker owned his own means of production in the form of a cottage loom, a potter's wheel, and the like. That altered relationship was the end product of a protracted revolution, commencing in the fifteenth century or even earlier, continuing through the nineteenth, and in some parts of the world still in progress, in which the enclosure movement, the destruction of protected crafts and guilds, the creation of a proletariat from the cellars of society, and the whirlwind forces of new technologies disrupted the social relations of older socioeconomic regimes and prepared the way for the wholly different regime of capital.

However varied the agencies of this immense revolution, its effect was always the same: established rights of direct access to one's own product were replaced by new rights by which peasants and workers were legally excluded from access to their means of livelihood.[18]

There is an enormous irony to be noticed here. For the ultimate justification of private property to which virtually all defenders of capitalism appeal (when they are forced to defend the legitimacy of something that they would much prefer to have simply taken for granted)[19] is that offered by John Locke in the *Second Treatise of Government*. According to Locke, the only thing that entitles one to claim ownership of something that had previously had no owner is the fact that one has mixed (in some appropriate fashion) one's personal labor with that which one is now claiming. Labor is, in this sense, the key to ownership. But there *is* a proviso, of course. According to Locke, one's labor does not entitle one to anything unless "as much and as good" (in the way of natural resources) is left for others to appropriate through *their* efforts. But how are we to square this explanation of the legitimacy of private property with the mechanics of capitalism? For on the one hand, the capitalist *as* capitalist *does not labor at all* and yet his wealth increases. This is supposedly because his assets "labor" for him. His profits, that is to say, are in a sense rents received for the employment of his capital by others. But why, one might ask, does the capitalist who has somehow come into possession of land on which a coal seam is to be found *own* the coal that is dug from the ground, while the laborers who actually place their bodies at risk by entering the mine (which they have dug), and wear their muscles out with pick and shovel, have no claim at all to the coal that, aside from their efforts, would continue to lie in the ground, of no use to anyone? If labor is the key to ownership, then surely on the basis of Locke's theory of property, *they* should be the ones to own the coal. This would be especially true if, apart from identifying the presence of a coal seam, no one had yet done anything to "improve" the stretch of land in question. For as we have already seen (in the first chapter), there is no sensible way to explain, on Locke's terms, how such a stretch of land could have come into anyone's ownership. And yet it is only because the capitalist is deemed to own the coal that his miners unearth that he is able to extract a "surplus" from their production—by paying them less in the way of wages than the market value of the coal that they have brought out.

This is not yet the main problem, however. The truly serious question is: how can the capitalist be entitled to his ownership of capital goods—in accordance with Locke's theory of property—when "as much and as good" is most definitely *not* available for his laborers to appropriate to themselves? After all, if the necessary land and resources were still available to be appropriated by anyone coming along, there would be no reason at all for his laborers to work for *his* benefit. Instead, they could work for themselves, keeping all of the fruits of their own efforts. In other words, in order for the capitalist's assets to bring him any rents in the first place—in order for the capitalist to be in a position to hire employees on favorable terms—Locke's proviso *must* be violated. Were it not violated, there would be no "class of workers dependent for their livelihood on access to the tools and land" of the capitalist, access to which the latter is legally entitled to deny them. As an economic system, then, capitalism is incompatible with the basic fairness that Locke attempted to guarantee by means of his proviso on the original acquisition of property. For capitalism *requires* a class of exploitable laborers (even if, in principle at least, no given person is compelled indefinitely to remain a member of that class).

Bluntly stated, the relationship between capitalist and wage-earner involves a form of domination. But as Heilbroner is quick to remind us, domination of the many by the few is historically the norm, and the exercise of power through capital at least has the virtue of being less violent and direct than the power traditionally exercised by a king or inquisitor.

> The power wielded by capital differs in subtle but substantial ways. The owner of capital is not entitled to use direct force against those who refuse to enter into engagement with him as buyer or seller. The merchant or the industrial employer may, of course, have recourse to the power of state to enforce contractual arrangements, and the state is usually—although not always or by legal necessity—willing to lend its punitive powers to break strikes, disband picketers, provide armed guards to protect the routes and outposts of trade or the establishments of production. Nonetheless, the coercive force itself belongs to the state, not to the capitalist; and when the capitalist employs strong-arm tactics it is a usurpation, not a proper use of power.
>
> In a word, there is a qualitative difference between the power of an institution to wield the knout, to brand, mutilate, deport, chain, imprison, or execute those who defy its will, and the power of an institution to withdraw its support, no matter how life-giving that support may be.[20]

One should be able to acknowledge this qualitative difference in the way in which power is exercised by means of capital, however, without losing sight of the fact that domination of any kind—as the failure to afford equal consideration to the well-being of those who are dominated—is incompatible with justice.

We can already anticipate, then, that just as it is difficult, if not impossible, for the idealist committed to the pursuit of truth and justice to participate wholeheartedly in politics, given its intrinsic nature, so too it will be difficult, if not impossible, for the dignified idealist to function effectively as the head of—or even as a reasonably senior executive in—a business enterprise. (We might do well to recall at this point the contrast between the attitude of Ralph Hopkins who, in order to build his "big successful business," was prepared to "lift it up regardless of anybody or anything else," and that of Tom Rath who, when called upon to sacrifice his family's welfare in order to advance his career, excused himself on the grounds that he was "one of those nine-to-five guys" that Hopkins had earlier disparaged.) In both cases the explanation for this incapacity on the part of the idealist is the same. Politics and the market are essentially competitive—often fiercely so—and achieving success in either consequently tends to require a single-mindedness and ruthlessness that the dignified idealist *cannot* adopt as his frame of mind and remain true to his ideals.

That the marketplace is a competitive environment is a truism, but it will be worth our while to consider for a moment why this is the case, and what implications follow from this fact. Again, we turn to Robert Heilbroner for his analysis:

> capital . . . exists in a constant state of vulnerability as it passes through its never-ending circuits of M-C-M' [that is, capital-as-money—capital-as-commodities—capital-as-more-money].
>
> The vulnerability results from the continuous dissolution of objects into money, which returns all embodiments of wealth to a common reservoir accessible to all other capitalists. . . . Capital is powerful only insofar as it continuously runs the gauntlet of circulation, each capitalist of necessity distributing his money into the hands of the public (his workers, his suppliers) in order to procure the labor services and materials from which his capital will be reconstituted as a commodity. Each capitalist must win back from the public at large the money capital he has disbursed to various sections of it, and each capitalist is simultaneously trying to win for himself as much as possible of the money capital of other capitalists that has been relinquished in similar fashion.
>
> *This continuous dissolution and recapture is the essence of the process of competition*, which can now be seen as an element in the working of the system that directly stems from the nature of capital itself. Competition . . . [means] the inescapable exposure of each capitalist to the efforts of others to gain as much as possible of the public's purchasing power. Competition therefore . . . is not directly connected with the exercise of domination, because competition does not [directly] pit capitalists against workers but capitalists against other capitalists. [Thus] competition is the instantiation in the economic world of the "warre of each against all" that Hobbes imagined to be the original and always latent

condition of the political world. In Hobbes's world, protection against the threat of mutual devastation was gained by the delegation of power to Leviathan, the state, in the form of a social contract; but in the economic war among capitalists no such protection is possible because . . . the very creation of the realm of capital requires the exclusion of Leviathan's power from its domain. The state can buffer competition in individual markets, but it cannot call off the "warre of each against all" that results from the M-C-M' circuit.

Thus capital itself introduces a form of social war, and social war brings a new intensity to the drive for wealth. . . . That new intensity derives from the motive of self-preservation, by popular repute the most intense and unrestrained of all instinctual responses. . . .

Because of its necessitous exposure to capture, . . . the defense of capital cannot be mounted like that of a citadel. On the contrary, the only defense available to any capitalist, large or small, is an unrelenting concentration on the successful recapture of capital-as-money from the hands of the public. Here is the root of the acquisitive behavior of the business world that we can now see as a necessary expression of the nature of capital itself.[21]

The economic "warre of each against all" that Heilbroner describes here may not directly pit the capitalist against his employees, but it most certainly affects their relationship. For one important way in which the capitalist can always strive to improve his "competitive edge" is by squeezing wages. Success in the capitalist's "war," after all, is a matter of maximizing profits, and profits are what is left over after wages have been subtracted from the production of his workers. Thus a reduction of wages, if it can be managed, is among the most surefire of ways to increase profits. But to think along these lines is, as Kant would say, to view one's employees as a means to the achievement of one's own goal, rather than as ends in themselves. For Kant, of course, that constitutes an *immoral* way of looking at human beings. And indeed, there will no doubt be some employers who feel now and then a conscience pang at the prospect of reducing their workers' wages, or cutting their benefits, or laying them off altogether because it has suddenly become possible to hire labor more cheaply elsewhere. These are the employers who notice, and care somewhat, that these straightforward business-minded decisions will, incidentally, disrupt and in some cases perhaps even permanently harm the lives of people who are dependent upon them—people who may have already served them well for some time as employees. These are the employers, that is to say, who are not entirely comfortable about dominating others.

But in "war," of course, even presumably a social "warre of each against all," as in love, "all things are fair." That puts, somewhat too glibly, what is nonetheless a serious consideration. Insofar as self-preservation does seem to be at stake for the competing capitalists, for many of them it will seem obvious that doing business successfully requires that laborers—like soldiers—are to be sacrificed occasionally. And those employers who are too squeamish to recognize and comply with this requirement—like the nation that is too squeamish to sacrifice its young men in battle—will fall before those possessing the necessary toughness. The competitive edge gained by ruthlessly reducing one's labor costs is, after all, an edge that can be used to increase one's market share. Thus the softhearted capitalist soon finds that the question over which he has been wracking his soul—the question of whether or not to reduce his own labor costs when this seems possible—has become moot, since in the face of competitors who experience no such doubts, he soon finds himself with no business left to conduct. In business competition, as in war, scruples are a liability. And this same working principle—that profit maximization takes precedence over considerations of fairness—holds with regard to *all* of the various ways in which profit can be increased. One must not (seriously) break the law, of course, at least not if there is a significant danger of being called to account for doing so. And one must not alienate one's customers or one's employees, at least not if there is a serious possibility that this will send them to buy from, or to work for, one's competitors instead of oneself. But where expectations have been lowered—so that employees will accept a wage cut or poor working conditions, customers will tolerate shoddy service or defective products, and the law will turn a blind eye to moderate infractions—the logic of capitalism dictates that one should take advantage of those conditions. Doing so will, after all, cut costs—and virtue itself is only a virtue in the business sense if it improves the bottom line.

There is, moreover, a natural tendency for expectations to diminish in the economic realm. It takes an effort, after all, to respond to infractions and insults, even if these are minor. And so, for the most part *minor* insults and infractions go unpunished. When, for example, one's employer demands that one take on a heavier workload or accept poorer working conditions, one is faced with an unpleasant choice—either to accept the poorer conditions or to spend time and effort looking for better conditions with another employer. Thus if the conditions are not too much worse than they were, the natural inclination will be to put up with them. But in time, of course, these slightly worsened conditions set the new standard of expectation for both employer and employee. As a result, when the employer again looks for a way to reduce costs, he once again increases the workload slightly or cuts corners on benefits. And again, the employee, faced with the same unpleasant choice as before, is inclined to knuckle under. Eventually, as this process continues, the employee reaches a point at which she is ready to rebel. The series of repeated small infractions will be seen to constitute, collectively, a significant reduction of the terms according to which she originally agreed to work, and she will now seriously begin to look for alternatives. The problem, though, is that the working conditions being offered by her employer's competitors are probably also not what they once were. After all, those competitors will have noticed what her employer was getting away with, and given *their* need to reduce costs to remain competitive, they may well have followed suit. This is one small (and obviously much simplified) example of what is known as a "race to the bottom." The same principle can be seen to operate in the reduction of product quality over time—another obvious way of cutting costs. Customers, that is to say, just as readily as employees, can be forced into accepting a reduction in quality by a process of gently chivvying their expectations. In the case of customers, this involves getting them used to the idea that things will not last quite as long, or taste quite as good, or perform quite as dependably, as they once did. This can be done, of course, only if it happens slowly and only if almost everyone providing a given kind of product is participating in the game of quality reduction.

It is not the case, then, that everywhere one looks in a capitalist system one finds a "race to the bottom" in progress. Certain conditions need to be satisfied if such a race is to get started and, generally speaking, these are the conditions that foster collusion. Where there is genuine competition between capitalists, they will seek to increase profits by improving their market share. And normally that will be accomplished by offering the best products, wages, and working conditions they can afford, in order to attract customers and the most productive laborers. But precisely because some firms do succeed in significantly increasing their market share, it follows that as an industry matures competition tends to falter. There come to be fewer, and bigger, firms dominating the field and, given the economies of scale, as long as the industry in question remains essentially the same, these few large firms have comparatively little to fear from upstart would-be competitors. As this stage is reached, the prospect of continuing to increase profits by improving market share begins to look less plausible than does the alternative approach to profit growth—cutting costs and raising prices. And so, sometimes even without any explicit program having been agreed upon—for that, of course, would be illegal in most instances—the few large remaining firms within an industry more or less cease competing with each other and "grow" instead by squeezing production costs and tacitly fixing prices. The primary losers in this situation, as economic competition gradually transforms from something occurring among firms (that is, among capitalists) into something occurring between firms, on the one hand, and their customers and employees, on the other, are those whose expectations are being driven down in both respects—that is to say, ordinary wage-earners, who are offered only poorer quality or increasingly expensive goods to buy with their shrinking wages.

This is not the place to recount the history of capitalism's abuses, but one notable instance might be taken as illustrative of the general tendency. The following passage comes from Howard Zinn's *A People's History of the United States.*

> [In 1900 J. P. Morgan] formed the U. S. Steel Corporation, combining [Andrew] Carnegie's corporation with others. He sold stocks and bonds for $1,300,000,000 (about 400 million more than the combined worth of the companies) and took a fee of 150 million for arranging the consolidation. How could dividends be paid to all those stockholders and bondholders? By making sure Congress passed tariffs keeping out foreign steel; by closing off competition and maintaining the price at $28 a ton; and by working 200,000 men twelve hours a day for wages that barely kept their families alive.
>
> And so it went, in industry after industry—shrewd, efficient businessmen building empires, choking out competition, maintaining high prices, keeping wages low, using government subsidies. These industries were the first beneficiaries of the "welfare state." By the turn of the century, American Telephone and Telegraph had a monopoly of the nation's telephone system, International Harvester made 85 percent of all farm machinery, and in every other industry resources became concentrated, controlled.[22]

The market offers no serious opportunity for wage-earners to resist this kind of pressure, given that it is exerted (when it is effective) by a monopoly or by means of tacit collusion on the part of an oligopoly within a given industry. As a result, there is little or no opportunity for the individual laborer or consumer to respond by agreeing to work for, or to buy from, those firms that are not involved in driving down wages or product quality. The only effective response that might be available is thus a collective quasi-political response. For the owner of a firm who can afford to be indifferent if one or two of his employees decide to quit or a handful of his customers decide to stop buying his goods may nonetheless have a serious problem if his entire workforce decides to walk off the job or a sizable number of his customers organize a boycott of his products. Faced with the pressure of a strike or boycott, the capitalist might attempt to win by simply outlasting his tormentors. But this is an unwelcome prospect insofar as it involves giving up the position of dominance that the capitalist normally enjoys. Historically, then, an alternative (and overtly political) response has always been preferred by capitalists whenever it was available. And that was to bring the full weight of the state to bear in breaking strikes by having them declared illegal and then suppressed.

In the United States, for example, virtually from the inception of the labor movement in the 1830s until the depths of the Great Depression in the 1930s, capitalists could almost always count on the willingness of governors, legislatures, and judges to comply with requests for measures (court injunctions, as well as intervention by police or National Guardsmen) to break up strikes and eliminate the influence of labor organizers (frequently through their imprisonment). In 1935, with the country seemingly on the verge of social revolution, given the enormous sufferings and numbers of the poor, the rights of unions to organize and conduct orderly strikes were finally recognized, with the passage of the National Labor Relations Act as part of Franklin D. Roosevelt's New Deal legislation. No victory is permanent, however, and in the past two decades, with exceptionally business-friendly administrations in Washington curtailing labor rights, and with capital that is increasingly free to move wherever it wishes to around the globe (and thus increasingly free to avoid having to deal with protected and unionized labor—by setting up shop in China or Indonesia instead of Ohio or Indiana),[23] the hard-won achievements of more than a century of struggle on the part of labor are visibly starting to evaporate.

Business firms, at least those that are successful, have always tended to have a deep and abiding concern for politics. This is because government plays such a powerful role in determining the quality of the business environment within which a firm must operate. The state determines, after all, how licenses, subsidies, and state contracts will be dispersed, how tariffs and taxes will be imposed, how communication and transportation networks will be developed, whether and to what extent the "commons" (that is, the nation's lakes, rivers, air, and parklands) will be protected, and finally, the shape of foreign policy, and thus the availability of foreign investment opportunities and the reliability of foreign markets. These decisions have enormous impact on the prospects of individual firms. For this reason, capitalists who could afford the costs involved have almost always considered the purchasing of political influence to be a sound investment. And so it has become standard practice for major firms to contribute "generously" to election campaigns, to keep batteries of hired lobbyists busy on their behalf, and to compete for the services of well-connected former politicians looking for employment in the private sector.

But the political influence that is purchased by a given firm is used, of course, for the express purpose of benefiting that firm—of maximizing its profits. The firm does not invest its own capital in politics in order to see that government does what is best for the nation as a whole—not if there is any possibility that whatever policy is "best for the nation" might actually diminish its profits. That is to say that firms invariably see the political arena in terms of the *market* model that we discussed earlier, rather than in terms of the *forum* model. But the market model, as we saw, is fundamentally flawed in that it fails to acknowledge that the pursuit of justice rather than private advantage should be the governing consideration of politics. And what that implies, moreover, is that capitalists have no serious commitment to democracy—not if we understand by "democracy" the idea that government policy should be established as far as possible in accordance with the principle of "one citizen, one vote." The whole point of investing in political influence, after all, is to substitute that which one has in abundance—money—for that which one has an inadequate supply of—public support. The tobacco industry, for example, did not have to invest millions in lobbying for political protection as long as the majority of average citizens took it for granted that smoking was both safe and enjoyable. Only as the health costs became clear, and public opinion turned against an industry that made its profits by hooking customers on a highly addictive substance with damaging (and often lethal) side effects, did it become necessary to start investing in political influence in a big way. The point of purchasing political influence, then, is to be in a position to sway government policy even when—indeed, *especially when*—public opinion is against one. (But this is not incompatible, of course, with also spending heavily on the effort to *change* public opinion in one's favor, through political advertisements.)

Robert Heilbroner puts the matter this way:

> Capital is a process oriented to the creation of profit, not to the attainment of freedom. Political goals of any kind, conservative or liberal, enter into the considerations of capital only insofar as they affect the M-C-M' circuit. The normal relation of capital to state power is therefore pragmatic, gladly accepting the use of military, bureaucratic, legislative, or other state interventions when they favor accumulation, resisting them when they do not. To put it differently, capitalists have no interests *as capitalists* in promoting the cause of freedom. They are indeed more likely to have opposed interests, insofar as freedom may create subversive attitudes toward the regime of capital.[24]

We need only recall, in this regard, the long and bloody history of labor strife in the United States—a history that has been largely effaced from the official sanitized and heroic account of America's development. Throughout the period of the worst excesses—from roughly 1870 to 1935—the majority of Americans, as laborers and small-hold farmers, approved of combinations (labor unions and agricultural cooperatives) that would improve their negotiating power vis-à-vis the capitalists. And throughout that period, the various branches of government—reliably under the control of capitalists—did their best to undermine such combinations.[25] It is revealing as well, in this regard, that the Fourteenth Amendment, introduced in 1868 to guarantee the newly acquired rights of blacks, was invoked almost exclusively throughout this period to protect the interests and extend the influence of *corporations* (while blacks were subjected to a system of Jim Crow laws that denied them their basic rights).

The fixation of capitalists on the private acquisition of wealth—a fixation that they pursue not only in the economic realm but also in the political realm, through lobbying and the purchasing of political influence—tends to make government's primary task something that many citizens would find inconceivable. Regardless of what political philosophy may say about the purpose of government being the pursuit of justice, in practice government is first and foremost an arbitrator settling the disputes and squabbles of rival capitalists. For different capitalists, having invested in different industries in different locations, will be lobbying for different distributions of government favors. And the activities of legislation, administration, and adjudication can probably best be understood as processes through which the actual distribution of government favors is worked out through the resolution of power struggles.

But just as a fixation on the acquisition of wealth tends to make one myopic—for the opportunities available here and now are what one has to keep an eye on in order to maximize one's profit from them—so too the perspective of government, fixated as *it* is on the balancing of immediately present competing claims for favors, tends to be disturbingly shortsighted. It is not, of course, that long-term consequences are of no interest to government. But insofar as long-term consequences are always somewhat speculative, while the immediate claims of lobbyists and power brokers are entirely definite, it is difficult if not impossible for an administration or legislature to give due consideration to the long term.[26] And even when an administration does acknowledge the existence of a danger in the offing—a danger (like the depletion of the ozone layer, for example) that clearly and urgently requires a solution—the government in question will find it difficult to address the problem through appropriate regulation of economic practices. This is because the firms operating within the government's jurisdiction will naturally tend to view these proposed regulations from an entirely selfish perspective. In other words, each of them will be inclined to see itself as being unfairly disadvantaged relative to its competitors by the imposition of regulations and will, insofar as this is possible, seek to bear a smaller portion of the collective burden than is its just share. Thus when regulations are first proposed, the firms liable to be affected by them will collectively oppose their imposition altogether. If the government is nonetheless determined to see *some* regulations introduced in order to deal with the danger in the offing, the firms liable to be affected by those regulations will do their best, through lobbying and the calling in of debts, to shape the regulations to their own relative advantage. All of this takes time, of course, so the passage of regulations is delayed, sometimes interminably. Finally, when regulations are actually imposed, the firms affected by them will often do their best to minimize their impact, by surreptitious noncompliance, and by co-opting as far as possible the agencies and individuals that the government has placed in charge of overseeing the application of the regulations.[27]

GROWTH VERSUS PROGRESS

Capitalism, in a word, is about *growth*. Each individual capitalist is concerned to increase his own share of the economic pie, and the natural consequence of their collective efforts is supposed to be a larger pie. Thus a healthy economy, according to conventional wisdom, is one in which GNP, and even more importantly, per capita income, are constantly growing. In 1958, during the halcyon days of America's postwar economic boom, John Kenneth Galbraith suggested that modern capitalist states tend to focus on ever-increasing production as a way of evading the political demand on the part of the poor for a redistribution of wealth.[28] If *everyone*'s lot is improving, after all, even the lot of the poorest members of society, there will tend to be less resentment about disparities of wealth. At the time that Galbraith advanced this idea, the upper classes were exhibiting a remarkable degree of self-restraint, perhaps because a greater measure of fellow-feeling existed then, occasioned by the recent wartime sacrifices that everyone had been called upon to make. To illustrate, in the late 1960s the average pay of corporate CEOs was only twenty-five times that of production workers. By 1988, in contrast, the ratio of average compensation for CEOs to the income of ordinary workers had swollen to ninety-three, and by 1999 it had ballooned to four hundred and nineteen.[29] In the 1950s and 1960s the share of the federal tax burden borne by corporations and the top percentiles of individual income-earners was also far higher than it is today. It is no longer clear, in other words, that it is still the case that *everyone*'s lot is improving as the economy grows. In fact, it is pretty clear that, for the lower and middle classes, their purchasing power peaked some time ago and is now declining. Nonetheless, the idea that a healthy economy is necessarily a growing economy—even if today this implies an increasing gap between rich and poor—is still an unquestioned article of faith among those who control the political and economic realms.

As Galbraith also pointed out, however, there is a problem involved with a perpetually growing economy. For if the purpose of an economy is to provide for the satisfaction of human needs and wants, then surely once the economy in question has reached a level of productivity such that almost everyone's needs and wants have been adequately satisfied, there should be less and less demand for further growth. In a sense, this is already implicit in the economic notion of marginal utility. But if we admit to ourselves, even in principle, that there might be a point beyond which an economy has no good reason to grow, the preferability of capitalism over all other economic systems begins to come into doubt. For capitalism's great advantage, as was mentioned earlier, is that it generates economic growth to an unparalleled degree. If we reach a point at which that is no longer a valued property, then capitalism might reasonably be set aside or superseded. And that, of course, would have enormous implications for those who currently dominate the economic and political realms—which is to say, for *capitalists*.

But given that capitalists have long been in a position to call the prevailing ideological tune, it was not too difficult for them to find a way around this unwelcome implication. As Galbraith explains, the fact that wants diminish in urgency as they are increasingly satisfied was simply *denied*.

> In part, this was accomplished in the name of refined scientific method which, as so often at the higher levels of sophistication, proved a formidable bulwark of the conventional wisdom. Obvious but inconvenient evidence was rejected on the grounds that it could not be scientifically assimilated. . . .
>
> The first step . . . was to divorce economics from any judgment on the goods with which it was concerned. Any notion of necessary versus unnecessary or important as against unimportant goods was rigorously excluded from the subject. Alfred Marshall, who on this, as on so many other things, laid down the rules to which economists have since adhered, noted that "the economist studies mental states rather through their manifestations than in themselves; and if he finds they afford evenly balanced incentives to action, he treats them prima facie as for his purposes equal." He almost immediately added that this simplification . . . was only a "starting-point." But economists ever since have been content to stay with his starting point and to make it a mark of scholarly restraint and scientific virtue to do so. . . . Nothing in economics so quickly marks an individual as incompetently trained as a disposition to remark on the legitimacy of the desire for more food and the frivolity of the desire for a more expensive automobile.[30]

All the same, there is a tremendous implausibility to "the notion that wants do not become less urgent the more amply the individual is supplied." As Galbraith puts it, "It is something to be believed only by those who wish to believe."[31]

But those who are determined at all costs to argue, for example, that the seventh luxury sports car in the multimillionaire's garage is as urgently desired as is the homeless woman's next meal have one significant debating advantage. It is not possible, after all, to directly compare the urgency of the desire that each feels. Thus one can, if one is so inclined, insist that they be treated equally. But there is still, as Galbraith observes, "a flaw in the case."

If the individual's wants are to be urgent, they must be original with himself. They cannot be urgent if they must be contrived for him. And above all, they must not be contrived by the process of production by which they are satisfied. For this means that the whole case for the urgency of production, based on the urgency of wants, falls to the ground. One cannot defend production as satisfying wants if that production produces those wants.[32]

And as we know full well, for some time now in the developed economies manufacturers have had to take an increasingly active part in *generating* wants.

The . . . direct link between production and wants is provided by the institutions of modern advertising and salesmanship. These cannot be reconciled with the notion of independently determined desires, for their central function is to create desires—to bring into being wants that previously did not exist. This is accomplished by the producer of the goods or at his behest. A broad empirical relationship exists between what is spent on production of consumer goods and what is spent in synthesizing the desires for that production. A new consumer product must be introduced with a suitable advertising campaign to arouse interest in it. . . .

Here is something which cannot be accommodated easily to existing [economic] theory. More pervious scholars have speculated on the urgency of desires which are so obviously the fruit of such expensively contrived campaigns for popular attention. Is a new breakfast cereal or detergent so much wanted if so much must be spent to compel in the consumer the sense of want? But there has been little tendency to go on to examine the implications of this for the theory of consumer demand and even less for the importance of production and productive efficiency. These have remained sacrosanct.[33]

And so the commitment to perpetual economic growth persists, even as the increasing reliance on advertising to generate consumption desires makes it clear that much of what is being produced in the perpetually growing economy is superfluous and trivial.

Outside of economics at least it is well understood that perpetual growth is far from a good thing. Perpetual population growth leads of necessity to overcrowding and famine. Perpetual physiological growth—especially when the growth is undirected by the organism as a whole—is downright disastrous. We call such things tumors and cancers. But in economics, capitalist ideology contends, perpetual growth—and most importantly, growth that is not centrally governed, but which proceeds haphazardly, driven by the countless disjointed and often conflicting investment decisions made by millions of greater and lesser capitalists—leads miraculously to a healthy, prosperous, and *just* society. And that faith, among true believers, is unshaken even as they pass (with deliberately averted gaze) the many destitute and homeless individuals who crowd our inner cities, even as they complain about the information-poor and unskilled graduates of our sorely underfunded public education systems, even as they drive by rivers and lakes in which no one any longer would ever dream of swimming, even as they watch the evening news reports about another ecological disaster as some decrepit tanker splits open and dumps its thousands of barrels of crude oil into the ocean, fouling beaches and smothering innumerable fish and seabirds, even as their elderly neighbors drive north to Canada to purchase the medicines they cannot live without and cannot afford to buy at home, even as *two million* of their fellow citizens (the majority of them poor and uneducated and far too many of them black) are incarcerated, even as they find themselves called upon by Washington to help bail out banks that have loaned enormous sums to uncreditworthy debtors in order to encourage consumption, and even as they watch war declared on a pretext in some far-off land at least in part so that a few politically favored corporations (Halliburton, Bechtel, etc.) can reap the benefits of rebuilding the economy that must first be shattered in order to make available the opportunity of reconstruction. The true believer in capitalist ideology sees no connection between any of these things and the exaltation of greed—the eagerness to cut corners wherever possible and to score big at someone else's expense—which lies at the core of capitalism.

The mere fact that things are getting bigger or more numerous is by no means a guarantee that they are also getting better. It is progress, not growth, that should interest us primarily. And it is progress, not growth, that does primarily interest the individual who possesses that more demanding form of dignity that is bound up with an intelligent dedication to the pursuit of truth and justice. This last claim comes close to being a tautology, given that the appropriate yardsticks in terms of which we should measure progress are precisely the regulative ideals of truth and justice. Because, speaking in very general terms here, truth and justice are things that all human beings desire to enjoy in greater measure, and because the pursuit of truth and justice is a communal enterprise, requiring contributions from many sources, an enterprise, moreover, in which the rewards of success are normally (and in some cases, necessarily) made equally available to all who participate, the pursuit of the regulative ideals is unproblematically good. This is why the regulative ideals constitute the correct yardsticks to employ in determining whether or not a community is genuinely achieving progress. A general increase in wealth is seldom unwelcome, of course, but a *community's* wealth—and even more so its welfare—is never to be identified with the sum total of the wealth possessed by its individual members. The pattern of its distribution, which is one crucial aspect of the measure of justice achieved in the community (given that wealth is power), is always at least as important as the mere aggregate amount of wealth in determining how progressive a society is. Moreover, insofar as all achievements effected in the pursuits of truth and justice reflect the expenditure of power, to some extent we already measure the meaningful possession of wealth in a community when we consider what strides it has managed to make in the pursuit of these regulative ideals.

The dignified idealist is by nature a reformer then. Given his concern for the promotion of truth and justice, he will seek to change people's opinions where this seems necessary to improve the quality of their understanding and their treatment of each other. And since much of our treatment of one another takes place within institutional settings, he will seek as well to improve the ways in which institutions function—promoting their efficiency where this seems possible (since the conservation of resources is always a good thing) but far more importantly, making them fairer insofar as he can. Thus the idealist, in spite of his distaste for the stratagems of political realists and his unwillingness to profit at his neighbor's expense, will nonetheless take a serious interest in both the political and economic realms, since he will need to make use of the tools of politics in order to resist the depredations of the power-hungry concentrators of wealth and to introduce safeguards for those people and things that most particularly require protection against exploitation. In all of this, of course, there will be a significant sacrifice involved on his part. His efforts will be time-consuming and exhausting and, to the extent that he makes a difference, they will focus upon him the unpleasant attentions of those whose schemes for exploitation he is trying to foil. Nor will there be any great pleasure to be had from contemplating the nastier inclinations of his fellow human beings. This, however, is simply the price to be paid for his genuine dedication to the ideals of truth and justice. And the particular form of self-restraint that defines his dignity in this sphere is to be found in his willingness to bear the costs that are inevitably involved in striving for reform.

It may appear to some that the reformer described here is well on his way to becoming a fanatic—and it was argued at the end of the second chapter, they might go on to point out, that fanaticism is incompatible with dignity. Certainly there is a fine line that the dignified idealist must walk in his pursuit of public reform. The evidence on which he bases his reforming efforts, he must acknowledge, is always incomplete. There is always information of which he is unaware that may have a bearing on the issue that concerns him. For this reason, and because of his dedication to truth, the dignified idealist is always ready to attend to important new evidence and to change his position and attitude should the evidence warrant it. But it does not follow that because, in principle, the evidence one possesses relating to a particular social issue is always incomplete, that the evidence available is necessarily inadequate to justify action. When the evidence that *is* available clearly seems to indicate that a serious injustice is being committed, anyone who *cares* about justice will not only inquire into the matter more deeply and critically, he will do what he can to end the injustice. If, as in many cases he should, he proceeds slowly, this will be a result of his circumspection, not a consequence of indifference on his part.

NOTES

1. See David Herbert Donald, *Lincoln* (London: Random House, 1995), 419–20.

2. The evidence for this, which is overwhelming, is to be found of course in any serious work of history. For an especially frank and thorough account of how this principle has manifested itself in American history, however, see either Howard Zinn, *A People's History of the United States* (New York: Harper and Row, 1980), or Kevin Phillips, *Wealth and Democracy* (New York: Broadway Boks, 2002) (especially chapter 5).

3. Thus have arisen in America in recent decades the many privately funded conservative "think tanks," the primary function of which is to challenge the influence of the more liberal and intellectually independent political philosophers working in the nation's major universities.

4. Jon Elster, "The Market and the Forum: Three Varieties of Political Theory," in Robert E. Goodin and Philip Pettit, eds., *Contemporary Political Philosophy* (London: Blackwell, 1997), 131–32.

5. I should stress that this is an entirely hypothetical example. There is no allusion intended here to any actual piece of legislation past or present, or to any particular politician from Arizona. The example names a particular state only in order to bring home the fact that in political decision-making there are always localized interests at stake. (This does not mean, of course, that the interests at stake will always be localized in a geographic sense. They may be "localized" instead in pertaining, for example, to one's socioeconomic class, one's gender, one's race, or one's religious sect.)

6. Someone familiar with Robert Axelrod's experiment with competing computer programs, the results of which he discussed in *The Evolution of Cooperation*, might be inclined to suppose that Nice TIT FOR TAT's having won Axelrod's tournament implies that virtue need not be permanently at a disadvantage relative to vice. But this conclusion would be mistaken on two grounds. First of all, as TIT FOR TAT's designer, Anatol Rapoport, repeatedly pointed out to those who misunderstood the "secret" of his program's success, in each and every direct encounter with a "nasty" exploitative program, TIT FOR TAT invariably came off worse. And second, it should be said that TIT FOR TAT was not *really* all that "virtuous" a program. It followed an absolutely unforgiving policy of retribution in its dealing with other programs, and in real life we would hardly call that "virtue." It is worth remembering, in this regard, that the crudely "virtuous" programs—those that always anticipated and offered cooperation in their encounters with others—all went under in short order in the

presence of "nasty" programs. In any event, if virtue in real life is more complicated than even Kant realized, it has to be admitted that it is far more complicated than anything capturable in Axelrod's tournament—revealing, in broad outline, as that may have been.

7. Elster, "The Market and the Forum," 134.

8. More technically, the realm of the Forms. But then, the Forms *inform* the world of appearances, so contemplation of the first does not occur to the exclusion of the second.

9. Those who cut deals and renege on them are not, of course, average religious fundamentalists, but rather the political leaders of religious fundamentalism. These individuals, given that they behave so much more like Machiavellian realists than does the average fundamentalist (who tends merely to mouth support), might well be suspected of *primarily* being Machiavellian realists—realists who have simply discovered that the religious fundamentalism of others is something that can readily be used as a powerful tool in pursuit of their own private and quite selfish goals within the political arena.

10. To mention only the most salient points of connection, it is the state that guarantees the protection of private property and that underwrites the legitimacy, and thus guarantees the purchasing power, of the various forms of currency in circulation—two indispensable conditions for any advanced economy. So too the state sets conditions (in the form of tariffs, investment in national infrastructure, and so on) that favor the growth of one or another sector of the economy (and often one or another company *within* a given sector of the economy), and it does so under the prodding of lobbyists representing various economic interests. On the other hand, it is the wealth generated in the economic realm that purchases—either directly or indirectly—political influence for individuals and corporations. That economic wealth is also tapped (through taxation) by the state for its own political ends—the most crucial of which, of course, are its military contests with other states, which are in turn almost invariably conducted with an eye to the achievement of (someone's) economic goals.

11. Robert L. Heilbroner, *The Nature and Logic of Capitalism* (New York: Norton, 1985), 36–37.

12. That is, an increase not attributable to mere inflation.

13. Heilbroner, *The Nature and Logic of Capitalism*, 33.

14. Heilbroner, *The Nature and Logic of Capitalism*, 33.

15. Heilbroner, *The Nature and Logic of Capitalism*, 38.

16. Heilbroner, *The Nature and Logic of Capitalism*, 41.

17. Adam Smith, *The Wealth of Nations* (Oxford: Clarendon Press, 1976), 84.

18. Heilbroner, *The Nature and Logic of Capitalism*, 41–42.

19. No one *currently* in possession of a significant amount of private property is normally too eager to acknowledge in public that *theft*—in its many variations—has traditionally been one of the most common ways in which property has come to "belong" to a given person, and subsequently, to his heirs. For as soon as one admits this, the challenge arises: how does the *current* owner of (originally stolen) property differ in principle from the individual who would *now* steal it from *him*? The answer, of course, is that the current holder of the wealth in question is in a po-

sition to enlist the power of the state to defend his ownership of the property. He continues, in other words, to enjoy the upper hand in the power struggle with those who would usurp his position of privilege. But the reason for never admitting too loudly in public that *this* represents, not the whole truth about property by any means, but nonetheless an important aspect of that truth, is that those "masses" of poor and acquiescently law-abiding citizens who take the rich man's entitlement to his wealth for granted might eventually come to think like the would-be thief, who sees no particular reason to respect the *current* distribution of property. And as soon as enough of the poor did that, the balance of power now favoring the wealthy would be disrupted. (Given human nature, a *new* hierarchy of wealth would no doubt soon emerge, but the point is that many of those who are *currently* wealthy might be swept aside in the upheaval.)

20. Heilbroner, *The Nature and Logic of Capitalism*, 39.

21. Heilbroner, *The Nature and Logic of Capitalism*, 56–59.

22. Zinn, *A People's History of the United States*, 251. J. P. Morgan had an interesting start to his career as well. "During the Civil War he bought five thousand rifles for $3.50 each from an army arsenal, and sold them to a general in the field for $22 each. The rifles were defective and would shoot off the thumbs of the soldiers using them. A congressional committee noted this in the small print of an obscure report, but a federal judge upheld the deal as the fulfillment of a valid legal contract." *A People's History*, 249.

23. See William Greider, *One World, Ready or Not* (New York: Simon and Schuster, 1997).

24. Heilbroner, *The Nature and Logic of Capitalism*, 127–28.

25. Government—in the service of the capitalists—for the most part did not directly attack agricultural cooperatives. Rather, it undermined the small-hold farmer's prospects of maintaining his independence by keeping the nation's money supply tight, in spite of America's burgeoning population growth during this time. In this way, farmers were forced to pay exorbitant interest rates on the supplies and equipment that they had to buy in order to run their farms; and as a result, they regularly fell into bankruptcy—and the necessity of having to hire themselves out as workers.

26. Consider, for example, Ronald Reagan's refusal to acknowledge, during his two terms as president, the dangers posed by global warming and pollution. Rather than attempt to head off these problems, which would of necessity have involved tightening regulations on manufacturing practices, and in the process would have antagonized some of his wealthiest supporters, it was easier for Reagan simply to deny the scientific evidence that the dangers are real and growing imminent. In startling contrast, in spite of the almost unanimous declarations on the part of disinterested scientists that the "Star Wars" antimissile defense system that he envisioned was entirely unfeasible, Reagan insisted on pouring tens of billions of dollars into this line of research. But here, one suspects, in spite of the rhetoric used to sell the system to taxpayers, the true motivation was not so much guaranteeing long-term national security as it was the provision of "pork"—in the form of research and development funding—to favored firms.

27. See Greider, *Who Will Tell the People? The Betrayal of American Democracy* (New York: Simon and Schuster, 1993), 105–40, and Cass Sunstein, *After the Rights Revolution: Reconceiving the Regulatory State* (Cambridge, Mass.: Harvard University Press, 1990), 97–101.

28. John Kenneth Galbraith, *The Affluent Society*, Fortieth Anniversary Edition (Boston: Houghton Mifflin, 1998), 101.

29. Phillips, *Wealth and Democracy*, 153.

30. Galbraith, *The Affluent Society*, 119–20.

31. Galbraith, *The Affluent Society*, 124.

32. Galbraith, *The Affluent Society*, 124.

33. Galbraith, *The Affluent Society*, 127–28.

Chapter Seven

Why Embrace the Regulative Ideals?

Kant thought that the requirements of morality were fairly obvious and were understood perfectly well by the ordinary "good folk" of his day. One of the central contentions of this book is that, even if that was true in Kant's day, it is no longer the case. We live in a very different moral landscape than Kant did. Determining with confidence exactly what morality requires of us is now often extraordinarily difficult because of the mature development of a political-economic system that was only just beginning to announce its appearance (in England and Holland) in Kant's day—capitalist democracy. The apparent simplicity of the moral law in the Age of Absolutism was a consequence of the fact that ordinary folk had no role to play in the determination of state policy. Kant's fellow Prussians, for example, fought and suffered through two dreadful wars between 1740 and 1763 without having anything to say about Prussia's involvement in those conflicts. It was the prerogative of their hereditary ruler, Frederick the Great, to take them into war if he so chose. Their role was merely to pay taxes, to fight, to suffer and, in no small numbers, to die in support of their king's pursuit of his chosen goals. In this regard, of course, ordinary Prussians were no worse off than their opponents and occasional allies—the French, the Austrians, and the Russians. All were silent supporters of their monarchs—or they were traitors and outlaws.

Today the role of a citizen is far more demanding intellectually. The right to vote in a democratic state carries with it, whether acknowledged or not, the obligation to inform oneself regarding the qualifications, the past histories, and the advisability of the proposed policies of candidates for office. But while this obligation is important, it is impossible to specify exactly *how much* research is required to satisfy it. A cursory glance at the candidates' party affiliations obviously *fails* to satisfy the obligation. On the other hand,

spending all of one's waking hours studying the politicians and their proposals is clearly more than can be expected of any normal citizen (who
makes his living outside of political journalism) even if this would significantly improve the reliability of his decisions about which candidates to support. That we cannot specify with confidence how much investigative effort
is necessary to satisfy the citizen's obligation to inform himself does not imply that the burden is a mere formality—for the policies enacted (or rejected)
by governments affect the lives of enormous numbers of ordinary people,
both at home and abroad. Given that one has some small measure of power
to determine the outcomes of elections, and thus the establishment of policy,
one also has some small measure of responsibility for what is every so often
an *enormously* significant improvement or worsening of the living conditions of other people. And if the achievement or debacle is enormous
enough, even playing a small part in bringing it about will be by no means
morally negligible. But then, neither is one irrevocably condemned to accept
a *small* role in the shaping of public policy. One's political involvement in a
modern democracy is never mandatorily restricted to the act of casting one's
vote at election time. One always has the option, if one is so inclined, of trying to shape the opinions of others—through lobbying efforts or through
public information campaigns. Sometimes the results of such efforts can be
extremely important, as the examples of William Lloyd Garrison, Harriet
Beecher Stowe, and the other major abolitionists illustrate. In principle at
least, even if political realities and one's financial circumstances significantly limit this, one also has the option of standing for office. This can be,
and often is, done from entirely self-interested motives, of course, but there
is nothing to prevent one from entering politics in order to serve some large
moral imperative—the abolition of slavery, say, or the need to end the war
in Vietnam.

Because of the opportunities available to us in a democracy to affect the establishment of public policy, the domain of our moral responsibility is larger
than it was in Kant's day. If we choose to ignore those opportunities, as many
people do, we are to some extent responsible for the disastrous policy decisions that our inattention to public affairs has made possible. If we embrace
those opportunities, however, it is crucial that we correctly understand the
moral implications of the policies being considered. Removing Saddam Hus-
sein as the leader of Iraq, for example, was not a *good* thing to do simply
because he was a tyrant. His removal by force had fully foreseeable consequences for Iraq, for the rest of the Middle East, and for the United States—
foreseeable, that is, *if* one was adequately informed, and also capable of being objective about the issue when it was first being publicly advocated late
in 2002. Those consequences, among which have been the deaths of hundreds

of thousands of Iraqis and the maiming of tens of thousands of American soldiers, have enormous moral significance. But then, so too does the fact that tens of millions of Americans continue to have no adequate health insurance. There are countless public policy issues that carry moral significance—the abortion issue, the gay marriage issue, the affirmative action issue, the homeless issue, the global warming issue, and on and on—and it is crucial that those involved in establishing policy understand in each case what justice requires *(and are committed to seeing it done)*. But that means that *all* of us have a responsibility to understand the moral implications of these many often complex issues, since we *all* are in a position to exert our influence—either for good or ill—in determining which policies will be embraced and which rejected. This is one important reason for contending that the moral landscape in which we live is vastly more complicated than it was in Kant's day. We need to know where we should stand on public policies that involve far more complicated moral issues than do the comparatively tame questions of whether or not we should cheat our neighbors, lie to our spouses, or beat our children.

But the increased opportunities for morally significant action that democracy provides us are not the end of the story. Capitalism too has contributed to the complication of our moral lives. Today each of us is bound into a web of economic relations that is far more intricate than anything that existed in the precapitalist world. We purchase articles and services from an enormous array of providers. We work, quite commonly, for huge corporations each of which is involved in an almost incomprehensible range of business activities. And almost invariably, in order to guarantee the security of our postretirement years, we are compelled to invest in a selection of those corporations. (If we choose not to invest directly, of course, the banks where we keep our savings will do this for us indirectly.) To say that we are *bound* into this web, however, carries slightly inappropriate connotations, for while there is no escaping the web altogether, it is a basic principle of capitalism that each individual is free to choose where to locate himself within this web of economic relations—which is to say, whom to work for, whom to buy from, and which opportunities to invest in. This freedom of choice, though—even constrained as it always is by personal circumstances—introduces the moral dimension into our economic lives, for whom one chooses to associate with and which projects one chooses to support are obviously matters of moral significance. No one working for the tobacco industry, for example, after the connection between smoking and lung cancer became clear, can pretend to be utterly innocent of the suffering and premature deaths that smoking has caused, given the highly addictive properties of nicotine. So too no one buying child pornography or sweatshop-produced running shoes can claim to be free of all responsibility for the harms inflicted upon the children involved in the production of these "goods."

There is big money to be made in a great many "shady" ways—some of them illegal, just as many of them merely immoral. As a result, the capitalist marketplace is rife with activities and projects that the moral individual will wish to avoid encouraging. The problem, however, is that the sheer complexity of the web of economic relations offers cover from the public eye for most individual and corporate wrongdoings. In spite of the occasional whistle-blower and public inquiry, we never see more than the tip of the iceberg of corruption and fraud. Our ignorance of what is being done in the marketplace sets us up to be exploited, moreover, in two different ways. Now and then our ignorance turns us into the direct victims of fraud or theft. More commonly, it sets the stage for our unwitting complicity in projects that we abhor. (This occurs whenever we work for, invest in, buy from, or sell to a company that is engaged in immoral profit-making practices.) Of these two ways of being exploited, the dignified individual will be more deeply troubled by the second. For while it is never pleasant to be robbed, at least one's own honor is unstained when this occurs. When one discovers that one has been unwittingly complicit in harming *someone else*, however, one's moral integrity is undermined. The fact that he was ignorant of the true nature of the projects that he voluntarily supported (even if only indirectly) offers no great comfort to the dignified individual in a case like this, for he will feel that there are things that one should be obliged to know about the activities in which one is involved. In practice, of course, there is always a limit to what one can know about the activities and intentions of those with whom one interacts. But his desire not to be used in any way as the instrument by which others are unjustly harmed will spur the dignified individual to a level of circumspection in his economic dealings with others that the average person would consider to be quite unnecessary.

Dignity, I have been arguing in this book, is a trait that reflects one's willingness—so long as this is not a grudging, but rather a natural and open willingness—to exercise self-restraint in the service of morality. Such willingness, moreover, will *not be* grudging insofar as it genuinely is directed to the exercise of *self*-restraint. For the individual who grudgingly does what is right does so only because he is compelled to, not by his own sense of self, but by external circumstances. He does what is right, in other words, in order to avoid losing the good opinion of his fellows, or from fear of punishment. In contrast, the individual who possesses genuine dignity restrains those of his natural impulses that it would be morally inappropriate to indulge because he has a simple and abiding desire to *avoid being wrong*. This is not a matter of priggish self-righteousness on his part. It is not, after all, as if he expects to be right on all occasions, by virtue of some moral infallibility on his part. On the contrary, his desire to avoid being wrong (in his *own* estimation)[1] — which includes, above all, his desire to play fair by others — has itself revealed to him that it is often difficult to know with anything approaching certainty what actually *is* right. The dignified individual, then, is fully aware that now and then, in spite of his own best efforts, he will find himself having acted inappropriately — even badly. But this is not a condition to which he readily acquiesces. The discomfort that he feels on discovering himself to have been in error is what motivates him, not only always to do what seems to him to be right at the time, but also to remain attentive for indications that his sense of what was right may have been mistaken. And there is, of course, no contradiction involved here. The dignified individual remains attentive for indications that he should *now* feel badly — almost as if he wished to feel badly — because in truth he wishes to learn from his mistakes as quickly as possible — and that in order to minimize the number of mistakes that he commits overall.

But this is an especially demanding regimen to impose upon oneself, and it must be acknowledged that most people do *not* impose it upon themselves. (We have been considering, remember, not the form of dignity that is often attributed to *all* human beings, but rather that "higher" form of dignity to which one might aspire and which only a comparatively few individuals ever exhibit to any considerable degree.) The question that remains to be addressed, then, is *why* anyone should wish to impose this remarkably demanding regimen upon himself. Why go looking for reasons to feel badly about how one has behaved? (Especially since those who will accuse one of having acted badly in particular instances will now and then be *wrong* in their accusations. They too are fallible, after all.) And perhaps more importantly, given that the individual who endeavors always to treat others fairly will inevitably be played for a dupe by at least some of those others, why disadvantage oneself by cultivating a sense of responsibility so much more stringent than the norm? The average person pays no serious penalties, after all, for being only moderately honest. In exploitative exchanges, he wins a few and loses a few, whereas the dignified individual invariably loses in such instances. So why concern oneself with the pursuits of justice and of truth, insofar as it falls within one's power to make a contribution, when simply getting by seems, not only so much easier, but also to pay off rather more handsomely?

WHY BE MORAL?
A FEW LESS THAN SATISFACTORY ANSWERS

Plato

The question is a very old one. We find the first attempt to answer it almost at the beginning of Western philosophy. For it is the question that prompted Plato to write the best known and most ambitious of his many dialogues, *The Republic*. In Book II of that work, having just seen off Thrasymachus with a less than thoroughly convincing refutation of this sophist's view that justice is whatever the powerful say it is, Socrates is challenged by two of his young followers—the brothers Glaucon and Adeimantus—to demonstrate that genuine justice really is worth pursuing unreservedly. And in this very first posing of the question "Why should one be moral?" Plato makes abundantly clear just how formidable are the arguments *against* pursuing justice unreservedly.

Glaucon begins by observing that justice as it is most commonly understood—which is to say, justice as the product of a social contract—is not in any sense an *ideal*. Instead, it is a compromise worked out among insecure individuals who agree mutually to forgo that which they would *like* (which is to be able to do whatever they might wish at any moment in time) in order to avoid that which they *fear* (which is to be wronged without the power of revenge). Having arrived at the compromise which they call "justice," these same insecure individuals now seek to reinforce that result by praising it as if it were a good in itself. But, Glaucon points out, it is only the insecure individual who will find this notion of justice at all attractive or feel compelled to abide by it. The man who has the power to do what he wishes without fear of retribution will be utterly indifferent to it. And that implies, of course, that there is a considerable measure of hypocrisy involved when the ordinary (insecure) individual praises justice as a good in itself. For presumably, had he the power to do whatever he wished, he would be equally indifferent to the claims of "justice."

In order to drive home this last point, Glaucon reminds Socrates of the story of Gyges's ring. According to legend, a ring was found by an ancestor of the Lydian Gyges—a ring which, when the embossed portion was turned inward toward the palm, rendered the person wearing the ring invisible. Gyges's ancestor, when he found the ring, was a mere shepherd, but by means of the near invulnerability that the ring provided him, he quickly took over the kingdom of Lydia, killing the former king and taking the queen to his own bed. Glaucon then asks Socrates to consider honestly whether *anyone*, in possession of such power, would have forgone the temptation to use it as Gyges's ancestor had done—to steal the property and position of another, and generally to have his way in all things. "The man who did not wish to do wrong with that opportunity," Glaucon remarks, "would be thought by those who knew it to be very foolish and miserable. They would praise him in public," of course, but only "for fear of being wronged" themselves.[2]

In short, Glaucon contends, while it may be advantageous to *appear* to be just (for then there will be no question of one's being punished for anything), to actually *be* just is not (for then one would have to forgo all of the advantages of cheating). In order to demonstrate that justice, at least as this is commonly understood, cannot reasonably be considered a good in itself, Glaucon and Adeimantus (who chimes in at this point) propose that Socrates consider the contrast presented by a pair of test cases—those of, on the one hand, the splendidly successful *unjust* man and, on the other, the truly just man who receives, however, no recognition of his being just. The former, by means of his skill at deception and crime, manages not only to amass a fortune but also to acquire a reputation for honesty, even magnanimity. And thus he enjoys not only power and influence, but a wide circle of admiring friends. The latter, in contrast, by virtue of his willingness to do what is noble and just regardless of the consequences, finds himself, let us imagine, unfairly convicted of serious crimes and, spurned by society, is imprisoned and subjected to terrible tortures before ultimately being executed. Given that this sort of fate *can* befall the just man in spite of—and to some degree even *because of*—his predilection for justice, how can justice be conceived of as good in itself? What is it about justice, Adeimantus in particular now challenges Socrates, that makes its possession beneficial for a man's soul—beneficial even if, as in the test case presented here, the fact of his being just brings him disrepute and torment instead of honor.

As an analysis of the problem posed, the first few pages of Book II of *The Republic* could hardly be improved upon. Plato's solution of the problem, however, which is developed in terms of his doctrine of the tripartite soul, is far from satisfying. Socrates (clearly speaking as Plato's surrogate in this dialogue) responds to the challenge presented by the two brothers with an elaborate analogy. Instead of explaining directly what justice involves in the case of the individual, he offers an account of what justice involves in the case of the polis or city-state. Socrates does this on the grounds that once we see what justice looks like in the polis, we will be better able to see what it really looks like in the conduct of an individual. For as he conceives of it, justice has nothing whatever to do with a (Hobbesian) social contract worked out among individuals in a state of insecurity. Instead, justice is a matter of harmony—the sort of harmony that is established when necessary tasks are performed by those people or things that are by their nature properly equipped to handle the tasks in question.

Thus on the basis of what must seem today an utterly implausible and more than slightly repellent view of "natural classes" among human beings, Socrates contends that in the city-state policy decisions and the establishment of laws must be left to those few who are born with the potential (which the state must then take care to nurture) to become philosopher-kings, for these alone possess the wisdom to govern disinterestedly. Defense of the city against attack is to be left to the lesser guardians, who possess the high spirit, courage, and sense of honor that are needed in this role. And the economic affairs of the polis are to be left strictly in the hands of that large majority of the citizens who lack the wisdom, courage, and sense of honor required of guardians, but who presumably do possess an acquisitive disposition and a taste for the things that money can purchase. Justice in the city-state, Socrates contends, is simply a matter of each of the three classes of citizens restricting its activites and interests to the realm of endeavor to which it is by nature suited.

Socrates then goes on to argue that, just as within the corporate body of the polis there is a rational component, a passionate component, and an appetitive component (represented respectively by the three classes of citizens), so too the individual human soul can be seen as composed of these three parts — reason, emotion, and appetite. And in the same way that justice within the polis was a matter of each class concerning itself exclusively with the appropriate realm of endeavor, so justice in the conduct of an individual is to be understood as a matter of the three components of the soul each playing its proper part. In other words, the appetites are to be satisfied in due measure, reason is to govern the individual's actions, and the emotions are to lend their weight in support of the governance of reason (as opposed to siding with the appetites). Justice, on this account, clearly becomes a kind of preeminent virtue, incorporating within its own structure as it does the other primary virtues of wisdom, courage, and temperance.

The qualms that we feel, and quite understandably, regarding the authoritarianism implicit in Plato's account of justice in the polis should not be taken as evidence that his conception of justice in the conduct of an individual is equally crude and equally flawed. For while Plato sees the two forms of justice as strongly analogous one to the other, we are under no obligation to accept that claim. There are, after all, fairly obvious *dis*analogies between a political state and an individual human being.[3] Moreover, Plato's notion that the just man indulges his appetites in due measure, but never to excess, and is naturally inclined to govern his actions by means of reason (as is shown by the disposition of his emotions) is remarkably similar to the position that we saw Friedrich Schiller develop. We are entitled no doubt to consider Plato's psychological theory somewhat crude, given how much better we now understand the nature and limitations of human reason and human emotions. But making appropriate allowances for the more subtle conceptions of reason, emotion, and desire that we now have to work with, we would, I think, still wish to endorse Plato's general sense of how the moral individual comports himself.

The challenge, though, that Socrates has been presented is not only to offer a plausible account of what justice consists in, but to prove that, given what justice involves, it is worth pursuing unreservedly. In Book IX of *The Republic* he finally attempts to meet that challenge head-on. He argues there that the individual who is *not* committed to justice—the *unjust* man, in other words, whose actions are, by definition, governed by his appetites rather than his reason—will be driven by those appetites, like a drug addict, from one meaningless pleasure "fix" to another. Given his inability to resist his own appetites, moreover, the unjust man will soon find himself at odds with his neighbors, for in seeking the means to satisfy his desires, he will not hesitate to take advantage of those neighbors and to make use of what is properly theirs. He will seek wealth and power the better to satisfy his desires, and if he has what Socrates ironically refers to as the *misfortune* to succeed in acquiring great power, his existence will inexorably become still more miserable. As the dictator of a political state,[4] for example, he will find himself beset on all sides by threats to his position. These threats he will have to meet preemptively, by eliminating his rivals. Soon enough he will find himself surrounded by nothing but servile yes-men as his immediate subordinates and, beyond them, by resentful masses who object to his appropriation of wealth and power at their expense. The efforts of these masses to win for themselves a reasonable share of the state's wealth will have to be met with force. And so the dictator will find it necessary to hire mercenaries to protect himself and his assets against his own people. In this way, the dictator comes to be isolated, deprived of any worthwhile form of human interaction, and most particularly of intelligent conversation—in Plato's estimation, the most important of all good activities (in that it constitutes the means by which wisdom is acquired).

The main problem with this analysis of the consequences of injustice is that here Plato refuses to take entirely seriously the challenge that he himself has posed (through the personae of Glaucon and Adeimantus). That is to say, he refuses to entertain the possibility that there might even *be* such a thing as a splendidly successful unjust man. Instead, he takes it for granted that the unjust man, entirely at the mercy of his uncontrollable appetites, must of necessity reveal his own true nature, which then sets everyone against him. But Plato himself must have known better than this. After all, the descriptions of hypocrisy and manipulation that he puts into the mouths of Glaucon and

Adeimantus in Book II are compelling precisely because they describe so accurately timeless forms of human behavior with which we are all (unfortunately) only too familiar. Moreover, the thrust of the argument throughout much of *The Republic* is that the average person is neither wise nor even all that intelligent. The cleverly unjust individual, in other words, on Plato's own admission, should not find it all that difficult to deceive the average person regarding his true intentions. And indeed, given that the average individual understands justice *not* as a harmony within the soul but rather, just as Glaucon suggested, as the upshot of a social contract, the average person would presumably not be all that disturbed in any event to discover that the powerful members of society for the most part pay only lip service to justice. Wasn't that, after all, precisely the significance of the tale of Gyges's ring—that each of us obeys the law only to the extent that he finds it prudent to do so?

There is another dimension of this problem to be noticed, however. For in drawing attention to the unjust individual's isolation and to the likelihood of his having everyone's hand turned against him as significant reasons for rejecting the life of injustice, Plato clearly implies that these consequences are undesirable. Yet he fails to consider at this point the implications of Glaucon's test-case: that the just man too, precisely by virtue of his personal commitment to justice, may become isolated from his fellows, and may find everyone's hand turned against him. Plato's avoidance of this issue is especially ironic, given that his own teacher, the historical Socrates, was subjected to public trial and subsequently executed by the citizenry of Athens for no better reason than that he was exemplary in both wisdom and his commitment to justice. For Plato, this was *the* traumatic event of his life. All of his early dialogues (in particular the *Apology*, the *Crito*, and the *Phaedo*) can be understood, in psychological terms, as attempts to cope with this crisis through "the consolation of philosophy." And *The Republic* too, though a somewhat later and more mature work, can easily be read in this way. In Book II of *The Republic*, that is to say, the fictional persona of Socrates is called upon to offer a convincing justification for the way in which the actual flesh-and-blood Socrates had chosen to live his life—a challenge that is rendered all the more difficult by the fact that Socrates' chosen path led to his own persecution and murder at the hands of the city-state to the welfare of which he was personally dedicated. It is revealing, then, that in the end Plato has nothing to say that would draw the sting from the more bitter half of Glaucon's test-case— the persecution that is now and then brought down upon the innocent individual *because* of his commitment to justice.

This is not to imply that there is nothing of value to be found in Book IX. The best part of Plato's analysis there is contained in the suggestion that justice, as this is revealed in the character of an individual, is a matter of the soul's health. What makes this an especially interesting claim is that it attempts to penetrate the motivation underlying the commission of unjust acts. What it means for a soul to be healthy, for Plato, and in a slightly different sense also for Aristotle, is that it is governed by reason. This claim is closely bound up with the tendency of both Plato and Aristotle to identify an individual's dedication to justice with his dedication to the life of the mind. And that connection in turn is established because, for both of these philosophers, the archetypal form of injustice is *pleonexia*—or the desire, when one has enough, to have still more[5]—and the individual dedicated to the life of the mind is presumed to be in large part immune to *pleonexia*. Nor is this an entirely unreasonable presumption on the part of Plato and Aristotle. There has always tended to be a significant price to be paid, after all, in terms of material wealth forgone, by those who choose to dedicate their lives to science or scholarship. And the willingness of the scientist or scholar to forgo these potentially much greater earnings (that would quite probably have come his way if only he had employed his intelligence in business or the practice of law) clearly implies an ordering of values in which the pursuit of knowledge and understanding ranks higher than does the acquisition of power or material possessions.

But surely one's dedication to the life of the mind does not guarantee one's dedication to justice in a larger sense. One can be jealous of reputation as well as wealth, after all, and neither scholars nor scientists have shown themselves to possess any special immunity to the lust for fame and honor. Someone may wish to argue, following Nietzsche,[6] that the desire for fame is in fact a *good* thing, promoting as it does competition that leads to the improvement of the arts and sciences. But this is plausible in exactly the same way, and for the same reasons, as the argument that human greed is in fact a good thing because it is the raw material out of which the machinery of capitalism generates perpetually increasing collective wealth. In some sense, each of these claims is undeniably true. But that has never prevented greed or the lust for fame from generating as well an enormous amount of suffering and injustice.

Justice in the larger sense, moreover, as this applies to the conduct of an individual, cannot simply be reduced to one's resisting the temptations of *pleonexia* or acquisitiveness—even if this is extended to include the lust for fame. A considerable amount of injustice stems, after all, not from greed of any variety, but from an insistence on acting in accordance with one's own misguided prejudices. The bigot who refuses to provide his professional services to a Jew or a black is clearly acting unjustly even though, in the process, he forfeits an opportunity to increase his wealth. In a milder sense, there is also an injustice to be found wherever an individual in a position of authority is so certain of the truth of his own prejudices that he refuses to allow those under his authority even to explore the possibility that he may be mistaken. In this sense, the scholar or scientist who rejects out of hand the work of an assistant or student simply because it conflicts with his own ingrained prejudices is also acting unjustly. Justice in the larger sense requires, in other words, an awareness of the fallibility of one's own judgment and a consequent willingness to "put one's prejudices at risk."[7]

Aristotle

If the author of *The Republic* was working with assumptions about the nature of reason that prevented him from fully grasping the significance of our fallibility as knowers, the author of the *Nicomachean Ethics* was at least somewhat more sensitive to the fallibility of human understanding—as is shown in his discussion of the nature of practical wisdom. And because Aristotle's understanding of the life of the mind includes a much richer appreciation of the importance of experience, we cannot fault, to anything like the same degree that we just did with Plato, the adequacy of Aristotle's conception of justice. It might be worthwhile, then, to turn our attention away from Plato at this point in order to consider what Aristotle has to contribute to the problem under discussion.

Unlike Plato, Aristotle does not explicitly raise the question of why human beings should be moral. Nonetheless, it is easy enough to discern what his answer to that question would have been. According to Aristotle, that which is good for humans—which is to say, that end toward which all human activity is ultimately directed—is *eudaimonia*. This is usually translated in English as happiness, although MacIntyre, in an attempt to capture a little more fully the connotations of the word, offers "the state of being well and doing well in being well."[8] Simply put, the best, and indeed the only, reason why we should be moral, in Aristotle's estimation, is that the cultivation and practice of the various virtues (courage, temperance, magnanimity, and most importantly, wisdom—both practical and philosophical) *constitute* happiness. This fact is not fully appreciated, however, by those who never receive a proper moral education. According to Aristotle, whether any given individual will in fact be moral depends in large part upon factors not immediately and fully under that person's control—most importantly, how the individual in question has been brought up. Those who, as children, are not compelled to acquire the habits of virtue will never fully come to appreciate how those virtuous habits contribute to one's state of well-being. Instead, they will be inclined to fix upon one or more of the narrower sources of satisfaction—pleasure, fame, or wealth—and to pursue those narrower ends with a single-mindedness that reflects a failure to appreciate the limitations of the chosen goal or goals. In this sense, Aristotle can be seen to share Plato's conviction, expressed most clearly in the later pages of the *Protagoras*, that no one consciously chooses that which is bad. It is undeniable, of course, that many people choose to pursue lines of action that in fact turn out very badly. But both Aristotle and Plato would argue that they do so out of ignorance, as a result of not knowing what kinds of action are most conducive to a well-lived life. In contrast, the individual who has acquired virtuous habits as a result of having been well brought up will understand, on the basis of personal experience, the significance of those habits. Her generosity, her temperance, and her courage will make her a valued companion of other worthwhile individuals like herself, and she will take a quiet satisfaction in doing the many fine things that accord with her character. Such a person, in short, has a fair chance of achieving a considerable measure of happiness in her life.

According to Aristotle, however, the fullest form of happiness can be enjoyed only by those who appreciate, and act on their understanding, that the activity most in keeping with the true end or *telos* of human nature is intellectual contemplation or the life of the mind. There are two reasons that Aristotle explicitly offers in support of this claim and a third that is at least implicit in his position. To begin with, the exercise of reason represents the expression of that which is distinctive of human beings. Humans, in other words, do not fully realize the possibilities latent within their own nature unless they engage in serious thought. And when they do, moreover, they discover that the kind of satisfaction afforded them by intellectual contemplation is richer and more rewarding than that afforded them by any other form of human activity. These are the explicit justifications that Aristotle offers in support of his contention that the fullest form of happiness must involve intellectual contemplation. The implicit justification for this claim has to do with the place of *phronēsis* or practical wisdom in the life of the mind. Practical wisdom, after all, is not merely a matter of experience. For if it were, every elderly person would possess it, simply by virtue of having had many experiences. Rather, practical wisdom is the product of *reflection* on the implications of experience. It is, potentially at least, one of the benefits of intellectual contemplation. It follows, then, that the life of the mind, insofar as it is dedicated not only to the cultivation of pure philosophical wisdom but also to the cultivation of one's practical wisdom, involves the refinement even of one's *non*intellectual virtues. For these latter can be properly exercised only in accordance with *phronēsis*. It requires fine judgment, in other words, in order to be able to distinguish, in widely varying circumstances, courage from recklessness and temperance from abstemiousness. The more practical wisdom one has achieved, the more reliable will be one's exercise of the other

virtues. And the more virtuous one's life overall, of course, the more fully it
is possible for one to achieve *eudaimonia.*

We can put this argument to the test, as it were, by considering how Aristotle might have responded to our contention a few paragraphs ago that the
life of the mind—judging at least by the actual behavior of many scholars and
scientists—does not appear to be in any way incompatible with an unseemly
lust for fame. A tactful, sensitive judgment of the value of one's own work,
Aristotle could have objected, would be inclined neither toward false mod-
esty nor toward arrogance. Nor would a person possessing such judgment be
inclined to overvalue the importance of being known and admired. In other
words, the individual who genuinely understood what the life of the mind
should involve—which is to say, the person who recognized that such a life
should include the cultivation of practical wisdom—would presumably *not* be
swept along by inappropriate ambitions (at least not insofar as she had succeeded in actually *acquiring* such wisdom).

There is a great deal to be said in favor of Aristotle's argument for the importance of cultivating one's virtues. Nonetheless, there are two weaknesses
to be found in his solution to our problem. The first of these has already been
mentioned back in chapter three. Aristotle's conception of a *telos* implicit in
human nature seems too strong. That is to say, the idea that there is something
which, in the very nature of things, we are *intended* to be does not fit at all
comfortably with the principles of evolutionary biology that today we have
very good reason to accept. But setting aside the notion of such an end or purpose implicit in human nature suggests the need for a considerably greater degree of freedom for individuals to explore the possible sources of personal
fulfillment than Aristotle thought was necessary. And some of the directions
in which such exploration may legitimately head will no doubt seem immoral,
or at least morally questionable, to those who have no desire to head in those
directions themselves. (Consider recently prevailing attitudes toward homo-
sexuality, for example, or toward intentional single parenthood.)

The second weakness is to be found in Aristotle's acknowledgment that
happiness is never guaranteed—that even the most virtuous of individuals is
subject to the effects of illness and misfortune, and that these will, if piled up
beyond a certain point, spoil all possibility of happiness. It is a point in Aristotle's favor that he is prepared to admit this fairly obvious truth. All the same,
it leaves the door open for someone to ask whether a better strategy for resisting the impact of those contingencies that undermine happiness might not
involve occasional deviations from virtue. The wealthy and influential, after
all, seem to be better situated to withstand the shocks of moderate misfortune.
And this presumably holds true regardless of how they came by their wealth
and influence. The quality of the happiness enjoyed by a less-than-fully-

virtuous wealthy individual may perhaps be lower than it would have been had he been equally wealthy *and* virtuous. But may it not, on balance, be considerably higher than that of the virtuous bankrupt, whose wife has abandoned him to his poverty and who is in no position to pay for the medical treatments that he has come to need? If that seems likely, then perhaps a willingness to compromise somewhat with one's virtue is not inappropriate, at least when the payoff for doing so is sufficiently impressive.

Let us take up the first of these objections to Aristotle's position and consider it somewhat further. Aristotle's contention that the life of the mind is an important aspect of the *telos* implicit in human nature may be unacceptable, given what evolutionary biology has to tell us. Nonetheless, the idea that intellectual reflection is a characteristic feature—even *the* characteristic feature—of human nature is an interesting and promising notion, *if* it is understood in the correct way. For while the principles of evolutionary biology are, strictly speaking, incompatible with the notion of a *telos*—with the notion that there is anything that our, or any other, species is *intended* to be—there is no reason at all to deny that within the evolutionary process (within, that is to say, the natural selection-governed drift of individual species through what Daniel Dennett calls "design space")[9] one can often identify specific developmental tendencies. For example, there was, evolutionary biologists will insist, absolutely nothing preordained about the remarkable increase in the brain size of hominids as they evolved over the past four million years from *australopithecus* through *homo habilis* and then *homo erectus* into *homo sapiens*. All the same, as a matter of fact, there has been during that time an enormous gradual increase in brain size, and with it an expansion of intellectual abilities that has in turn made possible the astonishing efflorescence of human culture in the past fifty thousand or so years. Given what humans have become, through evolution, the exercise of thought is as natural and important to *us* as is swimming to a dolphin, given what evolution has made of *it*. But as long as a species continues to exist, of course, its drift through design space is in principle unending,[10] which means that developmental tendencies that have prevailed for some time may slow, stop, and even reverse themselves. Distant descendants of today's dolphin, in other words, might conceivably no longer swim to any great degree. Similarly, it is at least conceivable that our own distant descendants (if there are any) might have no special aptitude for thought—nothing comparable to ours, at any rate.

One reason, however, for supposing that it is highly unlikely that our own descendants, no matter how distant, will be nonthinkers is that, with the development of serious intelligence in our species, a significant threshold has been crossed. Our current level of intelligence is such that, not only have we been able to discern the principles of evolutionary biology, but we are also in a position to intervene in various ways in the evolutionary process itself. And surely, one would suppose, insofar as we *can* shape the future development of our own species, we will do what we can to reinforce the development of human intelligence, rather than undermine it, given that it has proven to have such remarkable practical value. Insofar as this molding on our part of our own future identity takes place, moreover, our species will have chosen its own *telos*—will have decided for itself, that is, what it intends to become, and will have consciously included the capacity for intellectual reflection as an important component of that goal.

But while it is tempting to rehabilitate along these lines Aristotle's notion that the exercise of intelligence is an important component of the human *telos*, it is also dangerously misleading to suppose that our species ever acts or decides as one. Even if we might be said to act collectively, to at least some extent, in the process of establishing national or corporate policies, it should be clear that in our species there is nothing approaching a collective mind or collective will. If the exercise of intelligence allows us to recognize the practical value of cooperation (in some particular circumstances) and the means of achieving it, what motivates us are still private concerns. Granted, those private concerns *may* come to include, in a given individual, a concern for morality as such or for the pursuit of truth. And insofar as they do, such an individual will tend to find that the activities in which she engages in order to promote those particular concerns will now and then come to mesh, to some degree, with the independently pursued activities of other people who happen to share those concerns. A number of individuals, that is to say, on occasion will find themselves quite independently serving the same "good cause," for the simple reason that each is capable of recognizing the goodness of the cause in question, and finds in the goodness of the cause a motivation for serving it. Under these circumstances, it is unsurprising that some measure of spontaneous coordination should arise in their dealings with one another. But this is clearly the exception rather than the rule in human interaction. Normally we encounter each other as obstacles to be negotiated, even as rivals, and if we wish to cooperate, we must make a conscious effort to do so. All such efforts, moreover, are constantly susceptible to failure, given the many varieties of misunderstanding that can arise between us.

Thus even though the image of humanity voluntarily embracing the pursuit of wisdom and understanding as its ultimate aim is an appealing one, it has to be acknowledged that in fact this is the aim only of those individuals who actually do dedicate themselves to this end. Without appealing to the intention of some supernatural authority, it cannot be accounted the ultimate aim of our species as a whole. This is because those individuals who confine their attention to their own self-interested concerns are offered no compelling reason to change their outlook in this rehabilitated account of humanity's *telos*. In the light of what we know about evolution, one cannot legitimately say that they have missed something important about their own nature that they *should* have grasped. Instead, it has to be said that they have merely rejected one possible way of living their lives—on the basis, that is, of a serious personal concern for the pursuits of truth and justice—in favor of other less demanding ways that were equally available to them.

Dewey

The modern philosopher who argued most persuasively and unrelentingly that human beings should consciously embrace the pursuit of understanding as a crucially important aim in their lives was probably the pragmatist John Dewey. He did so, moreover, with a sophisticated appreciation of the significance of biological evolution. More than any other philosopher of the first half of the twentieth century, Dewey understood that evolutionary theory had powerful philosophical implications and, unlike the Social Darwinists, got those implications correct. As he explained in *Human Nature and Conduct*,

> The ethical import of the doctrine of evolution is enormous. But its import has been misconstrued because the doctrine has been appropriated by the very traditional notions which in truth it subverts. It has been thought [for example, by Spencer] that the doctrine of evolution means the complete subordination of present change to a future goal. . . . In fact evolution means continuity of change; and the fact that change may take the form of present growth of complexity and interaction.[11]

The central implication of biological evolution, in other words, is that the constant flow of change that we experience in our own lives and in the unfolding of history is not a mere play of appearances across the surface of an abiding and ultimately intelligible Reality. Disconcertingly, we must come to grips with the fact that change is all-pervasive. "There are . . . but two alternative courses," Dewey observed in "The Influence of Darwin on Philosophy."

> We must either find the appropriate objects and organs of knowledge in the mutual interactions of changing things; or else, to escape the infection of change, we must seek them in some transcendent and supernal region. The human mind, deliberately as it were, exhausted the logic of the changeless, the final, and the transcendent, before it essayed adventure on the pathless wastes of generation and transformation.[12]

There was nothing inappropriate in exploring first the resources available in "the logic of the changeless." But increasingly, as the natural sciences matured—which is to say, in the wake of Darwin's discoveries, most importantly, but also later in the wake of Einstein's work in relativity and the development of quantum mechanics—it became clear that flux and relation, rather than stasis and identity, are the more ultimately basic principles in terms of which experience must be understood. A new way of approaching philosophical problems, one which "forswears inquiry after absolute origins and absolute finalities in order to explore specific values and the specific conditions that generate them,"[13] was now required, Dewey felt. With the change of orientation effected by "the Darwinian logic,"

> Interest shifts from the wholesale essence back of special changes to the question of how special changes serve and defeat concrete purposes; shifts from an intelligence that shaped things once and for all to the particular intelligences which things are even now shaping; shifts from an ultimate goal of good to the direct increments of justice and happiness that intelligent administration of existent conditions may beget and that present carelessness or stupidity will destroy or forego.[14]

That the "intelligent administration" of conditions that we now find ourselves having to deal with can produce improvements in the measure of justice and happiness that we enjoy was a constant refrain and a central theme in most of Dewey's work, as was its corollary—that stupidity and carelessness can destroy those possibilities of improvement. But the "intelligent administration of existent conditions" depended upon one's understanding the principles that governed those conditions and the possibilities that arose relative to them. And such understanding, in order to be as reliable as possible, had to be theoretical and disinterested; it had to be, in a word, scientific. Thus even though, for Dewey, as a pragmatist, the significance of knowledge always resides finally in its implications for action, he was not incapable of appreciating the importance of deferring practical concerns for the sake of probing more thoroughly, through the various methods of science, into the relations holding between those changing things and conditions with which we hope to be able to deal effectively. Dewey, moreover, understood full well the coherentist epistemological implications of Pragmatism. This is shown in his willingness to acknowledge that Peirce's definition of truth as "the opinion which is fated to be ultimately agreed to by all who investigate"[15] is the best statement that one can offer finally of what "truth" has to mean—*if* we conceive of truth as the whole of what is permanently true. That said, however, Dewey's concern was not with the truth that lay at the hypothetical end of inquiry. What interested him, instead, were the many useful truths that could be put to work in the immediate or near future. This was truth as "warranted assertability" or the idea that we must accept, and act on the basis of, only those beliefs that are justified in light of the most rigorous epistemic standards of our own day.

There is in Dewey, for all of his interest in the promotion of improvements in justice and happiness wherever these are possible, a fairly strong resistance to the language and sentiment of idealism. We can see this already in his comparative lack of interest in the Peircean conception of truth as the ideal end of inquiry. Still, given Dewey's passionate concern for progress and his understanding of it as a perpetually open possibility, it is slightly surprising to come across the following passage in *Human Nature and Conduct*.

> Adherents of the idea that betterment, growth in goodness, consists in approximation to an exhaustive, stable, immutable end or good, have been compelled to recognize the truth in the fact that we envisage the good in specific terms that are relative to existing needs, and that the attainment of every specific good merges insensibly into a new condition of maladjustment with its need of a new end and a renewed effort. But they have elaborated an ingenious dialectical theory to account for the facts while maintaining their theory intact. The goal, the ideal, is infinite; man is finite, subject to conditions imposed by space and time. The specific character of the ends which man entertains and of the satisfaction he achieves is due therefore precisely to his empirical and finite nature in its contrast with the infinite and complete character of the true reality, the end. Consequently when man reaches what he had taken to be the destination of his journey he finds that he has only gone a piece on the road. Infinite vistas still stretch further before him. Again he sets his mark a little further ahead, and again when he reaches the station set, he finds the road opening before him in unexpected ways, and sees new distant objects beckoning him forward. . . .
>
> By some strange perversion this theory passes for moral idealism. An office of inspiration and guidance is attributed to the thought of the goal of ultimate completeness or perfection. As a matter of fact, the idea sincerely held brings discouragement and despair and not inspiration or hopefulness. There is something either ludicrous or tragic in the notion that inspiration to continued progress is had in telling man that no matter what he does or what he achieves, the outcome is negligible in comparison with what he set out to achieve. . . . The honest conclusion is pessimism. . . . But the fact is that it is not the negative aspect of an outcome, its failure to reach infinity, which renews courage and hope. Positive attainment, actual enrichment of meaning and powers opens new vistas and sets new tasks, creates new aims and stimulates new efforts.[16]

The position criticized in this passage is *very* close to his own, and yet significantly different, in Dewey's estimation. He objects, for example, to the postulation of a stable, immutable endstate toward which we are approaching, since this is clearly a vestige of "the logic of the changeless," which we need to move beyond. He objects vigorously to the idea that direction or inspiration can be received from this unknown and unknowable endstate toward which we are supposedly moving. After all, "instruction in what to do next can never come from an infinite goal, which for us is bound to be empty."[17] Clearly, our motivation is received instead from the concrete but localized improvements that we actually manage to bring about. Yet there is a legitimate challenge at least implicitly posed here that seems to be troubling Dewey somewhat (and which might account for the scorn that he pours upon a position so close to his own). For the pessimism and despair that attaches to this "moral idealism" also infects to some degree Dewey's own position. This is something that he acknowledges even as he defies it.

> The facts are not such as to yield unthinking optimism and consolation; for they render it impossible to rest upon attained goods. New struggles and failures are inevitable. The total scene of action remains as before, only for us more complex, and more subtly unstable. But this very situation is a consequence of expansion, not of failures of power, and when grasped and admitted it is a challenge to intelligence.[18]

What makes us take up the struggle, which is in principle never-ending, and resist despair, which might readily follow upon our recognition of the temporariness of our successes, is the fact that our localized achievements do nonetheless make a difference. This is obviously in an important sense correct.

But Dewey's disinclination to invoke the ideal whenever reference can be made instead to the localized concrete conditions that immediately affect us and that we may hope to improve upon does not always serve him well. For having acknowledged that the never-ending struggle for what can only ever be temporary and incremental solutions to the problems of injustice and unhappiness might conceivably induce pessimism and despair, Dewey then tackles head-on the question that we have been considering. Why should we even *bother* with the struggle, he asks. And the answer that he provides, with his eye once again on the concrete and immediate rather than the ideal, is disappointingly lame.

> But *why* act for the wise, or good, or better? Why not follow our own immediate devices if we are so inclined? There is only one answer. We have a moral nature, a conscience, call it what you will. And this nature responds directly in acknowledgment of the supreme authority of the Right over all claims of inclination and habit. . . .
>
> Why, indeed, acknowledge the authority of Right? That many persons do not acknowledge it in fact, in action, and that all persons ignore it at times, is assumed by the argument. Just what is the significance of an alleged recognition of a supremacy which is continually denied in fact? . . . [W]e live in a world

where other persons live too. Our acts affect them. They perceive these effects and react upon us in consequence. . . . They approve and condemn—not in abstract theory but in what they do to us. The answer to the question "Why not put your hand in the fire?" is the answer of fact. If you do your hand will be burnt. The answer to the question why acknowledge the right is of the same sort. For Right is only an abstract name for the multitude of concrete demands in action which others impress upon us, and of which we are obliged, if we would live, to take some account. Its authority is the exigency of their demands, the efficacy of their insistencies. . . .

Accordingly failure to recognize the authority of right means defect in effective apprehension of the realities of human association, not an arbitrary exercise of free will.[19]

This won't do at all. Insofar as "acting for the wise, or good, or better" involves engaging in a struggle against injustice, we can hardly explain why a person should engage in such a struggle by describing it, in effect, as the path of least resistance. If all that "acknowledging the authority of Right" meant was not doing things that others disapprove of, then Dewey's suggestion that what motivates us in this matter is the fear of unpleasant consequences would no doubt be adequate. It would be ignoble and slightly insulting, but psychologically plausible. But as we know, "acknowledging the authority of Right" is much more likely to mean standing up to others, resisting their selfish inclinations, and accepting their obloquy (and worse) all in the service of a vision of how things *should be* that one's mean-spirited fellows do not at the moment share. What Dewey has managed to explain, in other words, is merely the advisability of being "good" in the way that *most* people are good—which is to say, only moderately good. But following this line of argument, if one's neighbors are bigots or thieves, then it would be prudent not to be overly critical of their particular form of bigotry or thievery. No, what Dewey needs here instead is an explanation of why we should be willing to make sacrifices on behalf of a vision of how things *should be*—should be, that is, if we genuinely wish our social arrangements to be more just than they now are and genuinely wish our fellows to enjoy more happiness than they currently do. And *that* will require explaining why we should desire these things even when *most* of our fellows do not, and indeed even when *most* of them *stand in the way* of their achievement! Even the pragmatist, it turns out, needs to embrace a certain measure of the right kind of idealism.

MacIntyre

If we restrict ourselves to a naturalistic account of morality, and thus rule out any reference to the prospect of an afterlife or a divine reckoning, mere prudential considerations cannot possibly explain why an individual might exhibit an exceptional commitment to justice and honesty—the kind of commitment, in other words, that his more "easy-going" and "reasonable" neighbors would occasionally find excessive and disturbing. It is not necessary, however, to appeal to the intention of a divine agency in order to understand why and when such an exceptional commitment to justice and honesty might recommend itself on *other* than prudential grounds. Alasdair MacIntyre, for example, argues in *After Virtue* that a serious interest in any of the various cultural practices with which one might choose to enrich one's life can readily lead to the development of fairly robust virtues on the part of the individual who is caught up in such an interest.

MacIntyre's account of the natural development of the virtues, which owes a great deal to Aristotle, is both richly nuanced and highly plausible, and it will be worth our while to take a close look at it. To begin with, we have to understand what MacIntyre means when he speaks of a "practice."

> By a "practice" I am going to mean any coherent and complex form of socially established cooperative human activity through which goods internal to that form of activity are realized in the course of trying to achieve those standards of excellence which are appropriate to, and partially definitive of, that form of activity, with the result that human powers to achieve excellence, and human conceptions of the ends and goods involved, are systematically extended. . . . Thus the range of practices is wide: arts, sciences, games, politics in the Aristotelian sense, the making and sustaining of family life, all fall under the concept.[20]

The reference in this passage to *internal* goods relating to practices implies, of course, that there are also such things as *external* goods. The distinction between them can be roughly established as follows: external goods are the various rewards (prize money, fame, prestige, "groupies," etc.) that may come one's way as a result of excelling in some practice, while the internal goods related to a practice are the various forms of satisfaction that one can enjoy, and indeed, even come to know about, *only* by actively engaging in the practice in question. These include such things as the satisfaction that comes with accomplishment, the fascination one feels in exploring technique, and the creative thrill of discovering hitherto unrecognized avenues of development lying latent within the practice of which one is a devotee.

The crucial thing about practices, as MacIntyre conceives of them, is that they impose upon those dedicated to them a form of discipline.

> A practice involves standards of excellence and obedience to rules as well as the achievement of goods. To enter into a practice is to accept the authority of those standards and the inadequacy of my own performance as judged by them. It is

to subject my own attitudes, choices, preferences and tastes to the standards which currently and partially define the practice. Practices of course . . . have a history. . . . Thus the standards are not themselves immune from criticism, but nonetheless we cannot be initiated into a practice without accepting the authority of the best standards realized so far. . . . In the realm of practices the authority of both goods and standards operates in such a way as to rule out all subjectivist and emotivist analyses of judgment.[21]

Once we understand this, moreover, it is not difficult to see the relationship between practices and virtues. As MacIntyre explains,

It belongs to the concept of a practice . . . that its goods can only be achieved by subordinating ourselves within the practice in our relationship to other practitioners. We have to learn to recognize what is due to whom; we have to be prepared to take whatever self-endangering risks are demanded along the way; and we have to listen carefully to what we are told about our own inadequacies and to reply with the same carefulness for the facts. In other words we have to accept as necessary components of any practice with internal goods and standards of excellence the virtues of justice, courage and honesty. For not to accept these . . . so far bars us from achieving the standards of excellence or the goods internal to the practice that it renders the practice pointless except as a device for achieving external goods.[22]

In order to get as much as one can out of one's engagement in a practice, in other words, it is necessary to approach the practice and its standards of excellence *virtuously*. And if one does not yet possess the requisite virtues to any great degree, but one *is* keenly dedicated to some practice or other, one's willing submission to the discipline involved in the practice will go some way toward schooling one in the virtues of justice, courage, and honesty. (Something like this is no doubt what is meant by all those coaches who emphasize the "character building" dimension of engaging in sports.)

MacIntyre does not believe, of course, that *anyone* involved in any way with any practice whatsoever must necessarily possess the virtues of justice, courage and honesty. "It is no part of [his] thesis," he remarks, "that great violinists cannot be vicious or great chess-players mean-spirited." His point, instead, is that "the vicious and mean-spirited necessarily rely on the virtues of others for the practices in which they engage to flourish and also deny themselves the experience of achieving those internal goods which may reward even not very good chess-players and violinists."[23] But even if we now understand why the virtues will be important for the practitioner who wishes to improve, why should it also be the case, as MacIntyre contends here, that the virtues are required in order for *the practices themselves* to flourish? The explanation is that practices almost invariably depend upon institutions—institutions that sustain them, but which also inevitably threaten to corrupt them.

Chess, physics, and medicine are a few examples of what MacIntyre considers to be practices; chess clubs, universities, laboratories, and hospitals would then be the corresponding examples of institutions.

> Institutions are characteristically and necessarily concerned with . . . external goods. They are involved in acquiring money and other material goods; they are structured in terms of power and status, and they distribute money, power and status as rewards. Nor could they do otherwise if they are to sustain not only themselves, but also the practices of which they are the bearers. For no practices can survive for any length of time unsustained by institutions. Indeed so intimate is the relationship of practices to institutions—and consequently of the goods external to the goods internal to the practices in question—that institutions and practices characteristically form a single causal order in which the ideals and the creativity of the practice are always vulnerable to the acquisitiveness of the institution, in which the cooperative care for common goods of the practice is always vulnerable to the competitiveness of the institution. In this context the essential function of the virtues is clear. Without them, without justice, courage and truthfulness, practices could not resist the corrupting influence of institutions.[24]

One crucial part of what an institution does is draw in money and public attention in order to redistribute these as rewards for perceived excellence within the practice that it serves. But the availability of these rewards—these external goods—and the institutional emphasis on their importance will inevitably tempt some individuals to try to win them at all costs—which is to say, regardless of whether or not they are deserved. Insofar as these individuals succeed, of course, the practice itself suffers, for the standards that define excellence within the practice are in that case undermined. Neither exceptional effort nor exceptional talent receives its due. Instead, the techniques of cheating are encouraged, and in certain instances are even *seen* to be encouraged, with the result that, in some minds at least, the techniques that define the practice in question and the (illegitimate) techniques that have in fact led to success come to be confused with each other. This is one facet of the corrupting influence that institutions, by their very nature, are inclined to exert upon those practices that they are intended to sustain. There is another. For the institution, in order to play its sustaining role, must attract support, and this will occasionally be made available only with strings attached. A university, for example, in its eagerness to acquire money with which to encourage pure research in physics, finds that the money it has its eye on requires a commitment to engage in military research (of perhaps highly dubious scientific value). The temptation to prostitute its practice for the sake of "support" for the practice is often difficult to resist. And those who identify more closely with the administration of the institution than with the practice that the institution is ostensibly meant to serve will often succumb to this temptation all too easily.

When a practice is threatened with corruption in either of these ways, its only defense is to be found in the virtues of those who are loyally committed to the practice as it should be conducted. With respect to their own work, these individuals will refuse to receive either rewards or investment under false pretenses. Their sense of justice and honesty will not permit it. And if the circumstances require it, they will also courageously speak out against the prostitution of their practice, regardless of how unwelcome this message may be to those with the institutional authority to make decisions affecting the integrity of the practice (and with the authority as well, typically, to determine the treatment of individual practitioners — outspoken and otherwise). The virtuous individual will run these risks and accept the consequences involved, first, out of loyalty to the practice in question, but second, on the basis of a commitment to the virtues of justice, honesty, and courage themselves.

It is an important part of MacIntyre's thesis, in other words, that while the virtues originate in one's willing submission to the discipline imposed by particular practices, once the virtues take root in the character of the dedicated practitioner they will come to be exercised *whenever* they are called for. As MacIntyre explains,

> It is of the character of a virtue that in order that it be effective in producing the internal goods which are the rewards of the virtues it should be exercised without regard to consequences. For . . . although the virtues are just those qualities which tend to lead to the achievement of a certain class of goods, nonetheless unless we practice them irrespective of whether in any particular set of contingent circumstances they will produce those goods or not, we cannot possess them at all. We cannot be genuinely courageous or truthful and be so only on occasion.[25]

This is an important insight, and one that MacIntyre owes to Aristotle. For as Aristotle pointed out, the virtues are habits — deeply ingrained habits, one hopes — for it is only *as* deeply ingrained habits that they can be relied upon to override prudential considerations that would run contrary to their influence.

But where Aristotle stressed the role played by proper upbringing in the acquisition of such virtuous habits, MacIntyre stresses instead the possibility of these virtuous habits arising as the byproduct of a prolonged effort aimed, not directly at the acquisition of virtues, but at something else entirely — improvement within the context of a practice. This difference in emphasis is significant for our purposes for a couple of reasons. First, insofar as MacIntyre is correct, it would seem possible for the individual who was not as a child the beneficiary of a sound moral upbringing to make choices later in her life (albeit inadvertently) that could compensate for her deficient early moral education. That's a consoling thought. But more importantly, if we take it for granted that many people do in fact care about certain practices, some of the mystery is dispelled concerning how and why people acquire the virtues even though these tend *not to pay* in terms of the acquisition of external goods — even though, as MacIntyre puts it, "the cultivation of truthfulness, justice and courage will often, the world being what it contingently is, bar us from being rich or famous or powerful."[26] One has to care *deeply* about one's practice, of course, in order for one's submission to its discipline to foster in one's character the virtues of justice, honesty, and courage. And it is probably *not* the case that the majority of people acquire such virtue as they possess in this way, for the simple reason that the majority of people, it appears, never come to care all that deeply about any particular practice. They live, in this respect, comparatively superficial lives. (It is also not entirely clear, notwithstanding MacIntyre's conviction to the contrary, that an individual who was only seriously dedicated to *one* particular practice might not be able to compartmentalize her virtuous habits, so that they came into play *only* in that one aspect of her life.) Nonetheless, insofar as MacIntyre's account of the natural development of the virtues is correct, those individuals who do care deeply about one or more practices will never be at a loss to explain why the virtues matter to them. The virtues matter because they promote the welfare of that which they *already* care about.

This constitutes, I would argue, a much more plausible foundation upon which to build an explanation of why one should be moral than do appeals to prudential considerations. For as MacIntyre quite rightly points out, the virtuous individual regularly takes "self-endangering risks," and one cannot account for this at all convincingly as long as one remains committed to the idea that maximizing one's personal welfare is everyone's ultimate motivation. "There are things worth dying for," as the saying goes, and if so, then there must certainly also be things worth making more moderate sacrifices for. What those things are will vary to some extent from person to person. But MacIntyre's point in this regard, to simplify it somewhat, is that humans are capable of developing a deep and abiding interest in things *other than themselves*. And when they do, that interest — if it turns into the right kind of commitment — can bring out the very best in human nature. MacIntyre's implied answer to the question "Why should one be moral?" is thus nowhere near as unsatisfactory as are the answers offered by Plato and Dewey. It is, in fact, the answer upon which I wish to build, but it is not yet the last word.

What makes MacIntyre's position less than entirely satisfactory is an implication that he never quite manages to defuse, even though he was obviously concerned about it. (Were he not, he would hardly have given his next major work the title *Whose Justice? Which Rationality?*) That problematic implication can be posed in the form of a simple question: what happens when practices conflict? How are the conflicts that might arise between them to be resolved?

UNDERSTANDING THE VIRTUES OF JUSTICE AND TRUTHFULNESS

Almost at the end of *After Virtue* a point that has become increasingly clear in the course of the work is made perfectly explicit when MacIntyre announces that "the crucial moral opposition is between liberal individualism in some version or other and the Aristotelian tradition in some version or other."[27] And if this is ultimately the only choice available to us, MacIntyre contends, then even though liberal individualism has been the prevailing political-moral philosophy of the West ever since the Enlightenment, it is to some version of the Aristotelian tradition that we *must* turn. The problem with liberal individualism is that, having divorced morality from any conception of an end that humans by their very nature are meant to pursue, it has nothing better to offer for the guidance of human conduct than prudential considerations. Once the Kantian deontological experiment fails (as it does in MacIntyre's estimation), and the Enlightenment project comes increasingly to be defined by the Utilitarians and capitalists, the notion that each individual constitutes an end in himself is reconceived to mean that each individual is entitled by right to pursue the maximization of his own private welfare. And as recent history shows, MacIntyre would argue, this tendency to exaggerate the individual's right to pursue whatever may catch his fancy in turn causes liberal individualism to devolve fairly rapidly into narcissistic hedonism.

Confronted with this as the current deplorable state of affairs, MacIntyre counsels a return to a teleological conception of ethics. He knows, of course, that at the turn of the twenty-first century we can no longer embrace Aristotle's own conception of the human *telos*, but MacIntyre's focus upon practices and the traditions within which they are embedded is meant to offer the benefits of a teleological approach without committing us to any questionable metaphysical assumptions. In the process of embracing a practice and its tradition, after all, we simultaneously submit ourselves to the guidance of whatever purposes govern the practice and tradition in question. There is, however, a disturbingly inward-turning aspect to the proposal as MacIntyre presents it in the book's final paragraph. Invoking the Benedictine monasteries of an earlier time of (supposed) moral confusion, he declares that "[w]hat matters at this stage is the construction of local forms of community within which civility and the intellectual and moral life can be sustained through the new dark ages which are already upon us."[28] The implications of this sentiment for the question "What happens when practices conflict?" bear thinking about.

"Local forms of community," after all, have a notorious tendency to be insular, and the Christian Middle Ages were distinguished both for religious intolerance and for the Church's willingness to stifle inquiry in the interest of doctrinal purity. It is not that I wish to accuse MacIntyre of proposing to narrow the range of things that should concern us. But the challenge posed by the multiplicity of practices and traditions in our time of widespread emigration and instant communication is a serious one. Any suggestion that the way to meet this challenge is to close our doors and our eyes is clearly a nonstarter. Thus if MacIntyre's proposal that we renounce liberal individualism in favor of a teleological ethics grounded in our commitment to particular practices and their associated traditions is to be at all plausible, it is essential that this commitment (out of which the virtues are supposed to emerge) does not in fact warp those virtues by giving them too narrow a focus of application. In this respect, the reference to St. Benedict in the final chapter of *After Virtue* is portentous. For if leading a religious life constitutes a practice in MacIntyre's sense, as clearly it does, then the danger that truthfulness can become too readily identified with staunchness of faith and that justice can become too readily identified with adherence to the dictates of one's sect is obviously by no means negligible.

Liberal individualism, in contrast to many forms of religion, is deeply committed to the principle of tolerance, and this is an excellent thing. There are occasions, of course, when tolerance may not seem to be a virtue. This is the case, for example, when patterns of injustice and exploitation are excused on the grounds that they are merely "how things are done" in a particular place and by particular people. But this kind of blasé "live and let live" attitude, I would contend, is not properly characterized as tolerance at all. For tolerance is not a matter of being *indifferent* to the activity of others. (No one suggests that we "tolerate" crime, for example.) Rather, it is a matter of taking seriously the possibility that the activity of others may contain something of value from which we might learn. Tolerance in this sense is a form of intellectual humility. In contrast, *intolerance*, for all of its passionate antagonism, *is* in one important respect a matter of being utterly indifferent. What the intolerant are indifferent to, however, is *not* the possibility of learning from those that are significantly different from themselves, for the intolerant cannot bring themselves to believe that such a thing is possible. Their incredulity in this regard, though, is itself an expression of indifference toward whatever shortcomings there may be in their preferred way of doing things. They do not care to know, in other words, in what respects they may be wrong. Liberal individualism that is not lazy indifference, then, but which is grounded in a commitment to tolerance—the kind of tolerance that Mill advocates in *On Liberty*—is in possession of insights that must not be forgotten even if we choose to follow MacIntyre's lead in embracing a teleological ethics grounded in our commitment to particular practices. The most indispensable of those insights, I would argue, is that truth and justice are eternally elusive—that in order to approach them, we must be constantly prepared to be shown the errors involved in our current beliefs and practices.

Again, in asserting here that truth is eternally elusive, I do not mean to deny the obvious: that there are statements of fact—such as "The door is closed" or "Today is Wednesday"—the truth or falsity of which can be readily established. Were this *not* the case, thought would be utterly impossible. The point, rather, is that the kinds of things that primarily interest us and that we often need to understand are not those simple factual states. As soon as we consider even moderately complex states of affairs, the certainty that one can enjoy with regard to the closedness of doors and the current date begins to evaporate. One does not easily establish the true answers to such questions as, for example, "What does my boss think of me?" or "Why did our relationship fail?" And when we move on to the consideration of serious questions relating to social issues—"What does the First Amendment *mean*?" or "Why did the United States invade Iraq?"—any possibility of giving an absolutely definitive answer disappears. It is not only scientific truth, in other words, that needs to be understood as eternally elusive and yet crucially important.

Within MacIntyre's position there are, I believe, resources that can be used to carry us to this same insight—that we must always be ready to be shown the errors involved in our current beliefs and practices—but MacIntyre does not give them quite the emphasis that he should. He observes, for example, that practices may in some cases be seriously flawed. They may be badly structured, given their own internal goals, but even more disturbingly, they may be morally flawed. Torture, for instance, *if* it constitutes a practice in MacIntyre's sense (which he rather doubts, for reasons that he does not supply and that I cannot imagine), would certainly constitute an evil practice. Boxing and bullfighting, in any event, clearly *are* practices in MacIntyre's sense, and one might well argue that one or both of these are morally questionable activities. Now it may seem that an implication which follows from the fact that "the virtues . . . are defined not in terms of good and right practices," but simply in terms of practices in general, is that these have a kind of logical priority with respect to the virtues, and thus that no given practice as it is actually engaged in at a particular time and place *can* be subjected to moral criticism. But MacIntyre explicitly denies this.

> There is . . . no inconsistency in appealing to the requirements of a virtue to criticize a practice. Justice may be initially defined as a disposition which in its particular way is necessary to sustain practices; it does not follow that in pursuing the requirements of a practice violations of justice are not to be condemned.[29]

This is clearly a move that MacIntyre needs to make if his argument is to be plausible. But the move involves a shift, which MacIntyre seems not to notice, both in the meaning of "justice" and in the perspective adopted. We need to unpack the significance of this shift.

Justice as a virtuous disposition is one thing and justice as an ideal state that we wish to promote insofar as we can is quite another, even though the two are closely related. Thus when MacIntyre says that "in pursuing the requirements of a practice violations of justice" are still to be condemned, it is justice in the second sense that is being referred to, whether MacIntyre realizes this or not. The question that needs to be addressed, then, is how do we move from justice as a virtuous disposition, which comes first on MacIntyre's model, to justice as a general conception of *how things should be* in terms of which we can then criticize practices themselves.

Let us consider again a familiar example. The good soldier, within the context of military practice, is one who obeys orders promptly but intelligently, one who is skilled in the techniques of combat, one who exhibits courage under fire, and one who refrains from any activities that would damage the esprit de corps of his unit. All of these characteristics serve to make him a more effective "living bayonet" at the disposal of his superiors. And the military, of course, goes to great lengths to encourage the individual soldier's virtues—courage, justice, and truthfulness—*insofar as these contribute to his being a better soldier*. The military is not at all keen, however, on a soldier's developing the virtue of justice to the point at which he begins to question the moral legitimacy of his orders. The bombardier, for example, who is cool under fire, honest about whether or not the target was hit, and whose sense of fairness demands that he carry his share of the workload is respected. In contrast, the bombardier whose sense of justice leads him to question the morality of bombing innocent civilians is an embarrassment and a liability. The point, of course, is that in World War II there were a great many airmen "virtuous" in the more narrowly professional sense who were quite willing to swallow whatever qualms they may have had about the bombing of German and Japanese residential areas.

What this shows, I would contend, is that the transition from the virtues as these are rather narrowly exercised *within* a practice to a more broadly principled commitment to justice and truthfulness in general is by no means guaranteed or automatic. Truthfulness and justice, moreover, cannot really be adequately defined as virtues as long as we remain within the confines of a particular practice. It may well be, as MacIntyre contends, that often these virtues initially take hold within an individual's character as a result of his commitment to a particular practice. But even so, if those incipient virtues are to mature into what we mean in a more general sense by "truthfulness" and "a sense of justice," they must come to be applied as well *outside* of the practice, in *all* of the individual's activities, and thus in accordance with criteria that are not narrowly tailored to the needs of any specific practice. Finally, insofar as an individual is more concerned with the practice within which he first discovered the necessity of being (in some respects) truthful and just than he is with the virtues themselves, it is not likely that his virtues are going to mature to the point where they might ever incline him to criticize the moral import of that cherished practice. (The good soldier does not challenge authority.)

One's virtues may originate in one's commitment to a practice, just as MacIntyre suggests, but it is then possible for truth and justice to become additional and independent concerns that one has. To some extent, moreover, these *must* become independent concerns if one is to become genuinely truthful and just—which is to say, truthful and just *as a person* rather than merely as a particular kind of practitioner. And if one is not only concerned with truth and justice, but is also epistemologically sophisticated, one will understand truth and justice to be the kinds of things that I have been referring to as regulative ideals. To conceive of them as regulative ideals is to possess a powerful sense of the potential inadequacy of one's current beliefs and inclinations. It involves in this respect a pronounced awareness of the power to mislead that is contained within one's prejudices[30]—prejudices that are acquired in large part from the particular practices in which one happens to be regularly engaged. And that means, in turn, that one's concern for truth and justice inevitably tempers to some degree one's commitment to those practices from which one's prejudices derive. In "putting one's prejudices at risk," to borrow Gadamer's phrase, one must also to some extent put at risk one's commitment to the practices that shape one's prejudices.

This, then, is the point of asking what happens when practices conflict. When they do, one is never entitled simply to make one's choice between them on the grounds of familiarity or an unreflective personal inclination. Indifference in this respect is not an option insofar as one is genuinely committed to the pursuit of truth and justice. For a practice, even of long standing, may *deserve* to be extinguished, and it is in all likelihood another and better justified practice that will show us why. More commonly, perhaps, one practice will show us respects in which another should be improved, and to that possibility as well, if we are to be truthful and just, we must remain appropriately attentive.

LIFE AS (TRAGIC) ART

But the question still stands after this lengthy discussion of less than entirely satisfactory responses. Why should anyone enter upon an exceptional commitment to truthfulness and justice, given that such a commitment—for the sake of a vision of how things *should be*—will almost certainly involve significant sacrifices on one's part? As long as this question is posed in a *prescriptive* sense it is, I think, unanswerable. If we take the question in a *descriptive* sense, however, it suddenly becomes fairly easy to offer a convincing answer. MacIntyre provides the clue. We embrace a practice not because we must, after all, but because it appeals to us—because we recognize and value the goods latent within it. If it is possible, as I have argued, to embrace the virtues of truthfulness and justice over and above one's commitment to any specific practice, then the same principle applies here too. One embraces the pursuit of truth and justice not because one must, but because the enterprise "speaks" to one, in spite of the costs that it involves. In this respect the exceptional commitment to truth and justice falls within the realm of what Lon Fuller refers to as the morality of aspiration, in contrast to the morality of duty.[31] It represents, that is, a challenge that we may voluntarily take up in the effort to make of our lives the most that we can, but the pursuit of truth and justice (understood as regulative ideals) is not a task that we can be meaningfully *obliged* to undertake.

This phrase that has cropped up so frequently in the past few chapters—"the pursuit of truth and justice"—may be thought to have a rather pretentious ring to it. It may seem to suggest, in spite of my efforts to make clear that this is decidedly *not* what I mean by it, that truth and justice are goals that can actually be attained through the staunch efforts of the heroic individual acting entirely on her own. In that case, the seeming pretentiousness of the phrase stems from our awareness that truth and justice are nothing like the pinnacle of Mount Everest. The world is just too complicated for truth and justice to be reached once and for all in any meaningful sense. That was the point that the pragmatists in general, and Dewey in particular, were determined to impress upon us. But once having taken the point that ultimate truth and justice are unattainable, which is not all that difficult an idea to grasp, it is easy to draw the wrong inference. It is easy, that is to say, to conclude that we should settle for such understanding and such institutional arrangements as are readily available and not worry too much about what lies beyond our immediate reach. We only have so much energy to spare, after all. There is a danger, in other words, that this insight that truth and justice are eternally elusive will be seized upon as a justification for laziness and indifference. And that danger, rather obviously, needs to be countered, given that the world is far from perfect and those imperfections *matter*.

As I have been using it, then, the phrase "the pursuit of truth and justice" is meant to designate not so much a unified project as an unwavering attitude — an attitude involving, on the one hand, attentiveness to whatever possibilities present themselves of improving our understanding and our situation, and an attitude involving, on the other hand, the willingness to experiment, within reasonable bounds, in order to generate new openings for insight. The improvements and new insights that are achieved in this way will always be *local* achievements, of course, and in that sense it may seem a touch hyperbolic to refer to this attitude and enterprise as "the pursuit of truth and justice." But collectively those achievements represent — potentially at least — progress on a broad front and across considerable distance. It hardly seems excessive to say that science, which has come so far in the past five centuries, is concerned with the pursuit of truth, or that law, which has likewise come a tremendous distance in the past eight or nine centuries, is concerned with the pursuit of justice. And yet the attitude that I have been describing as a dedication to truth and justice (understood as regulative ideals) is the same attitude that informs both science and law insofar as these have managed to be progressive.

The attitude in question, it should be clear, given these connections to science and law, is also closely bound to what Aristotle meant by the life of the mind. The individual who embraces the pursuit of truth and justice, then, might be said to be consciously adopting *as her own* the *telos* that Aristotle erroneously attributed to all human beings. There is an interesting irony to be noticed here. For at a crucial point in the development of his argument in *After Virtue*, MacIntyre contends that Aristotle and Nietzsche represent the great polarity confronting us in ethics. He contends that we must choose to follow the lead of one or the other, and of course that we should do so on the grounds that the position of one of them is finally more plausible than that of the other. But those who choose to embrace the pursuit of truth and justice, and in the process embrace the life of the mind as Aristotle understood this, do so not because they must, but rather because it happens to "speak" to them personally. Thus in the process of following Aristotle's lead they are choosing *their*

own values in precisely the way that Nietzsche insists that we all should.
Those values that one in fact "chooses" are, of course, in some sense already
implicit in one's own nature; this explains one's inclination to choose precisely *these* values. It might be thought, then, that we have ended up siding
with Aristotle after all. But what prevents this discussion of the choosing of
one's values from collapsing entirely back into Aristotle's position is a fact
that we are obliged to acknowledge in the light of evolutionary biology—that
different individuals will be inclined to make different choices, and in each
instance will find them equally natural. It should be understood, moreover,
that Nietzsche would have seen absolutely nothing wrong in some particular
individual's choosing to embrace as her overriding personal value the life of
the mind. (As a philosopher and philologist that was, after all, his own choice
as well.)

Nietzsche's constant injunction was that the individual should strive to
make of her life an artwork.[32] An artwork, of course, is not restricted in terms
of what it can deal with; it can be built around any theme imaginable. What
accounts for its success, though, is the aesthetic satisfaction that we enjoy in
contemplating the way in which the details of the work are harmoniously integrated in the service of some governing purpose. It has to be admitted,
moreover, that not just any integration, however perfect, will afford us this
satisfaction. The artist, in order to please and impress us, must show us something original and interesting in the process of taking on a significant challenge. What this implies, for the process of making an artwork of one's own
life, is that the governing theme around which one constructs one's integrated
self must be sufficiently meaningful to make us appreciate the effort.

In chapter three, recall, we observed that a kind of integrity (or integrated
self) can be cheaply purchased simply by aspiring to nothing more demanding than the immediate satisfaction of one's animal urges. But as many
philosophers have pointed out, including both Aristotle and Mill, there is
nothing all that aesthetically appealing about the spectacle of a human being
living in a selfish and hedonistic fashion. As an "artwork" such an exhibition
is trite. We *know* what the basic urges are and what it takes to satisfy them.
Rakes and roués hold our interest, when they do, not because of their selfish
and hedonistic impulses, but because of the ingenuity they must occasionally
exhibit in order to escape the consequences of their own impulse-driven
choices. But even when they manage to have their cake and eat it too, their
success is rendered trivial by the comparative insignificance of the interests
that move them—money, sex, drink.[33]

In contrast, let us consider again the individual of grace and dignity, as
Schiller represents him. Here integrity of a much more demanding sort is
achieved. In all circumstances what *should* be done *is* done, with ease and

naturalness for the most part, and with evident nobility of character where an effort is required to restrain the natural impulses when these cannot be appropriately granted free rein. This, of course, is an ideal never actually achieved in life, but it is a worthy and aesthetically rich ideal precisely because it is so difficult to approach.[34] It is reason in the service of morality that determines, in all circumstances, what *should* be done by the individual of grace and dignity. And it is of course the complexity and changeability of circumstances that make integrating the facets of one's life on the basis of a dedication to truthfulness and justice such an enormous challenge. For as we saw in our discussion of Tom Rath's success and Ralph Hopkins's failure in this regard, it is by no means easy to take on the full range of responsibilities—to work and family, to humanity and country—that even a fairly average life typically involves and to balance the conflicting obligations that emerge so that each is given its due. On the other hand, the individual who succeeds in this regard will integrate the elements of his life in ways that are sure to involve original solutions to the difficulties that are thrown up by the unique combination of circumstances that are his alone to negotiate. As evidence of this, we can point to Tom Rath's own rather quiet and unprepossessing life (post World War II) which is nonetheless fascinating to watch as he deftly steers his way clear of having to sacrifice either his honesty or his family's welfare to the demands of his work, or his decency to the preservation of his family.

If it is felt, then, that it is still rather vague and unhelpful to claim that those who embrace the pursuit of truth and justice do so because the enterprise "speaks" to them, there is perhaps a somewhat clearer way of putting this. The individual making this choice recognizes that latent within one's human nature is the possibility of becoming something remarkably worthwhile—the sort of individual whose character and actions are a delight to contemplate—and he seeks in his own life to actualize that possibility. He seeks to make of his life, insofar as this is possible, an artwork. In doing so, moreover, he *cannot be cheated*. For the artist cannot be cheated of the aesthetic enjoyment of his own work as long as he is left free to create more or less what he will. True, the moral idealist, in his social interactions with others who do not happen to share his commitment to justice, will more than occasionally be exploited. But insofar as he achieves that meaningful integration that he seeks—the integration of the facets of his own life on the basis of a commitment to truth and justice—he himself will be able to take a creative aesthetic satisfaction in the result, even if no one else is in a position to appreciate the spectacle. It is important to note here the *creative* aspect of the satisfaction that is enjoyed. For if it were merely the disinterested aesthetic satisfaction that arose from the contemplation of a well-lived life that mattered, the life of

Socrates, say, or of Lincoln might be preferable as the object of contemplation. But much as he may appreciate the work of others, the satisfaction that
an artist takes in the successful production of his *own* work is always somewhat different, and more intense. So too, in the case of the moral idealist,
there will be a special intensity and significance to the satisfaction he feels in
having produced, out of the disparate resources available to him, that particular object of aesthetic contemplation that he wished to see realized—his *own*
exemplary life.

One might be inclined to object at this point that the individual's judgment
of his own success in this regard may well be delusional. He may attribute to
himself successes that he has not in fact achieved. And the quick answer to
this objection is: of course he may. Many people, in all likelihood, delude
themselves about their moral merit. For the most part, however, they do so by
avoiding the contemplation of the details of their own lives. Our task here,
moreover, has not been to explain how we can avoid self-delusion; it has been
to explain why someone might genuinely make an exceptionally strong commitment to the pursuit of truth and justice in spite of the fairly obvious disadvantages that such a commitment entails. The satisfaction that the moral
idealist is able to take in the creation and contemplation of his own life must
provide *some* compensation for his sacrifices. Presumably, the individual who
persists in his exceptional commitment to the regulative ideals of truth and
justice finds in this creative aesthetic satisfaction *more than enough* compensation for those sacrifices.

No one is compelled to make such an exceptional commitment to the pursuit of the regulative ideals. Increasingly, though, it seems that *whether* we
embrace the pursuit of truth and justice, and even more importantly *how many
of us* choose to embrace this enterprise are questions the answers to which
will have a crucial bearing upon the prospects of our species as a whole. The
problems confronting us today—the proliferation of "weapons of mass destruction" in a politically unstable world, the economic exploitation of the
many by the few, which promotes that instability, and the inexorable degra-
dation of our own environment—threaten our very survival, and yet they are
the problems of our own nature. If we are to survive as a species, it seems,
that nature will have to be dramatically altered and refined.

The challenge confronting us is daunting, for we must clearly become *more
rational* creatures if we are to find our way through the thicket of dangers that
our reason itself has played such a prominent role in generating. It was the
purely instrumental exercise of reason, after all, that armed us to the teeth and
gave us the means to exploit so exhaustively the resources of our planet. Reason, used almost exclusively as a tool for the fuller satisfaction of our blind
instinctive inclinations, merely renders us more dangerous animals—a more

volatile presence in the world's ecosystem. But reason is also the means—and indeed, the only means—by which the objective perspective can be approached. (Sympathetic identification helps, but unless schooled by reason it exaggerates the importance of what happens to be directly encountered.) The objective perspective, by definition, is that in which the legitimate interests of *all* things having interests are recognized and done justice so that an optimal balance is achieved.

Culture is the means by which reason has been cultivated and our basic human nature refined over the past fifty thousand or so years, and it continues to be the means by which our nature can be further refined. But only the right sort of culture will refine our nature in the manner necessary for our own survival, and that right sort of culture must be discovered as well as made. If the lessons of the past teach us anything, however, it is that the transformation of culture will always be resisted by those with a vested interest in the status quo. Those who have more than their share will tend to resist any restructuring of cultural practices that could involve their loss of privilege. Those who are comfortable will tend to resist any developments that might involve their discomfiture. And so, for the most part, we drift. Cultures continue to change, of course, as an unintended consequence of countless small alterations of circumstance that are generated, typically, by our own narrowly focused activities, but seldom in response to far-sighted proposals that can be articulated and the implications of which can be understood, for these almost invariably arouse overwhelming opposition.

Our situation, then, is not one in which optimism about the future of our kind seems appropriate. And yet, if there is to be any long-term future for our species, an effort to significantly change our situation must be made. Those who are seriously committed to the pursuit of truth and justice, and who can, as a consequence of this, see what is at stake, must struggle to overcome that opposition which makes meaningful change so unlikely. And they must do this, moreover, without in the process betraying their own commitment to the regulative ideals. They must struggle for social and political change, in other words, by means of rational persuasion alone. For insofar as they find it possible to *cheat* on behalf of the good cause, their commitment to the pursuit of truth and justice is seen to be a sham. In contrast, their opponents are free to resort—will resort, and are already resorting—to the use of force and deception, which have long shown themselves to be powerfully effective devices for directing the tide of political developments (as Machiavelli well knew). Which side will win this struggle on which so much hinges—on which, in a sense, *everything* hinges—is impossible at this point to say. Much will depend on just how responsive to rationality our species actually is. Can enough of us be persuaded (and inspired) by exemplars of rationality to make the difficult, costly, and ongoing effort to become significantly more rational ourselves?

NOTES

1. If the significance of this is not clear, I would suggest that the reader revisit the final few pages of chapter three.

2. *Plato's Republic*, trans. G. M. A. Grube (Indianapolis: Hackett, 1974), 360d.

3. Most of the problems involved in trying to make, for example, Benthamite utilitarianism plausible turn on those disanalogies.

4. It is interesting to note that virtually everything Socrates has to say here about the dictator could equally well be said of a ruthless business magnate—the American "robber baron" of the late nineteenth and early twentieth centuries, for example.

5. "*Pleonexia* is sometimes translated so as to make it appear that the vice which it picks out is simply that of wanting more than one's share. This is how J. S. Mill translated it and to follow Mill is to diminish the gap between the ancient world and modern individualism. . . . But in fact the vice picked out here is that of acquisitiveness as such, a quality that modern individualism both in its economic activity and in the *character* of the consuming aesthete does not perceive to be a vice at all. Nietzsche translated *pleonexia* with insight as well as precision: *haben und mehrwoll-haben*, because in the modern world . . . the notion that the wish to have more *simpliciter*, acquisitiveness as such, might be a vice, was increasingly lost sight of." Alasdair MacIntyre, *After Virtue*, 137.

6. See, for example, "Homer's Contest. "

7. Hans-Georg Gadamer, *Truth and Method*, second revised edition (New York: Crossroad, 1989), 299.

8. MacIntyre, *After Virtue*, 148.

9. See Daniel Dennett, *Darwin's Dangerous Idea* (New York: Simon and Schuster, 1995), chapter 6.

10. Although, if certain conditions hold, that drift may slow *almost* to a standstill. Crocodilians, for example, seem to have changed relatively little in over two hundred million years.

11. John Dewey, *Human Nature and Conduct* (Mineola, N.Y.: Dover, 2002, originally pub. 1922), 284.

12. John Dewey, *The Influence of Darwin on Philosophy and Other Essays* (Amherst, N.Y.: Prometheus Books, 1997, originally pub. 1910), 6–7.

13. Dewey, *The Influence of Darwin on Philosophy*, 13.

14. Dewey, *The Influence of Darwin on Philosophy*, 15.

15. *Philosophical Writings of Peirce*, ed. Justus Buchler (New York: Dover, 1955), 38.

16. Dewey, *Human Nature and Conduct*, 287–88.

17. Dewey, *Human Nature and Conduct*, 288–89.

18. Dewey, *Human Nature and Conduct*, 288.

19. Dewey, *Human Nature and Conduct*, 325–28.

20. MacIntyre, *After Virtue*, 187–88.

21. MacIntyre, *After Virtue*, 190.

22. MacIntyre, *After Virtue*, 191.

23. MacIntyre, *After Virtue*, 193.

24. MacIntyre, *After Virtue*, 194.

25. MacIntyre, *After Virtue*, 198.

26. MacIntyre, *After Virtue*, 196.

27. MacIntyre, *After Virtue*, 259.

28. MacIntyre, *After Virtue*, 263.

29. MacIntyre, *After Virtue*, 200.

30. I am using the word "prejudice" here in the value-neutral sense in which Gadamer uses the term in *Truth and Method*, to refer to our assumptions, predilections, and prejudgments.

31. See Lon L. Fuller, *The Morality of Law* (New Haven: Yale University Press, 1969), chapter one.

32. See, for example, *The Gay Science* (Cambridger: Cambridge University Press, 2001), 290.

33. That most marvelous of roués, Falstaff, constitutes no more than an exception that proves this rule. He commands our interest, after all, not by virtue of his carnal impulses but by virtue of those qualities that only an artist of Shakespeare's stature could have supplied him—that is to say, his all-penetrating skeptical genius and his ebullient gift for language.

34. As Nietzsche observes, it is not dancing but "dancing in chains" that is the epitome of art.

Bibliography

Aristotle. *Nicomachean Ethics*. Translated by David Ross. Oxford: Oxford University Press, 1980.

Axelrod, Robert. *The Evolution of Cooperation*. New York: Basic Books, 1984.

Beard, Charles. *An Economic Interpretation of the Constitution of the United States*. New York: The Free Press, 1965.

Bowler, Peter. *Evolution: The History of an Idea*, revised edition. Berkeley: University of California Press, 1983.

Cavell, Stanley. *Pursuits of Happiness*. Cambridge, Mass.: Harvard University Press, 1981.

Cicero. *On Duties*. Edited by M. T. Griffin and E. M. Atkins. Cambridge: Cambridge University Press, 1991.

Darwin, Charles. *On the Origin of Species*. Cambridge, Mass.: Harvard University Press, 1964.

Dawson, Coningsby. *Carry On*. London: John Lane The Bodley Head Press, 1917.

———. *Living Bayonets*. London: John Lane The Bodley Head Press, 1919.

———. *The Love of an Unknown Soldier*. Toronto: McClelland, Goodchild and Stewart, 1918.

Dennett, Daniel C. *Darwin's Dangerous Idea*. New York: Simon and Schuster, 1995.

Desmond, Adrian, and James Moore. *Darwin: The Life of a Tormented Evolutionist*. New York: Norton, 1994.

Dewey, John. *Human Nature and Conduct*. Mineola: Dover, 2002.

———. *The Influence of Darwin on Philosophy and Other Essays*. Amherst: Prometheus Books, 1997.

Donald, David Herbert. *Lincoln*. New York: Simon and Schuster, 1995.

Dostoyevsky, Fyodor. *The Brothers Karamazov*. Translated by Richard Pevear and Larissa Volokhonsky. New York: Farrar, Straus and Giroux, 2002.

Elster, Jon. "The Market and the Forum: Three Varieties of Political Theory." In *Contemporary Political Philosophy*. Edited by Robert E. Goodin and Philip Pettit. Oxford: Blackwell, 1997.

Ferguson, Niall. *The Pity of War*. New York: Basic Books, 1999.

Feyerabend, Paul. *Against Method*. London: Verso, 1988.

Fuller, Lon L. *The Morality of Law*, revised edition. New Haven: Yale University Press, 1969.

Gadamer, Hans-Georg. *Truth and Method*, second revised edition. New York: Crossroad, 1991.

Galbraith, John Kenneth. *The Affluent Society*, Fortieth Anniversary Edition. Boston: Houghton Mifflin, 1998.

Gould, Stephen Jay. *The Structure of Evolutionary Theory*. Cambridge, Mass.: Belknap Press, 2002.

Greider, William. *One World, Ready or Not*. New York: Simon and Schuster, 1997.

——. *Who Will Tell the People: The Betrayal of American Democracy*. New York: Simon and Schuster, 1992.

Hall, Kermit L., William M. Wiecek, and Paul Finkelman. *American Legal History: Cases and Materials*. New York: Oxford University Press, 1991.

Hamilton, Alexander, James Madison, and John Jay. *The Federalist Papers*. Edited by Clinton Rossiter. New York: New American Library Penguin, 1961.

Hamilton, W. D. "Extraordinary Sex Ratios." *Science* 156:477–88.

——. "The Evolution of Altruistic Behavior." The American Naturalist. Vol. 97: 354–56.

Harris, George W. *Dignity and Vulnerability*. Berkeley: University of California Press, 1997.

Heilbroner, Robert. *The Nature and Logic of Capitalism*. New York: Norton, 1985.

——. *The Worldly Philosophers*. New York: Simon and Schuster, 1953.

Hobbes, Thomas. *Leviathan*. Edited by Michael Oakeshott. New York: Macmillan, 1962.

Horne, John, and Alan Kramer. *German Atrocities, 1914: A History of Denial*. New Haven: Yale University Press, 2001.

Hume, David. *A Treatise of Human Nature*. Edited by David Fate Norton and Mary J. Norton. Oxford: Oxford University Press, 2000.

——. *Dialogues Concerning Natural Religion*. Edited by Richard H. Popkin. Indianapolis: Hackett, 1998.

——. *Enquiry Concerning the Principles of Morals*. Edited by Tom L. Beauchamp. Oxford: Oxford University Press, 1998.

Huxley, T. H. *Evolution and Ethics*. Edited by James Paradis and George C. Williams. Princeton: Princeton University Press, 1989.

James, William. *The Principles of Psychology*. Cambridge, Mass.: Harvard University Press, 1981.

Kant, Immanuel. *Groundwork of the Metaphysics of Morals*. Cambridge: Cambridge University Press, 1996.

——. *Lectures on Ethics*. Translated by Louis Infield. Indianapolis: Hackett, 1963.

——. *The Metaphysics of Morals*. Edited by Mary Gregor. Cambridge: Cambridge University Press, 1996.

Katz, Leo. *Ill-Gotten Gains*. Chicago: University of Chicago Press, 1996.

Kaufmann, Walter. *Tragedy and Philosophy*. Princeton: Princeton University Press, 1968.

Latour, Bruno. *Science in Action*. Cambridge Mass.: Harvard University Press, 1987.

Locke, John. *Two Treatises of Government*. Edited by Ian Shapiro. New Haven: Yale University Press, 2003.

Lorenz, Konrad. *On Aggression*. Translated by Marjorie Latzke. London: Methuen, 1966.

MacIntyre, Alasdair. *After Virtue*, second edition. Notre Dame: University of Notre Dame Press, 1984.

Mackie, J. L. *Ethics: Inventing Right and Wrong*. Harmondsworth: Penguin, 1977.

McNeill, William H. *Plagues and Peoples*. Garden City: Doubleday, 1976.

Mayr, Ernst. *This Is Biology*. Cambridge Mass.: Harvard University Press, 1997.

———. *Toward a new Philosophy of Biology*. Cambridge Mass.: Harvard University Press, 1988.

Midgley, Mary. *Beast and Man: The Roots of Human Nature*. London: Routledge, 1995.

Mill, John Stuart. *Three Essays: On Liberty, Representative Government, The Subjection of Women*. Oxford: Oxford University Press, 1975.

———. *Utilitarianism*. Edited by Oscar Piest. New York: Bobbs-Merrill, 1957.

Miller, William Lee. *Arguing about Slavery*. New York: Knopf. 1996.

———. *Lincoln's Virtues: An Ethical Biography*. New York: Knopf, 2002.

Nietzsche, Friedrich. *The Gay Science*. Translated by Josefine Nauckhoff. Cambridge: Cambridge University Press, 2001.

Nozick, Robert. *Anarchy, State, and Utopia*. New York: Basic Books, 1974.

Nussbaum, Martha. *The Fragility of Goodness*. Cambridge: Cambridge University Press, 1986.

Peirce, Charles Sanders. *Philosophical Writings of Peirce*. Edited by Justus Buchler. New York: Dover, 1955.

Phillips, Kevin. *Wealth and Democracy: A Political History of the American Rich*. New York: Broadway Books, 2002.

Plato. *The Republic*. Translated by G. M. A. Grube. Indianapolis: Hackett, 1974.

Rawls, John. *A Theory of Justice*. Cambridge, Mass.: Belknap Press, 1971.

Ricoeur, Paul. *Oneself as Another*. Translated by Kathleen Blamey. Chicago: University of Chicago Press, 1992.

———. *Time and Narrative*, vol. 1. Translated by Kathleen McLaughlin and David Pellauer. Chicago: University of Chicago Press, 1984.

Ridley, Matt. *The Origins of Virtue: Human Instincts and the Evolution of Cooperation*. Harmondsworth: Penguin, 1996.

Ruse, Michael. *Taking Darwin Seriously*. Oxford: Basil Blackwell, 1986.

Schiller, Friedrich. "On Grace and Dignity." In *Essays Aesthetical and Philosophical*. London: George Bell and Sons, 1916.

Sen, Amartya. *Inequality Reexamined*. Cambridge, Mass.: Harvard University Press, 1992.

Smith, Adam. *The Wealth of Nations*. Oxford: Clarendon Press, 1976.

Sober, Elliott, and David Sloan Wilson. *Unto Others: The Evolution and Psychology of Unselfish Behavior*. Cambridge, Mass.: Harvard University Press, 1998.

Sumner, William Graham. *Essays of William Graham Sumner*, two volumes. Edited by A. G. Keller and M. R. Davie. Archon Books, 1969.

Sunstein, Cass. *After the Rights Revolution: Reconceiving the Regulatory State*. Cambridge, Mass.: Harvard University Press, 1990.

Williams, George C. *Adaptation and Natural Selection*. Princeton: Princeton University Press, 1966.

Wilson, Edward O. *Sociobiology: The New Synthesis*, 25th Anniversary Edition. Cambridge, Mass.: Belknap Press, 2000.

Wrangham, Richard, and Dale Peterson. *Demonic Males and the Origins of Human Violence*. Boston: Houghton Mifflin, 1996.

Zinn, Howard. *A People's History of the United States*. New York: Harper and Row, 1980.

Index

About the Author

Ron Bontekoe was born and raised in southern Ontario. He received most of his higher education at the University of Toronto, which is where he earned his doctorate in philosophy in 1988. For two years he taught at the Ryerson Polytechnical Institute in Toronto. Since 1990, he has been a professor in the Philosophy Department at the University of Hawaii. In the late 1990s, he spent a year as a liberal arts fellow at the Harvard Law School. He is the author of *Dimensions of the Hermeneutic Circle* (Humanities Press) and coeditor, with Eliot Deutsch, of Blackwell's *Companion to World Philosophies*. He lives in Honolulu—somewhat reluctantly, given his preference for bookstores over beaches.